MODERNISM IN SERBIA

Published in association with the Harvard University Graduate School of Design

The MIT Press
Cambridge, Massachusetts
London, England

photographic preparation by Dejan Vlaškalić

MODERNISM IN SERBIA

THE ELUSIVE MARGINS OF BELGRADE ARCHITECTURE 1919–1941

Ljiljana Blagojević

© 2003 Massachusetts Institute of Technology
All rights reserved. No part of this book may be reproduced in any form by any electronic or mechanical means (including photocopying, recording, or information storage and retrieval) without permission in writing from the publisher.

This book was set in Gotham by Graphic Composition, Inc.

Printed and bound in Spain.

Library of Congress Cataloging-in-Publication Data

Blagojević, Ljiljana, 1960–
    Modernism in Serbia : the elusive margins of Belgrade architecture, 1919–1941 / Ljiljana Blagojević ; photographic preparation by Dejan Vlaškalić
      p. cm.
    Includes bibliographical references and index.
    ISBN 0-262-02537-X (hc. : alk. paper)
      1. Architecture—Yugoslavia—Belgrade (Serbia)—20th century. 2. Belgrade (Serbia)—Buildings, structures, etc. I. Vlaškalić, Dejan. II. Title.

NA1450 .B57 2003
720'.94971—dc21

2002038066

for M. V.

CONTENTS

ACKNOWLEDGMENTS
INTRODUCTION

	viii	
	x	

1 SHIFT — 2
  1.1 The Notion of the Noble Savage — 3
  1.2 The Concept of Barbarogenius — 8

2 CONSTRUCT — 24
  2.1 The Eslinger Case — 25
  2.2 Interior Identity — 44
  2.3 Group Identity — 57

3 EXPOSURE — 80
  3.1 A Distracted Gaze over the Image of the Nation at the World Expositions — 83
  3.2 Beauty Is ~~Not~~ in the Eyes of the Beholder — 95
  3.3 Nikola Dobrović (1897–1967): The Lateral Impact — 104

4 BYT MODE — 124
  4.1 The Problem of Dwelling — 127
  4.2 The Patterns of Dwelling — 140
  4.3 Dragiša Brašovan (1887–1965): The Style Master — 176

5 DEPARTURE — 190
  5.1 Milan Zloković (1898–1965): The Architect and His Ship — 191
  5.2 The House Rules — 197
  5.3 Readiness to Depart — 205

VISION — 226

NOTES — 232
ILLUSTRATION CREDITS — 274
INDEX — 278

ACKNOWLEDGMENTS

This book would not have been conceived if not for the initial idea on the subject put forward by Dejan Vlaškalić. He has been the silent partner in this project from the preliminary stages and throughout the lengthy process of putting the material together, providing continual support without which this undertaking would have been impossible. Impossible also to figure out how to acknowledge him properly; there is little left for me to do here but simply to thank him.

I owe a great deal to many people who contributed to the project in various ways. Perhaps my first thanks should go to Đorđe Zloković, whose advice and generous help guided me precisely through the meandering work of one of the central figures of Serbian modern architecture, his father, Milan Zloković. I thank Irina Subotić for her comments and encouragement in my research of the architectural discourse of *Zenit*.

For providing research and illustration material, I am indebted to: Gordana Stanišić and Dragana Kovačić of the National Museum in Belgrade, Bojana Popović and Dragan Živković of the Museum of Applied Art in Belgrade, Branislava Anđelković of the Museum of Contemporary Arts in Belgrade, Anica Medaković and Javor Rašajski of the City Museum, Vršac, Snežana Toševa of the Architecture Department in the Museum of Science and Technology in Belgrade, Predrag Milosavljević of the Photodocumentation Center Politika, Milena Marković of the Department of Bibliography at the Serbian Academy of Sciences and Arts, Vojislava Protić-Benišek of the Astronomical Observatory in Belgrade, Jelena Vasić of the Museum of the City of Belgrade, and Branko Bojović and Mileta Prodanović who lent me period publications from their private libraries. Special thanks should go to Nikola Belobrk for the photographs of buildings by his father, Momčilo Belobrk, from his family archive. I am grateful for the materials generously provided by Miloš Jurišić from his private collection.

I would like to thank Evelyne Tréhin of the Fondation Le Corbusier in Paris.

I am grateful to all the staff, and especially to Svetlana Nikolić, of the University Library in Belgrade for going out of their way to provide materials, and for making their institution one of the friendliest research environments.

For his unfaltering support, I would like to thank Branimir Stojanović, who invited me to deliver a series of lectures on the subject of this book at the School for History and Theory of Images in Belgrade that helped me sharpen my arguments. I also thank Branislava Anđelković and Branislav Dimitrijević for their encouragement, and the students at the School for the ever-so-rewarding feedback of the first audience.

Special thanks should go to Marija Milinković, Milica Lopičić, and Zlatko Haban, who not only made beautiful drawings and photographs but became my great allies in the project.

I am indebted to Roger Pain for editing the draft version of the text.

At the MIT Press, I owe a special debt to Roger Conover for his belief in the project, his continual support, and above all his unrelenting enthusiasm which kept me going through all its phases. I am grateful to Matthew Abbate for his subtle and precise editing, and to Tímea Adrián for her excellent design work. Finally, I am grateful to Peter Rowe for his interest in this project, which led to the cosponsorhip of this book by the Harvard University Graduate School of Design.

This book is dedicated to my husband Miša Vujošević for his intellectual and emotional support, and without whom it would never have happened.

INTRODUCTION

The identity of architectural modernism in Serbia, formatted by a kind of lateral reflection, to one side of and consecutive to the main body of work of the European modern movement, escapes definition by a slippery swiftness and a certain cleverness. It is an identity of the margins, or more precisely of a marginal topos of modernity, and it appears more as a crisis of identity than a conscious and stable one. The condition I am here analyzing is of the utmost elusiveness, not only for the lack of systematic archiving and the absence of an ethos of documenting, but for its essential quality of anonymity. The main actors on the modernist scene of the Belgrade interwar years were neither friends nor disciples of any of the masters of the European modern movement, they knew not their "gods" in person, they followed only reflections and translations, and they were not recognized by their idols as equals. This architecture belongs to largely unknown territory, where the question of its identity raises a debate on the extent of modernism's wider influence and the authenticity of its *translation* into other concurrent forms. In Serbia of the period, the ideas and texts of the international (primarily of the European) modern movement were translated into quintessentially local forms and were provincially colored, only in order to act as the primary vehicle of deprovincialization. The modern architecture of Serbia thus remained but a marginal and provisional construct of modernity. Yet it is within these very margins of the European modern movement, however elusive they might be, that we can attempt to comprehend the power of modernism's wider message.

On the changed political map of Europe after the First World War, the Kingdom of Serbs, Croats and Slovenes was one of eight newly established countries in the region between Vienna and Istanbul—where only a hundred years before had stood two empires, the Ottoman and the Habsburg. The capital of the former Kingdom of Serbia, Belgrade, became the capital city of this new, considerably enlarged, multinational state of some 12 million inhabitants. The English architecture critic Philip Morton Shand succinctly summarized this transformation:

In 1860, Belgrade found itself promoted to diplomatic significance and larger print in the maps on becoming the capital of one of the smallest and weakest of European States. For sixty years it remained the humblest and shabbiest of Balkan capital cities, insignificant in size, wealth, and everything except geographic and strategic importance compared to Bucharest, Athens, or even Sofia. The complete liberation of the former kingdom of Serbia as a result of the Balkan Wars of 1912–13 did little to enhance its development, if only because the national impoverishment was too complete, and the respite from war afforded altogether too brief, to allow of the sword being forged into a ploughshare. At this period the few

modest Government buildings, barracks, and schools, which this dingy town of under 60,000 inhabitants could boast, were unpretentious exercises in the usual frigidly academic "Italian Renaissance" of the latter half of the nineteenth century. At the end of the World War, Belgrade, then in Austrian occupation and badly damaged by a sequence of bombardments, awoke from its torpor to realize that it had suddenly blossomed out into the capital of a considerable, relatively powerful, and no longer land-locked State, peopled by some fifteen millions of consanguineous Serbs, Croats, and Slovenes; a triune kingdom in which Old Serbia, though the dominant, was by far the most backward partner.[1]

    As such, in the coming years Belgrade was to undergo a more profound transformation from a provincial border city into what was meant to be a modern European capital worthy of the victorious nation. The city experienced an immediate economic, administrative, political, and cultural expansion, paralleled by an overwhelming population increase and largely uncontrolled urbanization at an astonishingly rapid pace. The conditions after the First World War placed Serbian architecture in an ambiguous position between the will to be European and, at the same time, the will to create its own autonomous expression. The last remains of once-splendid Oriental Belgrade were disappearing under the potent drive of architectural Europeanization, manifested in a rather unselective importing of all sparkling signifiers of the new Westernized middle classes. On the other hand, the autochthonous Balkan architecture of old Serbia gave way to a national style based on medieval sacred architecture, the Serbian-Byzantine style. While the state in its public commissions opted for academicism, produced with panache by immigrant Russian architects, the church firmly embraced a new aberration of the Byzantine paradigm. The financial institutions, which were regarded as a Western invention, chose variants of Italian or French Renaissance styled by mainstream architectural offices from European countries. Private entrepreneurs had their houses and apartment blocks designed in all sorts of eclectic styles carried out by Serbian architects who were educated at European universities of varying academic traditions. The result was a violent clash of different-size buildings and conflicting architectural styles, ranging from poor and modest representatives of the Beaux-Arts tradition, Viennese Secession, and Italian or French Renaissance to the popular Serbian-Byzantine style.

    Turning from these models, young artists and intellectuals who settled in Serbia in the early twenties raised the vertical of *l'esprit nouveau,* and immersed themselves in free artistic experimentation influenced by the spirit of the European avant-garde. Their activities in the fields of art and literature helped set in motion an irreversible process of change in aesthetic perception, which was to mark the beginning of twentieth-century discourse. The space was opened for an emancipation and modernization of architecture too, and this project was enthusiastically carried out by four young men who, in 1928, established the Group of Architects of the Modern Movement in Belgrade: Jan Dubovy, Milan Zloković, Branislav Kojić, and Dušan Babić. In the short span of some fifteen years between 1925 and 1940, the four founders of the Group, together with a few other modernists, managed to achieve the primary goal they had set for themselves: to establish a characteristic identity for Belgrade modern architecture.

The quest for this identity is the main concern of this book, its aim being to reconstruct the modernist discourse of the architecture of the interwar period in Belgrade. As it is the first English-language publication that aims to systematically address these issues, its wider intention is to provide a baseline study of Serbian interaction with the international modern architectural context of the period. Of no less fundamental concern is the relevance of the modernist heritage for current architectural issues in today's Serbia. In the anarchic pluralization of post-communist society, the architecture of transition has been sinking into a commonplace of unsophisticated commercialism and disintegration of better architectural values. Belgrade is becoming a polygon of uncritical and retrograde architectural development locked in the uncertainty of contemporary paradigms. Original modern buildings are either literally disintegrating due to disrepair or are being altered, ruined, and transformed beyond recognition. At this point of evident annihilation of the architectural identity of modernism, the stability of our critical endeavor has to be anchored to the original *translation* of the authentic modernist text. The contemporary condition of crisis, therefore, urges a new *translation,* which will hopefully act again as a reconstructive key to modern Europe. To see forward, we need to direct our view backward, as Adolf Loos once said of Le Corbusier: "Er ist ein Prophet der nach Rückwärts schaut!"—"He is a prophet seeing backward!" Or better, "He is a prophet turned toward the past!"[2]

In the course of writing this book, I constantly revisited original texts, artworks, projects, and buildings of the main actors of the avant-garde and of architectural modernism, and concentrated on seeing them from more than one angle. The research is primarily based on the thorough investigation of primary sources, some of which are published here for the first time. Great support, however, was found in the up-to-date historiography of modern architecture in Serbia, and if the work of any one author could be singled out here, it would have to be the pioneering writings of the architectural historian Zoran Manević. Without aiming to produce a conclusive history of modern architecture in Serbia, or, for that matter, any history at all, my method is to critically elaborate the problematic through elucidation of specific issues and themes relevant to the subject. In the process, I was reassured that the structure of the book should follow the elusive character of the subject and its largely incoherent manifestation. A story of interwar Belgrade architectural modernism is, therefore, reconstructed in a series of seemingly independent critical essays, which enlighten specific phenomena that I find to be crucial to its development.

The main theme of chapter 1 focuses on the opposition of the notion of the "noble savage" as the "natural man" of the old Balkans and the new concept of "barbarogenius" introduced by the founder of the avant-garde magazine *Zenit* and the movement Zenitism, Ljubomir Micić. Through its publications and exhibitions, and especially through the work of Zenitist artist Jo Klek, *Zenit* generated an authentic and relatively coherent architectural discourse. It is my contention that Klek's works can be recognized as the reference point and the central event of architectural modernity in Belgrade, despite being both "theoretical" and marginal in their essence. Chapter 2 gives an insight into the changing paradigms of the period in retracing the tentative overlaps between the first modern building in Belgrade, the house of architect Milan Zloković, and the related contemporary concepts of the avant-garde movement of surrealism. The argument centers on the artists' and architects' awareness of the metropolitan tendency of Belgrade, and its reflection in art and architecture. The account also follows the formative role of the Group of Architects of the Modern Movement. The opposing notions of traditionalism and conservatism on the one side and modernism on the other are the main theme of chapter 3, with special attention given to the seminal role of the architect Nikola Dobrović. Analyzed in chapter 4 are patterns of dwelling and the character of the everyday. In this context, the analysis of the architecture of Dragiša Brašovan serves to point to the victory of modernism in the 1930s and its transfer into the mainstream. Chapter 5 explores the architecture of Milan Zloković, whose work, I would argue, marks the departure from the predominant stylistic and formalist understanding of modern architecture as the "modern style." Finally, in the concluding remarks the gaze is returned and observation is observed in order to put forward the question of the scope and the scopic field of modernism in Serbia.

PRONUNCIATION KEY

The letter đ (as in Đorđe) is the equivalent of the English-language *g* sound in *angel*. The letter j (Jan) is always read as *y* in *yes*. The letters ć (Zloković) and č (Zaječar) are both forms of the English-language *ch* (ć as in *rich*, č as in *chocolate*), while the letter c (Obrenovac) is pronounced as *ts* in *cats*. The letter ž (Žiča) is pronounced like the sequence *su* in *treasure*, and dž (Hadži) like the sequence *die* in *soldier*. The letter š (Dragiša) is pronounced as *sh* in *ship*. Pronounciation of lj (Ljubljana) is similar to the sequence *lli* in *million*, and nj (Knjaževac) is similar to the sequence *ni* in *onion*, both with the tongue tip lowered and the two sounds said simultaneously.

MODERNISM IN SERBIA

1 SHIFT

THE NOTION OF THE NOBLE SAVAGE 1.1

The solitude is incredible. . . . Like a white ghost, our boat floats in an elusive element.

Le Corbusier, *Journey to the East*

The twentieth century seemed scarcely to have commenced in Belgrade and Serbia when young Charles-Édouard Jeanneret, then a draftsman in the office of Peter Behrens in Berlin, and his friend Auguste Klipstein arrived in 1911, searching for intact lands on their now famous journey to the East. In his travel diary Jeanneret made notes and sketches of the seven-month-long journey, during which he and his friend traveled via Dresden, Prague, Vienna, Budapest, Belgrade, Bucharest, Tŭrnovo, Gabrovo, and Adrianople to Constantinople (Istanbul), then on to Mount Athos, Athens, and southern Italy.[1] Giving up on the Orient Express in Vienna, they boarded a "great white boat," going down the river Danube all the way to Ruschuk in Romania. In his travel journal Jeanneret wrote about his great expectations of Belgrade, imagining it as the magic door to the East "swarming with colorful life, populated by flashing and bedizened horsemen wearing plumes and lacquered boots!" But, after two days of bitter disillusionment, he wrote harshly about it: "It is a ridiculous capital, worse even: a dishonest city, dirty, and disorganized."[2] The picture was brightened only by the city's "admirable position" and the "exquisite" ethnographic museum where he

discovered Serbian folkloric art: kilims (*Pirottenteppiche,* as he jotted down in his *carnet*),³ peasant costumes, and "pots, beautiful Serbian pots." Jeanneret, *toujours seul,* sat in the Belgrade museum and made sketches of earthenware jugs and of the traditional string instrument, the *gusle*.⁴

For Jeanneret, folkloric art was like an overwhelming vision of the origins of man. In his travel journal he wrote: "Considered from a certain point of view, folk art outlives the highest of civilizations. It remains a norm, a sort of measure whose standard is man's ancestor—the savage, if you will."⁵ Fascinated by the traces of the "noble savage" he found in the Belgrade museum, Jeanneret promptly made a detour in order to look for a habitat of the proverbial "natural man" of the Balkans. He followed the trail, traveling by train, on foot, and by cart, to small Serbian towns near the Bulgarian border—Negotin, Zaječar, and Knjaževac. Jeanneret's sketch of Knjaževac displays the harmony of traditional architectural form in its natural setting, with a man and his kettle in the foreground and a rolling landscape behind.⁶ The drawing of a sleepy settlement has a quality of atemporality, as if it had been a conserved museum exhibit of a pastoral Europe where life is forever pure and simple.

"This Serbian countryside is ideal!" Jeanneret exclaimed as roads "fragrant with chamomile" took him to a landscape that might have seemed to him like a setting for the *soleil, espace, verdure* fantasy. The "natural" society he found there—a boring country wedding where he listened to divine Gypsy music while drinking ruby-red wine—he much preferred to the premodern dust of the capital city. Seeking to "flee from the invading and dirty 'Europeanization' to the tranquil refuges where—abating, and soon to be submerged—the great popular tradition survives,"⁷ he searched all nooks and crannies to retrieve objects of his desire from the inevitable oblivion. In the attic of a potter's house in Knjaževac, he found a jug with the Greek motif of the immortal winged horse, Pegasus. The photograph of this particular jug was later published in his *L'Art décoratif d'aujourd'hui,* the caption being its *in memoriam*:⁸

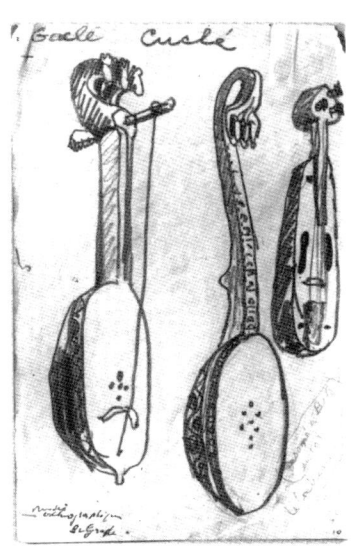

Folk culture in its lyric power. The lapse of centuries would bring Pegasus round again. The river, the tree, the flowers are transcribed into essential forms. Overflowing poetic feeling, whose expression has been fixed for centuries, makes this vase an outstanding artefact. The Serbian potter who made it in about 1900 had stowed it away with many others in his attic. The shelves of his house were filled with commercial pottery decorated in a vulgar way by machine. "Progress" had brutally crippled age-old traditions.⁹

Scarcely ten years after the notes and sketches of this Balkan idyll were made, however, the new era of modern times began, even there, in the depth of this other Europe. Jeanneret became Le Corbusier, hero of the new era, revered

1.1   (opposite page) Panorama of Belgrade, ca. 1910.

1.2   Le Corbusier, drawing of Serbian pottery from the Ethnographic Museum in Belgrade, 1911. (Courtesy National Museum, Belgrade.)

1.3   Le Corbusier, drawing of *gusle* from the Ethnographic Museum in Belgrade, 1911. (Courtesy National Museum, Belgrade.)

and admired by another Belgrade. The pottery Le Corbusier had found in Serbia served him as a paradigm for the true work of art, sharing a pedestal with "high" art: "There is no decoration which can summon up the feelings of a traveller: there is architecture, which is pure, unified, form—structure and modelling—and there are works of art: Phidias or the pot of the potter in the Serbian Balkans."[10] For him, folkloric art had universal value, it was *pensée-type* and the language of the hearts of all people. The jug he brought to La Chaux-de-Fonds from distant lands on the Danube was one of the first symbolic objects alongside which he decided to be photographed. Le Corbusier's penchant for juxtaposing his face next to current creative impulses can be seen as a lateral history of his life and work. Many a fascination and obsession interpreted in his oeuvre can be traced through photographs in the lifelong series of his portraits with things. It was at the time of writing *Après le cubisme* (1918) that he chose to be photographed with the jug he had brought from Serbia. In a photograph taken at his parents' home in La Chaux-de-Fonds, with his brother Albert Jeanneret and Amédée Ozenfant, Le Corbusier holds the Knjaževac jug on top of his head with both hands. He sits up with his back straight, crowned with Pegasus, and smiles toward the camera with an air both of the charade and of anticipation of the purist revolution.

The natives of Serbia, however, shunned any connection with the noble savage, whose very existence they ignored. Le Corbusier's "natural" man was too near, and too powerful an actor in the patriarchal *ancien régime,* for the new, aspiring class of intellectuals in Belgrade. For emancipation from their self-

CHAPTER 1 **SHIFT**

6

determining Balkan heritage they needed the new, self-referential forms offered by modernism. Belgrade was gasping for as much European air as it could inhale in order to achieve its metropolitan status, but the real change occurred in the 1920s, spurred on by the arrival of young intellectuals and artists. Many of them returned from France, where they had received their education after the First World War, and others came from a number of centers of the former Austro-Hungarian monarchy. They brought with them the atmosphere, the spirit of the age, and the modernist *Weltanschauung* from the European centers where they had been educated. Their arrival marked a belated yet fresh and promising beginning to the twentieth century: "In Belgrade new things should be built, and new things should be written, without any concern for what had been. Behind us, there is nothing that we could continue.... Immersions [in the new] are our necessity, free immersions, precipitous ones."[11] The lyrical prose and poetic image of a "'natural' society as a paradigm of 'rational' society" may have been the idea behind Le Corbusier's Ville Radieuse, but Belgrade developed a different model for itself.[12]

For all the evident direct impact Le Corbusier's doctrines had on Belgrade planning and architecture, any traces of direct contact with him are elusive.[13] One of the paths leads to 1932, when Belgrade architect Branko Maksimović sent his book *Problemi urbanizma* to a friend in Le Corbusier's office.[14] In this book Maksimović made a three-steps sketch proposal for the reconstruction of an urban block in central Belgrade, in which he suggested a new perimeter type of

1.4   (opposite page) Le Corbusier, *Knajewatz de Serbie* (Knjaževac in Serbia), 1911. (Courtesy National Museum, Belgrade.)

1.5   Earthenware jug from Knjaževac, ca. 1900, published in Le Corbusier, *L'Art décoratif d'aujourd'hui*. (Courtesy Fondation Le Corbusier, © FLC 46.)

1.6   Charles-Édouard and Albert Jeanneret with Amédée Ozenfant in the Jeanneret-Perret house in La Chaux-de-Fonds, ca. 1918. (Courtesy Fondation Le Corbusier, © FLC—L1 (6) 4.32.)

block with large internal courtyards. Le Corbusier freely took this example as a readymade and republished it, fourteen years later, in his book *Manière de penser l'urbanisme* (1946)—without any reference to its origin. With his characteristic acerbic tone, he criticized the original sketch as a superficial exercise in fashionable planning, and triumphantly proffered, in a fourth step, the "right" solution. He proposed the total destruction of all traces of the existing urban block and the erasure of the traditional urban matrix. In its place he introduced his orthodox open meandering block in order to liberate the city from the "tyranny of the street," thereby, demonstrating how a city can gradually be transformed into a park.[15] Yet again, he thus violently divested Belgrade of any serious consideration. He simply wrote it off as one of those notorious places where Europeanization, and pseudo-modern urbanization consequent to it, had utterly failed. Later still, in the 1950s, on seeing photographs of some of the most prominent buildings in Belgrade, Le Corbusier gave it no second thought. His comment was, as ever, unforgiving: "My God, how ugly it is."[16]

1.2 THE CONCEPT OF BARBAROGENIUS

LA
RÉVOLUTION
ZÉNITISTE EST LE
MOUVEMENT ÉLÉMENTAIRE
POUR LA SINTHÈSE DE TOUS LES
ARTS NOUVEAUX DE LA NOUVELLE HUMANITÉ.
PARMIS LES BARBARES LE ZÉNITISME EST LA LUTTE
POUR LA CULTURE! PARMIS LES CIVILISÉS LE ZÉNITISME
SOULÈVE LA CONSCIENCE BARBARE! VIVE L'ACTION
RÉVOLUTIONNAIRE DU PARADOXE ÉTERNEL
→ZÉNITISME!←

Branko Ve Poliansky, ***Toumbé***[17]

The Belgrade scene was set on fire by the arrival of its first twentieth-century hero, poet and critic Ljubomir Micić—"le poète d'après-guerre et le découvreur du sixième continent: des Balkans."[18] As the life and soul of the avant-garde movement Zenitism, Micić was the one true "barbarogenius," who loudly announced his onset:

MAN—That is our first word.

From the loneliness of stiff walls and condemned streets, from the dark depths of subconsciousness and ghostly nights, we come before you as apostles, as prophets, to preach: MAN ART.[19]

The movement, as conceived by Micić, was centered on the idea of the "Balkanization of Europe," as the optimal projection to be undertaken by pure Zenitist art in the name of barbarogenius.[20] The focal point of the movement was the high-profile "International Review for Zenitism and New Art," *Zenit*, published regularly from 1921 to 1923 in Zagreb, and from 1923 to 1926 in Belgrade.[21] Although by its content predominantly a literary magazine, *Zenit* stood for the synthesis of art forms, an assemblage under the highly subjective editorship of Ljubomir Micić, its owner. The Zenitist program presented an eclectic and contradictory mixture of conscious cultural barbarism, internationalism or supranationalism, and enthusiasm for Russia's October Revolution and its new art. In the course of the 1920s its orientation shifted from expressionist and futurist to an

1.7   Ljubomir Micić, ca. 1921.

elementarist/constructivist position and iconoclastic (dadaist) design. It disseminated the new intellectual content of Zenitist philosophy—"Zenitosophy"—a new syntax of words, images, and thought. In its political orientation, *Zenit* was anti-institutional, "anticlerical, antibourgeois, antibureaucratic, antiacademic," and leftist in the sense that its ultimate aim was to change the world with the new art.[22] For the magazine's radical use of the term "revolution" and its overt leftism, it had continual problems with the regime, both in Zagreb and Belgrade, and was finally banned in December 1926 for its alleged "Bolshevik propaganda" and its calls for "socialist revolution." It supported a "supranational" rather than the international European idea, trying to employ positively the energy generated by the Orient↔Occident interface, that is, the East↔West creative friction.

For his decisive point of departure Micić chose the authentic ground point of barbarism, advocating reversion to a zero point of culture with the seemingly naive concept of "barbarogenius": "We are all striving toward the common goal, toward the internationalization of culture. . . . I repeat: Zenitism aims at a synthesis of new art by means of Balkan creative elementalism, and it is struggling for the Balkanization of Europe."[23] He totally rejected any relation to an idealized "noble savage," opting instead for a radicalization of the notion of the antihero. The romanticized natural man, who so enchanted Le Corbusier, had no power to carry out the Zenitist will to revalue all aspects of art and life. For this task, a new symbolic figure of an artistic/creative genius invested with a pure barbarian force was needed. It is important to stress here that Micić decisively disassociated Zenitism from the Western idea of primitivism:

The West *consciously* imposes *primitivism* (which is a new imitation). They all are mistaken in becoming *modern naturalists.* Behind the old unconscious primitivism stood nature and the naiveness of man. Behind the new *conscious* primitivism stands culture and man's refinement. Here lies the difference. Culture has therefore been used for refining primitivism, which is *regression.*[24]

The *Zenitist Manifesto* elaborated the concept of barbarogenius and paid homage to the great barbarian models: "To be a barbarian means: beginning, potential, creation. (Nietzsche, Whitman, Dostoyevski are barbarians, for they are the beginnings.)"[25] A new Man was envisaged in these words, one capable of emancipating the Balkans by imbuing the region with an international, or rather supranational, ideology. Simultaneously, a sheer Balkan creative potential was to be invested into the building of one new Europe. To the noble savage simpleton invented by the West, *Zenit* opposed the ultimate genius: "man of the Balkans—killer of darkness—barbarogenius—conqueror of space—electrogenius—inventor of radiotelegraphy—Nikola Tesla."[26]

With an active orientation to (mass) communication, as part of its basic philosophical commitment, *Zenit* exchanged ideas and contributions with the wide network of European avant-garde magazines, most notably *Contimporanul, Der Sturm, L'Esprit nouveau, De Stijl,* Вещь *(Veshch)/Gegenstand/Objet, Noi, Ma, Stavba, Devětsil, ABC,* and *365*. From the very outset, the formative ideas of Zenitism stemmed from the common operative discourse of the international avant-garde, transmitted through this network. Perhaps the most telling document in this respect is the article "L'Esthétique du cinéma" by one of the first and most prominent Zenitists from Belgrade, Boško Tokin, published in the first issue of *L'Esprit nouveau* and quoted from, only six months later, in the pages of *Zenit*. In one of the first and most important programmatic articles published in *Zenit,* Tokin elaborates his thesis on the connection of new art to Henri Bergson's philosophy and "other intuitive ways of structuring (such as theories of time and space)." In quoting his definition of cinematography as "création plastique à travers la durée," Tokin legitimizes his theoretical position by a reference to his publication in *L'Esprit nouveau*.[27] The brotherhood of avant-garde magazines regarded *Zenit* as next of kin: Hannes Meyer included it in his selection of the seven most important avant-garde magazines in *7 Arts* (1924) and placed it among "magazines and books adequate to our time" in his article "Die neue Welt" (in *Das Werk,* 1926); and Theo van Doesburg's *De Stijl* singled it out as one of five especially influential magazines (1923).

Zenit's international fame may have followed from the fact that it made one of the most important contributions to avant-garde iconography, namely the first publication of Vladimir Tatlin's *Monument to the Third International* outside Russia, in February 1922.[28] During the rest of that year, *Zenit* became a springboard for constructivism in poetry and art in general, and especially for the promotion of new Russian art and architecture, which was largely unknown in the West. Micić strengthened his relationship with Ilya Ehrenburg and El Lissitzky, who had started publishing their magazine Вещь *(Veshch)/Gegenstand/Objet* in Berlin in March 1922, and it was through them that he had been given the Tatlin drawing a few months earlier. That same summer, Micić and his wife Nina-Naj (Anuška Micić) went to Germany, and not only published a special German-language issue in Munich in July (no. 16, 1922) but, on their return to Zagreb, issued a 10,000-copy *Zenit* broadsheet in September, and, in parallel, edited and produced an excellent double issue dedicated to Russian new art. The latter's front page was designed by Lissitzky, who was also, together with Ehrenburg, the editor of the Russian section. This issue was published in October 1922 (the symbolism of the month of publication was no accident). It offered completely new visual references, such as Lissitzky's *Construction,* Aleksandr Rodchenko's *Constructive Form in Space,* and, again, Tatlin's *Monument to the Third International.* Ehrenburg and Lissitzky also wrote, specially for this issue of

1.8   (opposite page) Cover of *Zenit*, no. 3 (April 1921): Egon Schiele, *Weltwehmut*.

1.9   Cover of *Zenit*, no. 10 (December 1921): Mihailo S. Petrov, *Rhythm*.

Zenit, an important article titled "The Russian New Art" in which they pointed out the progressive dislocation of art (especially painting) toward architecture. They saw Tatlin's work "in real space and with modern materials" as the forerunner of constructive art, but in criticizing his "fetishism of material" they offered a corrective view of Malevich's suprematism and his move to the "destruction of painting." The next shift of constructive art is represented by an orientation to "production art," from which a truly new form, constructed on the basis of function and economy of material, was developed. In this evolution, and through work in the new theater, according to Ehrenburg and Lissitzky, "the artist arrived at architecture."[29] This understanding of constructive arts became axiomatic in *Zenit*'s own artistic discourse, which for the first time included references to architecture as the ultimate possibility of a synthesis of the arts. This was reflected in Micić's own poetry cycle entitled "Words in Space" [Worte im Raum] and in his subsequent selection of images and texts reinforcing this position.

It was thus through Zenitist publications and exhibitions that the Serbian public first saw new European art and architecture, and it was *Zenit,* again, that first presented new (Yugoslav) Zenitist art to the international avant-garde scene. In 1924, Zenit organized the "First International Exhibition of New Art" in Belgrade, where 110 original works of avant-garde art were shown, by artists such as Louis Lozowick, Robert Delaunay, Albert Gleizes, László Moholy-Nagy, Ossip Zadkine, Wassily Kandinsky, Lazar (El) Lissitzky, Alexander Archipenko, as well as five Yugoslav artists.[30] This exhibition included nineteen paintings by the young Croatian artist Josif (Jo) Klek.[31] Klek's works were presented by Micić as the only true Zenitist painting, which is to say painting that "has, finally, been successfully emancipated from any literalness and history, and from any photographic likeness and amateur imitation."[32] Klek subsequently exhibited his work at international exhibitions in Bucharest ("La Prima expozitie Internationala a 'Contimpuranul,'" 1924) and in the Städtisches Museum in Bielefeld, Germany ("Internationale Ausstellung junger Kunst," 1924). Together with Micić, Klek also took part in the Zenitist presentation at the "Exhibition of the Revolutionary Art of the West and America" held at the Academy of Sciences on Art in Moscow in 1926.

Concomitantly, *Zenit* generated an authentic and relatively coherent architectural discourse, which was the first of its kind to inform the evolving Belgrade scene about what might be regarded as architectural modernity. While he never promulgated actual architectural modernism, Micić actively promoted an awareness of the architectural content of the zeitgeist, in parallel with the shift from the expressionist to the constructivist position of the magazine. Modernism was never an issue in *Zenit,* the actual word "modern" was consciously avoided, and yet it seems that in architecture *Zenit* was a harbinger of what was finally to be incarnated as the modern movement in Belgrade architecture. Although auxiliary to the main literature/art line, an architectural discourse had been built up by regular publication of international avant-garde architecture under Micić's editorship, and by promotion of Zenitist architecture designed by Klek. Nevertheless, in the historiography of the modern architecture of Serbia, the relevance of *Zenit* has been either ignored or relativized, since there are no obvious expressions of the Zenitist aesthetic in the built architecture of the period.[33] With no ambition to prove the direct influence of avant-garde movements on Belgrade modern architecture, I would still argue that the emergence of new aesthetic criteria owed much to the crack that *Zenit* managed to open in the stifling atmosphere of the prevailing provincial conservatism.

Zenit was used effectively by Micić to publicize his invention of Zenitism as a definitive movement for a synthesis of new art. In this, the architectural object had the uneasy status of the ultimate form of such a synthesis. At the end of 1922, Micić translated and published the text by the Hungarian activist Lajos Kassák, "Architecture of a Painting," that was crucial in settling *Zenit*'s architectural course of action. Kassák elaborates on the sequence that led to the possibility of a synthesis in art, from futurism's "discovery" of movement as an element essential to life, to Lissitzky's concept of the Proun and its constructivism of movement, and to cubism as a possible means of stability pointing to a new architecture. That new architecture was, for Kassák, "the architecture that is built on a constructive basis, as a possibility for a synthesis of the contemporary quests of art." Again, "The struggle for new constructive architecture started in two directions, in space and on surfaces. The first is the art of building, the second the architecture of painting."[34] This was fundamental for reaffirming Micić's position: new architecture was constructive and its form was cubist, or, conversely, for cubism architecture held the most powerful potential for its realization.[35]

While he uncompromisingly proffered and even forced his opinions in the domains of poetry, literature, and arts, Micić reserved his judgment with regard to architecture. When venturing into the relatively unknown territory of architectural discourse, he very occasionally chose texts concerning new architecture, thus securing himself an editorial position on the "right" side of the polemics but at the same time staying out of them as an interested observer.[36] In *Zenit,* however, new architectural issues were at least raised, not ignored as in the other Serbian avant-garde periodicals of the period. Regarding contemporary architectural tendencies in Yugoslavia, Micić commented only in one instance, and then with an atypical politeness and moderation: "One success was the work of Zagreb architect Viktor Kovačić, who built the Slaveks building on Starčević Square in a new spirit. It is appropriate to the purpose and the gravity of the times. Clarity of form is expressed. Mr. Kovačić took hold of cubism and, with partial success, realized it in architecture. Cubism is not a monster, as the

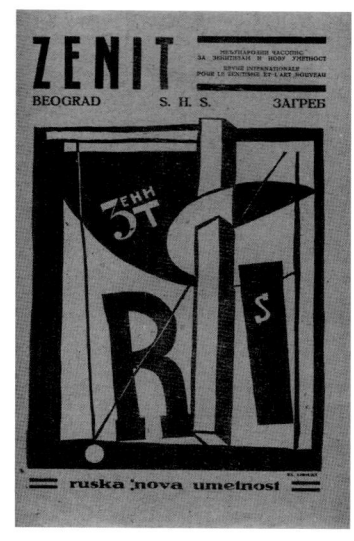

1.10   (opposite page) Cover of *Zenit,* no. 11 (February 1922): Vladimir Tatlin, *Monument to the Third International.*

1.11   Cover of *Zenit,* no. 17–18 (October 1922): El Lissitzky, *The Russian New Art.*

average citizen is inclined to think."³⁷ Two years later, Micić wrote an obituary for Kovačić giving the old master the honor of being the one and only modern architect in Yugoslavia, whose architecture had been under the strong influence of the great and famous Adolf Loos.³⁸

More often, paradigmatic (if somewhat eclectically chosen) images of new architecture served to corroborate the important Zenitist programmatic texts. The most striking example of the use of architectural images in *Zenit*'s ideological propaganda, without comment on the architecture they represented, is the illustrations for one of the most important texts by Micić, "The New Art." This text was written for a "conference held at the opening of the First International Exhibition in Belgrade, 9 April 1924," and was published in two parts. In the first of these, Micić gave an introduction to Zenitism, using slogans such as "Zenitism is a totalizer of contemporary life and new art" and "Creation, invention, originality, and work are our axioms," and he illustrated his points with photographs of the model of the Villa Moïssi (Lido, Venice, 1923) by Adolf Loos.³⁹ The choice of the architect and of the project cannot be regarded as random, since Micić was very particular in selecting the objects for assemblage in his magazine pages. At first glance, it seems odd that he chose Loos, who was not one of *Zenit*'s regular contributors, and that he took photographs from *Architecture vivante*, a French architecture periodical of a moderate modernist orientation, rather than from old friends in the network of avant-garde magazines. The explanation, however, is found in his texts on painting, which reveal how Micić saw architecture as a proper realization of cubism. For example:

Cubism cannot belong to painting as much as expressionism, since it is best affirmed in architecture and sculpture—Archipenko. And if those "neoclassicists" and retroactive "synthetists" were to comprehend that possibility as a result of cubism, and as its right realization (build houses, monuments, theaters, cinemas, Zenitheums!), they would quit painting, much sooner than seek help from Negro art as a means for Western rejuvenation (Zenitism in the Southeast!). Cubism brought in one new element: three-dimensionality.⁴⁰

In this sense, photographs of Loos's Villa Moïssi, and somewhat later publication of the Rosenberg house by Theo van Doesburg and Cornelis van Eesteren, clearly prove the point.⁴¹ But, as with avant-garde texts in general, Micić's writings cannot be read on a simple referential level, as they generally perform the function of aesthetic revalorization by creating an illusion of a definitive referentiality. The body of his text is far from being monolithic and, more often than not, concepts of expressionism, constructivism, cubism, and Zenitism are muddled, reinterpreted, or revised. The puzzling contrast of reproducing images such as Tatlin's *Monument* and Loos or De Stijl cubic architecture on the one end, against the expressionist aesthetic of Mendelsohn's Einstein Tower on the other, demonstrates this oscillation. However, in addition to reproductions in *Zenit* of texts and images of the international avant-gardes, the authentic architectural drawings/paintings of Jo Klek are of paramount importance for comprehending the true spirit of the Zenitist concept of architecture.

Zenit's darling, Klek joined Micić's inner circle as a student in his final year in gymnasium in Zagreb, only to find himself soon expelled from all schools in Croatia for his riotous Zenitist activity. Following his spiritual mentor, he moved to Serbia in 1923, where he marked *Zenit*'s Belgrade years with a series of extraordinary artworks. Totally self-taught, Klek became the epitome of Zenitist art in general, earning Micić's recognition as the only true Zenitist artist, and, more importantly for our present concern, he became the one and only actor in the Zenitist architectural discourse. He explored different art techniques and media, such as pencil or ink drawing, watercolor, tempera, collage, and typography, to produce Zenitist posters, illustrations and front covers for Zenitist publications, collages, and *Pafama* painting (the name derives from the German *Papier-Farben-Malerei*)—his own invention, which was christened by Micić as *arbos*.[42] Of more fundamental concern here are Klek's architectural proposals and drawings/paintings predominantly exploring issues of architectural space. The quest for the identity of new architecture through free experimentation with formal expression is vividly reflected in the development of his own personal architectural stance. Klek was committed to creating, and above all realizing, what he called "Zenitist, Balkan architecture and painting." As he asserted in a letter to Micić, it was the will to realize that very aim that made him study architecture at the Technical Faculty, first in Belgrade (1923–1924) and later in Zagreb where he graduated in 1929.[43] In the summer of 1923, he was preoccupied with the exploration of architectural space, as he wrote: "I have not held the brush in my hand for a very long time, and I don't even have the will for it. But I found a new thing, which is to make models of houses from paper. I have made, in fact, only one such house, yet I know that a great many brilliant models could be made."[44] These must have been models of Zenitist houses, as Klek was at the time commencing his autodidactic journey away from painting toward a new architecture. A sequence of his architectural proposals in three subsequent issues of *Zenit,* published in Belgrade in 1924–1925, is indicative of this process.

The first project was Klek's translation of the constructivist model in *Advertisements* (1923), published as an illustration to the article "Modern Advertisement." The text, which originated from *ABC,* was written, as Irina Subotić ascertained, by El Lissitzky.[45] The link established between Micić and Lissitzky remained strong after the latter's move to Zurich in 1923, and all communication was transferred from Вещь *(Veshch)/Gegenstand/Objet* to the new left-wing group ABC, and to their magazine of the same name. Through these contacts

BERSON
ARKO
BOR
SKF
REKLAM
KLEK
URUGUAY
FORD
BOX
KIOSK
VREME VAZNO
ЈОСИФ КЛЕК

Hannes Meyer, for example, also became a correspondent for *Zenit* and contributed illustrations of his Co-op works.[46] Klek's painting clearly follows the instructions from Lissitzky's text—clarity of message, color impact, accentuation, etc.—but despite its attractiveness and advertising effectiveness, it is architecturally rather conservative. Unlike its much-publicized close contemporary, Herbert Bayer's Newspaper Kiosk (1924), where architecture and advertisements are one, Klek's architectural object is a static, pure, and simple white box, physically separated from the constructivist structure of the advertising panels around it. The dynamics of the composition are provided solely by the latter, and, in that sense, the project is most functional and economic. The architecture is here reduced to the neutral function of a basic kiosk unit, providing only a necessary shelter, so that its form does not compete with the dominant communicative impact of the commercial message.

At the same time, Klek moved in the completely opposite direction, diverting his research away from constructivism. Two graphically related proposals for a Zenitheum, published only a month after *Advertisements,* with the final installment of Micić's text "The New Art," showed a lateral digression into the land of architectural fantasy.[47] This flight of fantasy is well described by Belgrade art historian Ješa Denegri:

Since it sufficed for it to be drawn and published in the magazine only as a reproduced image, the untenable planning of this architecture does not aspire to be realized; it is satisfied with the prospect of belonging to the category of visionary architecture, with which the history of European avant-garde "paper architecture," starting with Sant'Elia, is redolent—to the architecture, in other words, which, being unrealized, allows itself to dream up a new environment different from and more diverse than the contemporary reality, one that is puzzling and even mystical, full of symbolic connotations, such as its resemblance to a temple of a new religion (might it be the religion of Micić's vision of Zenitist art?).[48]

The two Zenitheums are rooted in expressionist iconography, as Irina Subotić noted, "fantastic prophetic projects whose vision can be compared with the ideas of Mendelsohn,"[49] but they are nevertheless strongly colored by Klek's own talent for phantasmagoria.

In subsequent projects Klek started to define his own architectural position. He began to question the character of new architectural space in a series of paintings which, as it were, displayed the unfolding of architectural elements. He painted walls, stairs, and floors as two-dimensional folded sheets that partly enclose, or direct, a fluid architectural space. These works show the influence of Lissitzky's concept of the Proun, "a changing-trains between painting and

1.12 Jo Klek, *Advertisements*, 1923. (Courtesy National Museum, Belgrade.)

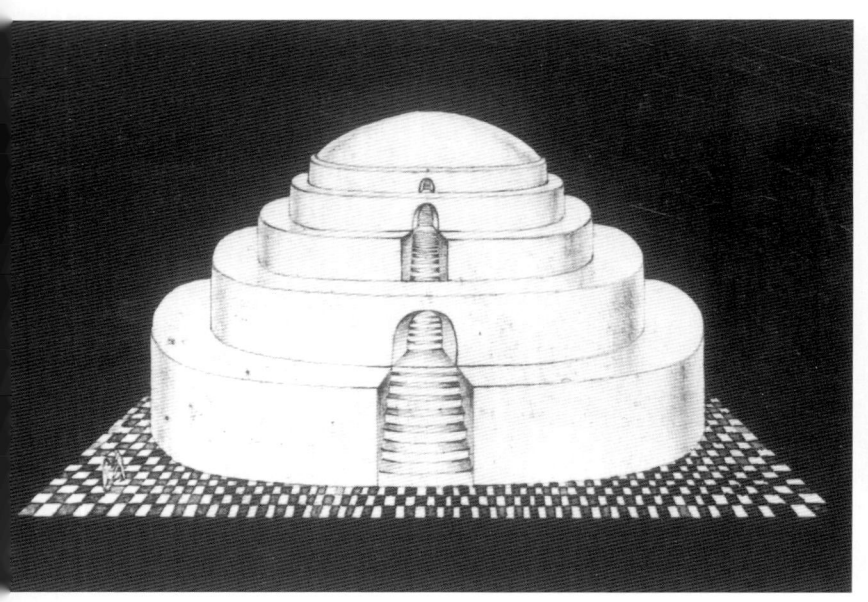 

architecture."[50] Nevertheless, Klek's paintings are of a simpler geometrical composition, and they are more symbolic, as if evoking the surrealist atmosphere that will actually characterize his post-Zenitist work in the late 1930s. One of the most interesting examples of this series is *Tavern* (1924). In this painting, the architectural volumetric is formed by the continual folding of one surface, which is transformed repeatedly from pavement to courtyard and then to walls, floors, and roofs of an endless house.[51] Spatial assembly of elemental planes is generated by nonhierarchical geometric manipulation, in which a sameness of object-house-city is achieved by the truly modern artist, as Mondrian wrote for the *De Stijl Manifesto:* "The genuinely modern artist sees the metropolis as abstract living converted into form."[52]

Much less pure and elemental are the particular spatial sequences or situations depicted in a decorative manner in the symbolic paintings *Playing Cards*. All these single spatial situations, strange houses or, more precisely, uncanny inhabited spaces, are painted as abstract objects, totally detached from reality, in their own universe. In his painting *Bayadere,* though, Klek portrays a city as a somber urban scene of a strange atemporality. In some aspects this painting of an imagined city, at the same time a fairly true portrait of old Zagreb, questions the traditional representation of space in perspective. Its method of cubist synthesis of space is authentic, yet its explorative intent seems close to the one in the painting *La Ville* by Léopold Survage, which was published on the front cover of *Zenit,* no. 6, in 1921.

1.13 (opposite page) Jo Klek, *Zenitheum I*, 1924. (Courtesy National Museum, Belgrade.)

1.14 (opposite page) Jo Klek, *Zenitheum II*, 1924. (Courtesy National Museum, Belgrade.)

1.15 Jo Klek, *Tavern*, published in *Zenit*, no. 34 (1924).

The final stage of Klek's Zenitist activity is marked by *Villa Zenit*, a work that symbolizes his shift away from Belgrade and *Zenit* and return to "normal" life, in which he would take his "real" name again and became Josip Seissel, student of architecture in Zagreb.[53] This drawing/painting approaches a definite architectural concept, and it strongly reflects Klek's desire for the realization of Zenitist architecture. Based on the combination of two points of reference, cubism and Loos, this work is critical to the establishment of architectural modernity in *Zenit*. All the crucial elements of a modern house or villa are displayed here: free plan, roof terrace, and spatial continuity of inside and outside, with an obvious reference to the identity of the Loosian aesthetic. With this painting, Klek finalizes his search, offers an unequivocal proposal for a house, and achieves what could be regarded as the first modern house of Belgrade, notwithstanding its painterly treatment.

If Jo Klek's paper architecture were to be regarded as the first operationalization of the modernist concept in architecture, it would not be too farfetched to place it as a predecessor to the first modern house actually built in Belgrade, the house of one of its most important modern architects, Milan Zloković. It is exactly in tracing the tentative overlaps of Loos, Klek, and Zloković that the difference between the modernist and the avant-garde architectural discourses becomes obvious.[54] The fact is that this difference, which is indeed inherent in the Belgrade modernist discourse, does not undermine the contribution of the avant-garde to the formative framework of the modernist stance. On the contrary, it raises an important question: what was the extent of the emancipation of society achieved by modern architecture in relation to the (mis)calculated failure by the avant-garde?

1.16 (opposite page) Jo Klek, *Playing Cards*, 1924. (Courtesy National Museum, Belgrade.)

1.17 (opposite page) Jo Klek, *Bayadere*, 1924. (Courtesy National Museum, Belgrade.)

1.18 Cover of *Zenit*, no. 6 (July 1921): Léopold Survage, *La Ville*.

1.19 (following page) Jo Klek, *Villa Zenit*, 1924–1925. (Courtesy National Museum, Belgrade.)

ЈОСИФ КЛЕК

2 CONSTRUCT

THE ESLINGER CASE 2.1

In the Serbia of the 1920s, understanding of the new spirit in architecture lagged far behind developments in the art and literary scene. Architecture played the role of a shock absorber between the radicalism of the avant-garde position and commercial imperatives demanding "habitations of style" based on historic or national paradigms. In the photodocumentation of Belgrade architecture of the 1920s, one photograph stands out from the prevailing commonplace of "sweet traditionalism" characteristic of buildings in eclectic styles. Taken some seventy years ago, this photograph shows an extraordinarily plain edifice with a man standing in front of it, positioned slightly off-center, his posture characteristically stooped, his arm in an elegant pose. He is dressed in proper gentleman's attire and wears a hat. His dress is modern in a Loosian sense, in that one does not notice it. His identity is impossible to establish: at first glance his position seems like that of an elite guard in summer military uniform; the shadow of a mullion on the door behind him appears like a parade weapon, the light is transforming the shape of his hat into a soldier's cap. On closer inspection, this is all just a fancy, a key that fails to open any door of recognition. The form of the building offers even fewer clues as to what it might be, or where it actually is. The man in the photograph is being photographed, yet it is not a photograph of him but of a building behind him. It is a portrait of architecture, a professionally taken shot of the building at its best angle, with none of the distortions of amateur photography. The photograph appears to be aimed at publicity, but the presence of a man transforms it into personalized documentary material.

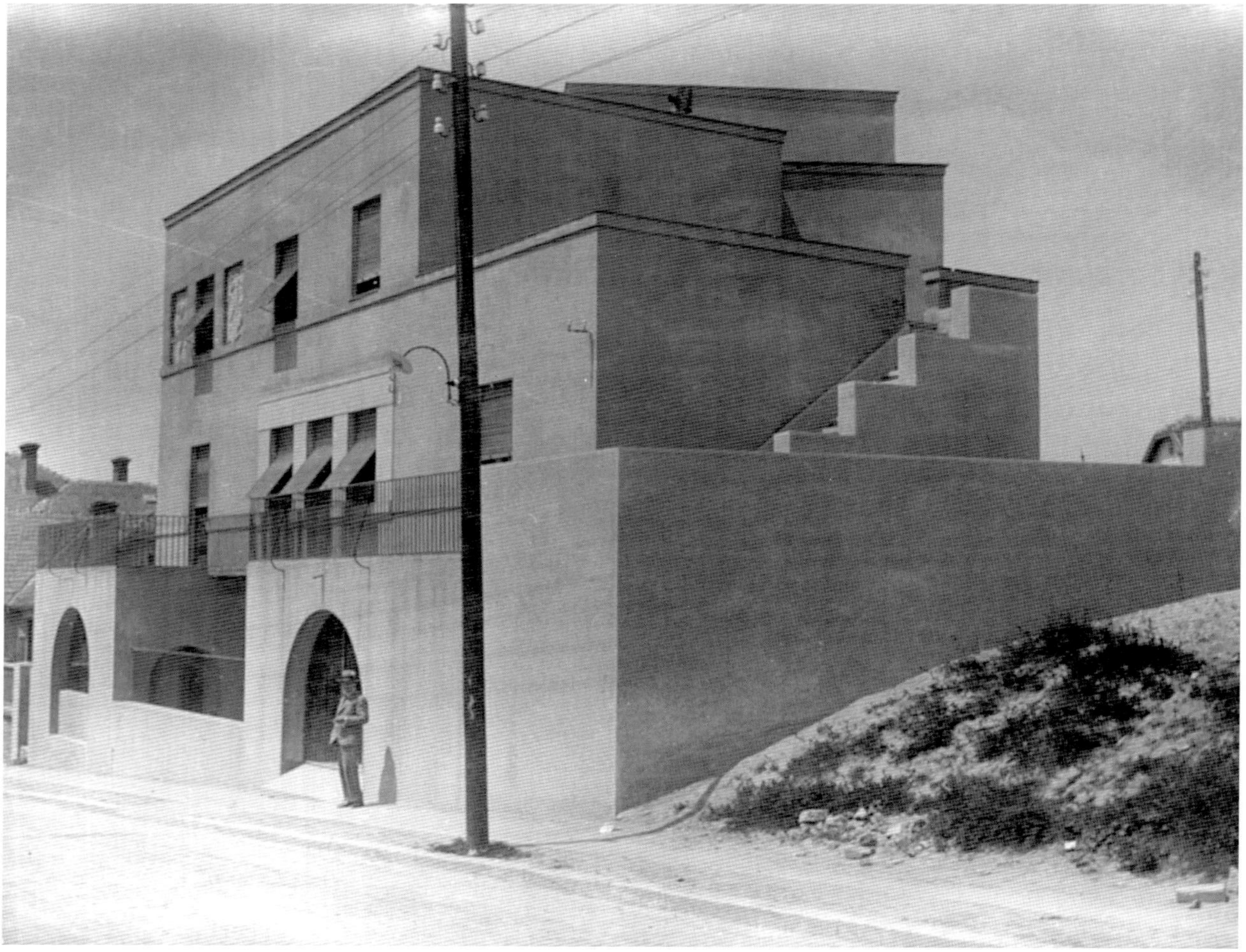

It is now widely known that this is a photograph of the first modern house in Belgrade, taken in the summer of 1929, and that the man in front of the house is Milan Zloković, the architect who both designed and owned it.[1] The facts being known, and the photographed object laid under our eyes (but, as Le Corbusier phrased it, "eyes which do not see"), we are left with no understanding of its genealogy. What actually is there to be seen?

The young architect, barely in his thirties, posing in front of his house must have been convinced of the importance of his achievement. But, in addition to the architect's pride in his work, the photo session also reveals the pride of a homeowner. What is most interesting is the photographically captured duality of the house's public function as the first realization of modernism in Belgrade, and its private function as the first home of a young family. The other photos from the same series document the highly conscious process of setting the scene for the camera that can be none other than Zloković's. The inhabitants of the house are always in the frame, but they do not obtrude on the main objective of photographing the architecture. It is as if the family were the backdrop for a portrait of architecture, in much the same way that picturesque landscape backdrops were used as portrait backgrounds in the photographic studios of the nineteenth century.[2] The family group portrait on the main terrace is composed so subtly that it does not subordinate the public image of the house to the private function of this picture in the family album. On the contrary, it actually becomes a most exciting photograph of the house. It shows the architect's uncompromising modernist stance, and his self-assuredness in setting a new aesthetic order.

The house is clearly self-referential and pays no homage to the idealization of a bourgeois "nice house"; it is noncontextual—and yet it uses the context's full potential for the architectural composition. If Jo Klek's painting *Villa Zenit* could be seen as a moment of rupture with the ornamental image of style and the precursor of the architectural discourse of the new epoch, then Zloković's house might be regarded as its first architectural realization in interwar Serbia.[3] Furthermore, this house marks the point of change for Belgrade from the city as *polis,* even if only as a matter of nostalgia, into the metropolis. To use Massimo Cacciari's argument, its antinatural or antiorganic, antiexpressive, antisynthetic, and nonnostalgic architecture opposes the mythical notion of the city as a community organism, and addresses the conditions of the metropolis as *Grossstadt,* with its "nervous life," alienation, and autonomous individuality.[4] It is in the opposition to sentimentality and petit-bourgeois reality that the architecture of this house manifests its metropolitan tendency.

In the photographic representation, though, the antiexpressive form is offset by the presence of a family, which serves as the key to understanding what the function of the building might be. By having a family inhabit the frame, the

2.1   Milan Zloković, Zloković house, Belgrade, 1927–1928. Architect in front of his house.

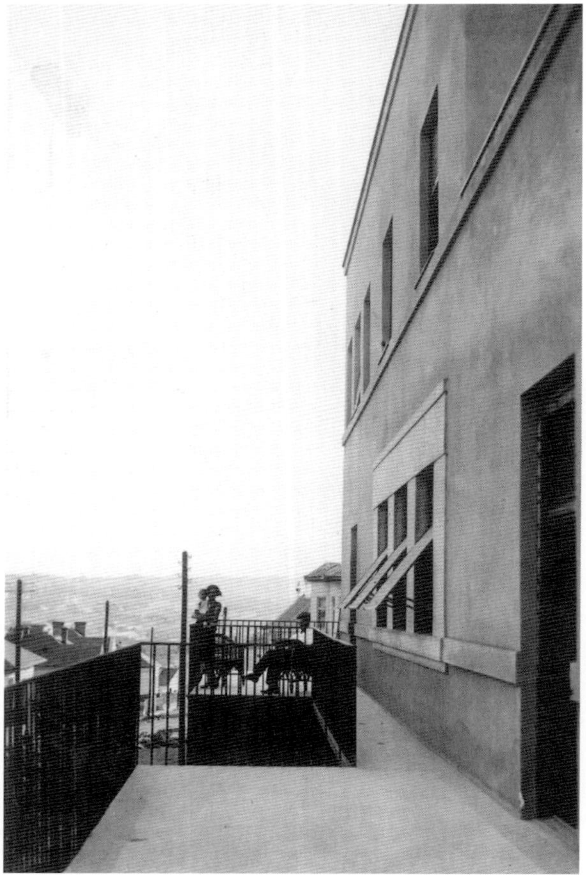
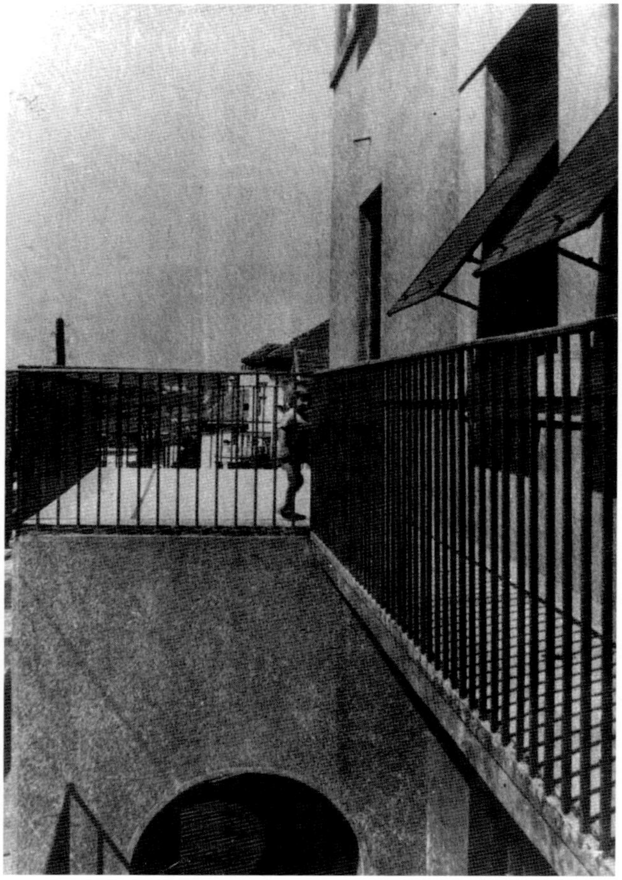

image clearly conveys a message that this is a house, but also that the notion of what a house looks like is to be changed forever. To paraphrase from Walter Benjamin's notes on photography, I would argue that in making the portrait of his house Zloković does not use the photographic medium just to reproduce the new architectural form with mathematical accuracy. Rather, he aims to grasp and to represent, while justifying and embellishing the image with the family as a backdrop, the notions and intentions implicit in the new understanding of modernity in (domestic) architecture.[5] Thus, the photographs were made to convey the concept of new architecture, and from the very outset photography became operative in enunciating the identity of modernist discourse in Belgrade.

The photographs of the Zloković house were first exhibited at the "First Salon of Architecture," organized by the Group of Architects of the Modern Movement in Belgrade and held in June 1929 in the Arts Pavilion. This was not the first time that Zloković exhibited his works, but it was the first time he presented his work through the photographic medium, using photography as a means of conveying the message of contemporary architecture. Curiously enough, the founding of the Group of Architects of the Modern Movement in Belgrade on 12 November 1928 virtually coincided with that of the Belgrade Photo Club, an organization "for the promotion of scientific, artistic, and amateur photography," on 4 December 1928. The "First Exhibition of the Photo Club" followed almost immediately after the "First Salon of Architecture," at the same venue, the Arts Pavilion, in September 1929. So the first public promotion of architecture, represented in photographs, coincided with the first significant postwar public exhibition of photography.[6] According to a period critic, the photographers exhibiting at the Photo Club exhibition generally aimed at artistic and pictorial effects.[7] While photographers mimicked painting, architects took to photography as the most practical means to communicate, and eventually to sell, their ideas and concepts. It needs to be stressed that, in addition to their first and foremost task of documenting the built work, architects used the potential of the medium to convey their changed perception of the built environment. In the photographs of his house, Milan Zloković presents the concept of the pure cubic form of the new architecture by dissecting the volumetric into a series of frames. These carefully framed fragments stand as images in their own right, almost totally independent of the architecture they represent. In fact, they form a set of references, not necessarily following the actual architectural narrative, but having an autonomous status as visual evidence of modernity.

The acceptance of concept as the main content of a photographic image, with the consequent understanding of photography as an independent art medium, came about in Belgrade with the unfolding of surrealism.[8] Whereas in the earlier publications of *Zenit* photography had been used merely as a means

2.2   Zloković house. Family group portrait on the terrace; child on the terrace.

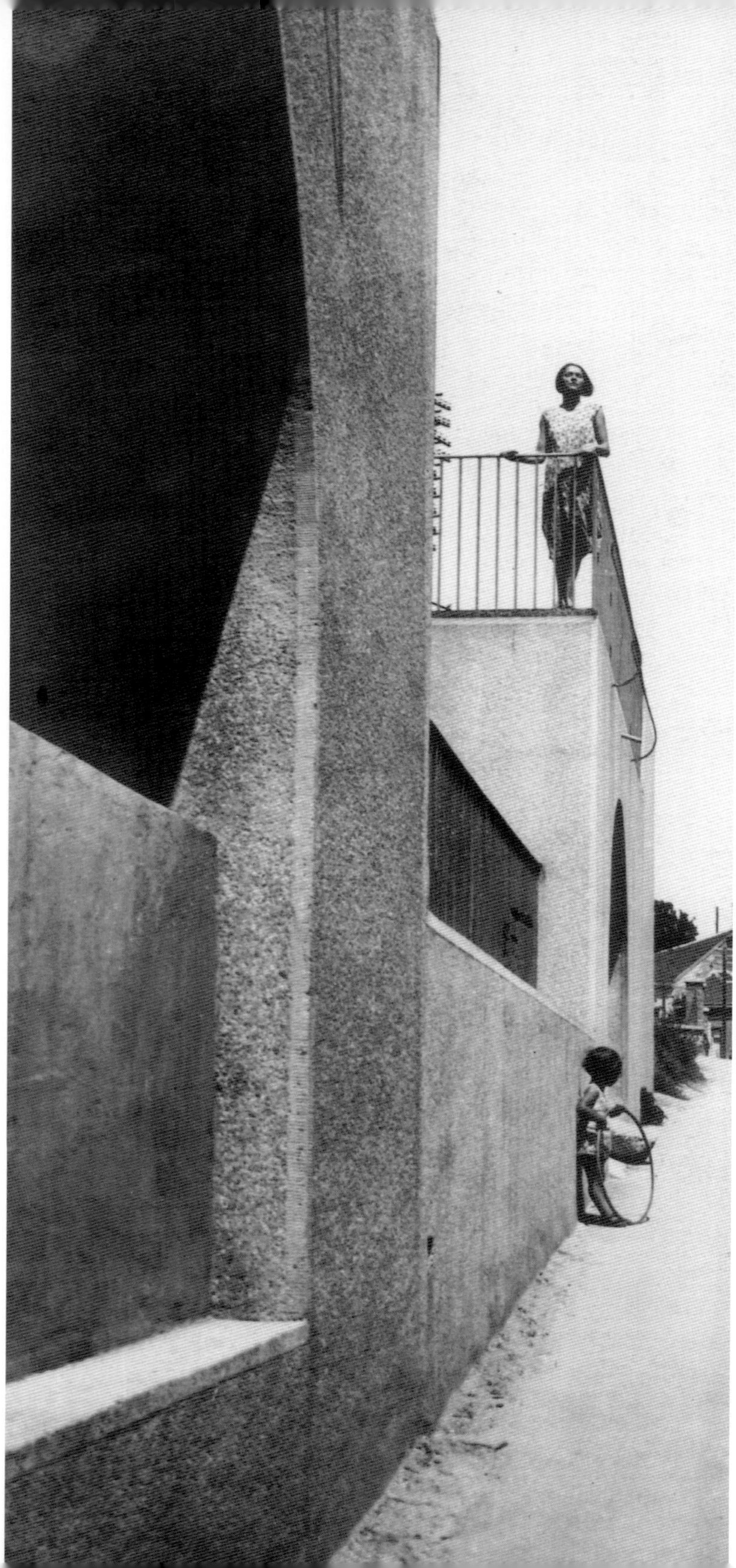

2.3 (opposite page) Zloković house. Mrs. Zloković on the terrace and her son Đorđe by the house.

2.4 Zloković house. Architect in front of his house.

of reproducing artworks and, in some instances, for documenting events,⁹ surrealist magazines brought a different attitude to the medium. It is clear that the photographic reproduction of artworks in *Zenit* had been no more than a phase in the struggle between photography and painting.¹⁰ While Micić unreservedly championed painting, the surrealists brought photography to the fore in their publications. Marko Ristić, one of the principal protagonists of the Belgrade surrealist circle, noted the importance of photography to the discourse of surrealism:

I do not care if this may seem unimportant and ridiculous, as gigglers will find anything to laugh at, but let this be noted once again as an example that one should look for signs of miracles outside the great scene settings and emphatic apparatus of visibility, that one evening in early summer 1928 I said, in front of The Russian Tsar, with no indications whatsoever that it would actually be so, that *Nadja* would be illustrated with photographs, only to find the next morning, when I suddenly received it, that it was really illustrated with photographs, which is by no means unimportant as a sign of the true, everyday, documentary, undisguised, and realistic in its connection to the supernatural, for these photographs,

ordinary, yet by their suppressed eloquence hallucinatory, are only signifying that the surreal is immanent in the real.[11]

Surrealism in Belgrade developed as a predominantly literary movement out of the activity of a group of artists, writers, and poets who initially advocated, much like all the avant-gardes of the period, an active orientation to all that was new and opposed to the retrograde and old in art and life.[12] The first magazine in which the future surrealists Marko Ristić and Milan Dedinac took a leading role was *Putevi* (Belgrade, 1922–1923). Among other references to modernism, *Putevi* published an article introducing *L'Esprit nouveau* and supporting its ideology of a constructive understanding of modern art.[13] In its second year, under the editorship of Marko Ristić, the magazine published important articles by André Breton, who became one of the most influential figures in the development of Serbian surrealism. The decisive shift from modernism to surrealism followed with the new magazine *Svedočanstva* (Belgrade, 1924–1925), started by Rastko Petrović, Milan Dedinac, Marko Ristić, Mladen Dimitrijević, Dušan Matić, and Aleksandar Vučo. The magazine was endorsed in Paris surrealist circles by being recommended by Breton in his *La Révolution surréaliste*.[14] Only eight issues of *Svedočanstva* were published, at

2.5 (opposite page) Nikola Vučo, *Portrait of Marko Ristić*, photograph, 1930. (Courtesy Museum of Applied Art, Belgrade.)

2.6 "Girl with tattoos," photograph published in *Svedočanstva*, no. 7 (1925).

intervals of ten days between November 1924 and March 1925. The first issue was dedicated to the Croatian poet Tin Ujević, followed by a series of different thematic issues: no. 2: Slavonic Issue; no. 3: Poetic Art; no. 4: Emotions of Intimacy and Devotion; no. 5: Christmas Issue; no. 6: Notes from the Home of Bedlamites; no. 7: Hell; and no. 8: Paradise.

The supremacy of text over other art forms in Belgrade avant-garde publications of the period (*Zenit, Svedočanstva, Nemoguće/L'Impossible,* etc.) did not prevent different art media from taking precedence at various points, according to the aims and orientation of each movement. Text was deemed the most direct way of sounding the call to new thinking and fresh action and the most important catalyst in the perception of abstract new ideas. It also served, however, to point to other art forms. As Miodrag B. Protić wrote: "Due to the solidarity, cooperation, and passion of talented individuals, there was no separation of the individual arts with their own problems and preoccupations during that period. This anti-guild attitude of generality and openness, sometimes coupled with the aim that art should be not only—and perhaps not at all—an art, but an attitude to life, was particularly important for avant-garde movements in the first postwar years."[15] An important aspect of Belgrade surrealism is that it gave photography the status of a work of art, thereby legitimizing its position and its right to free artistic experimentation.

In February 1925 the magazine *Svedočanstva,* in an issue thematically entitled "Hell," published three documentary photographs of tattooed human bodies, under a section headed "Settlements for Those Banished from the Garden of Eden."[16] While the first two photographs zoom in on tattooed parts of male bodies whose identity is obscured and irrelevant, the third photograph fully displays a young woman reclining on a (psychoanalyst's?) couch, her body entirely covered by tattoos. On closer inspection, however, one realizes that the tattoo is not genuine, that the girl's body is dressed in a fine tricot printed with tattoo pattern. It suddenly becomes obvious that the image is a fake if it is to be taken as a documentary photograph. As Milanka Todić suggests, "It is not a visual document of unknown 'surreal' things in the world around us, it is itself a false document on the plane of representation of reality. Its real function is revealed in the intention to use the photographic medium in representing an action conceived and carried out in the surrealist fashion."[17] I would argue that the girl's body is a backdrop for a surrealist projection, it is an object that has been edited—a montage. For the Belgrade surrealists, the evident reference to the famous essay "Ornament and Crime" by Adolf Loos is perhaps a memento of their earlier affiliation with *L'Esprit nouveau,* in which this essay had been published.[18] Loos wrote: "The modern man who tattoos himself is a criminal or a degenerate. There are prisons where eighty percent of the inmates bear tattoos. Those who are tattooed but are not imprisoned are latent criminals or degenerate aristocrats. If a tattooed person dies at liberty, it is only that he died a few years before he committed a murder."[19] But the tattooed woman in the photograph is not a criminal or a degenerate; she is merely having fun posing for an idea.

With no affinity to the avant-garde shock treatment, architect Milan Zloković nevertheless employed a similar method of montage for documenting his own built work. His method is particular in that the photographed object is edited before the photograph is taken, like the body of the "tattooed" woman. It is a montage of the content and not of the final product, the form of the resulting picture; a montage on site, as it were, and not an intervention in the chemical process in the darkroom or the actual surface of the photograph. In this way the documentary character of both architecture and photograph is retained. In the family group portrait on the terrace, mentioned earlier, Zloković, in the dual role of architect and father/husband, strikes a detached pose, as if uninterested and occupied by his reading, while his wife with a child in her arms stands by, gazing afar. The scene evokes Kurt Schwitters's prediction of the use of people to fuse all factors into a composite work: "Even people can be used. / People can even be tied to backdrops. / People can even appear actively, even in their everyday position, they can speak on two legs, even in sensible sentences."[20]

Aiming to draw attention to the composite effect of his work in a photograph, Zloković sets the scene with the most attentive planning, down to the last item. The most telling detail is careful control of the position of the wooden roller blinds, known generally by their trade name Eslinger.[21] By angling the blinds' metal frames, Zloković dramatizes the facade surface, and with this simple gesture he introduces a dynamism into the otherwise planar and static treatment of the wall. It seems certain that the angling of the frames is carried out deliberately, with the montage process in mind. In the photographs showing the whole facade, an asymmetrical arrangement of three-plus-two frames extended outward accentuates the stepped volumetric of the house. In other camera angles, where a compacted elevation is shown in exaggerated perspective, only the three lower frames are extended in order to achieve the desired dramatic effect.

The skewed geometry of the blinds is used as a counterpoint to the primary volumetrics of the house, thus acting as a catalyst to aesthetic perception and making the impact greater. It might seem only a trivial detail, were it not for its recurrence in photographs of Zloković's buildings in the years that followed.[22] This detail, which is highly informative of Zloković's method of tuning in architecture for photographic representation, became his signature in the photographs of his buildings that he himself controlled. In the photographs of Commerce Hall in Skopje, the blinds are pulled up, but the extended frames twinkle on top windows like the false eyelashes of a film star. The architect has here tried to correct the deadness of a two-dimensional representation of his

2.7 Milan Zloković, Commerce Hall, Skopje, 1933–1935. Details of the corner volume.

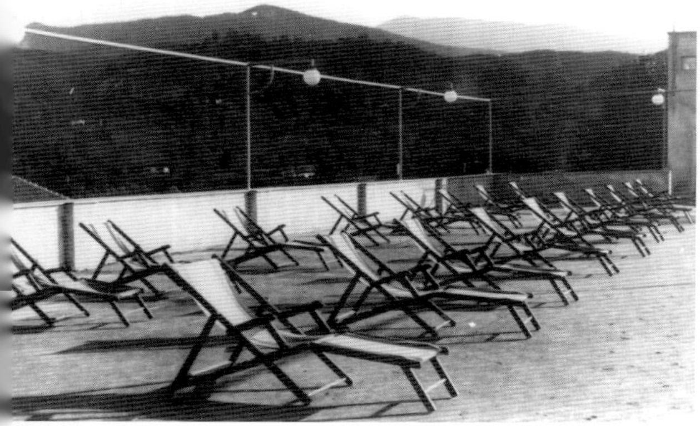

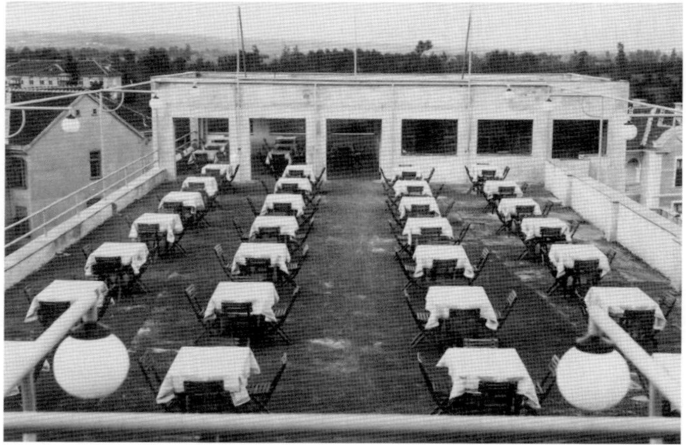

2.8 Milan Zloković, Hotel Žiča, Mataruška Banja, 1931–1932. Solarium setup on the roof terrace; café setup on the roof terrace; restaurant furniture setup.

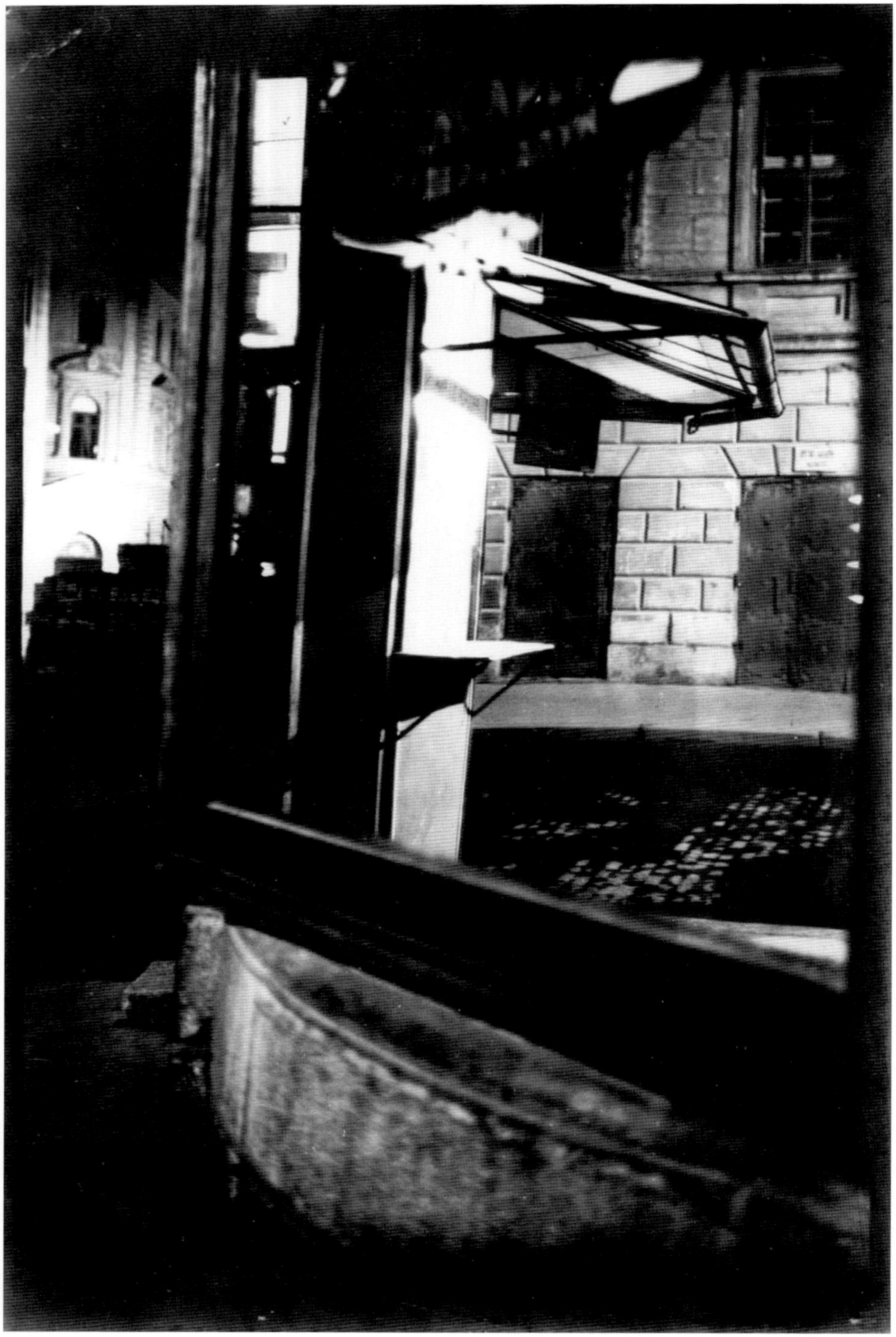

work by introducing a shifting focus to achieve a dynamic play of light and shade, thus making the photographically captured moment less finite. Also indicative are photographs of the Hotel Žiča's open-air cinema/sun deck with a regiment of empty chaises longues, or the ones of highly photogenic and geometrically intriguing setups of Thonet furniture in the hotel restaurant. The same sense of the medium's defect is evident in these interventions, a defect to which Adolf Loos famously referred: "However I contend: a real building makes no impression as an illustration reproduced two-dimensionally. It is my greatest pride that the interiors which I have created are totally ineffective in photographs. I am proud of the fact that the inhabitants of my spaces do not recognize their own apartments in the photographs."[23]

The deficiency of the photographic medium in recording the three-dimensional character of architectural space is used to advantage in the photographs published in the surrealist almanac *Nemoguće/L'Impossible* (Belgrade, 1930). I refer here specifically to two photographs by Nikola Vučo that were incorporated in the important programmatic article of Serbian surrealism, "Just in Passing."[24] The captions to both, thought out by Marko Ristić, are in fact references to some of the principal propositions of the article. The images themselves carry an autonomous visual message, however, not directly mediating the textual content of the article but acting on the parallel plane of visual "textuality." In this sense, I would argue that by eradicating the boundaries between reality and imagination in these images, Vučo also produced a striking testimony to the multifaceted character of the modern city. The reflections of, or on, the glass surfaces in the photograph entitled *We Have to Convince No One* refer to a characteristic urban experience, not as a document of a particular city but a picture of a nonplace. The image conveys the same notion as the words on the same page: "it is and it isn't, both black and white, both yes and no," but in a visual register unrelated to the text.[25] Similarly, the photograph entitled *Wall of Agnosticism* is timeless and placeless, and yet it precisely pinpoints the anxiety of the epoch. By focusing on the seemingly hidden detail of a familiar mass-produced object such as a hollow building block, Vučo extends the boundaries of the artistic and architectural fields of action. Yet, when its caption is cross-referenced to the footnote on the same page, this photograph reads differently: "Yet we demand the impossible, and always the impossible, from everything that still demands something, and finally from all that demands nothing. For could we allow—we are starting from that question, even with an instantaneous, tired wave of a hand, a smile of careful dissociation—for dare we contribute, even in a moment of skepticism, to that lair, to that persistently constructed wall of beds of agnosticism, irony, and indifference, erected in disgrace to the essential fire and real *cognizance?*"[26] It is this duality that connects back to the ambivalent status of photography in artistic and, to a certain extent, architectural projects of the period.

2.9   Nikola Vučo, *We Have to Convince No One*, photograph, 1930. (Courtesy Museum of Applied Art, Belgrade.)

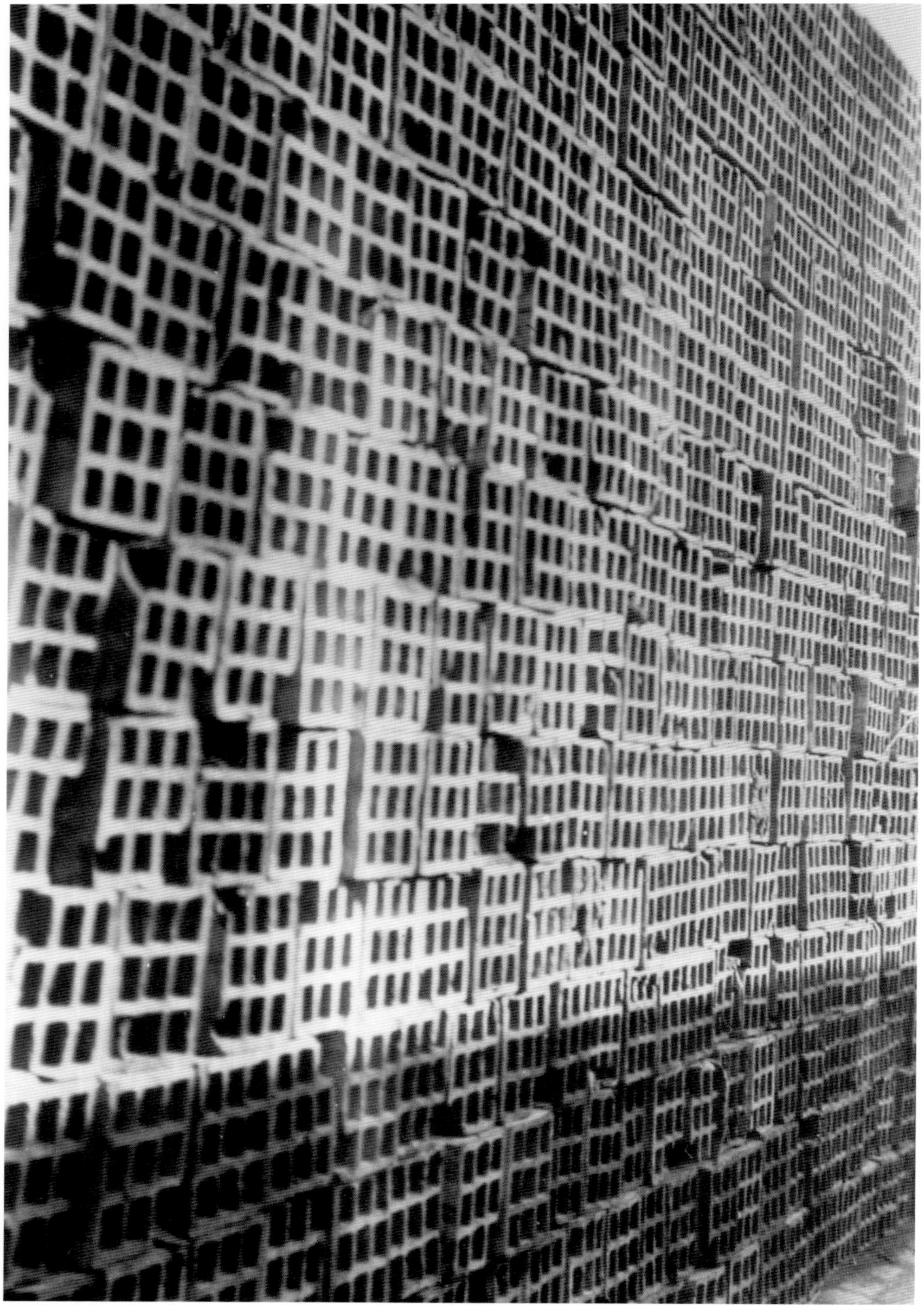

"The specific relation of surrealism to an object is articulated in a new manner with the technique of the rayograph or photogram," writes Todić, introducing the work of the surrealist artist and photographer Stevan (Vane) Živadinović Bor, who had experimented with photograms in the manner of Man Ray.[27] His photograms were published in the surrealist almanac *Nemoguće/L'Impossible* and in the magazine *Nadrealizam danas i ovde*. When he later turned to photographing life, Bor made the ordinary unfamiliar by the disquieting gaze of the camera. His photographs *Milica S. Lazović Like a Shadow* and *One Minute before a Crime* capture an uncanny moment of suspense in a perfectly ordinary Belgrade urban scene. As Dejan Sretenović observed in a recent rereading of these images, "it reminds one of the scene of the crime . . . , since the very gaze of the camera manifests itself as a threat. . . . In both cases the murder is frozen in the scopic field of the gaze directed toward the victim, and this means that the very act of committing the crime is manifested as an empty place which fills these apparently harmless scenes with the feeling of uneasiness."[28] There is a certain analogy between Bor's urban sequences and the photographs that Milan Zloković took on the roof garden of his house. Both sets of photographs have elements of the aesthetics of a film still, but more importantly the subjects present in these images are estranged by the method of photographic representation. In both, also, scenography is very carefully chosen to display unfamiliar architectural spaces that are further estranged by the subjects inhabiting them. Bor's photographs are set in a hard urban landscape with a road underpass opening toward a horizon, underlined by either a city skyline or a river bank. Those of the architect, limited to the scene of the private house, are set on a roof terrace—a much celebrated modernist reinvention—the Zloković family's concrete garden. Finally, both sets of photographs are taken in such a manner as to precisely represent the unyielding advance of urbanism in Belgrade, coupled with the anxiety inherent in a modern metropolis.

2.10   (opposite page) Nikola Vučo, *Wall of Agnosticism*, photograph, 1926–1929. (Courtesy Museum of Applied Art, Belgrade.)

2.11   Photogram by Vane Živadinović Bor, published in *Nemoguće/L'Impossible*, 1930.

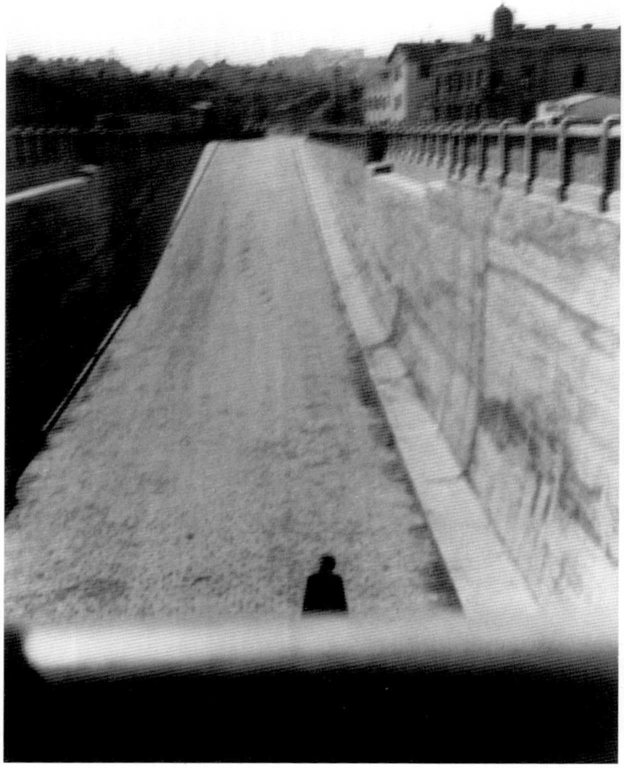
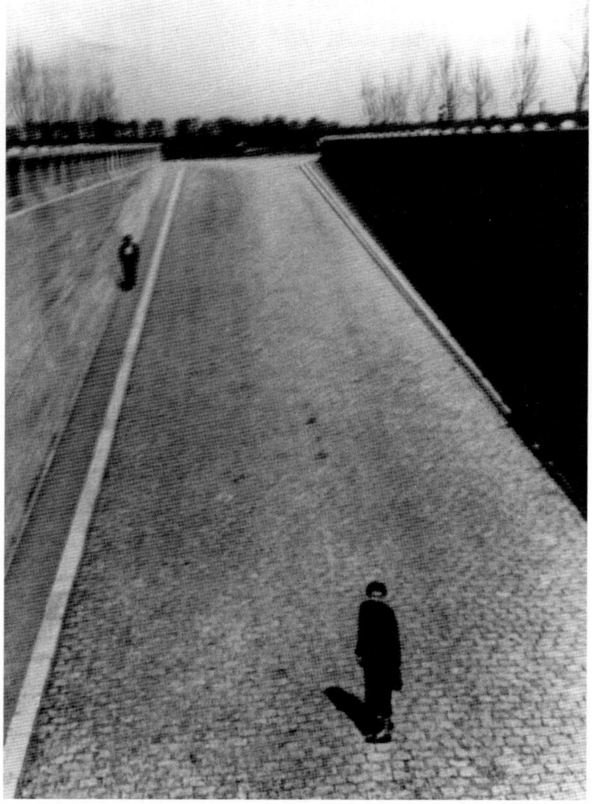

2.12 (opposite page) Vane Živadinović Bor, Milica S. Lazović *Like a Shadow* and *One Minute before a Crime*, photographs, both 1935. (Courtesy Museum of Contemporary Art, Belgrade.)

2.13 Zloković house. Roof garden.

2.2 INTERIOR IDENTITY

"The space disguises itself—puts on, like an alluring creature, the costumes of moods," wrote Walter Benjamin of the nineteenth-century domestic interior, in which "this mood involves, furthermore, an aversion to the open air."[29] Could this relation to the *plein air* be an essential parameter for distinguishing the mood of the century, or the mood of an architecture? Or was it the light, pouring into the mood of the twentieth century, that changed its identity completely? If we look at Serbian modernism from the interior, what prospects will be illuminated for understanding its narrative? Benjamin finds the "threshold magic," as if, looked at from within, the outside becomes clearer.

There is one particular interior that precisely reflected the mood of a Belgrade burgher in the 1920s: the "Bosnian hall" in the house of Krista and Đorđe Đorđević. The couple moved to Belgrade from Zagreb after the First World War, and soon made their new home in Strahinjića Bana Street a vibrant meeting place for many a young artist and intellectual of the period. The building itself was an existing house that had been thoroughly reconstructed in 1923 to accommodate the lifestyle of the new inhabitants and their bohemian friends, with the new lobby, central hall, and large dining room in the ground floor, and spacious private quarters in the mansard floor.[30] The house became known for its collection of artworks and ethnographic objects, and especially for the interior of the hall "in the Bosnian style," a room architecturally remodeled by Milan Zloković with reliefs by sculptor Sreten Stojanović, and the interior of the dining room with the large fresco by painter Milo Milunović.

The "Bosnian hall" was exquisitely designed by Zloković as a showcase for Stojanović's wooden reliefs.[31] The whole ensemble, comprising 36 reliefs in oak of various dimensions, was assembled in 1927, five years after Stojanović had started sketching the first elements for it. The reliefs were of decorative-ornamental character, with sharp and simple lines defining the highly stylized composition, low sculptural modeling of individual figures, and with color applied on some of the sculpted surfaces to accentuate the carved drawing.[32] The art historian Lazar Trifunović describes the coloring as selective, in the sense that "thick paint—red, blue, white, black—which he [Stojanović] applied in harmonic relationships . . . was functional to modeling and drawing, and was not an independent and aggressive element."[33] The reliefs depict people in Oriental costumes in scenes of life in Bosnia during the Ottoman rule, or just individual figures smoking. The architectural part of the interior was as stylized as the artworks themselves, especially in the synthetic structuring of spatial elements and their formal articulation of the low surface modeling. It is difficult to distinguish

2.14 Milan Zloković, the "Bosnian Hall" in the house of Krista and Dr. Đorđe Đorđević, Belgrade, 1927. View to the dining room with fresco by Milo Milunović in the background, reliefs by Sreten Stojanović.

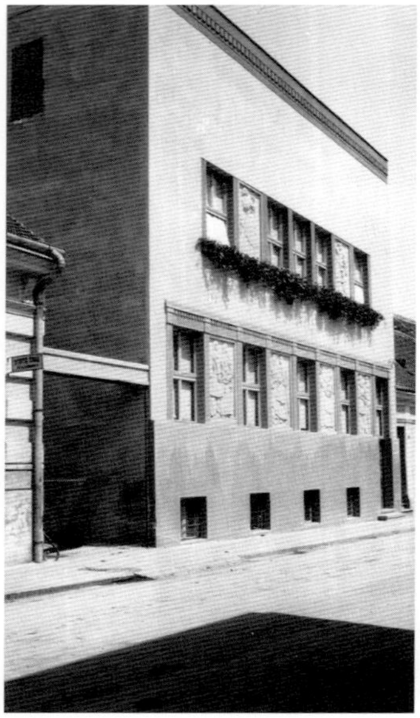

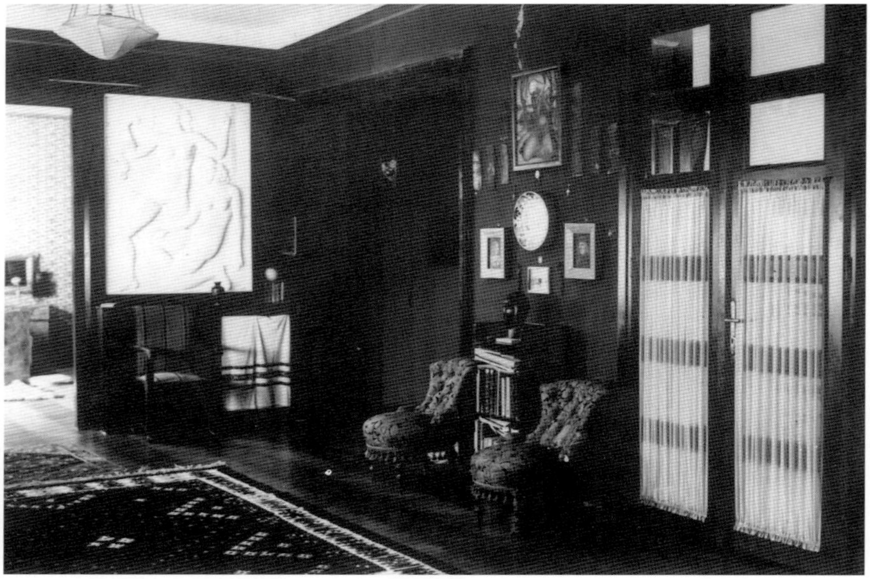

2.15 (opposite page, left) Milan Zloković, house of Đorđe Dragutinović, Zemun, 1929. Reliefs by Sreten Stojanović.

2.16 (opposite page and this page) Zloković house. Interior views of central room toward bedroom and toward dining room.

where the artwork stops and the architectural treatment of the space carries on, the two being complementary to each other in a subtle harmony of proportion, simplicity, and restraint. In contrast, the highly ornamental character of the loose ethnographic paraphernalia in the room (carpets, nargileh, and Oriental coffee tables) somewhat mars the hard, planar cleanliness of the encasing interior.

Stojanović believed that "if a work is to be done for architecture, the sculptor has to feel architecturally."[34] The architect, too, had to feel artistically in order to present the artworks as an independent yet integral part of the architectural space. Nevertheless, this was plainly not a modern interior. It belonged to the same protomodern domain as did the house of Đorđe Dragutinović in Zemun, which Stojanović and Zloković completed in 1929.[35] Here the static order of reliefs and windows alternating in a symmetrical, frontal composition makes the architectural articulation of the house appear as an art of the wall surface. As Stojanović wrote, "Architectural relief has a lot in common with wall painting. Both are intended for the wall, with no depth and set for frontal viewing, and their composition is designed to fill up space."[36] There is in these words a trace of apprehension related to empty, or maybe open, space, a kind of suppressed agoraphobia.

The "Bosnian hall" interior reflects this apprehension in the static precision of the wooden case that arrests movement in the center of the room, whereupon the reliefs separate and protect the private interior from the intrusion of the public exterior. Furthermore, the thematic content is, as Benjamin would suggest, "a stimulus to intoxication and dream" in which one feels secluded. In one photograph, the view through a pointed four-centered arch goes to yet another interior, this one of a diametrically opposite character but still set up as a kind of showcase. It is a dining room decorated to look European, with English-style furniture and wallpapering, ornate silver candlesticks, and, above all, a large fresco painted by Milo Milunović. Enveloped in the darkness of the dining room, the painted surface of the fresco provides the only discernible lucidity. As Benjamin suggests, "From this cavern, one does not like to stir."[37]

It was very characteristic of the domestic space of the period that rooms were set as frozen stage scenes, quite like tableaux, either Oriental or Western. The ultimate elaboration of this concept was carried out in the rooms of the two royal court buildings in the center of Belgrade. There, the image of private space was constructed to take on a highly representational role. As agents in the establishment of bourgeois taste, these rooms performed before the public eye, but only when the act was most carefully controlled. The photographs of the "Turkish room" at the Old Royal Palace and the "Bosnian room" at the New Palace, published in the weekly illustrated magazine *Nedeljne ilustracije,* imply the housebound condition of their owners/inhabitants. In their detachment and displacement from everyday life, the rooms appear more like exhibits than inhabited spaces. Within this kind of interior, to paraphrase Benjamin, architecture sought out an intimate view, as opposed to the modern image of a well-lit and ventilated domestic space that invites the public exterior into the domain of the home.[38] While conforming to a similar concept, in their design of the Đorđević "Bosnian hall" Zloković and Stojanović made a radical break with the suffocating elaboration of the tableaux theme. They purified the constituent elements of the interior to the point of ultimate stylization, and brought in the spirit of contemporaneity in a lateral and subdued fashion.

2.17   (opposite page) Dragiša Brašovan, Brašovan house, Belgrade, 1931. Interior of the hall.

2.18   (opposite page) Milan Zloković, State Mortgage Bank, Sarajevo, 1928–1932. Interior of the banking hall.

2.19   State Mortgage Bank. Street and courtyard facades.

Still, the interior stayed firmly rooted in the former paradigms, even though architectural concepts of space and form began to be transformed radically. In fact, it was precisely the interior that resisted most the movement to put an end to the dwelling in the old sense, and the reversal of aesthetic form and consequent visual difference. As Benjamin remarked, "Against the armature of glass and iron, upholstery offers resistance with its textiles."[39] When we look at Serbian modernism, where else should we look for clues to the change of its interior identity but in the house of Milan Zloković? It was there, in the three principal rooms that formed a continuous long space parallel to the street, that the gradual unfolding of the new context took place. The definition of space is provided by a simple matte black paint finish to the central room that neutralizes the cohabitation of sundry loose items on walls and floors, such as *kilims*, gaudily upholstered chairs, religious icons on wood, contemporary artworks by artist friends,[40] furniture designed by Zloković himself, and so on. In addition, a new interpretation of the relation between inside and outside creates here a new subject-object relation. The cast reliefs in this interior do not encase the room space, but relate to the articulation of the facade walls.[41] Even if the interior reliefs only mirror the instinct to enliven and adorn the otherwise plain wall surface, it is no longer an act of protection but of reference to the public exterior. In comparison, the interior of the hall in the house of the architect Dragiša Brašovan (1931) retains an autonomous status in relation to the external architecture. The luster finish of the inside surfaces contrasts with the plainness of the facade walls. Differing from the modest paint finish of Zloković's interior, the custom tailoring of the glossy cladding and the more rustic fireplace construction reflect the distinct sensuality and hedonism of Brašovan's lifestyle.

The real change came, as it did elsewhere, when functionality took priority over (life)style. Public interiors, such as those of banking halls, embraced the simple lines and the hard finish, although in more opulent materials. There is a solid and timeless Central European spirit, yet one that has been "modernized" by functionality, in the interior design and plain wooden furnishings in the banking hall of the State Mortgage Bank in Sarajevo by Zloković (1928–1932). The pronounced elegance in the articulation of structural elements, coupled with contemporary functional detailing of fixtures and furniture, has a Loosian refinement. The contrasting articulation of the building's facades is indicative of the competing notions of the former context and the modernizing impulse. The stone-clad front facades belong to an academicism particularly characteristic of bank buildings of the period, which speaks of a solidity worthy of a citizen's trust. At the same time, facades facing the inner courtyard are designed with a concern only for functionality and simplicity, with not one extraneous element. Notwithstanding the high level of stylization and modernization of the academic style in this building, Zloković's design still largely complied with the dominant

2.20 (opposite page) Hugo Ehrlich, Yugoslav Associated Bank, Belgrade, 1929–1931. Facade.

2.21 Yugoslav Associated Bank. Interior of the banking hall.

idiom. Only in the parts of the building where he felt unobserved were new formal solutions boldly anticipated.

At roughly the same time, the Croatian architect Hugo Ehrlich realized quite a different bank building in Belgrade, the Yugoslav Associated Bank (1929–1931). His design reflects an uncompromising shift toward contemporaneity, both in the articulation of the facades and in the treatment of the interiors. Precise and rational design of the central space of the main banking hall, lit from the large lantern above and furnished with original Marcel Breuer tubular steel furniture, manifested the most advanced thinking in the interior design of the period. Yet the static atmosphere of security and the orderly centrality of space were still the main points of departure here. New materials, such as steel, glass, and rubber flooring, were allowed only in areas hidden from the customers' view.

Evident transformation of the character of the interior can be seen in the restaurant of the Hotel Žiča in Mataruška Banja by Zloković (1931–1932). A bright and airy mood prevails here, implying the health-conscious atmosphere of a spa resort. In fact, the unadorned structure of the building, simply painted white, provides a neutral, almost sanitary background for the large dining hall, both in the indoor and outdoor parts of the restaurant. The glass facade merely divides the two, without forming a barrier. Continuity between inside and outside, with the unobstructed view and openness to as much light and air as possible, are the main characteristics of this space. This new attitude to health and hygiene is important to note. As Ernst Bloch bitterly remarked in his attack on the cold and empty new architecture, the interior has become "washable." An ethos of cleanliness starts to pervade the interior, mostly in new hospitals, schools, and workplaces. As Bloch wrote: "Its actual goal is the bathroom and the toilet that are the most undeniable and original accomplishments of this era.... But now washing-up reigns. Somehow water flows from every wall."[42] The recipe for a healthy architecture was simple: "In order to get air the buildings are placed to face the sun; to get light there are large openings and walls painted in bright colors; cleanliness is achieved by making the walls, floors, and ceilings plain and smooth."[43] In their struggle to promote modern architecture in Serbia, architects played up the hygienic aspects of their buildings as one of the main qualities. Even where the more visible parts of their architecture had to conform to the conservative standards of modernized academicism, the hygienic interiors allowed them to claim a modern identity. Notable examples of this inversion are a corridor and communal bathroom in schools by Branislav Kojić and the industrial interiors of the new mint by Josif Najman, which were published in the magazine *Arhitektura* as examples of the new, healthy architectural spirit—despite the quite conservative external appearance of these buildings.

The redefinition of the interior was also influenced by the new architectural principle established by Le Corbusier of the "architectural promenade, offering

2.22   (opposite page) Yugoslav Associated Bank. Elevator shaft.

2.23   Milan Zloković, Hotel Žiča, Mataruška Banja, 1931–1932. Interior of the restaurant and open-air restaurant.

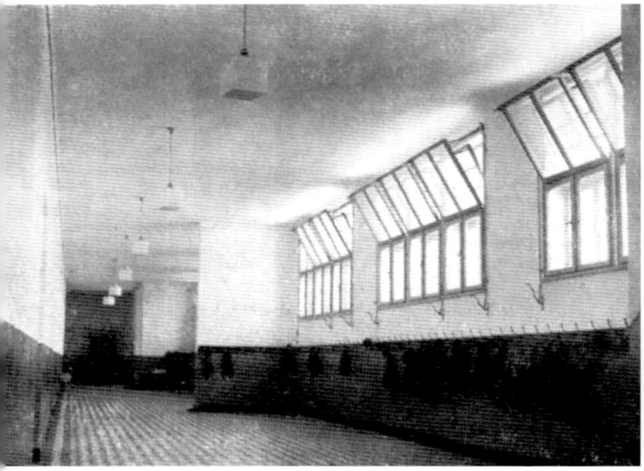

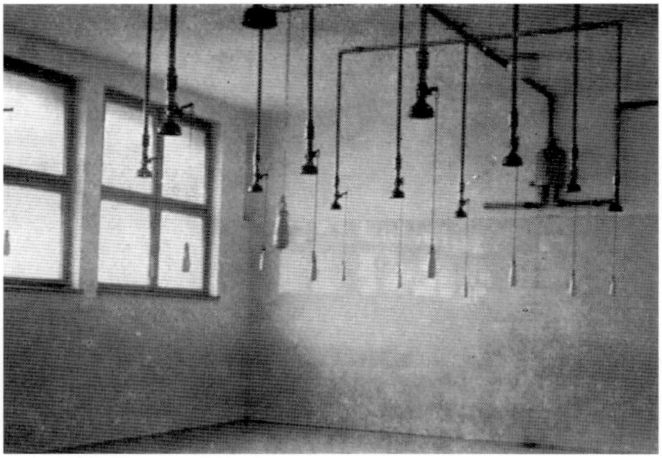

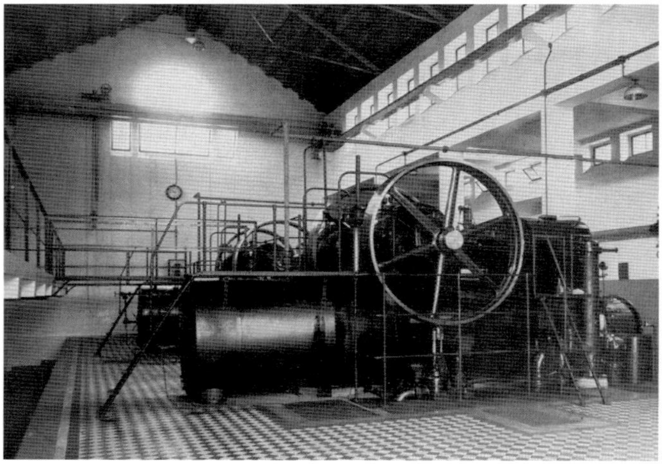

2.24　(opposite page, top) Branislav Kojić, school interiors: corridor in the Tsar Dušan School, Skopje, 1931–1933; communal bathroom in the Đura Jakšić School, Skopje, 1931–1933.

2.25　(opposite page, bottom) Josif Najman, Mint, Belgrade, 1929–1930. Interior.

2.26　Nikola Dobrović, Danube Station, Belgrade, 1931 (competition project). Ticket hall.

2.27　Nikola Dobrović, Municipal Café, Dubrovnik, 1931 (competition project). Interior.

Heslo : Urbanismus

9a

constantly changing views, unexpected, sometimes astonishing."[44] This interest in perception in movement affected the construction of architectural space in both its interior and exterior articulation. What is evident in the new notion of interior space is the destruction of centrality and the breaking out of the fixed point of inhabitation. This idea was introduced to Serbian modernism through perspective drawings of various interiors by the architect Nikola Dobrović. In his proposals, continual motion through architectural space is deliberately played up. For example, the design of the ticket hall in the competition project for the Danube railway station in Belgrade clearly conveys readiness to depart. It is surely not incidental that Dobrović chose to code-name this entry with the departure-evoking words "Trans-Balkan." While the expression of movement is logical in the design of a railway station, it comes as a surprising solution for the program of the Municipal Café in Dubrovnik. Here again Dobrović designed an interior for passing through, for walking and continuous moving in and out. The stationary positions of seating areas are only an addition, necessary to the function but not the main constituent of the café program. In his Terazije Terrace competition project, it is circulation that provides form and content to the underground interior streets. The transparent walls of these semi-interiors reflect precisely the new condition of urban space: simultaneity of perceptions in movement. Consequently, the mood has changed, and with light and air now central to the interior, the architecture has in turn to open up and change. It also has to make a move, to depart from the immobility of the former context and assume different referents.

GROUP IDENTITY 2.3

Faced with the great population growth and consequent rapid development of Belgrade in the 1920s, the architectural profession was divided on the issue of how to build the new capital. Battle was joined between the proponents of the national style and defenders of academicism on the one side, and those advocating modern architecture on the other. The latter group consisted of young newcomers to Belgrade who were adamant about establishing a contemporary identity for Serbian architecture. What they needed most was an impetus for their actions; joining forces into a high-profile group seemed to be the way ahead in their struggle against the hostile traditionalist environment.

The Group of Architects of the Modern Movement in Belgrade (GAMM) was formed on 12 November 1928 by the architects Milan Zloković (president),

2.28   Nikola Dobrović, Terazije Terrace, Belgrade, 1929–1930 (competition project). Longitudinal and transverse underground streets.

Branislav Kojić (secretary), Jan Dubovy, and Dušan Babić.⁴⁵ The four young architects met, as they did regularly once a week in the late afternoon, in the Russian Tsar café, and decided that the time had come to start an organized "ideological struggle" with group action to promote modern architecture.⁴⁶ The four founders brought to the Group a cross-cultural experience that was to be of great importance for their openness and the free spirit of their actions. Jan Dubovy (1892–1969) was a Czech and a graduate of Prague Technical University. Dušan Babić (1896–1948) was a Serb from Banja Luka (at that time part of the Austro-Hungarian monarchy) and a graduate in architecture from the Technische Hochschule in Vienna.⁴⁷ Milan Zloković (1898–1965) was born in Trieste (again part of the Austro-Hungarian monarchy) into a family of Serbs from Boka Kotorska in Montenegro; he studied at the Technische Hochschule in Graz (1915–1916) and at the Technical Faculty, University of Belgrade (1919–1921), and attended postgraduate lectures at the École Supérieure des Arts et Métiers, the École des Hautes Études, and the Sorbonne in Paris (1921–1923). Branislav Kojić (1899–1987), the only one who was born and grew up in Serbia, studied in France and graduated from the École Centrale des Arts et Manufactures in Paris. According to Kojić, not only did the four of them come from different countries with an education in completely different architectural traditions, but their personalities also differed greatly:

> **Babić was quiet, calm, and composed, Dubovy was quick and impulsive, with a great capacity for work, while I [Kojić] was methodical, persistent, and a planner. Milan Zloković was a complete and complex personality; at the same time he was an artist, a scientist, a bohemian, and a zealous, creative worker. These opposite character traits, however, did not hinder us from working together cordially and in harmony within the Group for the whole six years.⁴⁸**

At the time of the foundation of the Group, Kojić and Babić were employed in the Department of Architecture in the Ministry of Construction, Dubovy was chief of the Belgrade Master Plan Section in the City Council, and Zloković was an assistant at the Department of Architecture at the Technical Faculty of the University of Belgrade. At the same time they all worked as sole practitioners on their own projects. The four architects developed their own individual modernist identities, but as invariably happens with new ideologies, joining together in the Group provided them with a new stimulus in their ideological struggle.

The Group operated as a loose organization of individuals who held their meetings in cafés, never establishing themselves in any permanent premises. They had no employees, all the work being done by the members themselves, including technical chores such as organizing exhibitions, transporting and setting up exhibits, ushering at lectures and exhibitions, etc. Administration was kept to the minimum. Minutes of meetings were taken more or less regularly by the secretary, in the form of memoranda, equipment was limited to envelopes and a stamp made for official correspondence, and the secretary's private address was used by the Group. The necessary funds were provided by the members themselves from regular monthly membership fees and from their architectural competition prizes, out of which each contributed 3 percent. While all professional architecture matters were dealt with by the Architects Club of the Union of Yugoslav Engineers and Architects, Belgrade Section, the principal aim of the Group was to provide a modernizing impulse in the profession.[49] Despite the loose administrative setup, the Group formalized the "Rules of the Group of Architects of the Modern Movement," signed by the four founders and approved by the state authorities in June 1929. According to Article 1 of the Rules, the aim of the Group was to propagate "contemporary principles in architecture and decorative arts." The program, defined in Article 2, was to comprise "regular meetings, lectures, exhibitions, expert publications, formation of a collection of professional books and archive materials, and study excursions." Conditions of membership were stated in Article 3: only architects could be regular members; associate members could be artists or academics who would contribute to the principal aim of the Group; and auxiliary members could be artisans whose work was based on contemporary principles of technique and decorative arts. In practice, there were no members other than architects, two

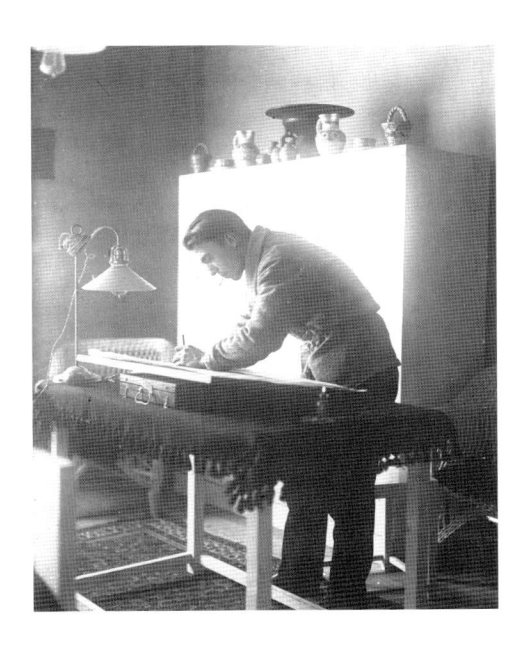

2.29 Milan Zloković.

2.30 Branislav Kojić. (Courtesy Architecture Department in the Museum of Science and Technology, Belgrade.)

of whom had construction firms as well as architectural practices. The cooperation with artists came through private connections and friendships. Through the artists Sreten Stojanović and Branko Popović, GAMM exhibited with the Oblik group of artists,[50] and Branislav Kojić exhibited his more folkloric projects with the Zograf association of artists.[51]

The Group's adherence to the modern movement was ambiguous, to say the least. Except in the name of the Group, the word "modern" was not used anywhere in the Rules, and its language avoided stating explicitly the aim of modernity. In fact, apart from the technical and organizational principles set down in the Rules, there are no articles that defined the Group's programmatic position. The wording was elusive, yet the words avoided were a prerequisite for the very establishment of the movement. The reasons behind this coded language were twofold. The dominant ones were of a political nature, since areas such as social issues of architecture and problems of workers' housing were taken to connote leftist propaganda, and were thus deemed dangerous to the system. GAMM was founded just days before King Aleksandar dismissed parliament and introduced his direct rule over the country, known in history books as the "Dictatorship of 6 January 1929." By coincidence, the Group's first public announcement was published in *Vreme,* a daily newspaper whose editorial orientation was close to government policy, on the same day as the dictatorship was announced. Hidden beneath the patriotic tone of the article, the subtext carried a message of the functionalism and internationalism of modern architecture. Yet, by depriving itself of a sociopolitical role, GAMM was left with nothing but the agency of style, i.e., its program had to be narrowed down to introducing a new formal paradigm. This is most clearly evident in the above-mentioned announcement, an article written by Kojić:

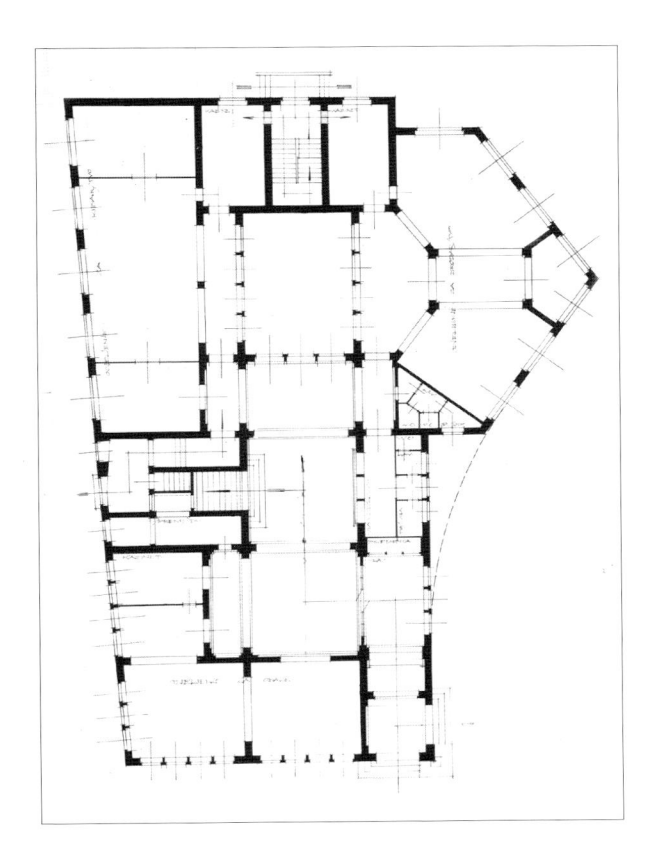

The basic need for better architecture in Belgrade has to be the creation of our own style.... Belgrade does not have to seek a remedy for the heterogeneity and colorlessness of its architecture in the national style based on our old sacred architecture. Belgrade has to look for its expression in free work and unlimited creativity. It has its own life, its own needs and habits. Its financial means, climate, work conditions, etc. will dictate the special and characteristic style of Belgrade Modern Architecture. That is the direction our architects should take in their efforts to create a national style. We shall, in that, very soon be driven by the example of the West itself.[52]

The other reason behind the Group's avoidance of a clear declaration of modernist aspiration was the weakness of conviction inherent in their movement. At the time GAMM was founded, the member architects were by no means uncompromising modernists, and in any case they still had to explore other paradigms in order to satisfy the wishes and demands of their clientele. In GAMM's program and published texts there is no firm theoretical position, no

2.31 Milan Zloković, Museum of the Adriatic Guards, Split, 1929 (competition project). Perspective view and plan of the ground floor.

critical and analytical relation to their own work that would have provided a stable foundation for an authentic declaration of modernism. Their ideological struggle had not been a merciless pursuit of untainted principles—as was the struggle of the avant-garde—and their blade was blunted by their choice to compromise between the modernist ideal and the conformity of the middle classes.

In their first years as GAMM, the four founders carried out an active lecturing and exhibition program. In his introductory lecture "Architecture: Principles and Past" held at the Architects Club in the spring of 1929, Branislav Kojić stressed that the first and main principle of architecture is truth—truth in composition, in the use of materials, and in relation of decoration to construction. Although Kojić stated that "modern architecture will be international, constructive, democratic, and aesthetic in its truth and sincerity,"[53] the actual practice of the Group members lagged behind their declared theoretical position. The first exhibitions of their projects took place alongside artists at the 1928 autumn show and the 1929 spring show in the newly opened Arts Pavilion.[54] A period critic found their works to be representative of "a very serious tendency to purify architectural design and to establish a relationship between local architecture and that of the European centers."[55] Somehow these presentations reflected the uneasy status of architectural objects at art exhibitions. Only Jan Dubovy showed photographs of his realized works, while the others displayed watercolor drawings of their projects, and even survey drawings of old architecture. The chosen projects were both modern and nonmodern. For example, Kojić included a survey of a traditional Balkan house at the autumn show; at the spring show he put a watercolor of the eclectic facade of the Arts Pavilion next to the project for his earliest contemporary building, the Urology Hospital in Belgrade. Similarly, Zloković displayed a watercolor of the medieval Gradac monastery alongside the images of his most modern project, that for the Museum of the Adriatic Guards in Split. In June 1929, the Group organized the "First Salon of Architecture," to which all Belgrade architects, regardless of their stylistic preferences, as well as painters and sculptors were invited. Although contemporary ideas were exhibited, such as the *Interior à la Corbusier* by Kojić, *Triangulation Point of Belgrade* by Dubovy, and his own house and railway station projects by Zloković, most of the exhibits reflected prevailing eclectic notions. A better-defined demonstration of the Group's aims was published later the same year in the Czech magazine *Stavba*. In a special section illustrated by the most advanced projects by Group members, Kojić gave a historical summary of Belgrade architecture, Dubovy wrote an article on the city's planning, and Zloković explained the nature of Belgrade architectural modernism in a few well-chosen words:

As for our modern architects, they do not propagandize violent solutions, such as we often meet today and which are really not appropriate. Their tendency is toward a logical plan and facade. Simplicity, often relying on the traditional plan, inasmuch as the latter is compatible with a contemporary understanding of architecture, is demonstrated in the majority of solutions. To be revolutionary does not always mean to be progressive, since, from our experience of many European faculties and art academies, it becomes opposed to what is logical to the contemporary architect and constructor.[56]

This publication was followed by the exhibition of GAMM at the Umělecká Beseda in Prague, in June 1930, in which eleven members took part.[57] The accompanying text from the catalogue explains that the works represent stages in the development of "new architecture in the international spirit, constructive and technical," which can be categorized in four groups. "In the first are copies of historical buildings with changes in detailing. The second is marked by modernization of the national style, related to our [Czech] Secession, while in the third there is a departure from tradition influenced by constructivism of an unclear character but still partly decorative and external. The fourth category contains results from the efforts made to achieve the new constructive architecture."[58] As the historian of architecture Zoran Manević noted, Belgrade modernists had proved themselves to be naive compared to the developed Czech functionalism.[59] This was most obvious in one particular example, the Hotel Prague in Belgrade by Đura Borošić, which even one local critic from the period, Đurđe Bošković, regarded as "insignificant." Also characteristic was the modest presentation, such as Dubovy's strangely drawn axonometric of his competition-

2.32   (opposite page) Branislav Kojić, *Interior à la Corbusier*, 1929, theoretical project. (Courtesy Architecture Department in the Museum of Science and Technology, Belgrade.)

2.33   Milan Zloković, railway station, Obrenovac, 1928 (project).

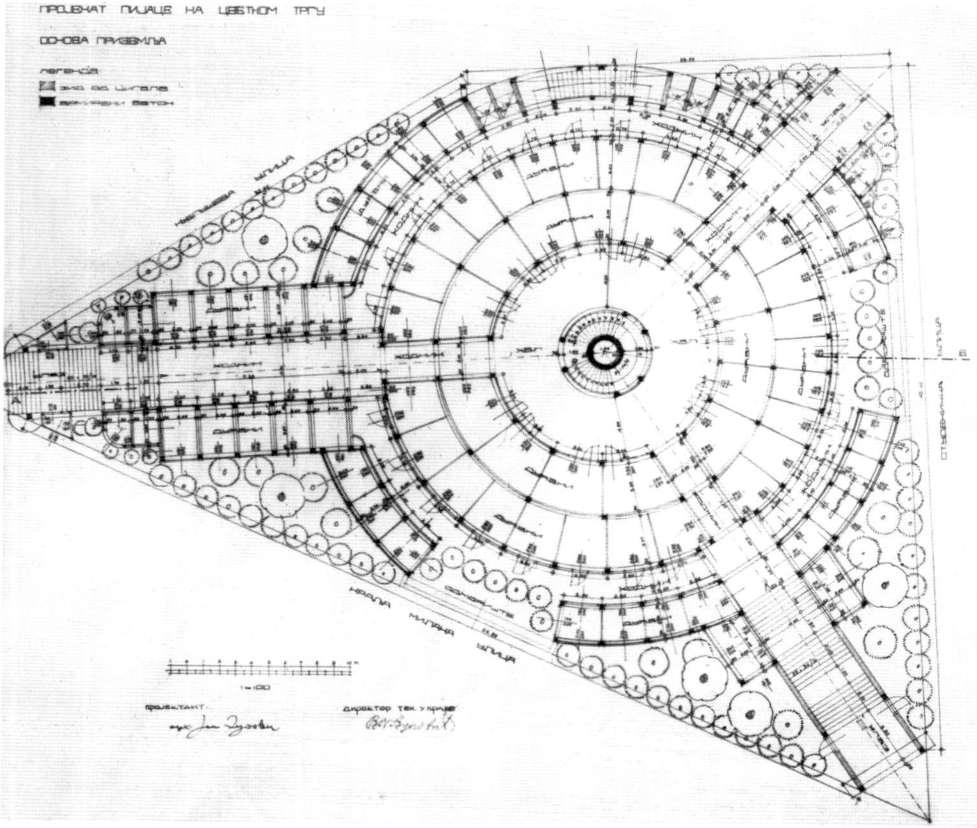
ПРОЈЕКАТ ПИЈАЦЕ НА ЦВЕТНОМ ТРГУ
ОСНОВА ПРИЗЕМЉА
ЛЕГЕНДА
ЗИД ОД ЦИГАЛА
АРМИРАНИ БЕТОН
КРАЉА МИЛАНА УЛИЦА
ХАЛ
1:100
ПРОЈЕКТАНТ
ДИРЕКТОР ТЕХ. УПРАВЕ

winning design for a Serbian Orthodox Church boarding school in Novi Sad. Although important for local history as the only joint exhibition of GAMM abroad, this exhibition passed unnoticed in Prague and did not succeed in establishing any relation to the European scene.[60] However, as the popularity and public exposure of the Group grew in Belgrade, other architects started to join in, so that by the end of 1930 there were fifteen members. An important indication of the Group's rising success was the joining of the architect Dragiša Brašovan, who was one of the most successful architects working in historical styles. Brašovan submitted to modernism in a splendid and victorious fashion, supporting the Group first in *Stavba,* where his perspective drawing of the Yugoslav pavilion at the 1929 International Exposition in Barcelona was published, and then by joining forces with it at the exhibition in Prague. Branko and Petar Krstić, Vojin Simić, Branko Maksimović, Momčilo Belobrk, and others also played active roles in the Group. At its high point the Group numbered eighteen regular members with one associate member from Berlin.

2.34   (opposite page) Jan Dubovy, Cvetni trg Market Hall, Belgrade, 1927 (project).

2.35   Đura Borošić, Hotel Prague, Belgrade, 1929.

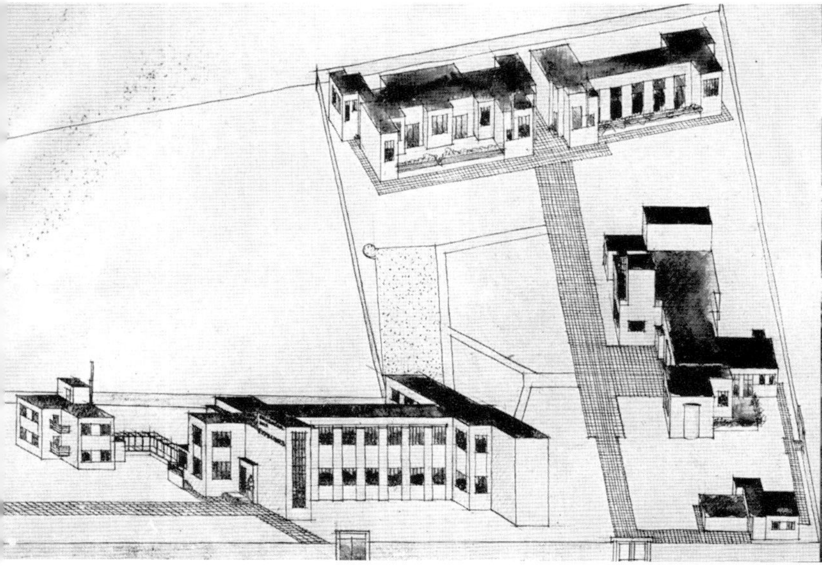

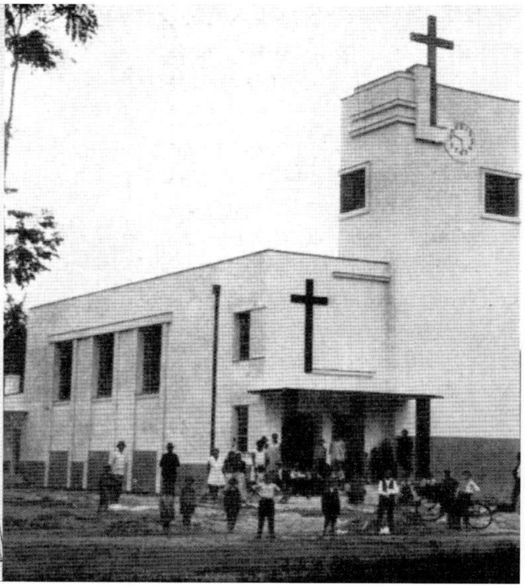

2.36 (opposite page) Jan Dubovy, Serbian Orthodox Church boarding school, Novi Sad, 1929 (competition project).

2.37 (opposite page) Jan Dubovy, Evangelical church, Ostojićevo, 1929.

2.38 Branislav Kojić, Municipal Administration Center, Novi Sad, 1930 (project).

2.39 Branislav Kojić, hall of the Sokol organization, Belgrade, 1930–1932.

2.40 Dušan Babić, UYEA building, Belgrade, 1930 (competition project).

The most important exhibition organized by GAMM was the "First Yugoslav Salon of Contemporary Architecture," held at the Arts Pavilion in Belgrade in 1931.⁶¹ In addition to Belgrade architects, members of the Zagreb Architects Circle and the Ljubljana Architects Club exhibited their works. Some of the most interesting proposals for towns in the Yugoslav province of Vojvodina were shown here, such as the Evangelical church in Ostojićevo by Jan Dubovy, the Palace of the Danube Regional Government in Novi Sad by Dragiša Brašovan, and the Municipal Administration Center in Novi Sad by Branislav Kojić. Also among the exhibits were perspective drawings of projects by Dušan Babić, including the UYEA hall and the Lektres building, in which, as a period critic notes, "a constant exploration and development can be felt."⁶² The presentation of Milan Zloković at this exhibition was probably the most informative example of the changing paradigms of Belgrade architecture at that time. On the one hand his project for the Hotel Žiča in Mataruška Banja demonstrated a genuine attempt at authentic contemporary architecture of simple volumetric and harmonic proportions. Yet his project for the international competition for the Columbus Tower in Santo Domingo, the Dominican Republic, showed a quite different point of departure.⁶³ According to Đurđe Bošković, the project represented a "hypermodernization of the Byzantine style" that "succeeds more in surprising than in enchanting."⁶⁴ In fact, this project contains somewhat confused references to expressionist models, especially in the construction of dramatic effects, but also hints at the geometrical quality of the cylindrical forms of grain silos, so dear to modern architects.

In 1933, Dubovy and Kojić took part in the Yugoslav presentation at the *Architecture d'Aujourd'hui* exhibition in Paris. There, as in previous exhibitions,

2.41   (opposite page) Milan Zloković, Hotel Žiča, Mataruška Banja, 1931–1932. Perspective drawing and commercial flyer.

2.42   Milan Zloković, Columbus Tower, Santo Domingo, 1929 (competition project).

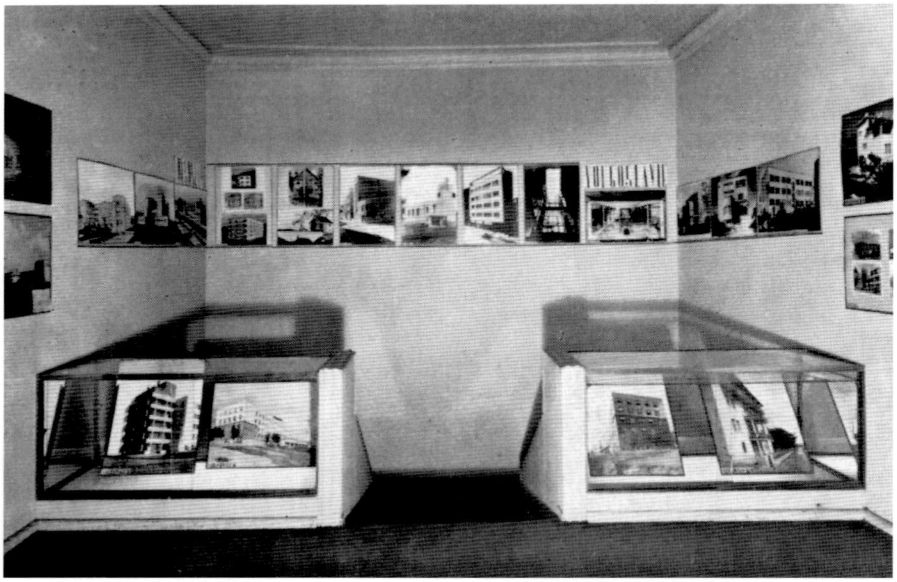

the predominant characteristic of the Belgrade architects seemed to be a profoundly unbalanced understanding of modernity in architecture. The uncertainty about the theoretical issues, and consequent formalist approach, inevitably led to the ambivalent position of most of the Group's members.

Despite all the progress made and the positive public reception of modernism, not all the members contributed equally to the common cause of GAMM. The first sign of crisis presented itself at the extraordinary conference held in the summer of 1932, when six members had to be asked to renounce their membership, since they had shown no interest in the work of the organization. The decline of the Group paradoxically coincided with the general acceptance of modernism as a fashionable new style. The principal and fundamental weakness of the Group had, from the very beginning, been the instability of its theoretical position. This is succinctly explained by Branislav Kojić:

In our meetings we had not discussed the essential characteristics of architectural modernism nor the different directions appearing within modernism, both in our country and abroad. The Group did not have a firm position on some tendencies in our architecture which still showed characteristics of the past, only in a new form, such as an inadequacy of functional and constructive principles, combined with a compromise with decorativeness in both primary and secondary forms. Alas, the Group had not been prepared for such studious work.[65]

The Group of Architects of the Modern Movement in Belgrade was disbanded by unanimous agreement of the remaining seven faithful members at their last meeting, held on 12 February 1934 in a private room of the café Damascus Sword. In his last report, Branislav Kojić, the president at the time, concluded that the aim of the Group had been fulfilled, and that it therefore had no concrete aim to strive toward. He also noted that the ideological interpretation of modern architecture had not been supported by all the Group members, and, finally, that the Rules had ceased to be relevant to the contemporary condition of Belgrade architecture.

In his book *Societal Conditions of Development of the Architectural Profession in Belgrade, 1920–1940*, published in the late 1970s, Kojić reminisced that the initiative for founding the Group had come from Jan Dubovy.[66] "Dubovy was, at the time, designing and supervising the construction of the Astronomical Observatory complex in Belgrade, which he realized in an entirely modern architecture, and which was, probably, the first monument of pure modernism here [in Belgrade]."[67] While Kojić's dating of events is arguable, I would support his thesis that the architecture of the Astronomical Observatory most notably reflected the aims and aspirations of the Group. As one of the most important

2.43 Yugoslav stand at the *Architecture d'Aujourd'hui* exhibition, Paris, 1933.

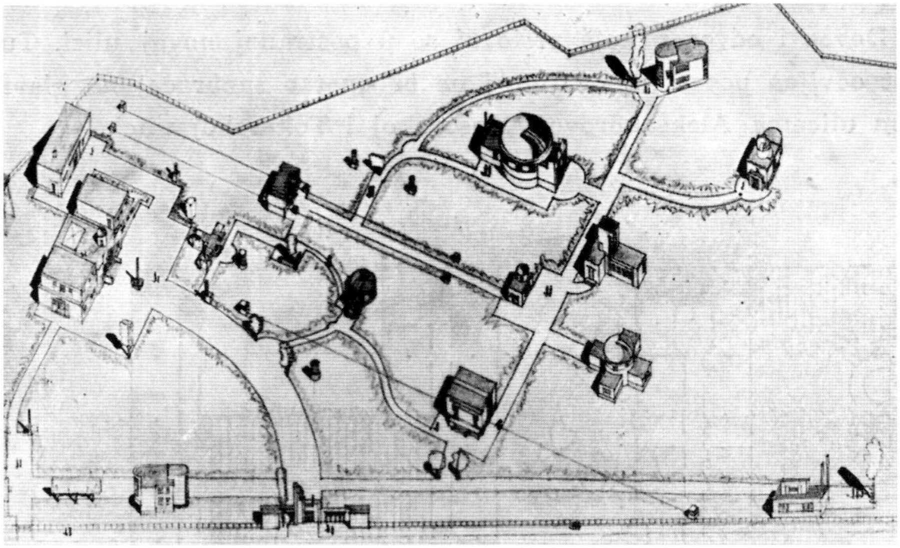

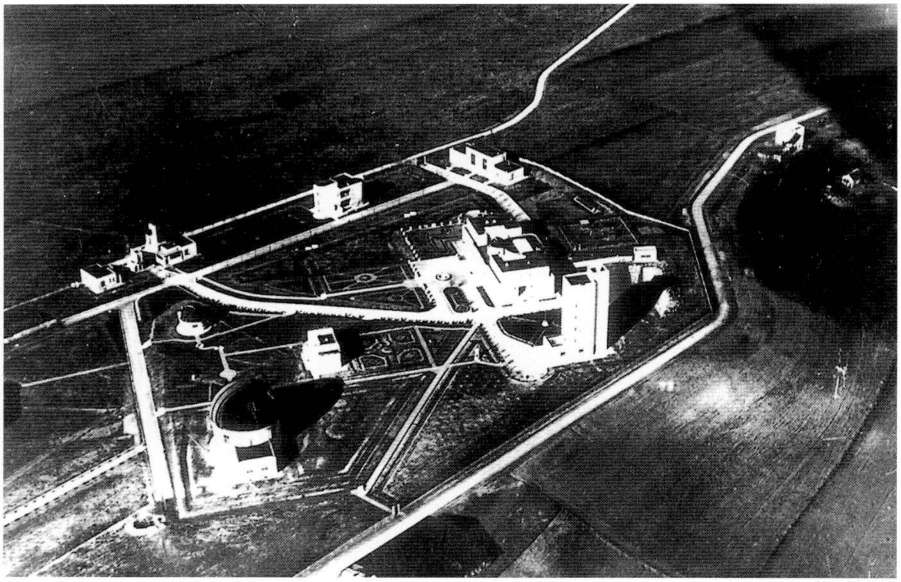

2.44 (opposite page) Jan Dubovy, Astronomical Observatory, Belgrade, 1929–1932. Axonometric drawing.

2.45 (opposite page) Astronomical Observatory. Aerial view.

2.46 Rajko Tatić, Milivoje Tričković, and Đorđe Lukić, Belgrade Fair, 1936–1937. Aerial view.

works of Serbian modernism in architecture, the Observatory complex marks the high point of the period of GAMM's activities, and not its point of departure, as Kojić suggests. The project at various stages—drawings, model of the complex, and photographs of finished buildings—was presented at exhibitions organized by GAMM, for example at the "First Salon of Architecture" (1929), at the exhibition in Prague (1930), at the "First" and the "Second Yugoslav Salon of Contemporary Architecture" (1931, 1933), and at the "11th Exhibition" of the artists' group Oblik in Sofia (1934), and was published in the reference book on modern architecture in Yugoslavia, *Problems of Contemporary Architecture*.[68] It also stood as the most significant achievement in the career of Jan Dubovy, for which he received the Doctorate in Technical Sciences.[69]

The construction of the new Astronomical Observatory followed the acquisition of extremely valuable, state-of-the-art optical and precision astronomical instruments, bought from the famous German producers Zeiss and Askania and paid for from First World War reparation monies.[70] Although the instruments were in place much earlier, it was not until 1929 that Professor Vojislav Mišković, the Observatory director at the time, managed to raise 10,000,000 dinars for the construction of the new complex. The site, an area of some 4.5 hectares in the hilly Belgrade suburb of Laudanov Šanac, was provided by the City Council. As a Council architect with experience in publicly funded projects and in urban planning, Jan Dubovy was put in charge of the design. Given the opportunity to realize his long-standing ideas on garden city planning and "healthy communal policy," on which he had regularly lectured and published articles since 1924, Dubovy produced an exceptionally modern scheme.[71] Envisaging Belgrade suburbia as a garden city, "all in vegetation, and full of happiness," Dubovy designed the Observatory complex as a loose composition of pavilions set in a park. Most notably, his design was of a nonhierarchical order, with the group of some fifteen buildings of varying size and content arranged freely, as seemingly unrelated objects, in veritable *soleil, espace, verdure* conditions.[72] Being unprecedented in the local practice of the period, this concept represented almost the sole example of modern urban planning in Belgrade. (The only other example is the complex of the Belgrade Fair [1936–1937] by architects Rajko Tatić, Milivoje Tričković, and Đorđe Lukić. Compared with the free planning of the Observatory, the centralized and formal planning of the Fair seems rather conservative, notwithstanding the fine architectural articulation of some of the exhibition pavilions.)

At the Observatory complex, the first structure to be realized was the column landmark, the Triangulation Point of Belgrade (1929), which marked its exact geographical position. When photographs were exhibited at the "First Salon of Architecture," its pure and simple design with a pronounced engineering aesthetic inspired the art critic Dragan Aleksić to proclaim it the only "sculp-

2.47   (opposite page) Astronomical Observatory. Triangulation Point of Belgrade, 1929.

2.48   Astronomical Observatory. Central Administration Building. (Courtesy Museum of the City of Belgrade.)

2.49   Astronomical Observatory. Small Refractor, Large Refractor, and Education pavilions. (Courtesy Astronomical Observatory, Belgrade.)

ture" at the exhibition that was worthy of excitement.[73] The buildings also share this clarity of expression, albeit with some concessions to the period taste for stylization. Each building is articulated as an architectural composition *sui generis,* with a primary concern for functionality and simplicity of form, and logical and pragmatic construction (brickwork construction, with structural elements in reinforced concrete and domes structured in steel, with wood lining on the inside and sheet metal covering on the outside surfaces). By a variety of compositional devices such as the arrangement of local symmetries, juxtaposition of cubic and cylindrical forms, configuration of apertures, and decorative application of reliefs and lettering, Dubovy made each building appear unique, yet related to all the others. He thus produced a series of disparate architectures articulated in the same formal register, with the discreteness of each pavilion lying in the different functional requirements.

But it is the unanimity and harmony of the whole complex that is the greatest strength of the design. Intensifying this perception is the renunciation of traditional planning that would organize the diverse parts in a hierarchical system, with the corollary that the overall effect would be built up gradually, through an architectural promenade. In this sense, Dubovy succeeded more than any other local architect of the period, as his innovative planning introduced a new understanding in the perception of architecture. It could be said that the Astronomical Observatory complex represented the new point of reference that the Group of Architects of the Modern Movement in Belgrade had been looking for. For, in the midst of interior motifs and individual identities, the Observatory complex stood firmly as the integral built manifestation of the Group's proclaimed ideology.

2.50 (opposite page) Astronomical Observatory. Water reservoir tower. (Courtesy Astronomical Observatory, Belgrade.)

2.51 Astronomical Observatory. Astrograph Pavilion. (Courtesy Museum of the City of Belgrade.)

2.52 Astronomical Observatory. Gate Pavilion.

2.53 Astronomical Observatory. Large Refractor Dome Pavilion with relief by Branko Krstić above the door. (Courtesy Museum of the City of Belgrade.)

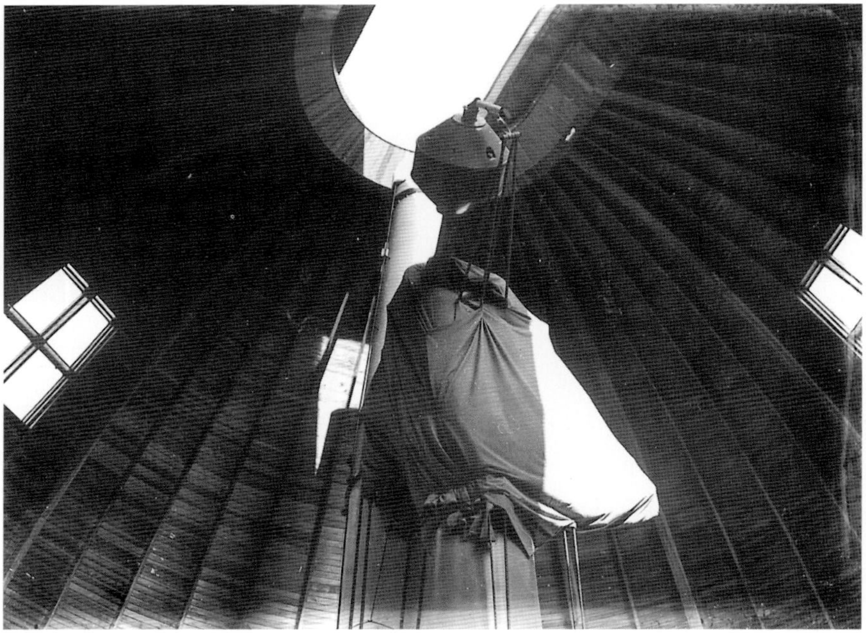

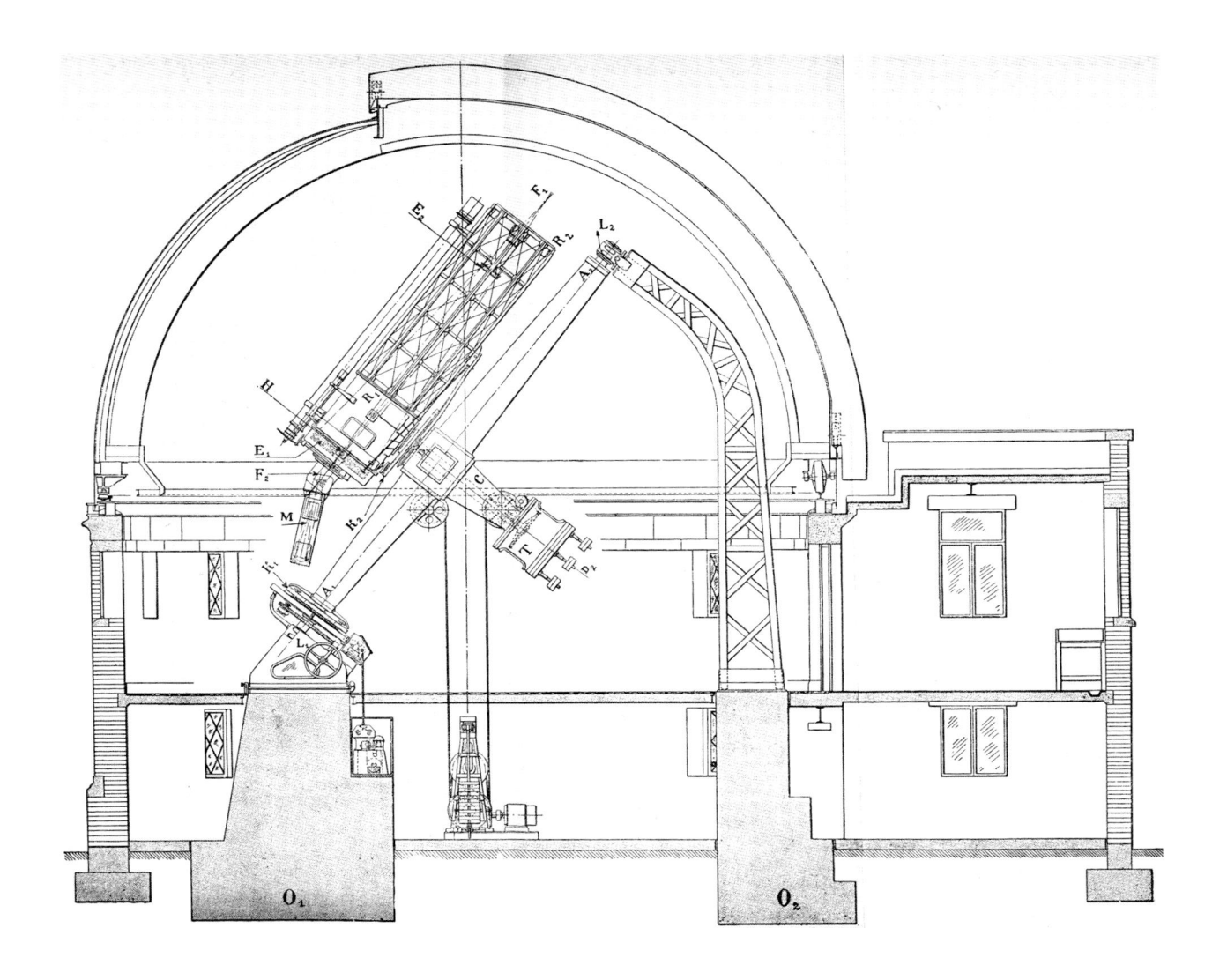

2.54 (opposite page) Astronomical Observatory. Interior of a dome. (Courtesy Museum of the City of Belgrade.)

2.55 Astronomical Observatory. Section through a pavilion with refractor.

3 EXPOSURE

> When a—Ball
> Be it the—Ball
> The great thinker Bothe & Ehrmann
> Invitation to the masked—masquerade—dance—riotous—ball—under masks. . . . In contrast to other balls of the kind, all invited *must be masked* (the mask of morality will not suffice) and possibly costumed as well—dressed in general; the worse the dress is, the better it will be. Transformation of gender is allowed exceptionally for this evening only (applicable solely to clothing).
>
> For the above purposes, a special organizing committee has been hastily assembled, members' names being a secondary matter, the most important thing is that the undersigned came to the unhappy thought of inviting you and your respected marital family (an empty site opposite the atelier is reserved for the extramarital ones)—to kindly adorn this dancing gathering with thy vanity and usually boring, yet for this evening specially pleasant, presence.[1]

The golden twenties atmosphere of Belgrade is well reflected in this text of an invitation to a party organized by painter Mladen Josić, to which architect Milan Zloković was an invitee. Despite the circumstances of the 1929 January Dictatorship and the consequent dissolution of parliament, the middle classes managed to carry on with their nonchalant lifestyle, provided they did not engage in any political or even intellectual activity critical of the system. Judging by the number of articles in newspapers of the period, the round-the-world journey of Count Zeppelin's airship was the most popular story in Belgrade in the summer of 1929. The daily coverage in *Politika* included reports and photographs of the airship's construction, interiors, technical equipment, hangars, and details of its itinerary. (Incidentally, the airship passed over Belgrade hours earlier than expected, so that its "historic" appearance was recorded only in an amateur photograph by *Politika* journalist Mihajlo Petrović.) Meanwhile, down on the ground, the new entrepreneurial class drove about the city in some 2,000 luxurious automobiles. Belgrade had not yet been hit by the great depression that all the Western press wrote about, and the urban population optimistically embraced all "mod-cons" (modern conveniences), partying along to the rhythm of jazz music.

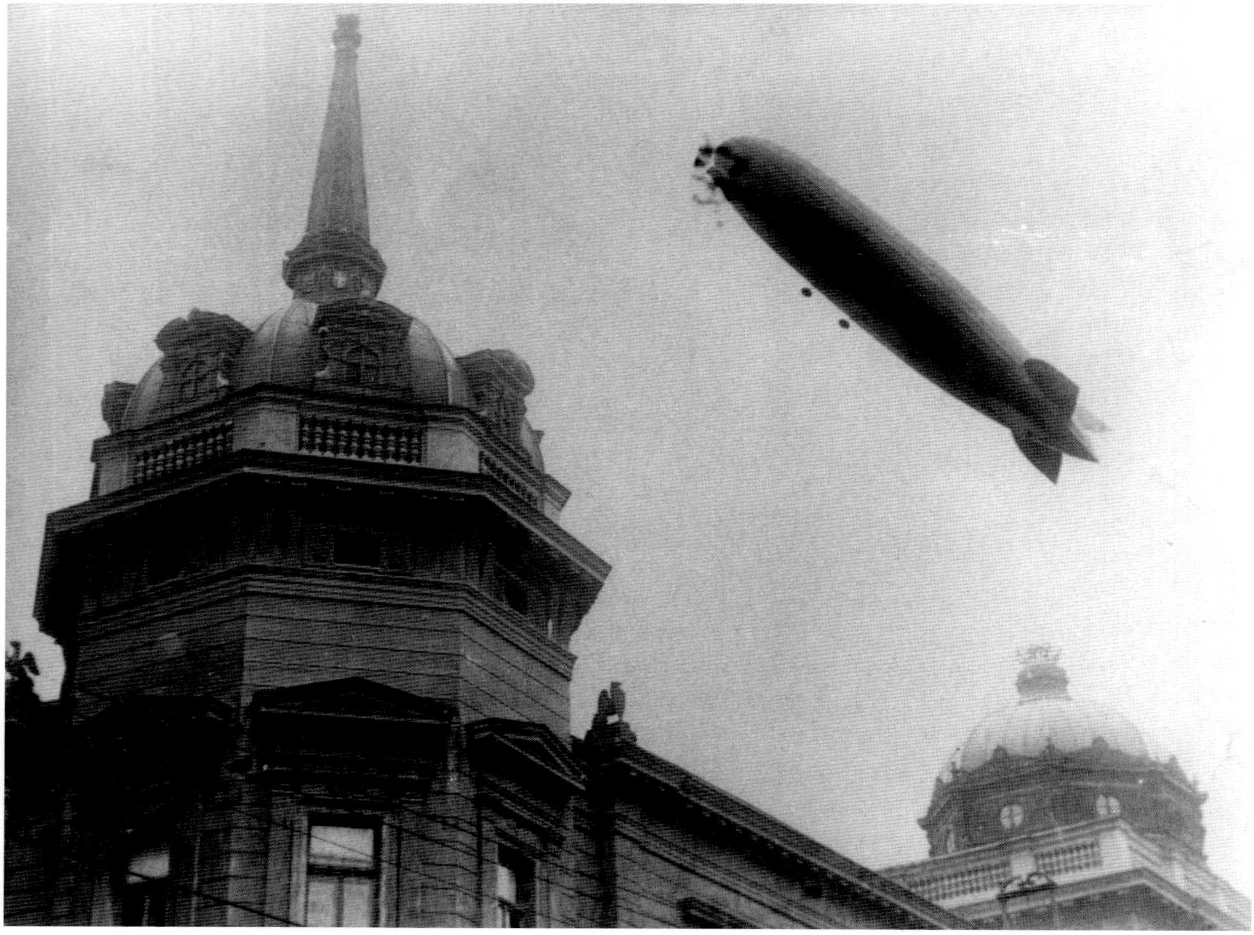

At the 1929 International Exposition in Barcelona, the Kingdom of Serbs, Croats and Slovenes, or, as it was renamed later that year, the Kingdom of Yugoslavia, was presented in a modern national pavilion by architect Dragiša Brašovan. By the summer of 1930, modern architecture had recorded an important victory in the international competition for the reconstruction of the central zone of Belgrade, Terazije Terrace. The winner of this competition, a legendary one for Serbian modernism, was architect Nikola Dobrović. Following these two events and the regular exhibitions of works by members of the Group of Architects of the Modern Movement in Belgrade, the public and, more importantly, the establishment were turning toward acceptance of modern architecture. Undoubtedly, the modernity of the Yugoslav pavilion in Barcelona and of the winning competition scheme for Terazije Terrace constituted a dramatic breakthrough, yet both represented only the antinomies within both modernist and conservative standard building practice of the period. In addition, both designs are closely connected with the problem of how to represent the national, whether as an image of the nation (in the case of the pavilion) or as the nation's center point of modernity in architecture (as the Terrace was supposed to be). In that sense, both played a symbolic role in forging an image of the nation's identity appropriate to the twentieth century. But what kind of architecture had represented the nation in the earlier course of the century? This question is related to the character of the national presentation on the international stage, most notably the changing paradigms in the architecture of the pavilions of Serbia and Yugoslavia at the world expositions.

A DISTRACTED GAZE OVER THE IMAGE OF THE NATION AT THE WORLD EXPOSITIONS — 3.1

As Walter Benjamin noted in *Das Passagen-Werk,* by the end of the nineteenth century the world expositions had lost their original character as celebrations of free trade and become highly representational of national ambitions and state entrepreneurship.[2] The Kingdom of Serbia entered the European nineteenth century, with its world expositions, "those popular phantasmagorias of patriotism and consumerism that glorified capitalism's technological progress,"[3] as late as 1878, when it finally gained internationally recognized independence from Ottoman rule. Although it had its unpretentious debut at the 1889 Universal Exposition in Paris, it was not until the exposition of 1900 (the Exposition Universelle Internationale) that Serbia showed its riches proper in its own national pavilion. In 1900 Europe was definitely "off to view the merchandise."[4] The expo-

3.1 Count Zeppelin's airship over the royal court in Belgrade, 1929.

sition, which spread over 112 hectares in central Paris, recorded some fifty million visitors. However transitory, the exposition left behind it the emblematic ensemble of the Grand and Petit Palais and Pont Alexandre III as permanent traces in the cityscape, so evidently inferior to the Eiffel Tower and even the Galerie des Machines left by the 1889 fair.

The pavilion of the Kingdom of Serbia at the 1900 exposition had a prominent location by the river Seine, right beside the Pont de l'Alma, the first in the line of foreign pavilions.[5] Its churchlike architecture of Serbian-Byzantine style constituted another nineteenth-century "house of the dreaming collective,"[6] one that was on a microcosmic journey through the national myth. In accordance with the established presentational practice, the Serbian display encompassed the state's entrepreneurial aim of national and commercial propaganda, but it rested on an eminently romantic notion of recalling the nation's long-lost ur-history. The pavilion promoted a utopian image of a regained pre-Ottoman grandeur, much in the sense of Benjamin's "collective wish images."[7] An identical notion was followed by the Serbian artists who exhibited their repertoire of mythical visions at a show that took place in parallel at the Grand Palais.[8] The design of the pavilion, inspired by the architecture of Serbian medieval monasteries from the end of the thirteenth century, was clearly intended to elicit the nation's collective phantasmagoria of an idealized image of the distant past. It is symptomatic of the acceptance of this ideology that the Belgrade architect Milan Kapetanović designed the pavilion in the Serbian-Byzantine style, despite the fact that he had never used this style in his architecture before 1900 and never would again. His adherence to the original Byzantine paradigm went so far as specifying brick and stone as the building materials, for the grandiloquent design required an appropriate material solidity. The reality of the pavilion's temporary character, however, meant that the subsequent project documents and detailing, carried out by the Ministry of Construction architect Milorad Ruvidić, would provide for a masterful imitation of stone and brick coursing and carvings, all to be executed in wood.[9]

The form of the pavilion was dominated by a large central gilded dome over a high octagonal drum, with four smaller domes—decorated archivolts between them—marking the corner volumes of the standard central-cross plan. The ecclesiastical paradigm was used in an unfettered manner, so that the central-plan church was transformed into an open-plan exhibition hall as easily as the religious content was transformed into a commercial one, and the patriotism into a commodity on display.[10] Inside the pavilion, it was the ethnographic wealth of Serbia and its agricultural products—the makings of the "noble savage"—that were the most fascinating part of the national display.[11] Particularly notable were the flat woven rugs, the *kilims* from Pirot, that decorated the interior walls, and the two weavers, Smiljka and Milica, who demonstrated their craft to the Parisian public day in and day out.¹² In a certain sense, the display of products clearly followed the displacement of the church paradigm, with the *kilims* that covered the walls taking the place of frescos, the hand-crafted gold jewelry, "which could be measured against the best-made products of the kind from Italy or the Orient," resting in vitrines instead of relics, and the natural mineral water by the entrance substituting for holy water.¹³

It is worth noting that the Serbia of the time was a predominantly agricultural country with little industry to speak of, and with an appallingly low literacy rate of only 21 percent of the total population, leaving aside schoolchildren. Despite the state of general underdevelopment, the dreaming collective paid no reverence to the one exception to Serbian myth-ridden exposure at the 1900 Paris exposition. That special case was a forward-looking invention by the mathematician Mihajlo Petrović, called the "hydro-integrator." This extraordinary machine for calculating approximate integrals in differential calculus on the principle of movement of liquid was also exhibited at the Pavilion of the Kingdom of Serbia. It was an original invention, the first to use a hydrodynamic model in solving various classes of differential calculus, and as such it was awarded one of the bronze medals at the 1900 exposition. It is my belief that its antinomic status within the context of the overall national culture of the time makes it the most pronounced sign of modernity, as well as of the nation's shifting paradigms. As Sigfried Giedion noted: "Wherever the nineteenth century feels itself to be unobserved, it grows bold."¹⁴ Beneath the deathlike masks of art and architecture, the *technē* dreamed of awakening. This condition was well understood by one of the

3.2 Milan Kapetanović and Milorad Ruvidić, Pavilion of the Kingdom of Serbia at the Universal Exposition, Paris, 1900.

3.3 Milan Kapetanović, original design for the Pavilion of the Kingdom of Serbia at the 1900 Universal Exposition.

architects of the 1900 pavilion, Milorad Ruvidić, who drew attention to the use of reinforced concrete as early as 1904.[15] Just a few months after the original publication of the German "Regulations for Construction in Reinforced Concrete," Ruvidić published his translation of this document in the *Srpski tehnički list* (Serbian Technical Journal) and initiated a campaign to introduce appropriate building codes.[16] Even in Serbia, in the depths of underdeveloped Europe, architects and engineers faced a Benjaminian dilemma: "Raging underneath was the battle between the academic architect, with his concern for stylistic forms, and the engineer, who dealt in formulas."[17] Artistic visions being wrapped in myth, it was the construction of buildings and machines that, as Giedion noted, played the role of the subconscious[18] and thus covertly announced the awakening to the advent of modernity.

By the time of the Exposition Internationale des Arts et Techniques dans la Vie Moderne, held in Paris in 1937, the curtain had fallen on the heroic phase of modern architecture, which had retreated back into the subconscious from the incursion of the emerging totalitarian models of architecture, such as the infamous German and Soviet pavilions at this exposition.[19] The pavilion of the Kingdom of Yugoslavia clearly manifested the retreat of modernity, articulating it in a form of an aloof restraint. It was designed by the Croatian architect Josip Seissel, the same person who in the 1920s as Jo Klek had been one of the main actors of the avant-garde movement Zenitism. The pavilion was located on the prominent platform raised by the left side of the main entrance to the Trocadéro.[20] Its front facade was conceived as a plain wall surface treated as an abstract relief composition of deep shadows in the entrance cutout and light bouncing off a large mosaic on a slightly protruding wall surface. The mosaic, *Three Girls,* which symbolized the idea of Yugoslav unity by three figures in national costumes of Serbia, Croatia, and Slovenia set into an imaginary garden of plenty, and which was awarded a Grand Prix, was made by the artist Milo Milunović.[21] The main architectural motif was formed by four columns in white Prizren marble, which accentuated the entrance. Of this feature Seissel wrote: "In this it was necessary to avoid empty and stiff stereotypes, in which stone is applied in a forced way to achieve false monumentality."[22] The columns' shafts, with no bases and no capitals, stood freely in front of the facade wall in line with the third essential element of the composition, a marble torso sculpture by Toma Rosandić, which was also awarded a Grand Prix.

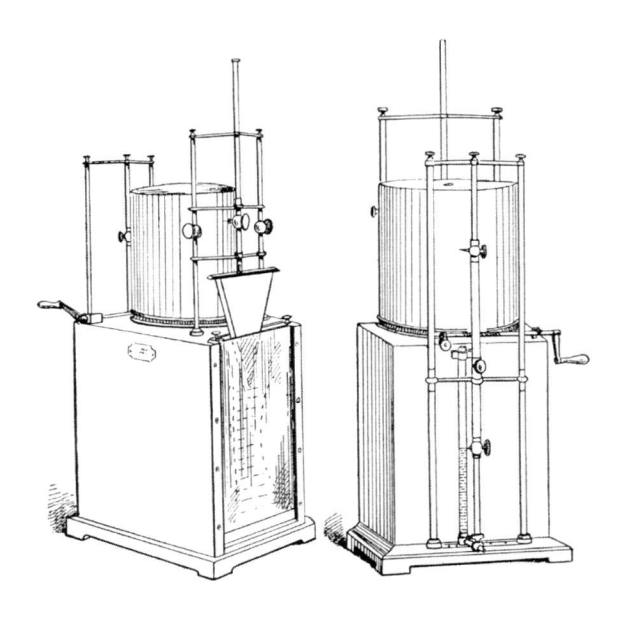

With this montage Seissel attempted to express a synthesis of painting, sculpture, and architecture, an aim so central to the avant-garde and which he himself achieved effectively in his Zenitist paintings, yet which became unattainable once his architecture had to make a compromise with the establishment. In effect, the architecture of the pavilion represented no more than a pictorial cliche of "the synthesis of art as a form of national self-representation," not too dissimilar to the classic carnival photograph of fairgoers posed in a cardboard airplane that Milunović and his artist friends chose to take home as a souvenir of the 1937 Paris exposition. Seissel's design did, nevertheless, fit in

3.4 (opposite page) Pavilion of the Kingdom of Serbia at the 1900 Universal Exposition. Interior.

3.5 Mihajlo Petrović, "hydro-integrator" exhibited at the 1900 Universal Exposition in Paris.

admirably with the current taste and was accordingly awarded a Grand Prix, but how very distant it was from the ingenuity of the mass education program of Le Corbusier's Pavillon des Temps Nouveaux at the same exposition! Still, what is of concern here is how the expression of the national style, the monastic form of the 1900 pavilion, was exchanged for an internationally recognized idiom in the 1937 pavilion in Paris. In these terms, it is also important to point to the consequent transformation of the display itself. While in 1900 railroad cars full of goods were brought to Paris to be shown in the flesh, at the 1937 exposition national presentation was done by large diapositive projections and the Pirot *kilims* were not a centerpiece of the show.

The first significant questioning of the appropriateness of the Serbian-Byzantine style for a national pavilion took place at the International Exposition of Art in Rome in 1911.[23] At the outset, the Italian organizing committee apportioned 74 square meters within the Palace of Fine Arts for the exhibition of Serbian art.[24] The situation changed drastically when a group of Croatian artists, led by the greatly revered sculptor Ivan Meštrović, refused to exhibit in either the Austrian or Hungarian pavilions and requested to be part of the Serbian show, thus promoting the political idea of unity of south Slav peoples—the Yugoslav idea. The Serbian government took up the challenge and decided to finance the erection of a separate pavilion of the Kingdom of Serbia in which both national and Croatian artists would be presented together. The architect of the pavilion, Petar Bajalović, understood well the underlying political agenda and successfully articulated it in a positively emancipatory design. The architecture of the pavilion complemented the character of the central display of the Vidovdan cycle by the sculptor Meštrović, inspired by Serbian national epic poetry. The display included 74 sculptures and a 5-meter-long wooden model of a memorial building, the Vidovdan Temple, envisaged as a monumental framework for the sculptures.[25] As one eminent period critic wrote, the triumph of the pavilion was in its *entelechy,* i.e., in the concord of Meštrović's work with the main idea that constituted the architecture of the pavilion.[26] Both emanated the spirit of modern Europe, inspired by the Viennese Secession, and both displaced the national myth beyond the deeply engrained

3.6   Josip Seissel, Pavilion of the Kingdom of Yugoslavia at the Exposition Internationale des Arts et Techniques dans la Vie Moderne, Paris, 1937. View of the main facade and view of the entrance.

nationalist conservatism and provincialism.²⁷ However, while Meštrović's genius decisively influenced the architectural presentation in Rome, at the concurrent International Exposition of Industry and Labor held in Turin, the national style firmly persisted. The spirit of the machine civilization clearly did not have enough force to change the architectural form of the pavilion. Its architect, Branko Tanazević, produced an absurd composition with the centerpiece being an imitation of a five-dome medieval church extended sideways with long wings, thus clumsily attempting functionality but ending up as an architectural paradox.

In the period after the First World War, following the unification of the Kingdom of Serbs, Croats and Slovenes, Serbia was in the contradictory position of being submerged in the newly formed tripartite state while holding onto the mechanisms of domination within it. The reassuring prewar image of a historical restitution of Serbian medieval glory was transformed into an eminently suppressive image of hegemony. Consequently, the Serbian-Byzantine style survived as the exclusively Serbian notion of a national style, to be challenged and finally relinquished as the official style for the pavilions of the new state at world expositions in the mid-twenties. Its end was marked by a fierce discussion over a competition-winning scheme for a pavilion of the Kingdom of Serbs, Croats and Slovenes at the Sesquicentennial International Exposition in Philadelphia of 1926. At this competition, organized under the auspices of the Ministry of Trade and Industry, the first and second prizes were won by the architects Petar and Branko Krstić.[28] The perspective rendering of the winning scheme shows a building of romantic character in a predominantly Serbian-Byzantine style, in which some authors also see a sort of "latent expressionism."[29] What strikes me is that at that point in time, sixteen years after Le Corbusier's Maison Dom-ino, and after all the avant-garde movements and magazines, including the local movement Zenitism, were well past their zenith, the architects Krstić totally ignored any reference to the zeitgeist in their proposal. Their design for the pavilion contained no correspondence between architectural form and internal planning, the plan itself was restrictive and rather constipated, and articulation of form was formalistic and conservative. The proposal lacks even the clarity and simplicity that characterized the transformation of the church central-cross plan into the light and airy exhibition hall of the 1900 Serbian pavilion in Paris. In the sequel to the competition, because of opposition by members of the Ministry of Construction who would not accept the Serbian-Byzantine style as representative of the new country, and after a controversial "Philadelphia War of Artists,"[30] the government decided not to erect the pavilion after all.[31]

Overt critical negation of the Serbian-Byzantine style for exposition architecture was also manifested in the choice of architect and architectural style for the pavilion of the Kingdom of Serbs, Croats and Slovenes at the 1925

3.7 (opposite page) Petar Bajalović, Pavilion of the Kingdom of Serbia at the International Exposition of Art, Rome, 1911.

3.8 Ivan Meštrović, the Vidovdan Temple model exhibited in the Pavilion of the Kingdom of Serbia at the 1911 International Exposition of Art.

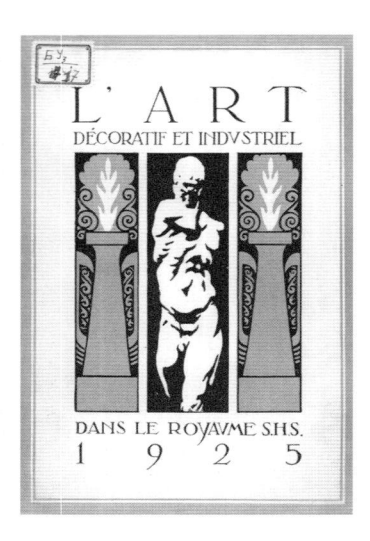

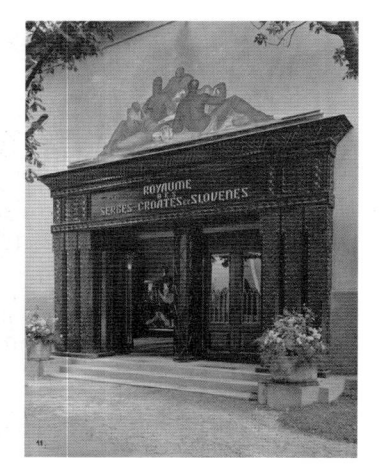

Exposition Internationale des Arts Décoratifs et Industriels Modernes in Paris. In the original design, Belgrade architect Miroslav Krejček attempted to produce a "politically correct" architecture in which motifs from different Yugoslav regions were combined in a highly eclectic manner.[32] The project was, however, turned down by the French Exhibition Committee on the grounds that its "synthetic architecture" was not adequate to the requirements of the program.[33] Following this embarrassment, the national committee hastily appointed architect Stjepan Hribar for the design of the pavilion and Tomislav Krizman for the interior decoration, both from Zagreb. The pavilion thus produced was of simple cubic form decorated with a prominent oak wood portal with stylized folk ornamentation and a fresco painting above it, and stained glass windows. Sculptural work on the portal was carried out by Croatian artist Vojta Braniš, who was awarded a Grand Prix, and the fresco, which symbolized decorative arts, was carried out by painter Jozo Kljaković. The architecture of the pavilion was criticized in Belgrade as "monotonous and common," while the only noteworthy part of the national presentation was deemed to be the "modernized Bosnian room" designed by architects Helen Baldesar and Dušan Smiljanić in collaboration with painter Karlo Mijić, all from Sarajevo.[34] Again, it was the *kilims* lining the interiors that saved the day. The national shop, located at the Esplanade des Invalides, in which "pure Turkish coffee was served from copper pots from Sarajevo," was designed by the Belgrade architect Branislav Kojić. It was conceived as a fairly modern system of kiosk units, albeit with decorative elements in a nationalized Art Nouveau style.

Nevertheless, the 1925 Paris exposition marked a turning point for Belgrade architects, however arguable the performance of their national architecture there. The Belgrade Architects Club organized an excursion to the exhibition, and for the first time Serbian architects encountered significant new architectural tendencies, all in one place, including Le Corbusier's Pavillon de l'Esprit Nouveau, Frederick Kiesler's Cité dans l'Espace, and Konstantin Melnikov's pavilion of the USSR. And so, once the imperative of the former national style had been overcome, the question remained of the appropriate character of contemporary national architectural representation. In essence it was Walter Benjamin's question of the problem of the form of new art (and architecture).

When and how will the worlds of form which, without our assistance, have arisen, for example, in mechanics, in film, in machine construction, in the new physics, and which have subjugated us, make it clear for us what manner of nature they contain? When will we reach a state of society in which these forms, or those arising from them, reveal themselves to us as natural forms?[35]

CHAPTER 3 **EXPOSURE**

3.9 (opposite page) Cover of the promotional booklet of the Kingdom of Serbs, Croats and Slovenes for the Exposition Internationale des Arts Décoratifs et Industriels Modernes, Paris, 1925 (design by Tomislav Krizman).

3.10 (opposite page) Stjepan Hribar, Pavilion of the Kingdom of Serbs, Croats and Slovenes at the 1925 exposition.

3.11 Helen Baldesar and Dušan Smiljanić, the "Bosnian room" in the Grand Palais at the 1925 exposition.

3.12 (following page) Branislav Kojić, national shop at the 1925 exposition.

21.

The discourse of Serbian architectural modernism constantly surfaces in the fissure between myth and fact, never actually transcending the condition of historical uncertainty. This instability causes perpetual restructuring of the very core of the discourse, as is seen when the reliability of the actual events is closely examined. A case in point is one of the most intriguing and fundamental stories in the history of the modern movement in Serbia. It concerns the first international exposure of Serbian modern architecture at the International Exposition at Barcelona in 1929, since regarded as its ultimate success story on the international stage. This particular modernist myth, however, has been contorted by coinciding actions, actions missing or avoiding each other, and spirited parallel actions[36] that twisted the facts beyond reliability. In retracing this route one stumbles upon "perverse natives," as José Quetglas calls them,[37] who aimed at elevating the image of the Yugoslav pavilion—an object that was itself no more than an architectural ephemeron—to the status of a national legend.[38] Eventually, when a more rigorous comparative analysis between the German and Yugoslav pavilions was undertaken, the latter ended up among "any other of the rancid exercises that vulgarly combine . . . poorly evoked expressionist effects."[39] The story thus bifurcates into two readings of one and the same object, i.e., into two parallel histories of the same architectural narrative that is central to the advent of modernity in Serbia, the first one being a glorious praise and the second a scornful critique. The main question here is what the origin was of this particular bifurcation, and what it was that profiled it as a narrative of modernity.

By the time of the 1929 International Exposition in Barcelona, Serbian architects were well aware of the new design directions. As Susan Buck-Morss notes, "no one in Europe (or the United States) could have lived through the decade of the thirties without being aware that international expositions, having become less frequent after World War I, suddenly came back with a vengeance during these Depression years. They were seen as a means of enhancing business, creating jobs for the unemployed, and providing state-subsidized, mass entertainment that was at the same time public 'education'."[40] The Yugoslav pavilion at the Barcelona exposition boldly confirmed that even the most resistant masters of historical styles, such as the pavilion's architect Dragiša Brašovan,[41] had made a decisive step toward a new epoch. Although the government placed an order for a pavilion that would represent, as it were, true patriotism and true progress of the true national architecture, and directly appointed Brašovan as a safe option, the pavilion unexpectedly turned out to be the first modern building commissioned by the state. In order to finalize the national presentation under conditions of tight deadlines and a relatively low budget, Brašovan made a virtue out of necessity by opting for simple form and detailing of the pavilion. Of all the national attributes, the final design retained wood as the traditional building material of Serbian vernacular architecture, and used it as the principal national commodity on display. All construction work was carried out by builders and workers from Serbia,[42] using only Serbian building materials and components shipped over to Barcelona, so the pavilion represented a national product par excellence.

Conceived as an exhibit in itself, as an object to be on view, the pavilion was designed as a formal exercise in modernity. The hierarchical composition of the dominant prow with symmetrically arranged side wings had an acceptable, pleasant modern outlook. There was no complexity to this architecture, no transparency or simultaneity of spatial experiences; its vision of space was firmly based on perspective, with effects sought from expressionist models.[43] The facade, in horizontal stripes of wood stained in gray and white and devoid of any ambiguity, did not pretend to reveal, nor in fact to hide, the interior. It can be argued that Brašovan, the great stylist of Belgrade architecture and master of bourgeois finesse, looked to expressionism as a mirror image of the winning new style, but it seems more that this was an "excess of pure subjectivity" (Ernst Bloch). Notwithstanding that the pavilion represented one of the very few examples of new architecture at the Barcelona exhibition, as noted in the comprehensive survey of the whole site by Ignasi de Solà-Morales,[44] its modernity seems contrived, especially if compared with the German pavilion.[45]

However, according to newspaper articles from the period, the Yugoslav pavilion had a glorious public reception in Barcelona, and it was one of the most visited national pavilions, with a record of 60,000 visitors in a single day.[46] By the end of the exhibition it had also become the most successful national presentation, winning 97 of a total of 180 Grand Prix awarded by the international jury for specific exhibits. As usual, the most effective exhibits were traditional products of the Serbian noble savage, particularly the *kilims* by the brothers Garotić from Pirot. The architecture of the pavilion had also achieved considerable success and, apparently, caused quite a furor. At the royal visitation, the Spanish King Alfonso XIII "expressed his liking of the architecture of the pavilion" and his wish to write about it to the Yugoslav King Aleksandar.[47] Soon after the royal blessing, in an interview given on his return from Barcelona Tomislav Krizman, one of the authors of the pavilion's interior decoration, reported that Dragiša Brašovan was awarded the highest prize of the exhibition, the Grand Prix, and that the pavilion was considered to be among the three most successful at the exposition.[48] It is at this point that the reports turn into a national myth.

The mythical reading of the pavilion's architecture starts with a newspaper review by Stanislav Vinaver, published in the popular daily newspaper *Poli-*

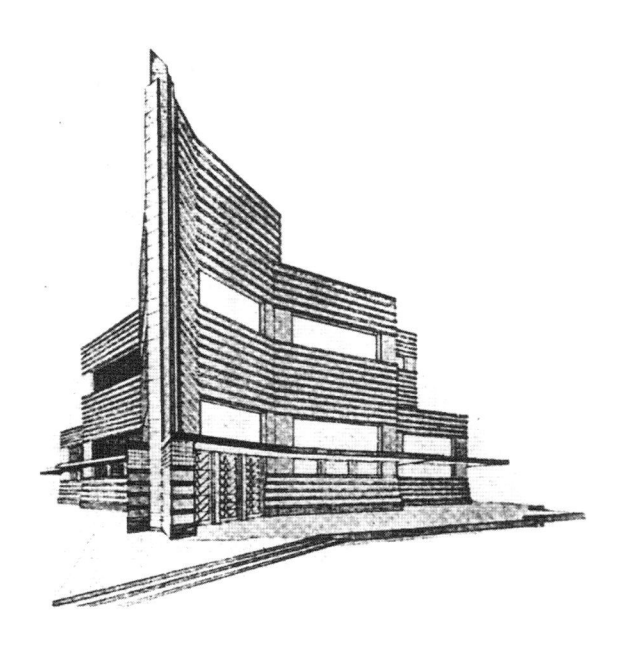

tika at the time of the exposition.⁴⁹ The author of the article was a person of extraordinary literary talent and considerable intellectual authority. One of the most important authors of the Serbian avant-garde, he was a poet, essayist, critic, translator, journalist, publicist, at one time a contributor to *Zenit,* and a prominent author of avant-garde short stories.⁵⁰ All through the twenties and thirties Vinaver regularly published newspaper reports from abroad, either as a foreign correspondent or as a press attaché in diplomatic missions of Yugoslavia throughout Europe; at the time of the Barcelona exposition he was serving at the League of Nations in Geneva. His report furnished the most significant support for the appropriation of modernity in the expression of the nation, and as such it is of particular importance here. The central issue of the article concerns the polarity of national vs. universal, based upon its author's discovery of the original national genius in the modern concept of the pavilion. Vinaver's reading of the pavilion offers a *dialectical image* wherein the ur-past comes together with the present in a true unity of seemingly opposed notions of the ancient "patriarchal household" and "modernist daring, calm monumentality." For him, this architecture aroused poetic feelings of "pleasant excitement, familiar exaltation," and of intimate identification with the archetypal ancient patriarchal house.⁵¹ He regards the pavilion as a "precisely used national emotion" and "a sum, an integral of experience and inspiration": "It immediately became clear to each one of us that this was the route that can be taken, that has to be taken . . . the whole national originality used with nothing held back in creation of one totally modern notion."⁵²

3.13   Dragiša Brašovan, Pavilion of the Kingdom of Serbs, Croats and Slovenes at the International Exposition, Barcelona, 1929. Perspective drawing.

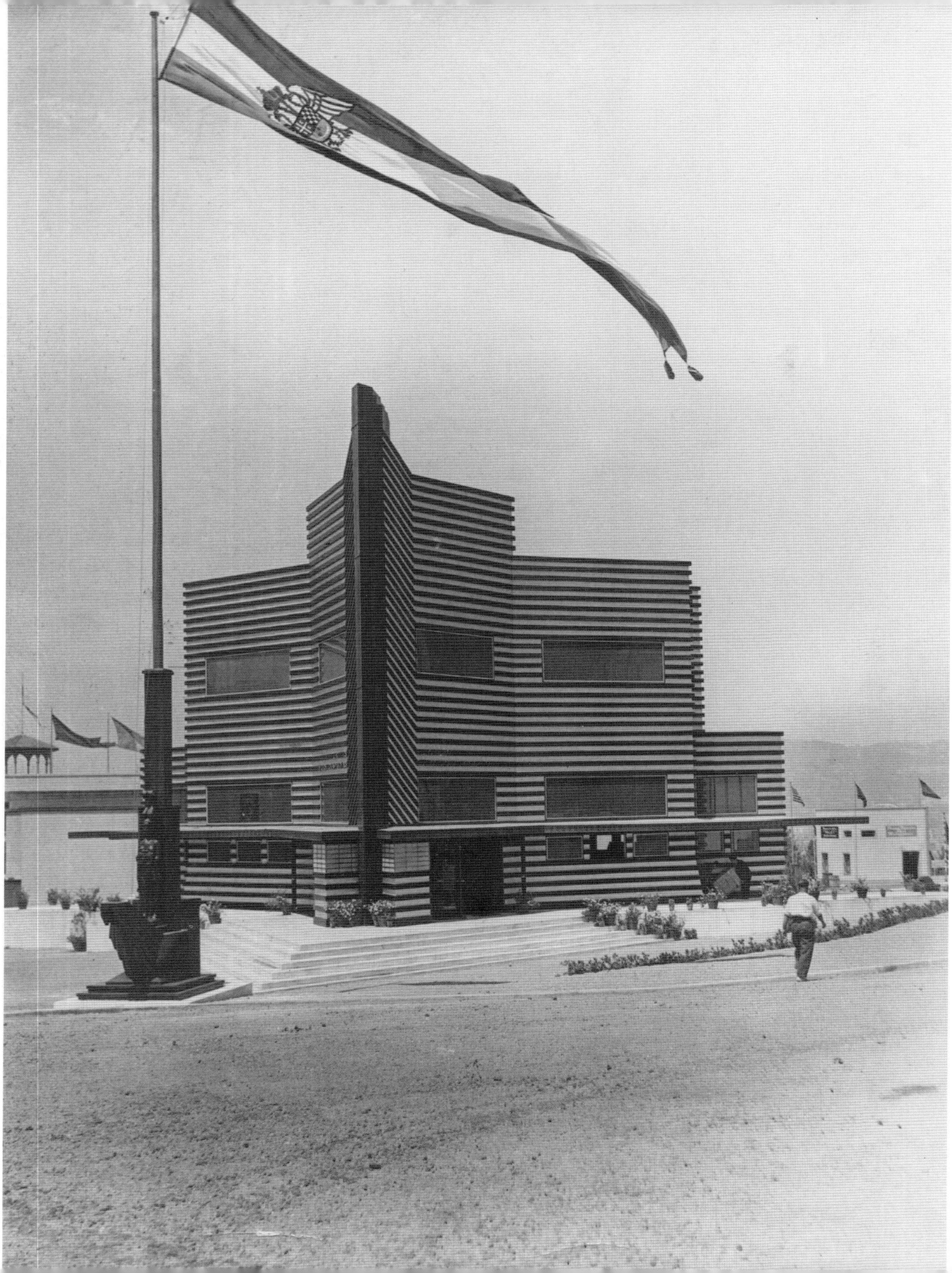

3.14   Pavilion of the Kingdom of Serbs, Croats and
Slovenes at the 1929 International Exposition. Entrance
and rear facades. (Courtesy City Museum, Vršac.)

Vinaver's distinction between the past, i.e., the former context, and the actualization of the past within "one totally modern notion" is very close to what interests Benjamin when he writes: "The dialectical penetration and actualization of former contexts puts the truth of all present action to the test."[53] The article argues for the pavilion's modernism, "with daring modern simplifications, with the power of clear and intelligible architecture corresponding to our time, our aspirations, and contemporary taste,"[54] all of which is symbolically charged by being infused with the aura of the ancients, to use Buck-Morss's expression. Within its architecture, myth and the present are brought together in such a way as to lead out of the national style's conservative practice of banal reincarnation of the past.

While transcending the stage of the mythical Serbian-Byzantine style, Brašovan's design still evoked images of the house as a protective case, the quintessentially nineteenth-century idea of a primal form of dwelling. *Kilims* and folkloric embroidery lined the walls of a wooden-case interior, in which the distracted gaze of the visiting crowd was enveloped in soft tissues. It was a version of a luscious bourgeois interior,[55] and therefore did not belong to the realm of the modern but merely took on a mask of new form. It did not attempt to reach the "twentieth century, with its porosity and transparency, its tendency toward the well lit and airy, [which] has nullified dwelling in the old sense."[56] The consciousness of modernity in this architecture is apparently more a matter of vogue, not a fully enlightened consciousness but the self-consciousness of an architectural dandy. In contrast to the German pavilion which "had no function to perform other than to look worthy of the country it represented,"[57] the Yugoslav pavilion was a showcase that literally represented national products for sale. Its evident success, nevertheless, opened up perspectives for modern architecture that were appreciated by the national establishment, and in that sense its effects were invaluable. The reception of the pavilion assured Brašovan of subsequent state commissions for the national pavilions in Milan (1931) and Thessalonica (1932). In an interview concerning the success of the pavilion in Milan, Brašovan said:

My intention was to bring a contemporary and modern pavilion to this exhibition, where all other pavilions are either of old classic monumentality or in national styles, and to show with it that we are a new and young state that steps forward, a strong nation capable of leadership, which wants to be modernized and to advance freely.[58]

In the national consciousness, however, it was the Yugoslav pavilion in Barcelona that stirred a lasting reverence. The story of the pavilion's success was institutionalized in a study on the architecture of Brašovan written by the architect

3.15 Dragiša Brašovan.

Nikola Dobrović, who was commissioned for the task by the Serbian Academy of Sciences and Arts.[59] With no references to the sources of his research, Dobrović wrote that the decision to award the Grand Prix to Brašovan was reversed, and that the international jury awarded it to Mies van der Rohe instead. This "procedural mistake," as he refers to it, was "mitigated" by a consolation prize of 150,000 Spanish pesetas awarded to Brašovan, which he used to tour Spain and Italy.[60] Dobrović's version of the story has been repeated verbatim in all subsequent studies on Brašovan, but, despite local apocryphal accounts, in all the standard sourcebooks on the history of modern architecture there has been no mention whatsoever of Mies being awarded a Grand Prix for the German pavilion in Barcelona. On the contrary, according to the findings of Ignasi de Solà-Morales, there is no evidence of any awards being given for the architecture of the pavilions.[61] The national legend thus stems from a fabrication of facts, creating the false conviction that, at least in this case, Serbian modern architecture had its minutes of fame and glory, and that the old master Brašovan rubbed shoulders with such a modernist hero as Mies van der Rohe.

In the perpetuation of the myth, the original intent of Dobrović's text to question and ultimately criticize the integrity of Brašovan's modernism got completely shrouded. The argument is gradually built up by sharp and direct criticism of the work being analyzed, which turns unforgiving when dealing with those of Brašovan's buildings generally regarded as modern. In assessing the pavilion in Barcelona, Dobrović writes: "The external appearance of Brašovan's pavilion does not reveal or sufficiently indicate the relevant structure of the building and its internal spatial resolution." He contrasts it with Mies's pavilion, which he regards as "new from every aspect, new in a logically made conjunction of all elements of the composition, new in its structural idea, in the manner of connecting the internal and external spaces, new by the quality of continual experience of what is represented by the pavilion."[62] Brašovan's pavilion is dismissed as reflecting something merely personal, a wanton decision with no depth and no completeness to it. In the sequel, the critique slashes further through Brašovan's architecture, sparing not even the most important buildings of his career, the Palace of the Danube Regional Government in Novi Sad and the building for the State Print Works in Belgrade. In his study Dobrović could not and would not pay lip service to the old master, as his mission was to finally unmask the essentially formalist character of Brašovan's architecture in particular and Serbian modernism in general. This is best manifested in his final assessment of Brašovan's contribution to Serbian modernism:

It could be added: at the turning point between the backwardness of the past, the present, and the immediate future, a complete man was needed. Such a man would have become a timely starter of new processes—and by fulfilling his role he would have become a symbol for future generations. Brašovan's success is irrefutable, for he was the first to realize modern buildings in our local environment—yet the message was not written with all the

3.16 Dragiša Brašovan, Pavilion of the Kingdom of Yugoslavia at the International Fair, Milan, 1931. Views of the main and rear facades. (Courtesy City Museum, Vršac.)

available tools of an architect. He was not in all senses a complete man, and consequently his lifelong function has not become a completed message.[63]

It is clear from the text that Dobrović writes from his own bitter disillusionment with the reception of modern architecture in Belgrade and Serbia. His writing reflects his own lifelong crusade for "constructive architecture" and his sense of isolation in his "mission of a chaste architect-constructivist." While Brašovan's "transitional forms," as Dobrović refers to his rival's modern works, had all the official and public support and reverence, his own radical modernism had been largely marginalized. Yet it was his winning project at the international competition for the reconstruction of the very center of Belgrade, the project for Terazije Terrace, that proved to be the seminal and, probably, the ultimate event of authentic modernity in Belgrade.

3.3 NIKOLA DOBROVIĆ (1897–1967): THE LATERAL IMPACT

In the local historiography, the name of Nikola Dobrović resounds gloriously in the hall of architectural fame as "the greatest name of Serbian Modernism in architecture."[64] At its face value this may just be the case, but there seems to be an underlying elusiveness inherent in this statement. To start with, in his forty-odd-years-long professional career Dobrović realized only one project in Serbia, the Ministry of Defense Headquarters in Belgrade, and that was as late as in the years between 1954 and 1963.[65] For the greater part of his professional life, until he permanently settled in Belgrade in 1944, he was living and practicing outside Serbia. In the period between the world wars, his contribution to modern architecture in Serbia amounted to several competition projects, exhibitions of his work, and published articles. He was not a member of the Group of Architects of the Modern Movement in Belgrade, and he took no part in their activities whatsoever. The ideas and concepts and the authentic architectural discourse raised by Nikola Dobrović far exceeded the local or, indeed, the national bounds. In his work he chose to act critically and to resist ideologies, including those of "national" and "international" categorization. His architecture belonged to the supranational domain of a trans-European movement for contemporary architecture, and could by no means be fitted simply into the Procrustean bed of Serbian modernism.

Theo van Doesburg correctly observed that Dobrović was, in fact, an exception, in the sense that he was the first Serbian architect whose realized buildings were in line with concurrent general architectural developments in Western Europe.⁶⁶ Notwithstanding van Doesburg's confused notions regarding Yugoslav nationalities, it is quite indicative that he saw the Slovenian architect Jože Plečnik and the Croatian architect Viktor Kovačić as Dobrović's direct predecessors. As representatives of the best emancipatory spirit in Yugoslav architecture, all three of them, Plečnik, Kovačić, and Dobrović, transcended the boundaries of national categorization and were, in fact, proponents of modern European ideas. Van Doesburg thus justly sees Dobrović as the harbinger of a European free spirit of new architecture, liberated from the limitations imposed by Yugoslav tradition. Yet it was this very quality that distanced or even disqualified him from taking a leading role in Serbian architecture of the time, a position he surely deserved on account of his work. Being a free agent of liberal ideas, and also a foreigner in his homeland, he was denied access to the establishment and its corridors of power. Having to rely solely on the unstable capacity of competitions and exhibitions of his work to introduce a structured discourse of architectural modernity, Dobrović actually failed in his mission

3.17 Nikola Dobrović, 1939. (Courtesy Architecture Department in the Museum of Science and Technology, Belgrade.)

to institute an authentic contemporary architecture in Serbia of the period. Although he was understood and appreciated by a number of critics and contemporaries, his ideas and projects did not manage to penetrate the local armor of traditionalism and provincialism until the sociopolitical circumstances changed drastically after the Second World War.

Nikola Dobrović came to Belgrade soon after his graduation from the Department of Architecture at the Technical University in Prague in 1923, with the intention of staying and settling there.[67] As noted in a biographical article by Ljiljana Babić, he came to Serbia with great enthusiasm and energy for work, aiming to be "at the full disposal of his homeland."[68] Moving in the artistic circles of his elder brother Petar, a well-known Serbian painter who had settled in Belgrade two years previously, he was aroused by the atmosphere he found in Belgrade. Unsuccessful in attempts to find work, he was compelled to return to Prague where there were more prospects of starting a professional career. However, the thrill and love of Belgrade felt at that first acquaintance remained an inspiration for many return visits. Back in Prague, he was initially employed by the firm of Bohumil Hübschmann and Antonin Engel, and later by the large construction firm Dušek-Kozák-Maca, and in 1929 he started to practice on his own.[69] As Tanja Damljanović suggests, Czech functionalism, and especially its "scientific" line promoted by Karel Teige and the left-oriented group Devětsil, had exerted an important influence on the students graduating from the Technical University in Prague, including Dobrović. Their ideas were disseminated through the Architects Club, an organization of university graduates promoting functionality, rationalism, and objectivity in architecture close to the ideas of *Neue Sachlichkeit,* and its magazine *Stavba* edited by Teige. The character of Dobrović's early works, such as the house of Dr. Burliž in Prague and especially a house with a pharmacy in Krč which was published in *Stavba,* could be seen as relating to the ideas promoted by this circle.[70] Apart from the modest appearance in *Stavba,* other important reviews included publication of his winning entry in the international competition for Terazije Terrace in Belgrade, together with a highly commendatory article by the art critic Kosta Strajnić, both in the Czech magazine *Architekt* in 1930.[71] Dobrović's projects were also critically acclaimed following exhibitions of his work alongside that of his brother Petar, both in Yugoslavia and abroad, most notably in reviews of their shows in Pulchri Studio in The Hague (1930) and in the Denisův Institut in Prague (1932).[72]

His most significant work realized during the Prague period was King Aleksandar I College (1932–1933), the Yugoslav student hall. Conceived as a social condenser in which "collective friendly life, work, fun, etc. are made possible to the extreme limits,"[73] the building is designed as an open, H-plan structure with recreation facilities in the courtyards. The building follows Le Corbusier's five points: reinforced concrete skeletal structure, roof terraces, free

3.18 (top and middle) Nikola Dobrović, villa of Dr. Burliž, Prague, 1926.

3.19 Nikola Dobrović, house with a pharmacy in Krč near Prague, 1926.

plan, free facade, and horizontal windows. The state-of-the-art construction of the reinforced concrete structure was carried out by the well-known firm Kapsa & Müller.[74] At the time of the construction, Dobrović wrote about his design intent: "Architecture wants to be the expression of a new building objectivity. *Purposefulness* in the internal connection of rooms, as well as in the use of structural elements, *purism* in logical expression of internal functions on the external facades—these are the strongest points of this project."[75] In the pursuit of objectivity and purposefulness as his central design concerns, Dobrović had developed a characteristic architectural syntax that he often reelaborated and reinterpreted in his later works. So, for example, in the articulation of the south-facing facade of the Prague college, the architect boldly anticipated some of his later solutions, particularly those of the Ministry of Defense Headquarters building, realized some thirty years later in Belgrade.

The turning point of Dobrović's career, however, and his long-awaited homecoming coincided with the construction of the Grand Hotel (1934–1936) on the island of Lopud near Dubrovnik. Following this commission, Dobrović left Prague and moved to Dubrovnik in 1934, where he continued to work in his own practice until the Second World War. Some of the best examples of his modernist opus, all built in the Dubrovnik region, were produced in this period, most notably a series of villas and the Student Vacation Association Hall in Dubrovnik.[76] Regarding the Grand Hotel as a "masterpiece of significant physical dimensions," the authoritative scholar Ranko Radović writes: "Clear solution of plan, to which Dobrović, as much as Le Corbusier, gives great importance and the role of the generative force of the building; economy and rationality of construction and of the whole structure; use of concrete as the appropriate material; and connection to the surroundings—these would constitute a general characterization of his architecture in this period."[77] I would add one other characteristic of the hotel and of subsequent buildings realized in Dalmatia, namely their appropriation of the logic and aesthetic of a ship.[78] This aspect also connects back to Le Corbusier, but, as Marina Oreb Mojaš pointed out, in his villas Dobrović combines the symmetry and typology of a traditional Mediterranean house/palace with the contemporary spirit embodied in ships, in quite his own manner.

Another important aspect of Dobrović's particular approach, the use of natural stone as a cladding material, is also present in his buildings in Dalmatia. Introducing the contemporary construction technique of reinforced-concrete skeletal structure, yet retaining stone as the traditional building material of this region, he had to invent a cladding technique that would provide a logical, economical, and aesthetic solution to the problem. In this he was compelled to find a way to transplant modern architecture, as conceived and developed in continental Western Europe, into the subtropical region of Dalmatia. While he researched quite a few cladding patterns, the one he finally elaborated and later transplanted back into Belgrade consists of identical stone parallelepipeds measuring about 25 by 25 by 7.5 centimeters, each with a roughly embossed external face. These were set into a regular square grid with lined-up joints. In his recent study of the Ministry of Defense Headquarters in Belgrade, where the same sort of stone cladding was applied in the late 1950s, Bojan Kovačević suggests that Dobrović first proposed a variant of this system in his competition project for the PRIZAD building in Belgrade in 1937, and that the cladding originally meant for Belgrade was, in fact, realized instead in Dalmatia. Supporting his thesis with an in-depth chronological analysis, Kovačević claims that, although the stone cladding was generated on motifs from the traditional architecture of Dubrovnik, it was not actually worked out until his design for the PRIZAD building in Belgrade.[79] As this competition project was unsuccessful, not even gaining a commendation, Dobrović had to wait some twenty years before realizing his ideas in the place for which he initially intended them. Nonetheless, it is important to note that the particular detail of lined-up joints between stones, which Dobrović often accentuated by contrasting color or by inserting into them small round pebbles, contradicts the logic of building in stone and manifests the architect's concern for a true and honest representation of stone as cladding. Referring to the square grid used in the Student Vacation Association building in Dubrovnik (1938–1940), Dobrović gave a scientific explanation: "By extending

3.20 Nikola Dobrović, Yugoslav student hall, King Aleksandar College, Prague, 1932–1933. Main facade, rear facade, and courtyard.

regularly with its multitude of stone cubes, the grid motif falls on the same place of the retina, and is then registered by the same region of the brain, thus giving rise to the formal effect. That is an important realization, if the quality of artistic energy is brought into relation with the finding and cognition of new aesthetic values."[80] As he said in the sequel to this passage, this experience from the 1930s impelled him to propose the application of white cement joints for the grid to contrast the red sandstone cladding on the Ministry of Defense Headquarters building.[81]

Despite being displaced from the territory of Serbian modernism of the 1930s, Nikola Dobrović had a decisive influence on its identity. In view of the character of the period, I would argue that his work in fact represented the most important antinomy in Serbian modernism. A case in point is the presentation of his projects in the small exhibition salon at the Arts Pavilion in Belgrade at the joint show with his brother, painter Petar Dobrović, and sculptor Rista Stijović, held in November 1930. Here for the first time Belgrade saw an exhibition of uncompromisingly contemporary concepts in architecture from a single hand, displayed in more than fifteen live projects for various cities in Yugoslavia. This exhibition marked the end point of his efforts to gain recognition in his own country. All through the 1920s the main agency of Dobrović's communication with the homeland were exhibitions of his work alongside his brother Petar and other artists, in Ljubljana (1925), Novi Sad (1927), Sombor (1928), and Zagreb (1928), but the one held in Belgrade in 1930 can be regarded as the most significant. According to notable period critics, Dobrović's projects were well understood and very highly regarded in Belgrade. For example, Todor Manojlović wrote: "These are the constructions of clear and grand ideas, severe and comprehensible even in their rich complexity, and full of a fresh, modern zest."[82] Yet Dobrović's intention to implement the principles of contemporary architecture and to build his projects in Serbia clashed with the general unreceptiveness to modern architecture and opposition from the traditionalists and proponents of the national, Serbian-Byzantine style. His work was still regarded merely as a display of new tendencies, not as a realistic option, and was appraised accordingly: "That is why his works, together with those of Rista Stijović and Petar Dobrović also displayed, make this exhibition, as much by its presentation as by the high artistic value, one of the most beautiful, perhaps the most beautiful one that Belgrade ever had."[83]

A significant part of the exhibition comprised various competition projects for Yugoslav cities, which Dobrović prepared in parallel to his regular practice in Prague. By the end of the 1920s Dobrović concentrated his efforts on systematic competition activity, through which he exerted a decisive influence on the development of modernism in Yugoslavia. This was brought about by the extraordinary success he recorded at both national and international architectural competitions organized in Yugoslavia in 1929–1931. The first was the 1929 national competition for the theater in Novi Sad, for which he received a commendation.[84] The proposal shows a building of symmetrical organization of plan and strong cubic volumetrics, of which a period critic exclaimed: "and how much elegance and sonority in those simple square surfaces and volumes!'[85] The design rested on a structural system of reinforced concrete columns and frames, which allowed for free plan, free facade, and horizontal windows in the rear of the building, as well as for the large glazed openings of the front facade.[86] Compared to the highly formalist character of contemporary "modern" projects by local architects, such as the art deco proposal at the same competition by the architects Petar and Branko Krstić, this design represented an innovative and contemporary approach to functional architecture.

In the sequel to this, in 1930 Dobrović won the highest prizes in three international architectural competitions, those for Terazije Terrace in Belgrade, the Regional Hospital in Split, and the bathing complex at Bačvice Bay in Split. The jury of the Bačvice competition, presided over by the revered Slovenian architect and professor Jože Plečnik, unanimously awarded Dobrović the highest prize among twenty-three projects, of which eight were by Yugoslav architects and the rest from Germany. In the jury report, Plečnik pointed especially to the powerful architectural concept and strong technical aspects of the winning design. A few months later, it was the contemporary spirit and artful articulation of the complex that were singled out as the strongest points of Dobrović's archi-

3.21   (opposite page) Nikola Dobrović, Grand Hotel on the island of Lopud near Dubrovnik, 1934–1936. View of the facade facing the sea, and detail of the facade.

3.22   Nikola Dobrović, hotel at Lapad in Dubrovnik, 1931 (project).

3.23   Nikola Dobrović, Villa Vesna on the island of Lopud near Dubrovnik, 1939.

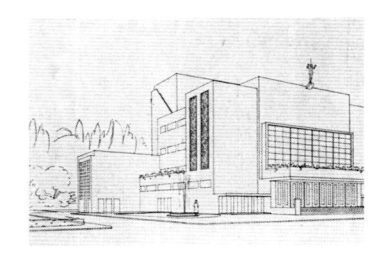

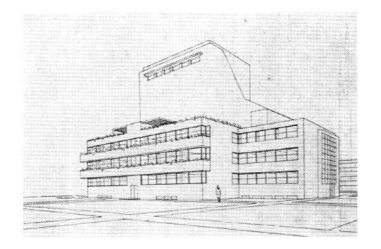

tectural proposal for the hospital in Split, which was awarded one of the two highest *ex aequo* prizes in an invited international competition. The last of the three projects Dobrović sent to Split in 1930 was an entry in the open competition for the Palace of the Coastal Regional Government, for which he was initially awarded one of five commendations (but after the reversal of the jury decision, the prizes were annulled and all awarded architects were given equal compensation prizes).[87] In the same year he also entered the national competitions for the Palace of the Vardar Regional Government in Skopje (second prize) and the Agrarian Bank in Belgrade (commended), and carried out a project for a *Hotel-Kursaal* in Dubrovnik. In 1931 the streak of competition successes continued with the projects for the railway station in Skopje (third prize), the Danube railway station in Belgrade, and the adaptation of the City Café in Dubrovnik (first prize). Yet not one of these projects was ever realized. Reacting to the fierce discussion concerning his controversial design of the *Hotel-Kursaal* in Dubrovnik, Dobrović published an article "In Defense of Contemporary Building" in which his uncompromising stance is well summarized:

What is today is but an early renaissance of contemporary building. . . .
I write for the colleagues who are convinced that in Dalmatia there are many
more places where, in the shortest time and with new building methods,
new settlements, far more perfect and more poetic than Dubrovnik,
could be created. I dedicate these lines to the ones who are convinced
that this century of ours would be too poor if it did not know how to create
unique deeds, in a technical and artistic sense, with all the natural and
artificial materials we have today. For the possibilities of today, the old styles
would represent just a limited accomplishment.

And something else. In contemporary building, in terms of building
methods, there is no left or right wing. That is a pejorative expression that
was used for my work during my stay in Split. There are only contemporary
and not-contemporary experts.[88]

It may be that conservative and clerical circles in Split and Dubrovnik rejected Dobrović because they saw his architecture as an "extreme left wing," in contrast to the acceptable modernity exemplified by Plečnik, whom they saw as the right "right wing." Or it may be that the provincialism of Belgrade's elite, fascinated by the grandness of European historical styles, coupled with the desperate need for national self-determination by the agency of the Serbian-Byzantine style, prevailed over the modernizing and emancipating impulses. In the context of this particular research, I would argue that the crucial point of rejection of modern architecture and planning in Belgrade could be explained by the example of the winning competition project for Terazije Terrace.

CHAPTER 3 **EXPOSURE**

3.24 (opposite page, top) Nikola Dobrović, theater in Novi Sad, 1929 (competition project). Perspective views of front and back.

3.25 (opposite page and this page) Nikola Dobrović, bathing complex at Bačvice Bay, Split, 1930 (competition project). Restaurant, main entrance, and aerial perspective view.

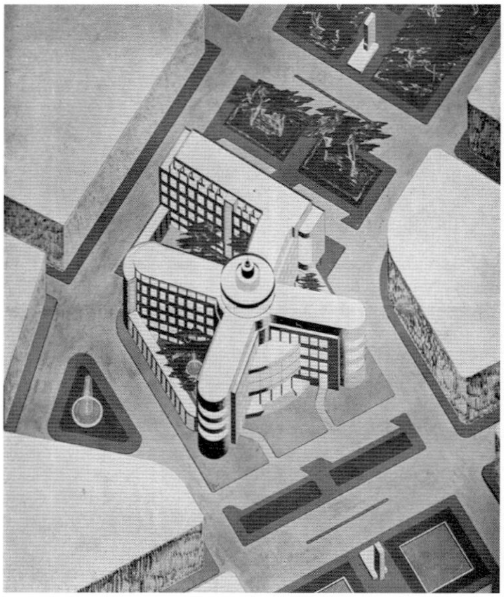

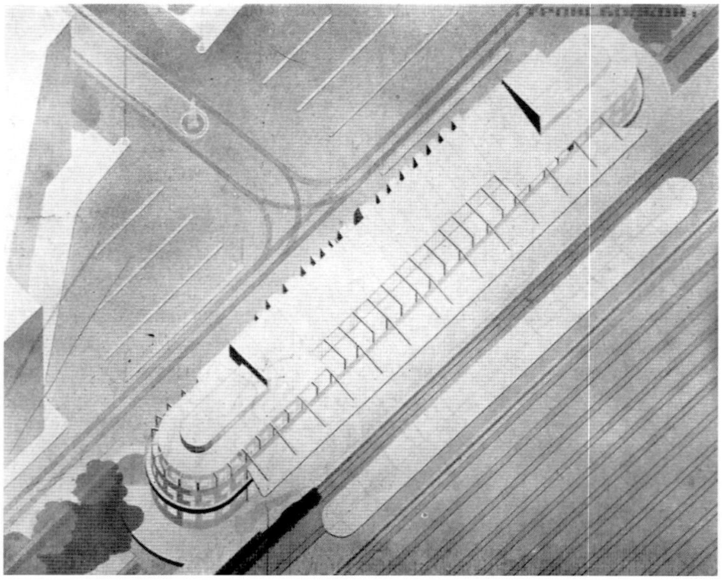

3.26 (opposite page, left) Nikola Dobrović, Palace of the Vardar Regional Government, Skopje, 1930 (competition project).

3.27 (opposite page and this page) Nikola Dobrović, Danube Station, Belgrade, 1931 (competition project). Aerial axonometric view and view of the main facade.

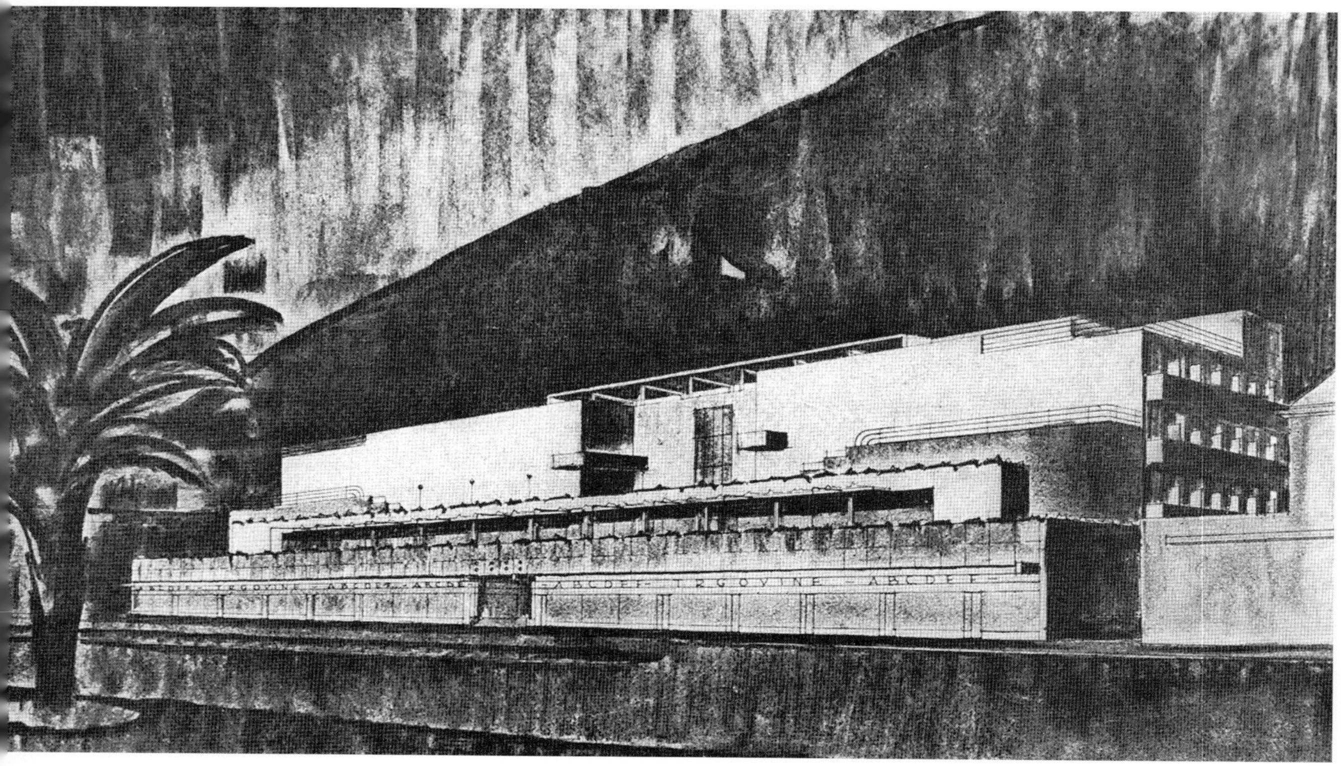
ABCDEF - TRGOVINE - ABCDEF

The competition site, Terazije Terrace, is an urban block by the side of the epicenter of Belgrade, Terazije Square, with a natural slope of the terrain toward the river Sava of some 15 meters in height between the perimeter streets, and with dramatic views to the large plain of the west bank. Dobrović made full use of the site's potential with a project that treated not only architectural aspects of the design but also much wider planning issues. With a simple incision through the existing urban tissue he connected Terazije with the river quay and the railway station square, thus opening a stepped cut-through along the principal longitudinal axis. The proposal extended the level of the Terazije plateau and formed a monumental square stretching over the whole length of the site. The rectangular open space of the Terrace, flanked by two long side buildings arranged in total axial symmetry, followed from the initial urban plan. In addition to these primary gestures, two towers were set to grow boldly out of the basic form, in order to mark the entrance to the Terrace from Terazije. On the opposite side of the site, an appropriate scaling down was achieved by cascading volumes and roof terraces. The complexity of spatial experience was underlined by the superimposition of longitudinally positioned solid volumes over the transverse layout of circulation areas and by the organization of underground spaces.

The architectural composition of the Terazije Terrace project was generated from the new perception of space in which an integral constellation of plastic volumes and the void between them create the spatial dynamics. By rejecting the notion of an inactive hollow space between plastic volumes, this approach developed a concept of interaction between the architectural object and the urban space, termed "space set in motion."

In one of his key theoretical texts from 1960, "Space Set in Motion—Bergson's Dynamic Schemes—New Image of Environment," Dobrović explains the concept of montage of spatial experiences in which solid volumes and void together, as equal partners, make a series of plastic conditions for an architectural composition.[89] Referring to the French philosopher Henri Bergson as a point of departure, he goes "further by uniting a dialectical-materialist truth, confirmed by notable representatives of scientific dialectic materialism, with the problems of spatial morphology."[90] Dobrović declares the perception of continuity in a dynamic architectural composition to be an illusion equivalent to the nature of perception in cinematography, yet as being prerequisite for understanding the law of the new aesthetic. The central point of his argument is the cinematographic character of cognition for modern man, "the new urbanized individual, 'homo spatiosus,' brought up to see and experience the city as a color film (*macro film*) on the Cinemascope of urban prospects."[91] Although the text refers specifically to the Ministry of Defense Headquarters building, some of its essential premises could be applied to the Terazije Terrace project as well. This is particularly notable in its integral compositional effect of positive vs. negative, with the square, as a grand urban void, that is,

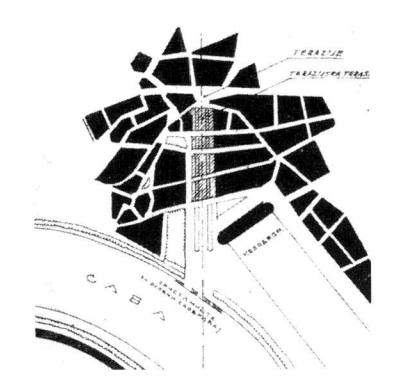

3.28   (opposite page) Nikola Dobrović, *Hotel-Kursaal*, Dubrovnik, 1931 (project).

3.29   Nikola Dobrović, Terazije Terrace, Belgrade, 1929–1930 (competition project). Location plan and axonometric view of the site.

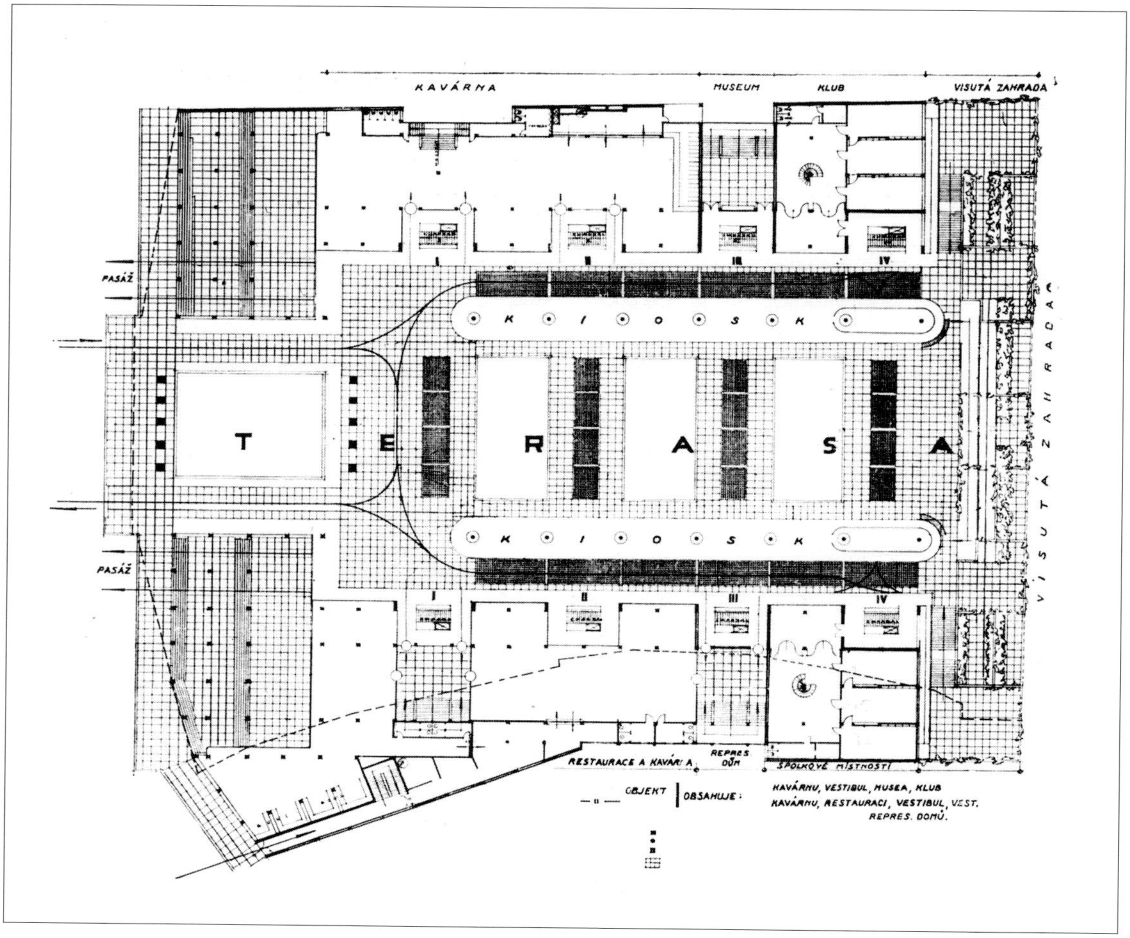
KAVÁRNA
MUSEUM
KLUB
VISUTÁ ZAHRADA
PASÁŽ
KIOSK
TERASA
KIOSK
PASÁŽ
VISUTÁ ZAHRADA
RESTAURACE A KAVÁRNA
REPRES DŮM
SPOLKOVÉ MÍSTNOSTI
OBJEKT
OBSAHUJE:
KAVÁRNU, VESTIBUL, MUSEA, KLUB
KAVÁRNU, RESTAURACI, VESTIBUL, VEST. REPRES. DOMŮ.

negative volume, contained by the severe geometry of the buildings' positive volumes. With the Terazije Terrace project Dobrović also anticipated the syncretism of cinematographic and architectonic discourses in the unfolding of the experience of an architectural composition. The actual presentation of the project rests on a series of colored perspective drawings that possess the character of film frames, through which the architect attempted to simulate the motion of spatial sequencing.

In broader terms, this design proposed a radical transformation of the scale and, consequently, the character of the existing urban pattern, while staying in keeping with the natural relief and historical matrix. Uncompromisingly modern in its articulation of planning and form, Dobrović's design envisaged the future metropolitan development of Belgrade and pointed to the logical direction of growth of the city center. The fact that this project was chosen as an outright winner in the competition among twenty-five entries, half of which were from the European centers (Germany, Czechoslovakia, and France), speaks of great hopes and aspirations for the city's future planning strategy. Yet the ever-competing forces of traditionalism and conservatism undermined the initial enthusiasm and delayed realization. In an article published in 1932 in the daily newspaper *Vreme,* Dobrović concluded his arguments with a questioning lament: "Is this idea, so full of life energy, need, vitality, and imperative, going to find ardent defenders and representatives? Here ends the mission of a chaste architect–constructivist. Let the experts of the national economy speak now."[92] In 1938, Dobrović's project was incorporated into the Regulation plan of Belgrade, but the momentum had been lost, and so had the chance to have it realized. For the "eyes which do not see" could not perceive its authentic value.

The final act of the Terazije Terrace drama took place in the new socialist/communist Belgrade. Dobrović finally came to the war-ransacked capital after the liberation, soon to be appointed director of the Urban Planning Institute of Serbia in 1945 and then to the position of Belgrade Chief Urbanist, the director of Belgrade's Town Planning Department, in 1946–1947. With unrelenting persistence, Dobrović returned to the problem of Terazije Terrace in his first postwar publication *Reconstruction and Construction of Belgrade* (1946).[93] In his renewed proposal for the Terrace he employed the original planning strategy, extending the scheme over the new underground rail line all the way to the riverbank. The character of the postwar scheme was, however, significantly changed in relation to the original one, notwithstanding its outline stage of design. The pure expression of horizontal layers of the original project gave way to a more cubic composition of form, and the whole scheme seems more of a directive kind of gesture. In some ways, the new scheme foresaw the ethos of the modern city of New Belgrade which was about to be built on the vast marshy plain opposite the Terrace.

3.30   Plan of the top level of Terazije Terrace.

Geslo : Urbanismus

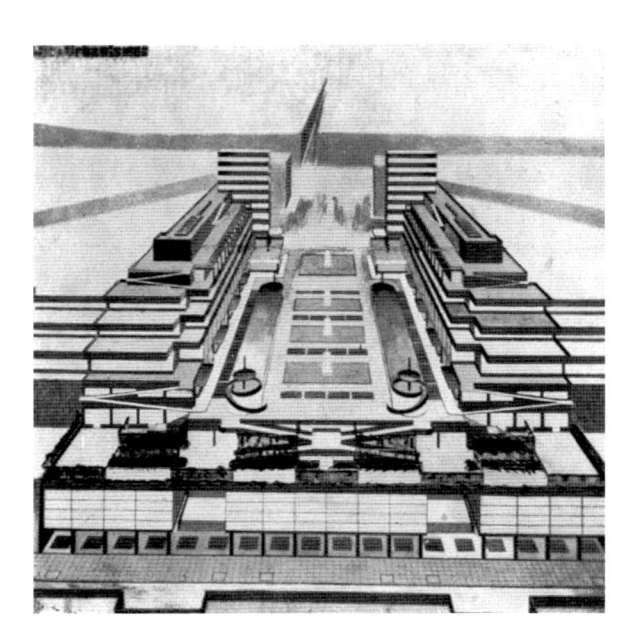

3.31 Terazije Terrace. Aerial perspective view from Kraljice Natalije Street; perspective view from Terazije Square with the existing urban context; perspective view from Terazije Square; perspective view of the side building with the tower.

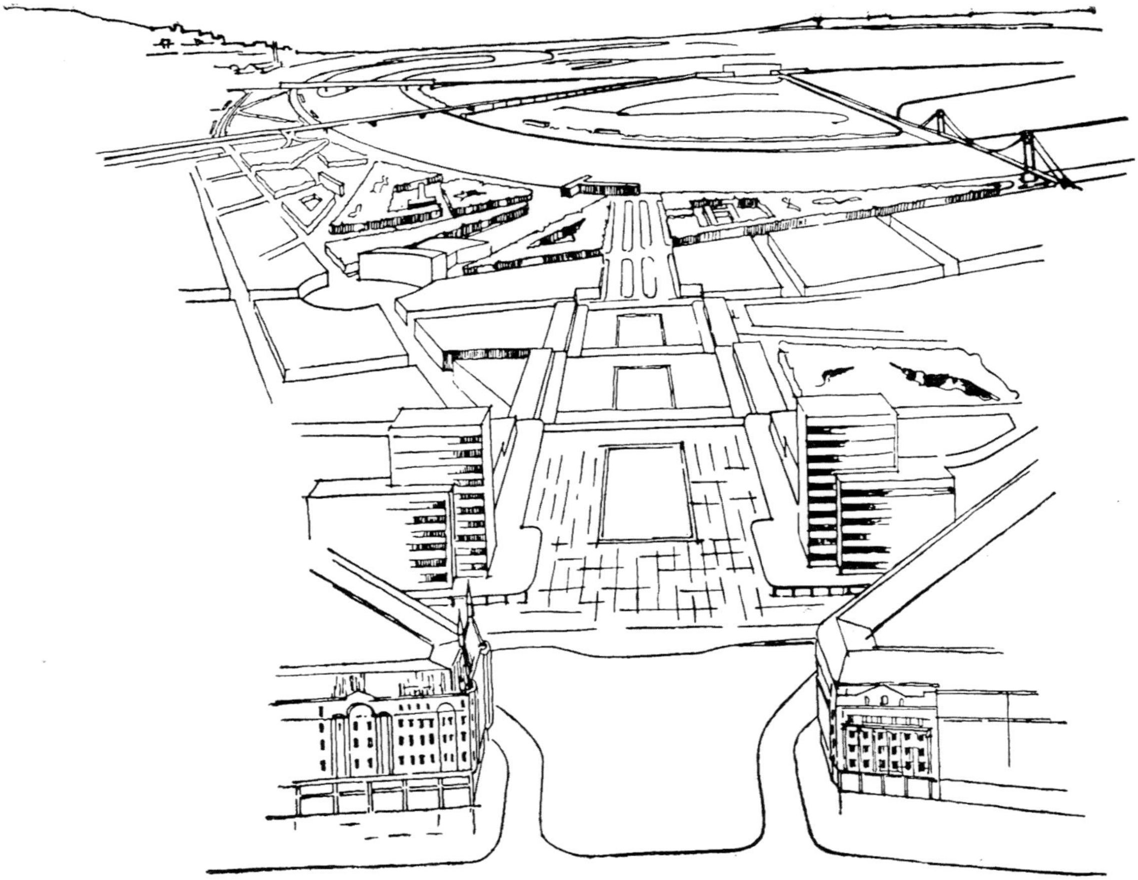

As it turned out, the new city took precedence, and it was Dobrović who made the first sketch for it, while the Terrace forever stayed a chimera.

Even if traces of its "space set in motion" are present in the Ministry of Defense Headquarters, there is the tremendous time lag of some thirty years, which is still perplexing. As Dobrović himself wrote in 1966, the feeling of lost opportunity with the Terrace far outweighed the success in building the Ministry thirty years later. I would suggest that the latter came as an anticlimax and that, despite its indisputable importance for Serbian modernism, albeit in its postwar aberration, it stands as evidence of the much too belated will to modernity. Strategies, concepts, and details developed and realized in Dobrović's 1930s buildings are just reenacted in the Ministry of Defense Headquarters, notwithstanding the integral ingenuity of its complex structure. The obvious time lag clearly manifests the slowdown in the process of internalization of modernity in Serbian architecture. Thus it may be said that the one truly modern notion epitomized in the architecture of Nikola Dobrović could not be seen, because the eyes of Belgrade were fixed on the wish image of the colorful balloon of the fashionable new "modern" style. The furthest their distracted gaze could reach was Count Zeppelin's airship, the image of engineering modernity to be admired from afar. But when action to materialize an architectural reflection of this image was needed, courage evaporated. As a result, against the integrated void of the Terrace the hollow space of New Belgrade won the day.

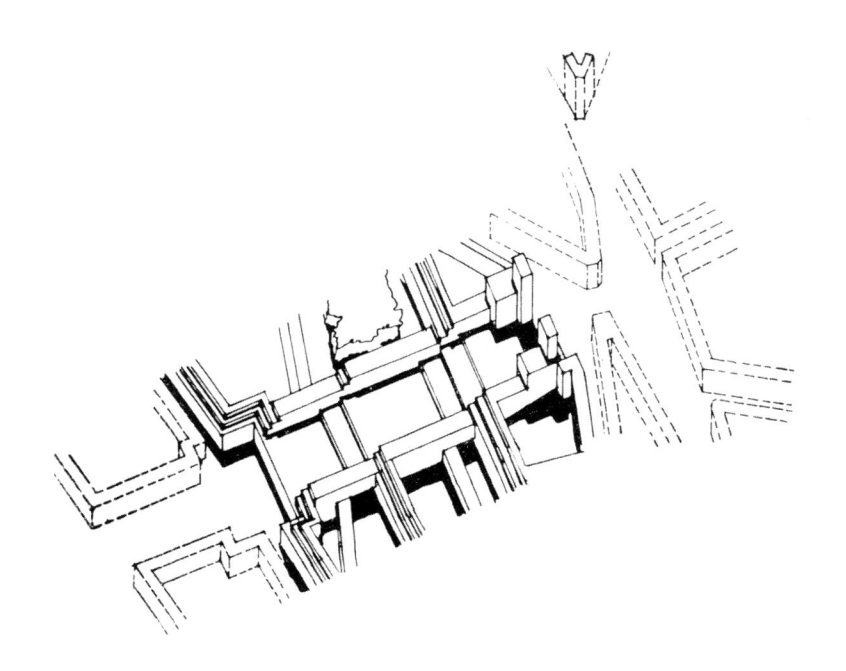

3.32 Nikola Dobrović, revised project for Terazije Terrace, Belgrade, 1946. Aerial view from above Terazije Square; axonometric drawing.

4 BYT MODE

byt—Russian for everyday life, the quotidian. It was much used by the Soviet avant-garde as a negative value for the traditionally conservative framework of society, signifiers of which are "infamous geraniums, canary birds, curtains . . . ," and which is embodied both in dwellings and in streets. "Languor and petrifaction" of *byt* is seen by *LEF*'s author, Boris Arvatov, as the "art of dwelling," subjected to institutional art, and as the "art of the street" which is somewhat more functional and dynamic. *Byt* is essentially a bourgeois category, which was, according to Arvatov, to be liquidated by the new Soviet art aiming at "revolution within art, within production, and within the *byt* itself." Kazimir Malevich denied not only *byt* per se but its representation in bourgeois figurative art as well, and claimed that *byt* cannot be immanent to the proletariat, for the proletariat is in its essence abstract, *bespredmetny*.[1]

mode—1. a manner or way of doing, acting or existing. 2. the current fashion or style. (*Collins English Dictionary*)

When Milan Zloković wrote in 1932, "The postwar enthusiasm, strong and convincing in resolving and carrying out practical problems in the social sphere, raised architecture to its proper level—the truthful and dignified expression of needs and desires of contemporary civilized people," he was only reiterating the more-than-a-decade-old discourse of the modern movement.[2] Being entangled in the time lag of Serbian modernism, Zloković carried on with the same argument even as late as 1938, when he recapitulated the claim: "The world war accelerated the crystallization of a new societal ideology, set up on a social basis, which, despite being interpreted differently in various countries, seriously acted to make living conditions better and more humane."[3] Reflecting this ideology, and with the new structural possibilities and great choice of products of a building industry and rationalized craftsmanship and, *nota bene,* "renewed views on people's health and closer relations between the social classes," the postwar architecture forever distanced itself from "the sterile, academicist formalism with its lack of understanding of real-life requirements." Finally, he concluded, contemporary architecture rests upon the following premises: it is a "social art" based on "concise program," "in-depth, true, and technically correct solution,"

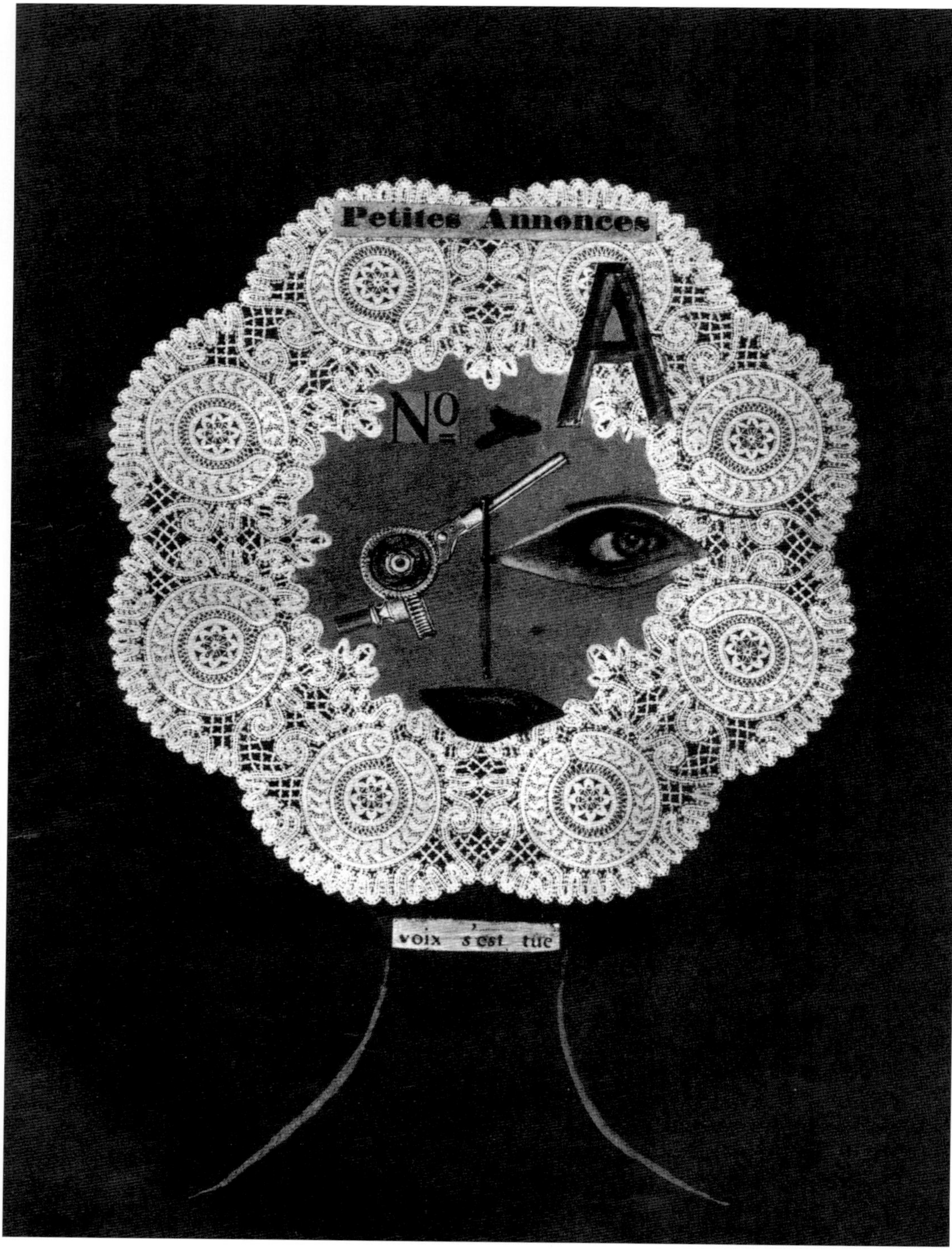
Petites Annonces
No
A
voix s'est tue

"lively, logical, and sober treatment of the essence of architecture," "wide collective understanding of the order of urbanism," and, above all, "honest collective cooperation" among architects, engineers/constructors, and all other professionals who "incise into the complex organism of the contemporary architectural object."[4]

But the messianic promise of a better world must have echoed hollowly against the actual situation of interwar Belgrade's urban housing conditions. For, despite the proclaimed aims and desires, Belgrade ended the modern epoch not as a city of dwellings worthy of a civilized person, but as one schizophrenically split between the modern center of houses and apartment buildings in all modes, and the nondescript sea of unhygienic suburbia full of nonarchitectural bare dwellings. Between the fashions of the one and the destitute *byt* of the other, the "optimal projection" of modern architecture largely failed. Could it be that, foreshadowed by the prospect of the new war, the main objective of Zloković's text was a conscious action of repetition in which the blind spots of the local modern movement are recognized as such and then reactualized for the end-of-the-epoch discourse? Could the above text, then, be seen as an un-played-out scenario that reads in retrospect the things that ought to have happened but did not—a kind of "retroactive manifesto" for the long-lost utopia?

THE PROBLEM OF DWELLING 4.1

In the short interwar period of just twenty years Belgrade was transformed from a provincial Balkan center into what could be seen as a modern European capital of the 1930s. Its population and the city's built-up area almost quadrupled, with the population increasing by an average of more than 10,000 people per year.[5] The great population influx in the first postwar years, into a city in which at least one-third of the building supply had been ruined or demolished, caused the most severe housing crisis. The first phase (1918–1921) of tackling this problem was characterized by the short-lived interventionist policy of limited ownership, requisition of flats, and directive minimization of rent prices. With the loosening of interventionism, and with no state-run programs for social housing, the resolution of the crisis had to rely entirely on private investment. With no legal provisions for separate ownership of individual flats, landlords ruled over the feverishly growing rental property market, and the steady flow of the homeless urban crowd was forced to rent anything, anywhere, at any exacted price.

4.1   Radojica Živanović Noje, *Horse Is Dead*, photo collage published in *Nadrealizam danas i ovde*, no. 1 (1931).

TABLE 4.1 Increase in Population and Built-up Area in Belgrade, 1921–1938

Year	Population	Built-up area (hectares)
1921	111,740	1,000
1929	226,070	2,600
1938	350,000	4,000

TABLE 4.2 Construction of Flats in Relation to Population Increase, Belgrade, 1919–1932

Year	New buildings	New buildings with ground floor only	New small flats	New large flats	Number of inhabitants
1919–20	100	61	118	125	
1921	172	99	250	177	111,740
1922	388	166	799	567	131,510
1923	405	157	879	798	145,462
1924	270	127	606	460	159,420
1925	236	108	409	271	173,375
1926	428	189	909	525	187,330
1927	612	215	1,040	1,029	201,285
1928	521	201	1,052	624	215,240
1929	280	109	542	400	229,195
1930	273	123	639	349	242,000
1931	531	244	910	796	260,000
Total	4,216	1,799	8,153	6,121	

Consequently, two types of furiously fabricated rental dwellings saturated the market by the end of the 1920s: expensive, large flats in the rental palaces on one side, and cheap, unhygienic, and uncomfortable dwellings in ramshackle ground-floor quarters on the other, with virtually no middle bracket.[6] As sociologist Slobodan Vidaković argued in 1932, the city lacked what it needed the most, *Existenzminimum* dwellings:

Belgrade is predominantly a city of clerks, small retailers, craftsmen, especially workers, all recruited from the great army of rural paupers and small-town proletarian craftsmen. This economically weak world is made up of some 200,000 people. The insignificant number of some 30,000 more affluent and just 10,000 wealthy citizens of Belgrade cannot be taken into account. That is why the housing problem of an entirely social character, manifested by the shortage of small, cheap, and hygienic dwellings, represents a most acute and very painful issue in Belgrade.[7]

In effect, the closely knit clusters of small inhabitable spaces (e.g., 8 persons living in a room of some 18 cubic meters and subletting the kitchen to a "fine" single tenant)[8] grew "with cinematic speed" into the illegally built suburban city of the poor, infamous as the world's no. 1 center of infant mortality, tuberculosis, and high rents (on average amounting to 50 percent of total income).[9] If, as Kracauer observed, "each social stratum has a space that is associated with it," then the sordid hovels in unregulated suburban quarters, "which cannot even be enlarged by the radio," corresponded precisely to the narrow living space of the anonymous Belgrade city dwellers completely deprived of their individuality.[10] More to the point, being temporarily rented, these were traversable, nomadic spaces, impersonal living containers to be exchanged for other, equally barren ones on the expiry of the tenancy contract.

4.2   Old and new Belgrade: Skadarska Street, ca. 1934.

But what of modern architects? "It cannot be forgotten that the [new] style, so to speak, comes from poverty," wrote Stanislav Vinaver on the results of the German *Neue Sachlichkeit* experiment.[11] Those in the Belgrade modernist circle, however, serviced the middle-class market, and stayed within the psychic mood that Georg Simmel defined as the "*blasé* attitude." It is not that they did not perceive the distinctions between things when they spoke and wrote of modern architecture as being a "social art" (Zloković) or that its most important characteristic was that "it is social" (Kojić), but their practice directly reflected the predominant money economy, and was thus leveled and discolored by it.[12] Very few of the modernist circle, perhaps only architect Jan Dubovy, addressed the issues raised by the rise of Belgrade into a metropolis, and argued the possibilities of its becoming what Simmel posited in his seminal essay "The Metropolis and Mental Life" as "the center of freedom" charged with an aura of "individual freedom."

Following the acceptance of the Belgrade Master Plan (1923), Dubovy gave a lecture titled "Garden City" in 1924 at the Belgrade section of the Union of Yugoslav Engineers and Architects (UYEA). Starting from ideas discussed at the Anti-Tuberculosis Conference held in Prague in 1923, specifically Dr. Ružička's paper on "eubotics" (the pseudo-science of the proper way of living) and its correlation to eugenics (the pseudo-science of methods of improving the quality of the human race), Dubovy postulated that the principal role of architects and engineers is to lead in the making of the fitting environment of "health, joy, and happiness" for future generations. In this he saw garden city planning as the most appropriate, and he introduced his public to Ebenezer Howard's *Tomorrow: A Peaceful Path to Real Reform* (1898), with lateral references to its prehistory in the ideas of Thomas Spencer, Charles Fourier, James Silk Buckingham, and others, as well as to more contemporary ideas such as Antonio Sant'Elia's futurist city, Auguste Perret's megabuildings for 10,000 inhabitants, Tony Garnier's Industrial City, and Le Corbusier's Ville Contemporaine.[13] In the conclusion, he spoke of Belgrade as the metropolis of all Yugoslavs, which could develop economically and culturally to transcend national and Balkan boundaries and become the cosmopolitan south metropolis of all Slavs.

This projection very much corresponds to what Simmel saw as the metropolitan condition: "It is not only the immediate size of the area and population which, on the basis of world-historical correlation between the increase in the size of the social unit and the degree of personal inner and outer freedom, makes the metropolis the locus of this condition. It is rather in transcending this purely tangible extensiveness that the metropolis also becomes the seat of cosmopolitanism."[14] Dubovy insisted on the geopolitical position of Belgrade and its potential for being "naturally" connected to Europe both north and south, to the north via the Danube to Czechoslovakia and Poland, and potentially further to the

North Sea, and to the south to Russia and the Black Sea, and via an envisaged future Danube-Morava-Vardar canal to Thessalonica and the Aegean Sea. It is clear that his argument was about the importance of dynamic extensions and an understanding of Belgrade in a functional magnitude beyond its actual physical boundaries, quite in line with what Simmel wrote: "For the metropolis it is decisive that its inner life is extended in a wave-like motion over a broader national or international area."[15] But Dubovy's vision was bounded by pan-Slavic ideas, as for him the metropolitan identity (or could it be Simmel's individual freedom?) was to be gained in the development of Slavism: "The garden city idea in our Slavic countries will have to be realized at last, for we have to resolve the housing problem and to give to our generation a dwelling that would be a foundation for healthy development of all Slavism."[16]

As for its architecture, he suggested, both monumental buildings and the simplest of houses should be "tasteful artistic-architectural works." For the garden suburbs, he proposed simple and practical typical houses, though infused with the aura of the ancients: "architecture Slavonic, architecture of our national soul, which represents our folkloric art." In this architecture, Dubovy said, "our Slavonic detailing in wood, our richly carved columns, bright colors around windows and doors, would in truth look beautiful in the green environment of the garden city, and this garden city would become the Slavic city."[17] The accompanying drawings by Dubovy's fellow graduate from Prague, Belgrade architect Svetomir Lazić, of "family houses in the Serbian style," dressed in the national or rather in pan-Slavic costumes, reflected the undercurrent of nostalgia and the search for a form of being different, but a form that still belonged to the objective spirit of the production of housing.[18]

In two subsequent important programmatic texts on social housing in urban and rural areas, illustrated with his own projects for typical workers' and peasants' houses and published in the Belgrade City Council journal *Savremena opština*, Dubovy reconfirmed his position.[19] In the text "Workers' House and Workers' Hall," the condition of urban working-class housing was diagnosed as the acute illness of society:

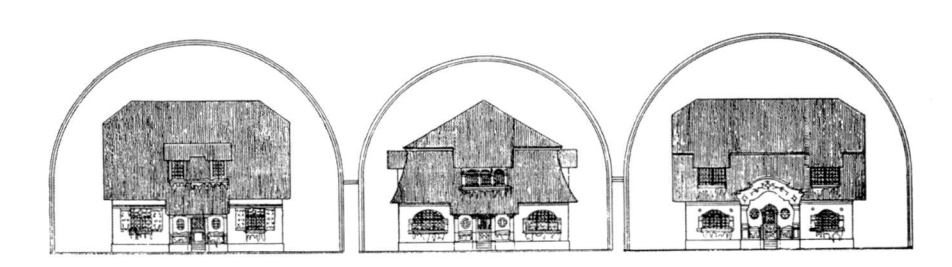

4.3 Svetomir Lazic, family houses in the Serbian style, 1925 (theoretical project).

The culmination of this misery is the housing problem, which has not been taken account of enough here, and which should be the first one with regard to workers' issues. Only pure social issues are being addressed, while the fundamentals of the "housing problem" are completely forgotten.... The present epoch has to lead the workers into their houses, their homes, where they will find familial happiness, life's pleasures, necessary physical and spiritual rest, opportunity for cultural education, and opportunity for work in free nature, in their own garden.[20]

In the following proposal for a small and simple semidetached worker's house, with a total ground-floor area of some 80 square meters, Dubovy produced a pragmatic and contemporary solution of, as he put it, "simple, harmonious, and tasteful" outlook. At the end of the article he suggested that the worker's house "has to represent our epoch, which requires from us not only order in life, but in art as well."[21] The concept is related to the architect's earlier views on the architecture of the garden city, which "should be simple and beautiful, and in accordance with the practical sense," but here the pan-Slavic costume is shed and the form of the house appears undressed, totally naked. It is in this very nakedness that Dubovy's worker's house project comes closest to the impersonal object of the modern epoch, the standard product. Although unrealized in the absence of major state programs for the construction of workers' housing, this design produces a "diagram of the present age"[22] by precisely pinpointing the nomadic condition, impersonality, and collectivity of the steadily increasing urban working population. The faint trace of this concept can be detected, but just so, in the few modest houses Dubovy designed for members of the working-class Paroci family, finalized in 1934, just before Dubovy, "financially wrecked, and morally and physically ruined," decided to leave the big city and move to Bitola in Macedonia.[23] In these, however, the nakedness of the worker's house prototype was veiled by the commonplace of suburban existence: as Kracauer put it, "the characteristic location of the small dependent existences who still very much like to associate themselves with the sunken middle class."[24]

It is most notably in three humanitarian institutions, the Workers' Shelters for Men and Women and Kindergarten realized in 1928–1929 as part of the social program of the Belgrade City Council, that Dubovy produced a space for the ultimate modern nomad, the unemployed working-class person.[25] As noted in one of the official speeches at the opening, the shelters were to have "as much a human and social as an economic and national task" in keeping the young working force healthy and protected in times of unemployment. As transitory homes offering overnight protection from the "destructive currents" of the big city, the shelters were based primarily on the idea of "absolute hygiene."[26] At the

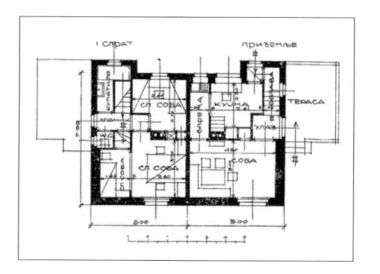

CHAPTER 4 **BYT MODE**

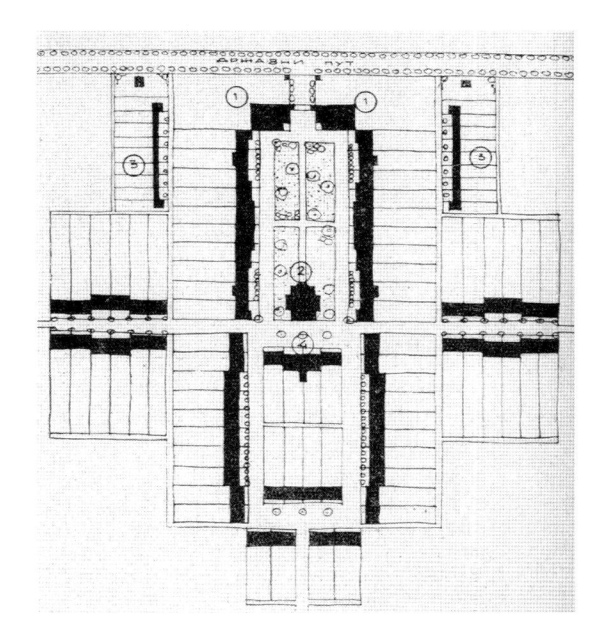

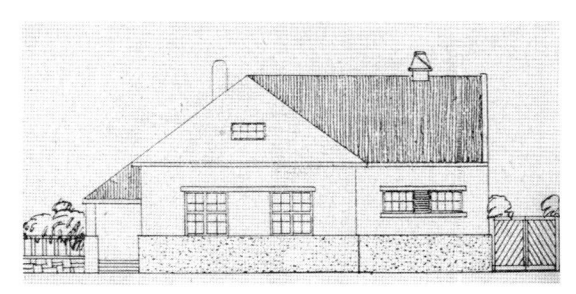

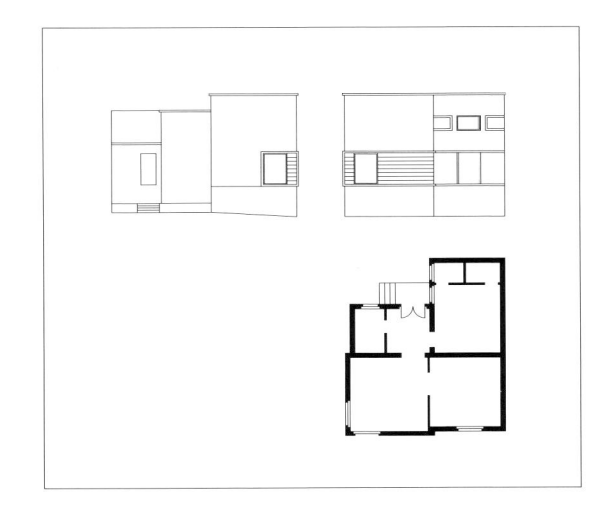

4.4 (opposite page) Jan Dubovy, worker's house, 1926 (project). Elevation, perspective view of the interior, and plan.

4.5 (top and middle) Jan Dubovy, Regulation plan for rural settlements, 1926 (project). Site plan and peasant's house.

4.6 Jan Dubovy, house of Josef Paroci, Belgrade, 1934. Elevations and plan.

low price of 10 dinars per night, each individual was first relieved of his or her clothes and then provided with a bath, disinfestation from lice if necessary, clean night shirt, towel and slippers, medical checkup, dinner and breakfast, and a fresh linen-covered bed in a centrally heated room. The men's shelter was combined with the job center, and the women's shelter also provided accommodation for women just out of maternity hospitals, as well as overnight shelter for their babies and children, while the kindergarten offered children day care.[27] With the clear concept of designing these as most economic, functional, and hygienic environments, in the three buildings Dubovy finally produced his "simple and beautiful" architecture of the real contemporary world. There is no division between the actuality of the shelters and Dubovy's "artistic-architectural work"; the two cooperate and yield the real within this architecture. While a pronounced hierarchical character of the facades still evoked the compositional strategies of academicism, the functional organization of plan, typifying of elements, and particularly the purist aesthetic of poverty of the interiors manifested the abstract, *bespredmetny* character of the new subject-object relationship and the consequent rationale of new architecture. While the frugality of design and fitting out was a corollary of the tight social program budget, I would argue that the architecture of the shelters' interior space is as impersonal, naked, and disinfected as the bodies of the faceless crowd moving in and out every day. In its bareness, this is the dwelling space of the uprooted individual, the home of the "intensification of emotional life."[28]

Beyond the protective hygiene of the shelters, the reality of the underprivileged bred tuberculosis in the home. On average, out of the total number of dead, every third citizen of Belgrade died from tuberculosis (amounting to 338 per 100,000 inhabitants per annum).[29] Twenty times that number were infected,

4.7   (opposite page) Jan Dubovy, Workers' Shelter for Men and Kindergarten, Belgrade, 1928–1929.

4.8   (opposite page) Jan Dubovy, Workers' Shelter for Women, Belgrade, 1928–1929.

4.9   Workers' Shelters. Registration and admissions room in the men's shelter; dining room in the men's shelter; bedroom in the men's shelter; playroom in the kindergarten.

which amounted to one person with tuberculosis living in every second home. The statistics worsen in the poor quarters, where about 70 percent of tuberculosis sufferers did not even have their own bed, let alone a separate room. While the well-off could afford the long sanatorium treatment, the idle world of Thomas Mann's *Zauberberg,* the workforce could not. And again the war provided useful solutions, as the president of the Anti-Tuberculosis League, Dr. Ljuba Stojanović, wrote: "[the world war] taught us many useful things, among others that: for successful treatment of tuberculosis patients it is not necessary that they live in mountains, in luxurious buildings, and that they be stuffed with select expensive meals, but that all of that can be achieved in wooded plains, in modest but comfortable buildings, if need be in timber houses, sheds, even tents, and with common food, only, of course, in plentiful quantities."[30] Subsequently, the idea of colonies or villages for tuberculosis sufferers, where they would live and, more importantly, work and earn their upkeep, became one of the most forward-thinking concepts for the development of the city perimeter: "Simply, a village for tuberculosis sufferers should be like a modern city, or better said, a suburb, the difference being only that in suburbs healthy citizens live, while these villages are inhabited by those infected with tuberculosis."[31]

One of the most notable theoretical proposals for the colony of tuberculosis sufferers was drawn up by a medical buildings expert, architect Dragan Petrik, for the Central Department of Hygiene in Belgrade. The project focuses on the functional distribution of dwellings for the sick, separate housing for their families, workshops, medical facilities, and community center. Set along a garden path—an idealized *soleil, espace, verdure* setting—the houses for the sick are designed as individual containers slightly raised off the ground with a removable front wall, a bed inside, and a terrace in front, all open to as much sun and fresh air as possible. The simple and economic architecture of these houses aimed at achieving a higher level of culture, one that could be measured by the level of tuberculosis mortality, as Dr. Stojanović argued: "The nation is more cultured the less people die of tuberculosis."[32]

The experts struggled in vain, as the Belgrade City Council managed not to make their ideas a reality. The provision of social housing as the more permanent solution to the problem of habitation for the healthy working population proved difficult enough for the Council, without venturing into the expensive development of colonies for the sick. As part of its communal policy, over the whole interwar period the Council funded the construction of just over 500 flats—a negligible number when thousands were needed for the constant housing crisis. Erected haphazardly in unattractive free council sites, with the aim of demonstrating that the Council, after all, did care for the poor, these ended up being urbanistically, architecturally, and hygienically substandard. As such, they acquired the disreputable character of "social asylums."[33] In an attempt to create a more fitting council housing, architect Branko Maksimović was appointed to design two Colonies for the Poor as part of the communal social project.[34] Constructed in 1928, the colony in Topčider comprised five independent buildings, each with eight small flats of some 40 square meters area. It was equipped with a sewage system, running water, and electricity, each building having a common laundry room and cellar storage, and each flat having a big room, a kitchen with pantry, and an "English water closet." At the cost of 400 dinars monthly rent, these represented affordable and comfortable dwellings for the underprivileged.[35] Conceiving it as a group of independent pavilions, the architect envisaged the Colony as only the first phase in the construction of a much larger housing estate, which was intended to have been planned as a modern *Siedlung,* with rich vegetation, children's playgrounds, and its own center.[36]

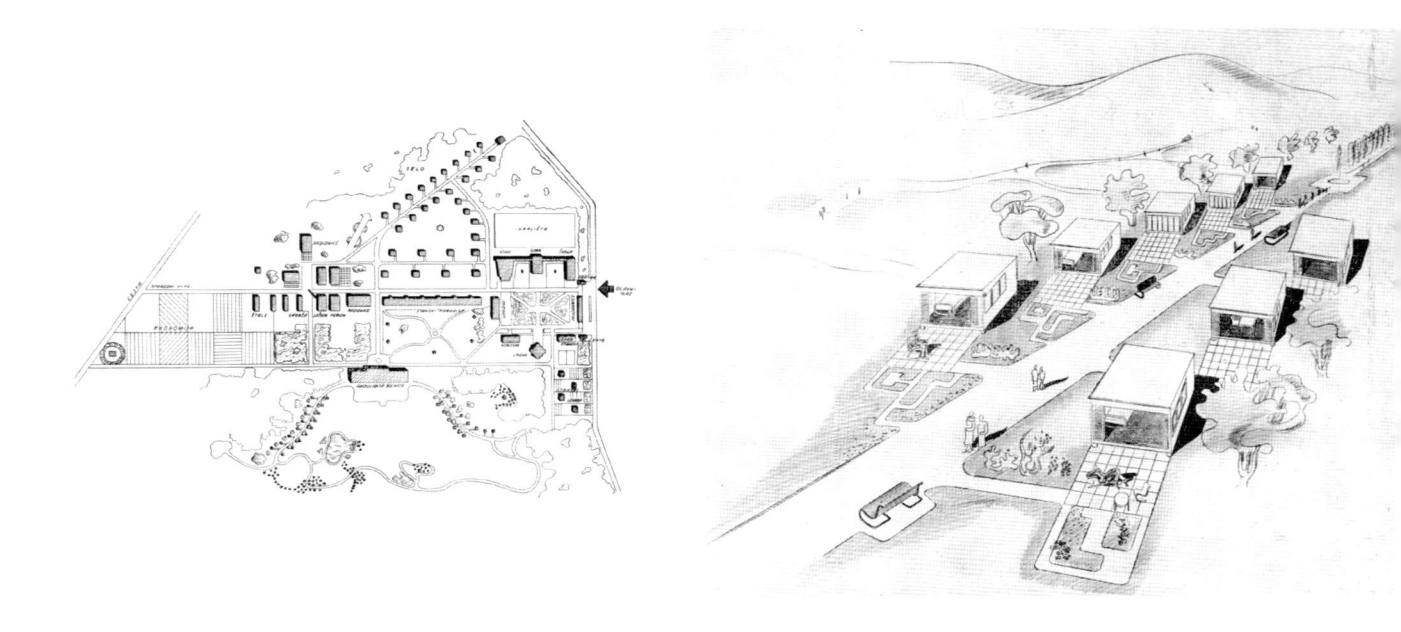

Oscillating between the concept of the *Siedlung* and the more romantic image of the garden city, the Council chose the strategy of evasion, and acted only when it found it absolutely necessary. For example, following a city sewage development project, plans were drawn up for the demolition of the notorious poor quarter of Jatagan Mala and the displacement of its inhabitants onto a new site. The plan envisaged that each household would be offered the chance to buy on credit a small plot of council land of 300 square meters, and that individual owners would build their houses according to specifications and recommendations given by the Council urbanists. The whole concept, therefore, relied again on private investment, though initiated and at first aided by the Council.

4.10 Dragan Petrik, village for tuberculosis sufferers, 1938 (project). Plan of the village; perspective view of the main street with accommodation units for the sick.

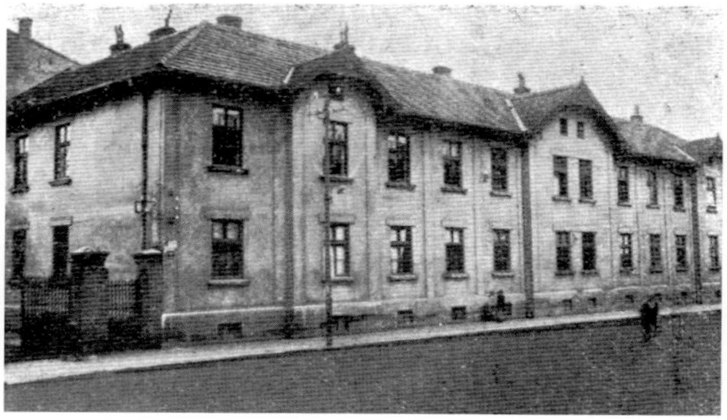

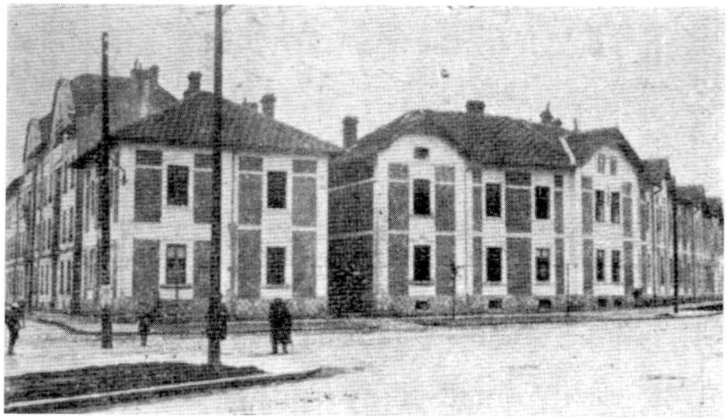

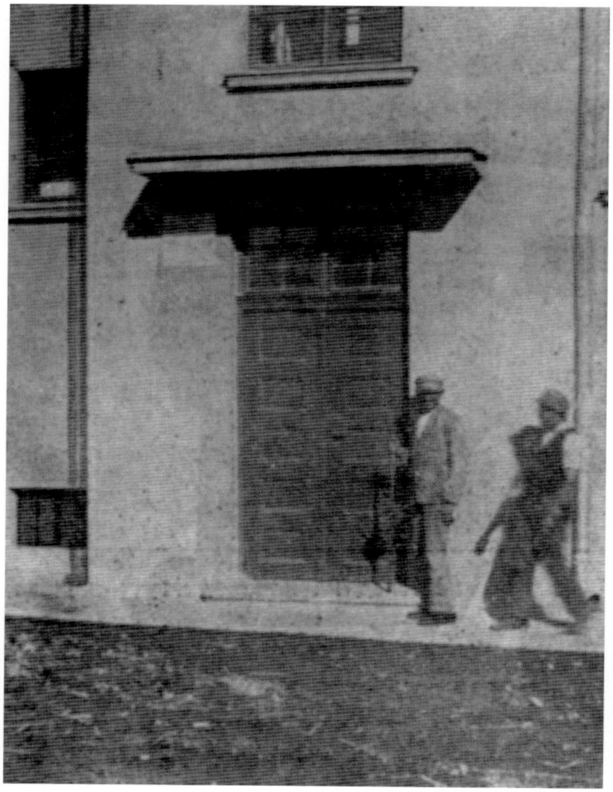

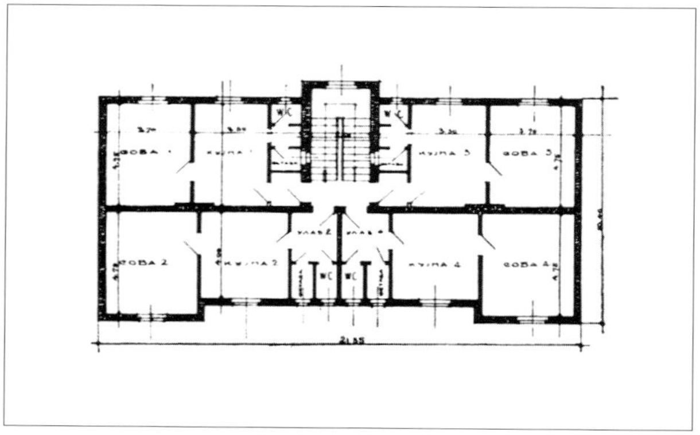
WC
WC
SOBA 2
WC
WC
21.55

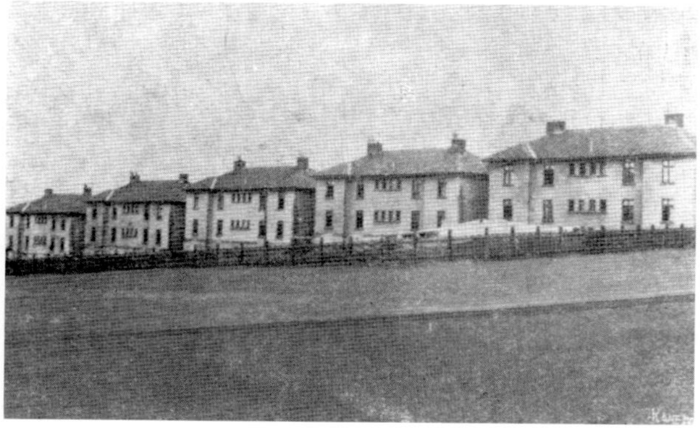

Social unrest being unlikely with the suppression of political freedoms and interdiction of workers' movements following the 1929 dictatorship, the Council could simply stall without anyone being too worried about the possible consequences. Le Corbusier's alternative "Architecture or Revolution" did not apply here, and the production of dwellings got diverted from social and political issues into those of commerce and, consequently, of style and fashion.

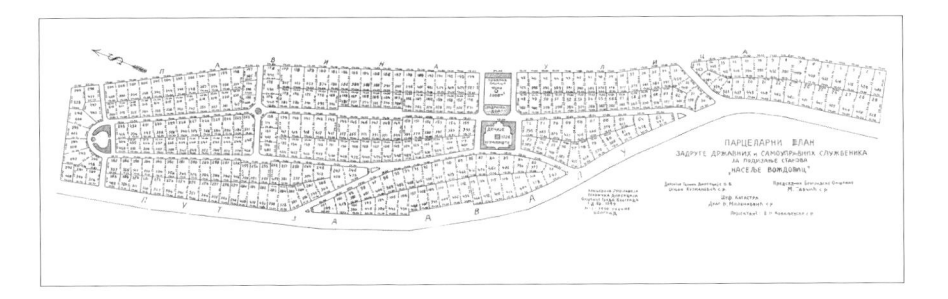

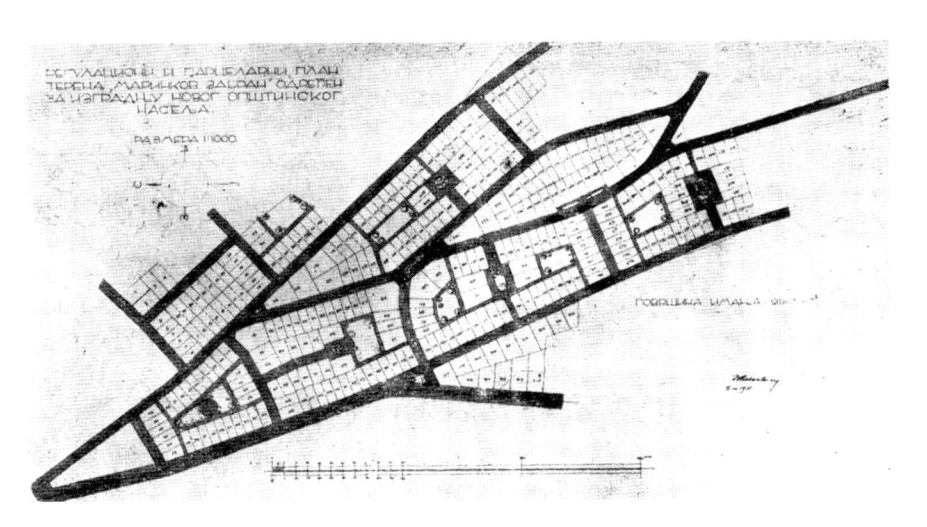

4.11 (opposite page, top) Council housing in Belgrade. Block of 24 flats in Drinčićeva Street; block of 114 flats in Radnička Street.

4.12 (opposite page, bottom) Branko Maksimović, Colony for the Poor, Belgrade, 1928. View of the Colony, typical floor plan, and entrance to one of the buildings.

4.13 Đorđe Kovaljevski, Regulation plan of the Clerks' Colony, Belgrade, 1932.

4.14 S. Burmazović, Regulation plan for the Marinkov Zabran district, Belgrade, ca. 1931.

4.2 THE PATTERNS OF DWELLING

In general architectural practice, it was the realm of bourgeois habitation, the houses and villas of the privileged class and the rental apartment blocks of the middle classes, where stylization got most intensified. At the end of the 1920s Belgrade was, as Toša Fodor, commentator to the magazine *Nova literatura*, saw it, "something that had not been sufficiently demolished, nor sufficiently reconstructed . . . the city that is not a ruin any more, but is not in the present yet . . . not a reminiscence of what once was, and still not the aspiration to something new . . . the city constructed on a feudal foundation with an American speed and in chaotic Balkan ways."[37] Its new architecture, he continued ironically, was best made according to a recipe:

Take 200 grams of Renaissance, add 50 grams of Romanticism, well crushed and sieved, 6 yolks of Moorish style, 2 cups of imbecile *fin-de-siècle* chaos, stir it well over low Gothic heat, and then add, slowly, as much impotent fantasy as needed for it all to get an indeterminate color and an overly sweet taste. . . . By all means, do not forget pilasters and columns. . . . Where there are no columns, use stucco decoration. As much as possible. Angels, vases, small nudes, garlands, whatever is at hand. Monograms above the entrance, and most importantly, domes with patina are not to be forgotten.[38]

Yet, at roughly the same time, the pro-modernist English architecture critic P. Morton Shand argued that forceful new advocates had entered the scene to struggle against the forces of historical styles, "the Jugoslav followers of Le Corbusier, Dudoek, and Gropius . . . , still few in numbers, but militantly enthusiastic, as a forcible reminder that within a very short time no continental city is likely to remain immune to the uncompromising intellectual austerity of the evangelists of doctrinal puritanism in reinforced concrete."[39] In this passage, written from his position as one of the most ardent supporters of the modern movement in the ever-resisting Britain, Shand optimistically suggested that his Belgrade counterparts were developing into a force to be reckoned with. The photograph supplied as the corroborative evidence showed a new block of flats, plain, white, and modern.[40]

The accounts of Fodor and Shand are, in fact, mirror images of the old style/new style pair of historic/modern paradigms, as they were worked out in general architectural practice of the period. Both are references to the process of Europeanization, one via the historical styles of Western culture, the other via the international puritanism, or would-be purism, of modern technology.

4.15 Vojislav Zađina, apartment block in Ivankovačka Street, Belgrade, 1928, published in *Architects' Journal*, no. 1734 (11 April 1928).

Beneath the surface, both articles speak of an attempt to break with the old Balkan past and switch, at high frequency, to an all-inclusive changeableness. At the turn of the century, Adolf Loos saw the same happen with Balkan men's underwear: "And so the good man from the Balkans decides with a heavy heart to make the attempt to wear socks. In doing so, he arrives at a new rung of human culture."[41]

The victory of modernism in the 1930s was manifested as a cycle of rapid stylistic change to the ordinary, everyday architecture, but the old style remained largely in operation under the camouflage of the "modern style." The traditional structural system of load-bearing walls was covered by cubic composition of form, hipped roofs were veiled by attic parapet walls, and ornaments were repatterned into modern decoration. Being out of view and in no need of stylistic mimicry, the plan and, more to the point, the structural system stayed largely unchanged. Could we then assume that modernism came as a change of dress, heavy-heartedly worn like Loos's socks instead of the less comfortable but more customary foot wrappings? And if so, could the paradox by which architects swiftly processed the stylistic change, while denying any relation to fashion, be explained outside the very mechanisms of fashion's operation? Or was modernism in Belgrade more than a mode? In the midst of the style processing, could there still be found a disparate group of ordinary architecture pertaining to structured modernity, and not to a practical exercise in formalism?

As Walter Benjamin noted in the sections on fashion in the *Passagen-Werk,* "fashion functions as camouflage for quite specific interests of the ruling class."[42] The bourgeois villa resisted violent change, while the dwelling of the poor barely changed at all. When the "modern style" came on the scene, celebrated as a novelty and appropriated by the upper stratum of society, in keeping with Simmel's assertion that "fashions differ for different classes," it started to be absorbed and controlled by the mechanisms of the fashion system. Conscious of the betrayal of the principles of social justice advocated by the GAMM founding members, Branislav Kojić saw death creeping in: "In a modernist view, today's villa is, from a social aspect, a noncontemporary object that will become obsolete in the future, and we are, therefore, only mentioning it *ad memoriam.*"[43] In everyday practice, it was precisely the houses and villas in the "modern style" that effectively offered material evidence that contemporary architecture could operate as an autonomous artistic practice devoid of political and social content, and could thus offer a safe and even fashionable option for the establishment. But modern architects argued that it was *truth* and *honesty* that mattered, not the transient and commercial qualities of fashion with the associations to masquerade, frivolity, and superficiality of ornament. "It [modern architecture] is a 'fashion,' they say! Let us just see if it is only a fashion!" exclaimed Kojić in one of his lectures, and offered counterarguments of "sincerity, rationality, and truthfulness" in the work of Henri Labrouste, Viollet-le-Duc, H. P. Berlage, Frank Lloyd Wright, Loos, and Le Corbusier.[44] As Mary McLeod suggests, for architects of the modern movement fashion (here meaning women's fashion) was the antithesis of functionality, rationality, and simplicity of modern architecture. Furthermore, she writes, "the spoken and unspoken assumption was that it was feminine or effeminate."[45]

Denied rights of equality, Serbian women, as bearers and/or victims of fashion as well as all things feminine or effeminate, had no place in the genealogy of local modernism.[46] Women were confined to home, bound by the duty to husband and family. Out of the home, their space was the soft and hidden interior of the beauty parlor or the couturier's salon. Even when designers in their own right, as was Danica Kojić, women's domain was almost invariably the interior. Photographed in the interior of the house of Mihajlo Kojić, which she designed, the woman-architect is posing not as an author of the project but an inhabitant of the house. Yet it may be worth looking at the more obvious parallels between the operation of fashion and the concurrent styling of architecture, in order to demonstrate the direct associations between the two.

Bourgeois ladies' fashion in the 1920s followed the dicta of Paris stitch for stitch, as Belgrade salons frivolously made exact copies of the French models

4.16 (opposite page) Helena Rubinstein Beauty Institute, Belgrade, 1931. (Courtesy Museum of the City of Belgrade.)

4.17 Danica Kojić, interior of the villa of Mihajlo Kojić, Belgrade, 1933–1934. (Courtesy Architecture Department in the Museum of Science and Technology, Belgrade.)

and sold them at ten percent of the original price.⁴⁷ With a similar disregard of copyright, when ordering architecture the client often demanded a replica of stylish homes seen in magazine reproductions. The ladies loved exoticism of fashion à la Tutankhamen, while architects of taste fashioned villas in "Provençal, English, Colonial, Asiatic, etc., etc. styles."⁴⁸ A most illustrative example, albeit from the late thirties, is the case of Pera Milanović, a local merchant, who requested that the facade of his building with rental apartments be an exact copy of the sixteenth-century Palazzo Principe Dorio in Via Nazionale in Rome—"famous for its beauty, one would assume, in the whole world," as he said—but, of course, modeled in cheap stucco.⁴⁹ In the translation of the paradigms, the fine details got lost: the evening toilettes were inappropriately worn for the daily promenade,⁵⁰ the palazzo frontage was planted onto rental apartments, the skirts of Belgrade coquettes were cut much too short,⁵¹ and the windows were cut too narrow to make space for columns and pilasters.⁵²

Similarly, when dwellings in the modern style made their way into the marketplace, it was in the manner of *haute couture*. They were not generated on notions that radicalized or even objectified the reality, such as workers' and peasants' houses by Jan Dubovy, but on the desirable image of modernity, in which the reality was displaced and marginalized. As Val Warke argues, the formulation of fashion tends to follow a pattern in which "the sources are deradicalized, their 'roughness' is tempered; they are subtly transformed from being sources of antagonism to being objects of desire: the eroticism of animus."⁵³

The earliest proposal for a new type of stylish bourgeois dwelling was drawn up in 1923 by Dušan Janković, artist and designer but also a *couturier,* who was living and working in Paris at the time.⁵⁴ His sketch shows a villa of a plain exterior with large glazed surfaces and thin flat slabs as roofs, with no historical reminiscences whatsoever. Notwithstanding the naivety and simplified presentation of the project, the transparency and lightness of the ground floor, the size of the windows, and the exposure of the spiral staircase clad in glass implied radical change not only of the exterior but of the character of the internal space. The drawing of the villa followed immediately after Janković's first interior decoration design for the Bohemian Ball, entitled "The Thousand and Second Night" and held in the Hotel Kasina in Belgrade on 16 February 1923. As can be seen in the tempera painting perspective of the buffet, more painterly than architectural, Janković freely combined fashionable themes in this interior: jazz, motifs of primitive African art, stylized cubist patterns, and various types of Thonet furniture. In a similar spirit he also designed costumes for *The Servant's Broom*, a futurist ballet in one act with text by Marko Ristić, music by Miloje Milojević, and choreography by Klavdija Isačenko, which was performed at the Ball.⁵⁵ In this instance, the wrapping of the ballroom matched the veiling of the dancers' bodies, and the two had the same rationale, to dress the *byt* for the event. The

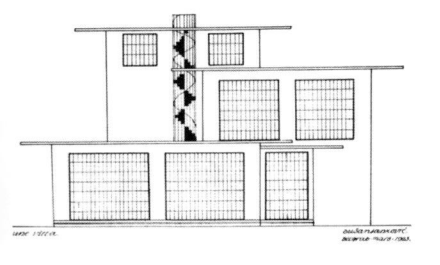

4.18 (opposite page) Dušan Janković, sketch for a villa in Belgrade, 1923. (Courtesy Museum of Applied Art, Belgrade.)

4.19 Dušan Janković, interior decoration of the buffet at the Bohemian Ball in the Hotel Kasina, Belgrade, 1923. (Courtesy Museum of Applied Art, Belgrade.)

highly decorative character of the costumes and the interior, with their bold colors and emphasis on the exotic, are clearly very different from the plain whiteness of the villa. Still, in both cases the original text of the avant-garde was deradicalized and fashioned so that it could operate within the social and cultural space of the aspiring middle classes. Although it is not known for whom the little villa was meant, if for anyone at all, I would argue that it reflected the highest fashion of the intellectual and artistic elite that attended the Ball. Its design gave the image of a desirable Parisian lifestyle, far from the stuffy domesticity of provincial Belgrade.

Another notable example of a desire to design a house fit for an imaginary modern lifestyle is the project of a villa "for a small family of three persons" (1929) by Branislav Kojić. The design displayed what may be seen as a total misrepresentation of reality, both formally and technically. Kojić wrote of his design intent: "In summer periods, glass walls are, naturally, lowered into the basement, so that the space is completely opened to the garden. All rooms on the ground floor are connected by large openings, and they form one representative space."[56] The invention of glass walls disappearing at a push of a button may have been possible for Le Corbusier in the Charles de Beistegui apartment in Paris (1929–1931), or for Mies van der Rohe in the Tugendhat house in Brno (1928–1930), but for Belgrade architects it represented a technological fiction, far from their everyday reality. Even more idealistic was a theoretical project for "Villas for Artists" (1929) designed by Branislav Kojić at the request of sculptor Sreten Stojanović. The perspective drawing of the villas was exhibited at the first exhibition of the Oblik group, held in the Arts Pavilion in December 1929. It showed the image of a new city as an ideal and harmonic community, in which simple houses of cubic form are freely, but regularly, set into a communal green site with no party walls. Front and back gardens have the character of a public space, a modern garden/park, along the lines of contemporary *Siedlung* concepts. Also present in this project is an image of artists as perfect inhabitants of a visionary city, but one that was far beyond the market reality of town planning in Belgrade of the period.

If ever a villa in Belgrade featured as a cinematographic space, or an object fashioned to the cinematographic aesthetic, it would be villa Miletić (1932) by Jan Dubovy. The project stayed unrealized because of the architect's rejection of his client's reality instructions.[57] As an architectural project it simply manifests the architect's aim to integrate the principal features of a modern villa: continuity between the internal and external space, reinforced concrete structure (albeit implemented partially), free plan, flat roof terraces, abstract composition of form, and, to some extent, free facade. But, more importantly, the design implies a subtext that could be read as a hypothetical scenario of a modern life. Once beyond the strict frontage and symmetrically positioned entrance zone, the

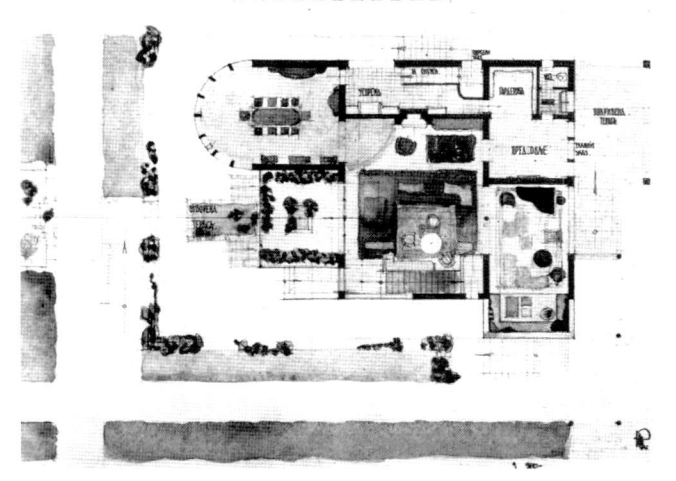

4.20 (top and middle) Branislav Kojić, villa for a small family of three persons, Belgrade, 1929 (project). Plan of the ground floor and perspective view of the villa.

4.21 Branislav Kojić, Villas for Artists, Belgrade, 1929 (project).

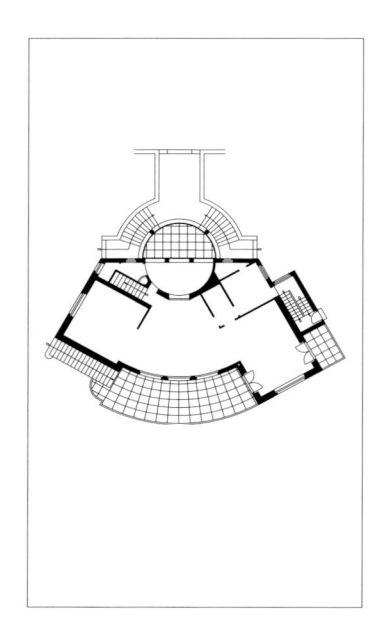

internal space unfolds as if through the motion of a movie camera and opens up onto the frames of the exterior, with terraces in the foreground and landscape in the background. The spatial sequencing culminates on the very top roof terrace in the space of health consciousness, with the solarium and shower cabin. One can easily see this space as a setting for scenes of gymnastics in the sunshine, as filmed in Pierre Chenal's and Le Corbusier's film *L'Architecture d'aujourd'hui* (1929). To paraphrase Val Warke, being *haute couture,* Dubovy's project "speaks the language of the manifesto," and as such it does little to convince the practical client, barrister Miletić, the proverbial *pret-à-porter* consumer, who rejected it outright.

Faced with the market reality, thus, architects had to produce a ready-to-wear line. By and large, they developed individual strategies of gradual transformation and modernization alongside their continuing practice of historical or national styles. Neither clients nor architects were ready for a radical change, and the first realized modern houses of the late twenties kept the interior of the bourgeois dwelling untouched, being modernized solely from without. Hybrids often substituted for authentic species, in the operative manner of the phantasmagoria of fashion: "Most often . . . [fashion] creates hybrids."[58]

The architecture of brothers Branko and Petar Krstić serves here as the most illustrative example of this trend. Their design of the villa of barrister Milićević (1929–1930) can be seen as the hybrid form of the transitional stage in the definition of the modern style. The form of the villa is a simple cube set into the sloping terrain, appearing from the street as a single-story house with raised ground floor and opening toward the garden with full height of two levels. The duality is accentuated by the facade decoration in bold horizontal striping of the *piano nobile,* the quite elaborate design of the approaching footbridge and external stairs, and the front garden layout. The porch over the main entrance is supported by caryatids, set in front of the asymmetrical facade as a direct historicist quotation. The villa reflected the architects' aim of a harmonious synthesis of art, decoration, and architecture, which was to become a trademark of their particular style.[59]

In their design of Villa Vukosava for Professor Dušan Tomić[60] (1930–1931), for example, the hybrid is created by crossing the traditional structural system and plan with an externally modernized form. The compact plan, constricted by the massive load-bearing wall structure, is organized around a central hall in a traditional manner, with no exploration of the continuity of space between the ground and first floor. The staircase is literally built in between the thick brickwork walls, and the private quarters on the upper level simply repeat the arrangement of rooms from below. The formal interpretation, however, moves away from historicist paradigms: the cubic composition is simple and restrained, and the facades are plain and smooth. The cubic purity, however, had to be given the proper dress: clear style signifiers such as the elaborate, decorative moldings signifying modern style planted onto the wall surface. The final touch of luxury to the otherwise modest villa was provided by the articulation

4.22 (opposite page) Jan Dubovy, villa of Arkadije Miletić, Belgrade, 1932 (project). Plan of ground floor and elevations.

4.23 Branko and Petar Krstić, villa of Stevka Milićević, Belgrade, 1929–1930.

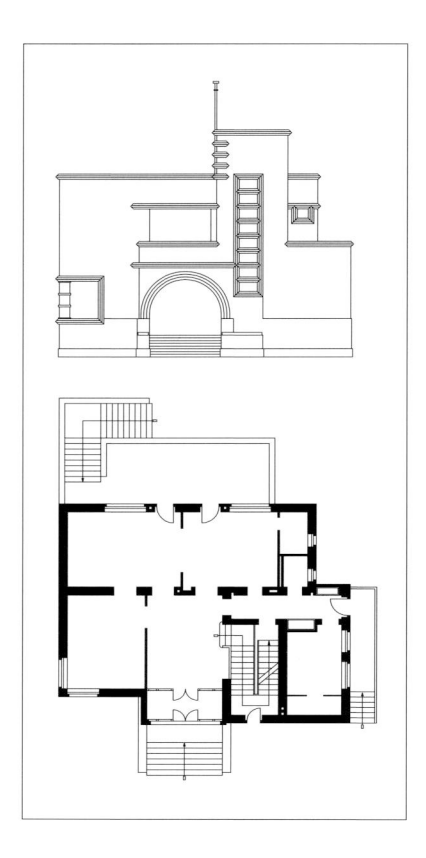

of the entrance zone with generously curved portal and wide external stairs, originally envisaged with an asymmetrically positioned sculpture by Branko Krstić, a draped nude leading two mythical dogs, and a shallow rectangular pond in front.

    With the double villa of Olga Lazić (1931), I would suggest, the brothers Krstić achieved the high point of their modernist career and managed, at least for a brief moment, to leave the territory of fashion. The atypical site of the villa, with a very limited depth and stretching longitudinally parallel to the street, was sold by the neighboring owner on condition that only one house be built on it. The architects were, however, requested by their client to design two independent houses, which they did by resolving the riddle in a clever, rather ambiguous manner. They designed two identical, totally separated houses mirrored in corner positions of the site, yet positively connected by an elongated, one-story-high gazebo, thus achieving the effective appearance of one integral structure. The effect was enhanced by the planar treatment of the facade cladding in sleek marble slabs laid in a continual pattern, in which subtle variation of the grid emphasized the longitudinal stretch of the composition.[61]

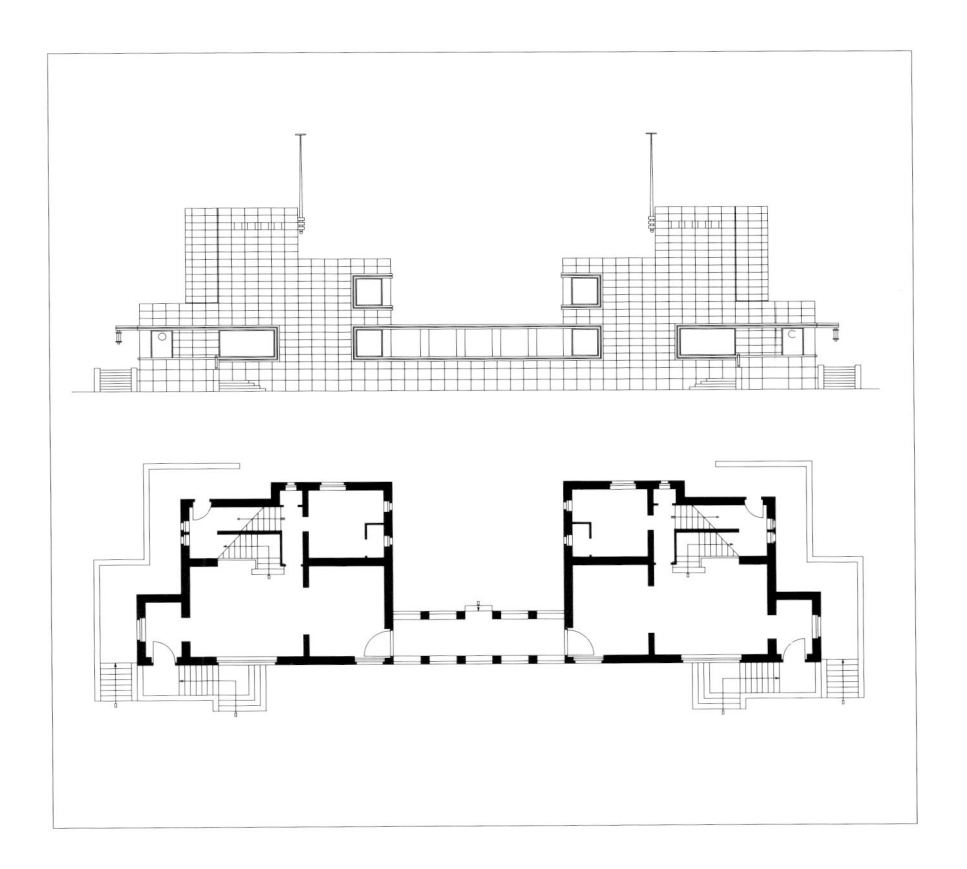

If anything, the brothers Krstić were masters of finishes. Even today, after decades of neglect, their buildings have to be appreciated for the finesse and quality of detailing in the use of materials. The facade of the rental apartment building of Mrs. Jelinić in Kumanovska Street (1930–1931) is perhaps the most telling example of their skill. It is no wonder that they themselves chose this building to represent them on the pages of the magazine *Arhitektura*.[62] The facade surface is formed by the inlaid materials of dark polished granite, matte gray-green stone, Terranova plastering, and Branko Krstić's cast reliefs in reconstituted stone, which are all carefully fitted together as a piece of marquetry. It is this skill in putting together different textures, patterns, and materials that distinguishes the Krstić label, however much the designs, or even styles, of their facades varied from case to case. In this sense, a Krstić facade is easily recognized, whether it is the ball gown style like the elaborate stucco-decorated Veterinary Foundation apartment block (1927) with caryatids, vases, reliefs, and so

4.24 (opposite page) Branko and Petar Krstić, Villa Vukosava, Belgrade, 1930–1931. Plan of ground floor and front elevation.

4.25 Branko and Petar Krstić, double villa of Olga Lazić, Belgrade, 1931. Plan of ground floor and front elevation.

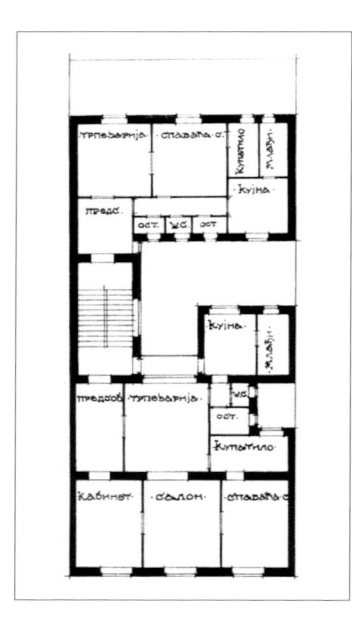

on; the starkly elegant column dress cut like the Igumanov Palace (1936–1937); or the simple little all-purpose black dress like the rental apartment building for Josif Šojat in Brankova Street (1934). And if the sartorial metaphor is cast aside, the Krstić brothers still hold prominence as one of the most representative creators of the Belgrade modern style.

Another architect who brought a particular finesse to the expression of the modern style was Dušan Babić, one of the four founders of the Group of Architects of the Modern Movement in Belgrade.[63] Despite his role in setting up the Group and his active participation in its activities, only fragmentary documentation on his life and work exists today: not even the years of his birth and death are confirmed, there is not one photograph of him published, and his biography is largely unknown. Only a few remaining houses bear witness to the work of this architect in Belgrade, most notably two neighboring villas designed in 1930: villa Protić and villa Reich. Both villas reflect a sensibility that characterizes modernist projects by Babić: expression of dominant horizontal planes supported by freestanding columns, and the use of horizontal profiling texture on the facade surface. The villa of Karl and Maria Reich (1930) represents the finest example of Babić's particular understanding of modern form. The most striking feature of villa Reich are columns of gigantic order on the garden side of the house, which support the overhanging flat roof. From an analysis of the primary volumetric, it becomes clear that the final form and balance of solid and void is a result of volumetric subtraction from the basic parallelepiped form. The intri-

4.26 (opposite page) Branko and Petar Krstić, apartment block in Kumanovska Street, Belgrade, 1930–1931. Plan of typical floor, facade, and detail with the relief by Branko Krstić.

4.27 Branko and Petar Krstić, apartment block in Brankova Street, Belgrade, 1934.

4.28 Branko and Petar Krstić, Igumanov Palace, Terazije, Belgrade, 1936–1937.

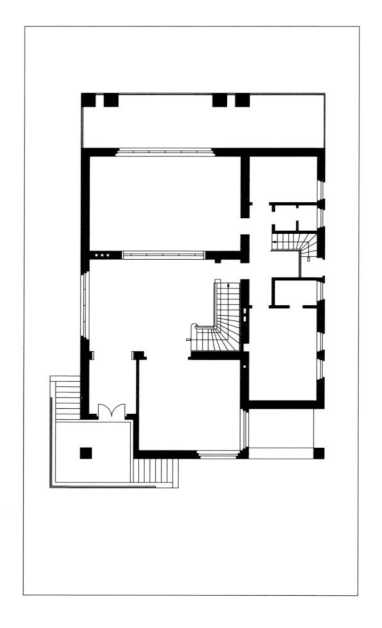

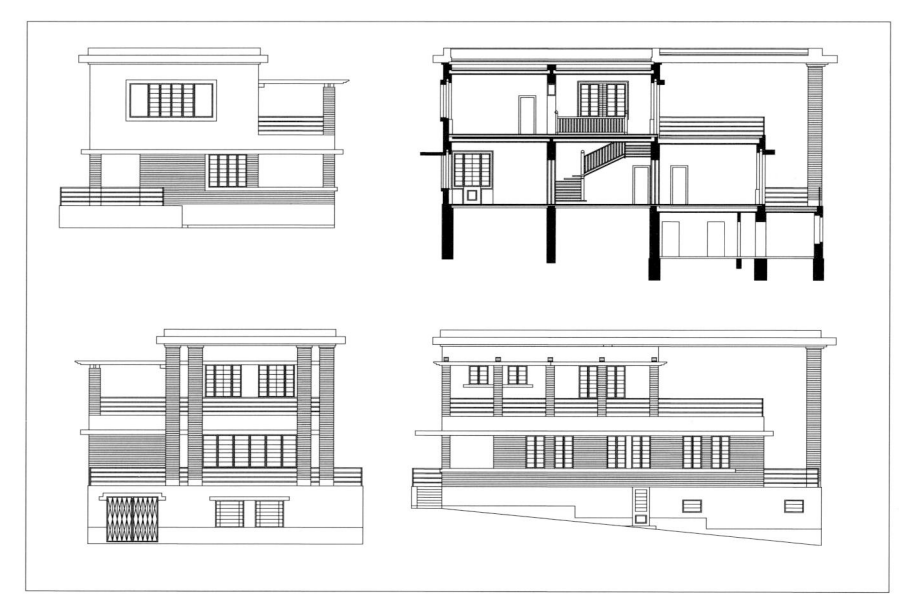

cate rhythm of columns and pergolas and the unfolding of terraces as the house opens toward the garden are regulated by the lines of the imaginary primary form. While the total floor area of the villa is quite modest, the extent of the outline points of form explicates the villa's actual and psychological domain. In plan, there is a clear distinction between representative, public space in the ground floor, private quarters on the first floor, and service rooms in the ground and basement levels. The formal accents, such as the elaboration of the main entrance and corner loggia on the main street facade and the arrangement of grand terraces toward the garden, follow the functional logic of the house. The external surface treatment reflects the design intent to play up the relation between weight and lightness: rustication in regular horizontal profiling is applied to the supporting elements, the foundation of the house and the square-section columns, while the supported elements are plain and smooth. Babić took great care in the elaboration of modern decoration in his projects, even in those for houses in less prestigious locations, for less demanding clients, such as the villa of Jelena Plevan (1933) and that of Dragutin Smejkal (1934). These modest houses are made representative in his perspective drawings, displaying a vision of the bright new world.

A further shift of the margins occurred in the modernization of the national paradigm in the work of Branislav Kojić.[64] In parallel to his most earnest work in promoting modern architecture and related design efforts, he researched the vernacular architecture of the Balkans and Serbia and designed a series of

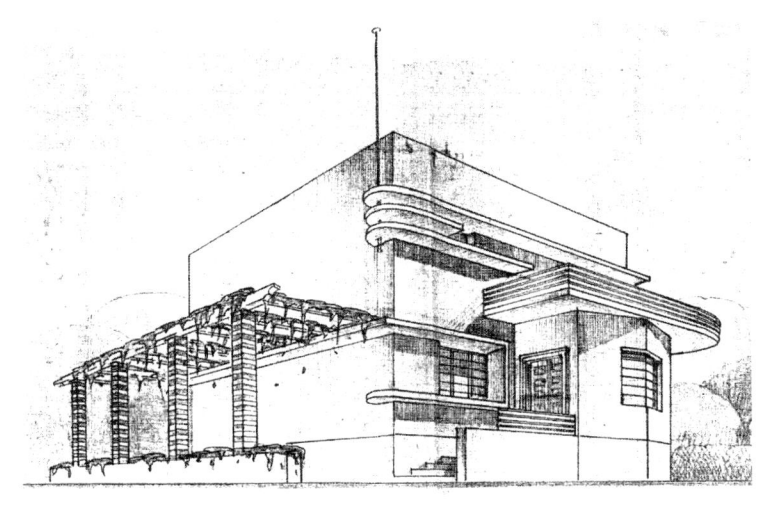

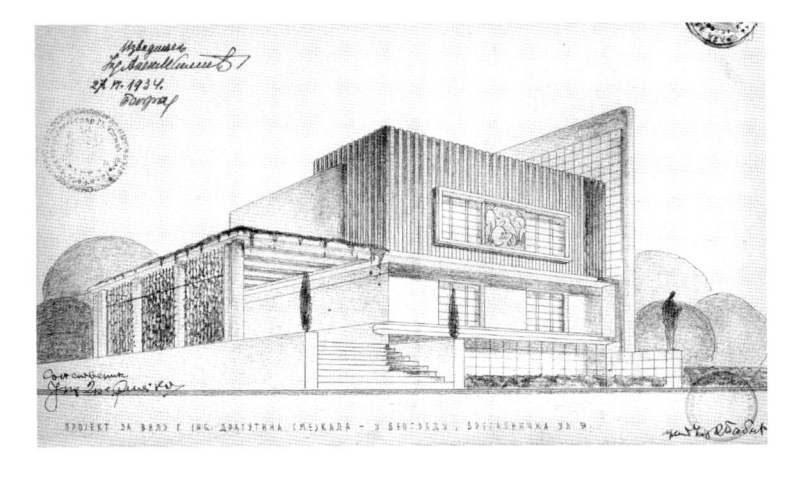

4.29   (opposite page) Dušan Babić, villa of
Karl Reich, Belgrade, 1930–1931. Plan of ground floor;
section and elevations.

4.30   Dušan Babić, villa Protić, Belgrade, 1930–1931.

4.31   Dušan Babić, villa of Jelena Plevan,
Belgrade, 1933.

4.32   Dušan Babić, villa of Dragutin Smejkal,
Belgrade, 1934.

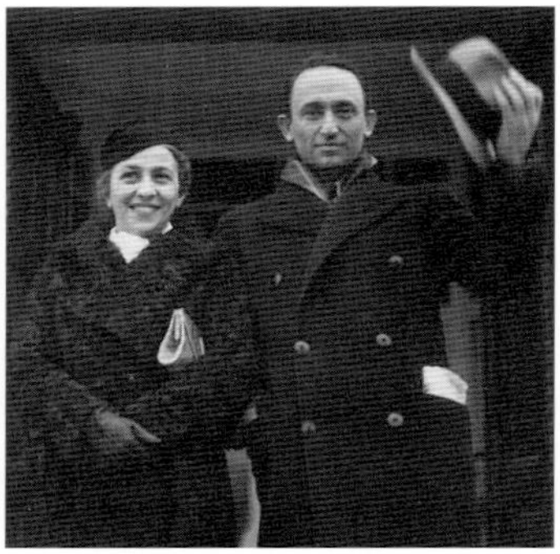

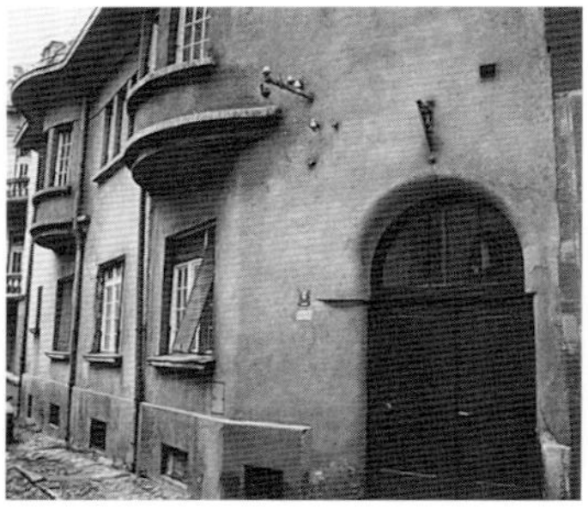

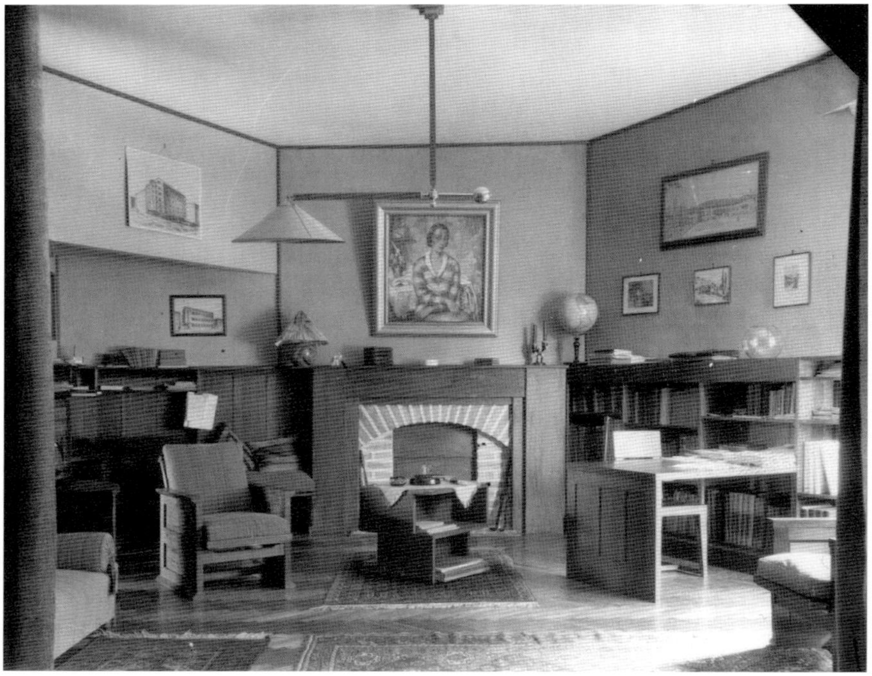

houses and buildings in the folkloric style derived from that heritage.[55] His interest in the vernacular started in 1925, when he was surveying old secular architecture of Belgrade, continued all throughout the interwar period through research and documentation along with projects and realizations in the folkloric style, and became predominant in the period after the Second World War when his professional practice had to cease and he took to systematic research and theoretical work in this field.[66] Kojić's built opus is singular in that it has to be seen against the constant sway between the two paradigms, the national originating in the vernacular, and the international immanent to the modern movement. This ambivalence is particularly manifested in projects where he attempted to achieve a symbiosis of the inherited and the contemporary forms and rationale, such as in the house he designed for himself and his architect wife Danica in Belgrade (1926–1927). The site of Kojić's house backs onto the historic *konak* (mansion house) of Princess Ljubica—one of the first "European" buildings in the Oriental Belgrade of the nineteenth century.[67] The plan (comprising a rental apartment on the ground floor and the owner's apartment on the first floor) is logically organized, with principal interconnected rooms on the street front and service rooms and circulation areas toward the back. In his design of the form of the house, Kojić introduced elements characteristic of vernacular architecture, such as the *erker,* an overhang protruding beyond the surface of the exterior wall, and semicircular alcoves in the interior. The old *konak* had evidently been the inspiration for the gentle undulation of the main facade and for the softening of the wall edges. In the secondary modeling Kojić renounced ornamentation and decoration, thus confirming both his modernist and vernacularist positions. Being a translation of the vernacular in quite a purist fashion, this house represents an authentic digression from the domineering period eclecticism into a territory of the modern. The interior of the house, of fairly contemporary spirit with no reminiscences of the vernacular heritage, was designed by Danica Kojić.[68]

In his practice, Kojić never quite accomplished the fine distinction of a modernized vernacular as he did in his own house, but he was quite successful with his buildings in the folkloric style, such as villa Marinković (1926), awarded a prize for "the most beautiful facade in Belgrade" in 1930, and villa Đorđević (1929), as well as a number of projects for Skopje. It is important to note that in all his works the national paradigm was closely related to regional specificity and the vernacular heritage, and strongly opposed to ideological readings such as that of the Serbian-Byzantine style.

More relevant to this research are Kojić's modernist works, which are distinctively set apart from those influenced by the vernacular. One of the most illustrative examples of this line is the small private house of Svetislav Marodić (1932). Despite its modest size and finish, the house represents one of the finest examples of modern architecture in Belgrade. While the plan of the dwelling

4.33 (opposite page) Danica and Branislav Kojić, 1936. (Courtesy Architecture Department in the Museum of Science and Technology, Belgrade.)

4.34 (opposite page) Branislav Kojić, Kojić house, Belgrade, 1926–1927. View from the street; interior by Danica Kojić (courtesy Architecture Department in the Museum of Science and Technology, Belgrade).

4.35 Branislav Kojić, villa Marinković, Belgrade, 1926. (Courtesy Architecture Department in the Museum of Science and Technology, Belgrade.)

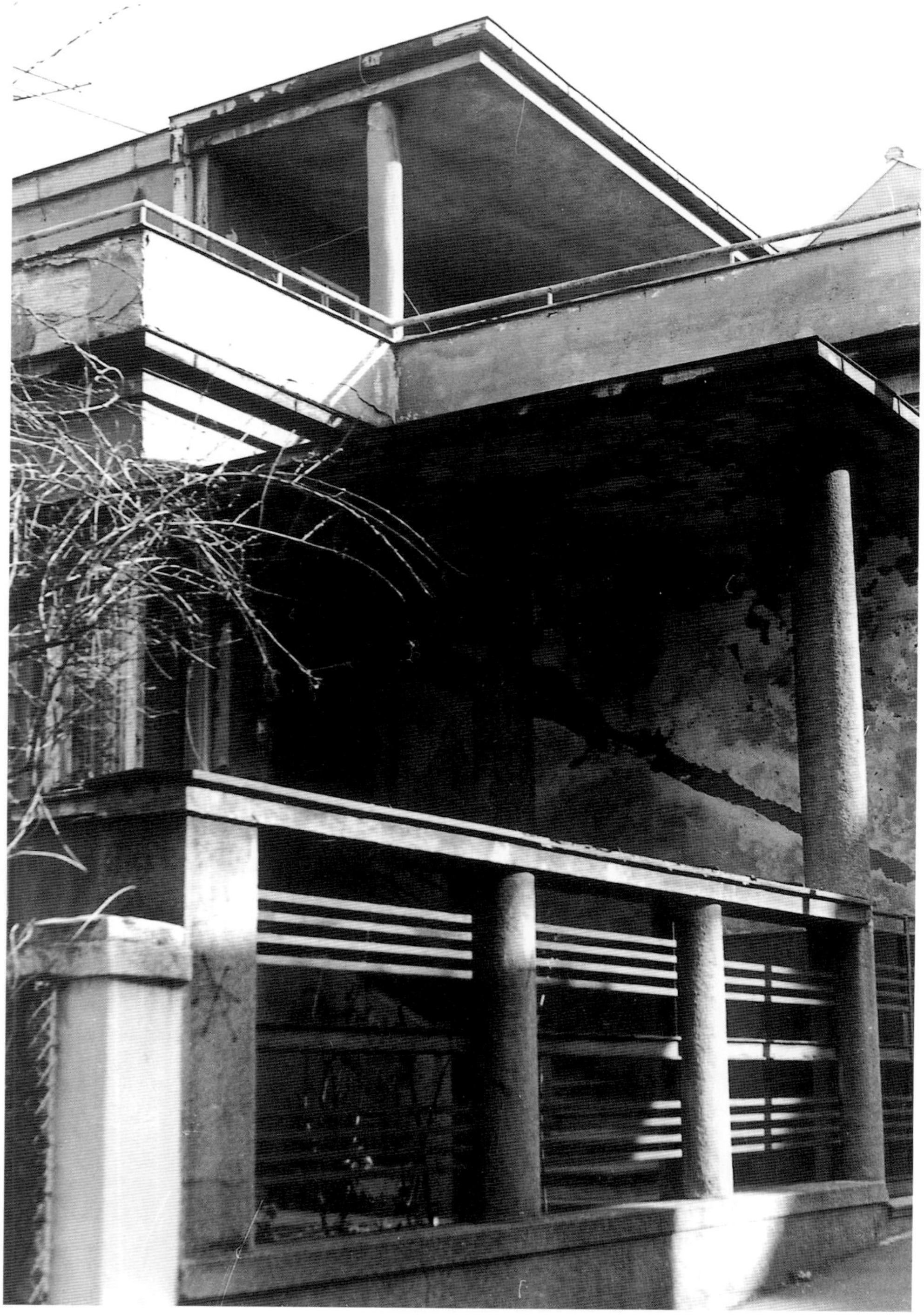

areas on the ground floor is standard, organized around a central dining room with two additional rooms at the front, the section reveals an intriguing spatial game. In order for the house to have a more prominent appearance from the street, Kojić resorted to dividing the roof into two parts: the flat-roof terrace at the front, and the hipped roof hidden behind the attic wall at the back. The height of the facade thus appears to be two stories, while in fact it is a single-story house with an attic. The effect is reinforced by the insertion of columns to support the thin concrete canopy above the roof terrace, as well as by the geometry of solid concrete parapets hovering above the cubic body of the house. The resulting interplay of plane surfaces, round-section columns, and the primary sculptural shape evoke the abstract aesthetic of neoplasticist spatial experimentation.

But of all Kojić's works, it is the apartment block of Dr. Đurić (1933) that is regarded as one of the most successful examples of Belgrade modernism.[69] The clever use of the site's potential, coupled with the bold articulation of the form, make this building quite unique in its context. The design rests on the fairly common functional organization of the commercial areas on the ground floor and mezzanine and apartments on upper floors, but the specificity of the solution follows from the conditions imposed by the corner site. As it is located on the perimeter of Terazije Terrace, on the top edge of the natural amphitheater sloping toward the river Sava, the back side of the site benefits from dramatic views toward the west. Since all facades exposed to the views from the rivers Sava and Danube had to be architecturally treated, as required under the Construction Act of 1931, Kojić took special care to promote this aspect of the context in his design. He stratified the volume into three distinct parts, functionally and formally defined: the horizontally layered podium with the public commercial program on the ground floor and mezzanine, the vertical corpus as the main body of the building with the private dwelling program, and the cornice pronounced by the thin overhanging concrete plane sheltering the roof terrace. The exposed corners of the corpus are accentuated by terraces, with particular attention to the balance of solid and void and the consequent spatial expression, whereby the dynamic of the river-facing corner volume is played up by the sinuous facade along the side street. The composition is further articulated by the shallow plastic variation of the facade surface, and underlined by the shadows of the slits under the terraces' parapets. Even though much of the initial concept was carried out in construction, one particular detail speaks of the architect's unfulfilled intentions: the window with a horizontal axis. Kojić often proposed this type of window in his modern projects, including the house of Marodić, but he never managed to implement it; instead, standard types were invariably used.[70]

In the local building practice, there was little room for invention of new details, technologies, or materials, let alone application of special window types.

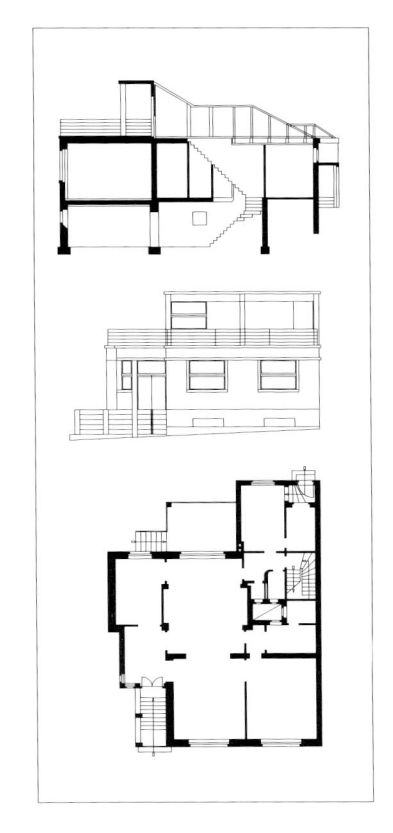

4.36   Branislav Kojić, house of Svetislav Marodić, Belgrade, 1932. View of the entrance porch (contemporary photograph by Marija Milinković); section, street elevation, and plan.

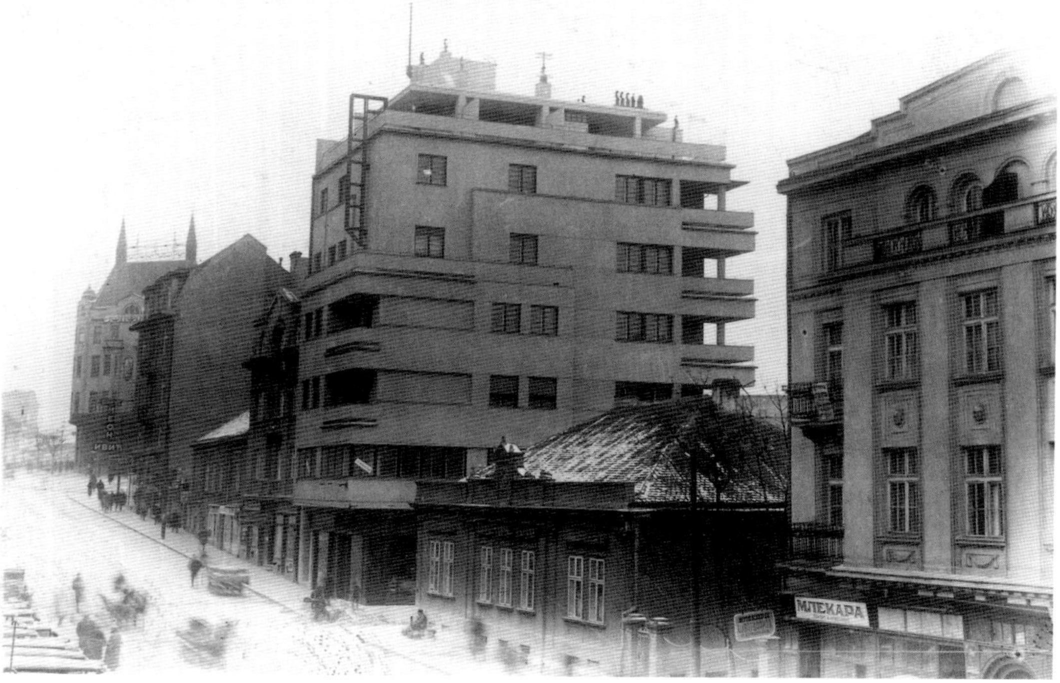
МЛЕКАРА

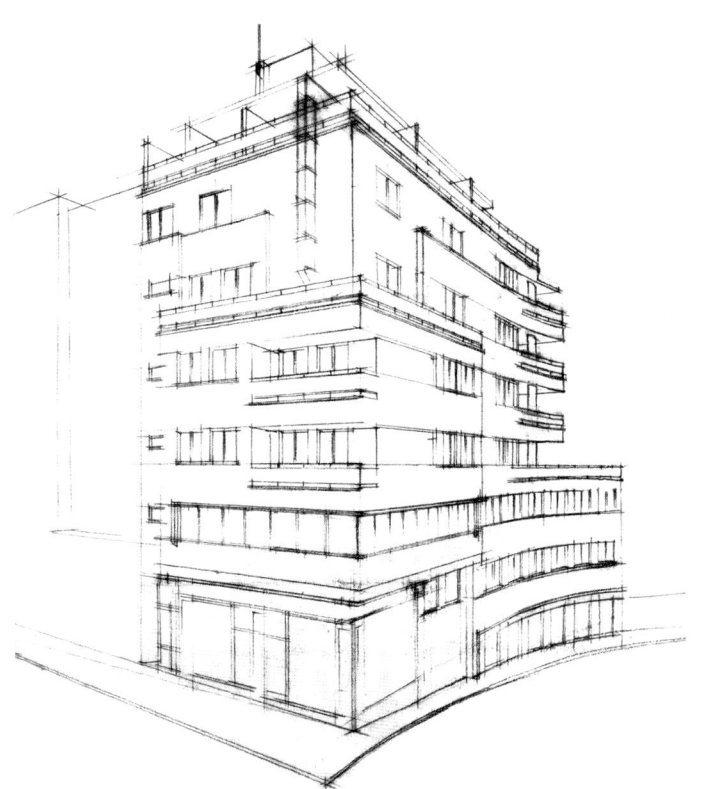

4.37   Branislav Kojić, apartment block of Dr. Đurić, Prizrenska Street, Belgrade, 1933. View from the street, perspective view (courtesy Architecture Department in the Museum of Science and Technology, Belgrade), and axonometric view.

Ђорђе Гоtпић

4.38 (opposite page) Dragiša Brašovan, apartment block in Braće Jugovića Street, Belgrade, 1934.

4.39 Miladin Prljević, apartment block in Kneza Miloša Street, Belgrade, 1932–1935.

4.40 Miladin Prljević, apartment block in Kosančićev Venac Street, Belgrade, 1938.

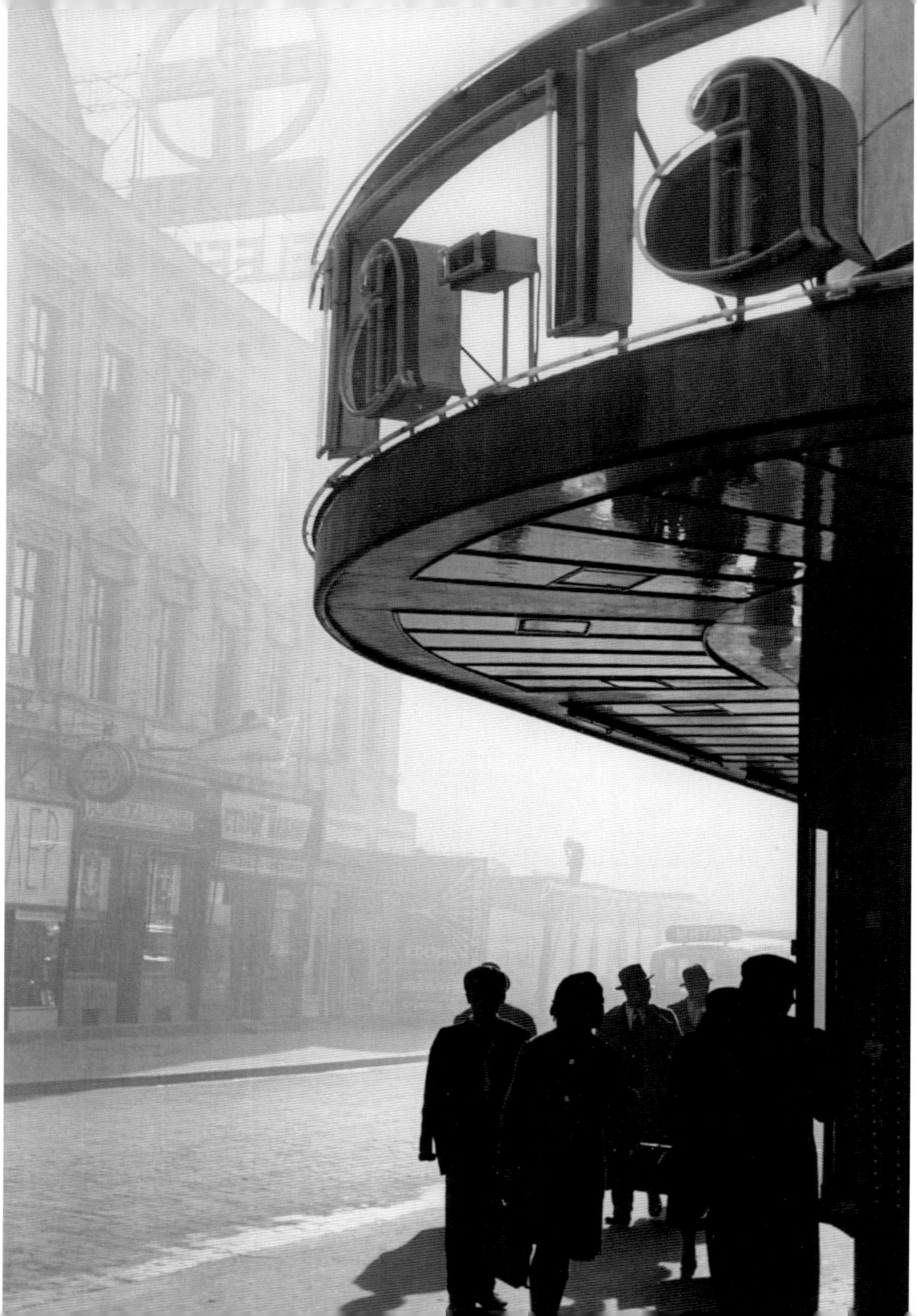

This detail, which may seem quite secondary, reveals the principal weakness of Kojić, and by and large of the local modernism in general, namely the rift between the architect and the building industry. In fact, in the conditions of traditional building technique, architecture had no chance to advance beyond the first stage of simple formal transformation, as there was no technology to instigate the fundamental structural change. Additionally, as technological, functional, and structural principles were brushed aside by the commercial demand for the economy of the new style, the allegiance to purism and renouncing of ornate stucco decoration served to increase the profit margins. Speculative construction business thus effectively operated under the cover of fashionable pseudo-modernity. The architecture of numerous apartment buildings realized in the 1930s is very indicative of this trend, such as the blocks of flats designed by Dragiša Brašovan (1934), Miladin Prljević (1932–1935), and Branislav Marinković (1938), or the one redesigned into the Ta-ta Department Store by engineer Đorđe Lazarević (1935), and many others.

In the 1930s, apartment buildings became uniform, rather like the women's dresses on the streets. As the economic crisis took its toll, both architecture and fashion went into what Warke designates "the fourth phase, ... marked by the repetitive atrophy of its forms' associated contents, with the eventual loss of virtually all original significations; ... most fashions descend through the various consumer classes."[71] In both buildings and dresses, it was the street that had became the polygon for the operation of fashion, and it was the street fashion that took the lead. Style columnists commented that women rather looked up to each other on the streets than to the newest models from the magazines.[72] Paradoxically, even in fashion shows there was hardly any difference between the models on the catwalk and the dresses in the audience, as can be seen from the photographs of the fashion show held in 1936 by Belgrade tailors for women. The photographers' shops were the first to realize the potential commercial effect of this change, so they sent dozens of their street agents out to photograph people, and especially women, on spec. They would capture them by chance, in movement, as they went about their business in the city center, and then try to sell them the quickly developed pictures as evidence of their *byt* mode. It is these snapshots, the first non-pose photos—which inundated almost every family album—that provide accurate evidence of the look of everyday life in 1930s Belgrade.

The property developers and landlords, of course, followed the trend; they too looked at the street movement and kept alert to the changes of street fashion. Since, under the property law, individual ownership of apartments was not possible (only houses or whole buildings could be bought or owned), most of the urban population was renting. The price and the lease period were fixed in the standard tenancy contract and could not be altered until the contract expiry

4.41 Period details. Office of Đorđe Lazarević, Ta-ta Department Store (period photograph by Zvonimir Janović, courtesy Miloš Jurišić); Herman Hus, house of Lojze Dolinar (contemporary photograph by Milica Lopičić); Branislav Marinković, apartment block in Kičevska Street (contemporary photograph by Milica Lopičić); all in Belgrade.

dates, which were also set down by law, as 1 May and 1 November. As a consequence, on these two dates every year the whole city was in commotion as people rushed around in their moving carriages looking to find a flat to rent. The streets were swarming with crowds in a state of anxiousness and panic, or, as one period commentator put it, "in the psychologically abnormal state."[73] In the effort to find a fitting temporary home, the only permanence for everyone was constant moving.[74] This fact greatly affected the development of the rental apartment building type and its perpetuation in the housing market of the striving middle classes. To be commercially viable, the plan had to be standard; there was little diversion from the usual organizational pattern around the central dining room, with large rooms facing the street and service spaces at the back opening onto internal courtyards. The buildings were constructed in one building season, usually between May and October, and they tended to be as standardized as possible, notwithstanding the traditional structural system of massive brickwork load-bearing walls with reinforced concrete floor slabs, and tile-covered pitched roofs over timber structure. It was the seasonal workers from the Serbian town of Crna Trava, rather than modern contracting firms from Belgrade, that constructed most of the apartment buildings. Custom-made interiors with more expensive materials and finishes were only made for the

4.42   (opposite page) Fashion show in the Engineers' Hall in Belgrade, 1936. (Courtesy Museum of the City of Belgrade.)

4.43   Josif Najman, photocollage of buildings designed by the architect, made as a Christmas card for 1936. (Courtesy Miloš Jurišić.)

entrance halls, as these were deemed representative of the social status of the inhabitants and could thus increase the price of the flats.[75]

The size, and consequently the form, of buildings were regulated by the provisions of the 1931 Building Act, which distinguished five types of urban space: "dense," "medium," and "sparse" settlements, areas for villas and summer houses, and industrial and agricultural areas.[76] For each type the Act regulated the minimum size of sites, minimum width of street front, maximum site use ratio, and maximum height of buildings. Except for public buildings and monuments, the Act prescribed a maximum of five floors above ground, with a provision for mezzanine and mansard floors in the city center. Following this, apartment blocks developed into a recognizable type of building of 4–5 floors, typically with two apartments per floor, and either shops or a caretaker's flat on the ground floor. Taller buildings were rarely constructed; table 4.3 shows that

TABLE 4.3   Number of Apartment Buildings Constructed in Belgrade, 1937–1938, by Number of Floors

Year	GF	GF+1	GF+2	GF+3	GF+4	GF+5	GF+6	GF+7	Total
1937	142	112	43	38	24	19	6	–	384
1938	201	125	52	40	40	24	10	2	494

GF= ground floor

only two buildings of more than seven floors were erected in Belgrade in 1937–1938, for example.[77]

The wide acceptance of the modern style furthered the typification of apartment blocks, and specifically the proliferation of what Milivoje Tričković, an architect of Beaux-Arts background, called architectural "nudists."[78] Notwithstanding his plea for a return to the national paradigm, the arguments he used in his critique of modern architecture in Belgrade are very indicative. Tričković claimed, and rightly so, that the victory of local modern architects had been an easy one, without the hard toil and blood and sweat shed in the long struggle of their European predecessors. He criticizes the local modernism for being fabricated as a "matter of fashion," inspired by principles of "fashionable retailing" and brought onto the market as a foreign product of the "latest style of architectural fashion" to satisfy the vanity of the public, with an added bonus of the nudes being cheaper to produce. Could we then assume that "nudism" was the latest architectural fashion of 1930s Belgrade? I would suggest that the distinction between nude and naked could be seen as the very point at which fashion and modernity diverge.

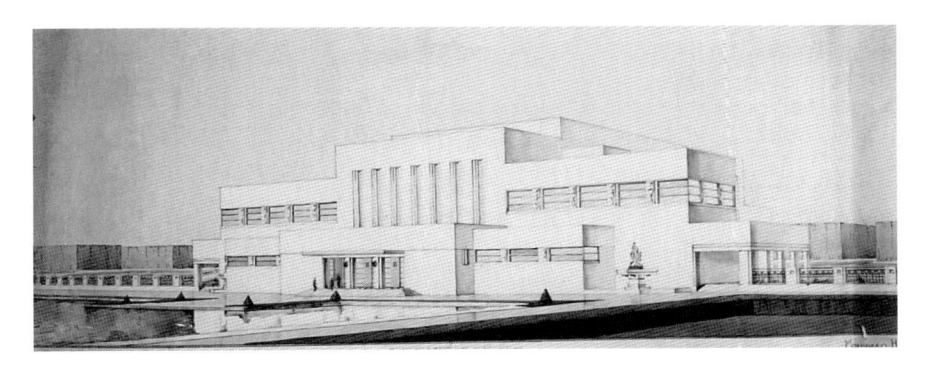

Of all Belgrade modern architects, it was the youngest member of the Group of Architects of the Modern Movement, Momčilo Belobrk,[79] who really made his mark with the rental apartment block building type. Before turning thirty-five years of age, in the short period from 1932 to 1940, he realized as many as 28 of these, all but one of them being representative of the best spirit of Belgrade modern architecture. An uncompromising orientation to the modern movement, consistency in applying the principle of pure form and cubic composition, and perseverance in the exploration of the aesthetic of purism are the main characteristics of his design method. In his most successful modernist works, Belobrk renounced reminiscences of the historical styles, ornamentation, and decoration. He made his apartment blocks products of extreme economy, rigorously established in line with the purist "Law of Mechanical Selection" as set down by Amédée Ozenfant and Le Corbusier in *La Peinture moderne* (Paris, 1926). By the purist law, "objects tend toward a type that is determined by the evolution of forms between the ideal of maximum utility, and the satisfaction of the necessities of economical manufacture, which conform inevitably to the laws of nature. This double play of laws has resulted in the creation of a certain number of objects that may thus be called standardized."[80]

In Belobrk's work, two types of objects came out of this process, the built-in block with exposed street frontage in one plane, and the corner block exposed as a volume. In both, the architect expressed nothing more than the natural, nonidealized body of residence, the plain dwellings container with windows and balconies. In effect, these apartment buildings are not just unadorned, they are stark naked, objects with no qualifications, which are inhabited by transient families with no shield or protection of ownership. Belobrk's design expresses the bare utility of rental housing, quite along the lines of functional-

4.44   Momčilo Belobrk, student project, 1929.

4.45   Momčilo Belobrk, ca. 1946.

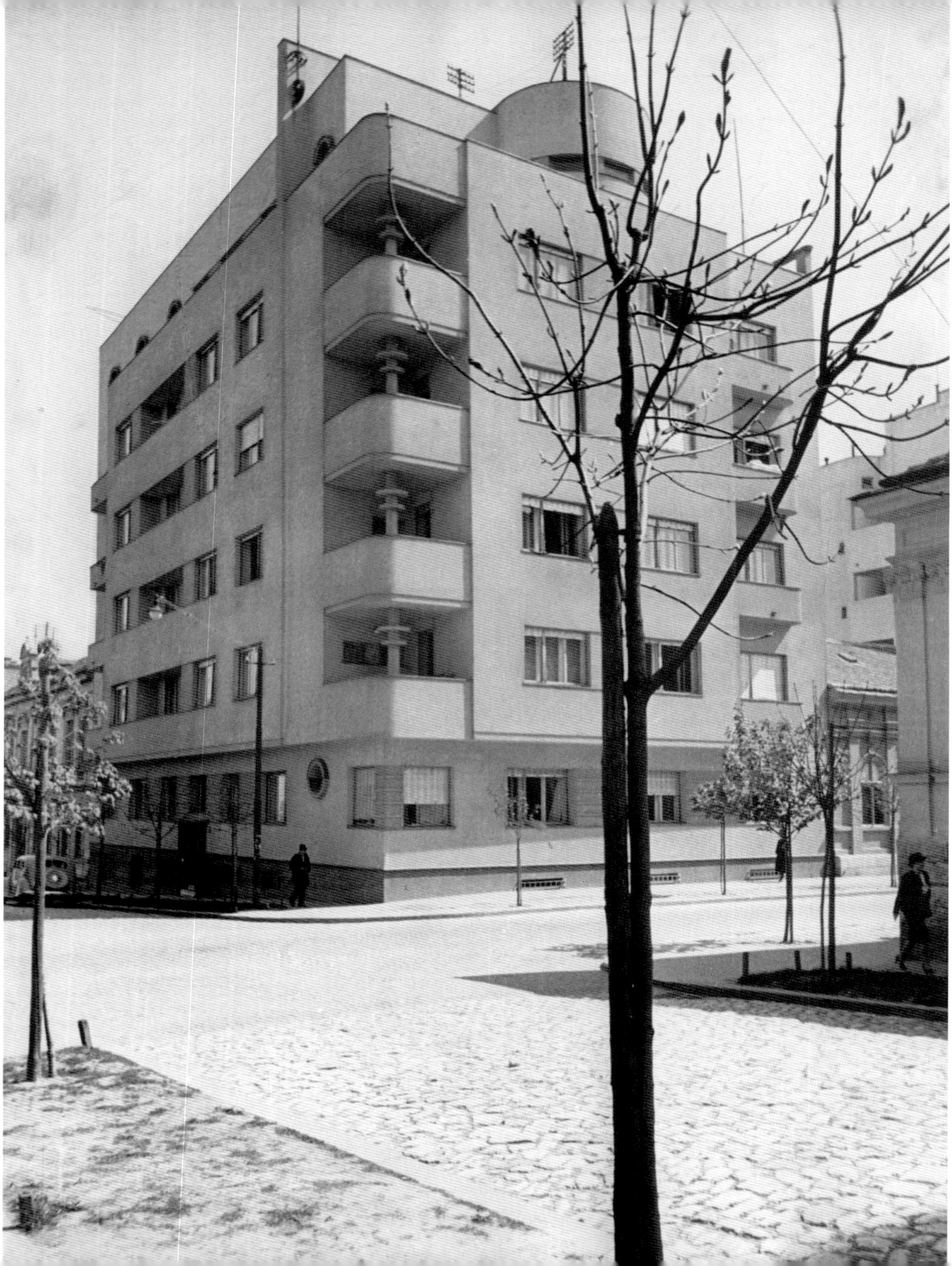

4.46   Momčilo Belobrk, apartment blocks in Belgrade, corner type. 14 Dobračina Street, 1934; 17 Dositejeva Street, 1937; 26 Gavrila Principa (Bosanska) Street, 1940.

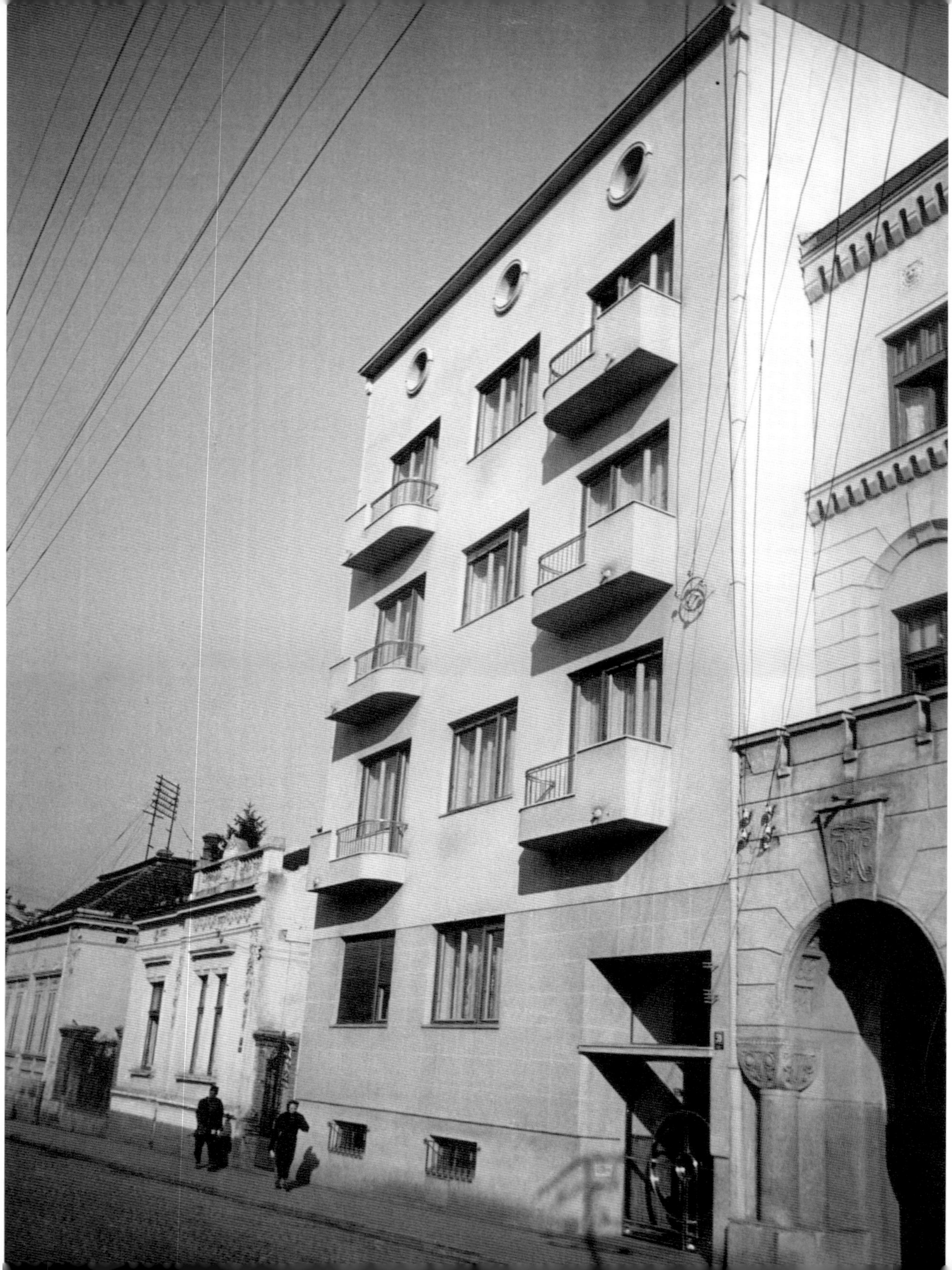

4.47   Momčilo Belobrk, apartment blocks in Belgrade, mid-perimeter-block type. 59 Njegoševa Street, 1935; 37 Francuska Street, 1937; 6-8 Svetogorska Street, 1938.

ism. It is by the "isolation of utility," as proposed by Joan Copjec, that any reminiscences of style and ornament take on the sartorial role:

The isolation of utility as the essential parameter of a building's definition resulted not only in the assigning to style and ornament the task of *expressing* this essential definition, of linking themselves to use, it resulted as well in the underlying assumption that obliged this task: namely, that style and ornament were separate from and secondary to function. It is at this point that style and ornament began to be considered precisely as *clothing;* their connection to the building, in other words, was taken as arbitrary rather than necessary, and they were thus viewed, for the first time, as the wrapping or covering of an otherwise nude building. . . . Functionalism, in the form of architectural purism, peaked, then, in a rending of clothing.[81]

If we look at the whole series of Belobrk's apartment buildings, the difference between the ones where facades are somewhat decorated with ornamental secondary modeling and the totally stripped ones appears to be in the phase of undressing. Once the clothing is completely removed, as from the villa in Kaćanskog Street (1933) or in Belobrk's last prewar apartment building in Bosanska Street (1940), it is not the fashionable nude/nudist body that remains but the naked nature of dwelling, and, consequently, the buildings that stand the test of time.

4.48 (opposite page) Momčilo Belobrk, entrance doors to apartment blocks; interior of the underground carpark in the apartment block at 6-8 Svetogorska Street, Belgrade.

4.49 Momčilo Belobrk, villa at 16 Kaćanskog Street, Belgrade, 1933.

4.3 DRAGIŠA BRAŠOVAN (1887–1965): THE STYLE MASTER

"Hallmark of the period's fashions: to intimate a body that never knows full nakedness," wrote Walter Benjamin with regard to the opposition of fashion to the natural or organic, and the fetishism that lies at the base of the appeal of the inorganic.[82] While the naked nature of modern architecture might have suited the habitus of the anonymous city dweller, it was seen as lacking the essential condition to render works of lasting value. Wealth and power ordered custom tailoring, and someone else, someone of masterly status, was needed to cut the appropriate contemporary style. That figure was the architect Dragiša Brašovan.[83] From 1920, when he left his position as city architect in the provincial town of Veliki Bečkerek and arrived at the capital in a "modest, cautious, and silent" way,[84] to the end of the decade, Dragiša Brašovan had became one of the most successful architects of the historical styles in Belgrade. His clients were among the wealthiest and most prominent representatives of the boisterous new bourgeois class of entrepreneurs and businessmen for whom he produced residences and business premises of quality and style.[85] Success and pleasantness pervaded his life and his career, as architectural historian Zoran Manević well observed:

The life of Brašovan, when it is being retold, is mostly like a scenario for a pleasant novel from bourgeois life in which success is built upon success, in which the transitions from one sphere of ideas into another are made easily, with no visible effort. A life that seems as if it were all made up of joyful and pleasant anecdotes. Friends, acquaintances, even those who only met him once . . . simply competed for who should be the first to retell some event from Brašovan's life, thus to corroborate with an anecdote their claims that Brašovan was "a born gentleman," or that in him "were united Hungarian gentry and Banat carousers," that all in all he was "a man of success," a man of lively spirit, short-tempered yet deeply human, and sociable.[86]

While he stayed forever faithful to this image of a grand lifestyle, in 1929 Brašovan walked out of the picture fashioned on historical styles, and swiftly walked into a different scene of contemporaneity. After his triumph in Barcelona, he joined the Group of Architects of the Modern Movement in Belgrade in 1930 and became one of the most prominent and realized architects of the new style. As Branislav Kojić noted, Brašovan's conversion to modernism and his joining GAMM marked one of the most important victories of the modern movement in Belgrade.

This process of transition is, perhaps, best manifested in the four private houses that Dragiša Brašovan completed in the years 1927–1932. The first of these is villa Škarka (1926–1927), the house of the director of the Prague Bank, Richard Škarka,[87] of which art historian Aleksandar Kadijević writes: "Done in a planar way like a painting, it was conceived as an intimate edifice with a fine, tactile plastic decor. Contributing largely to the impression of the picturesque is the rich romantic ornamentation of the facade, derived from the historical styles of the Mediterranean cultural circle. Obvious is the influence of late Gothic Venice, as well as the architectural detailing of Arabic and Catholic-baroque architecture."[88] Although Kadijević continues to find the elements of the modern style in the planar treatment of the facade wall, I would argue that the house represents the very example of high style, with no concern for the issues of modernity whatsoever. The symmetric arrangement of rooms and the strict formality of the interior spaces, with the plan focusing around the central salon shaped into a perfect circle, and, above all, the intricate decorativeness inherent in the design, confirm that the architect aimed, to use Nikola Dobrović's expressions, at "seducing," "winning," "forming," and "supporting" the bourgeois taste, and not at emancipating it toward the modern paradigm.[89]

In the genealogy of Brašovan's modernism, it is the architecture of villa Genčić (1929) that poses a perplexing dilemma. Is it a capital example of the well-thought-out period academicism, or could it be regarded as the breaking point of the architect's preoccupation with the historical styles? If a formal analysis is applied, the answer seems to be rather clear cut, as Kadijević asserts:

4.50   (opposite page) Dragiša Brašovan (seated) with Andreja Papkov in the office. (Courtesy City Museum, Vršac.)

4.51   Dragiša Brašovan, villa of Richard Škarka, Belgrade, 1926–1927.

4.52   Dragiša Brašovan, villa of Đorđe Genčić, Belgrade, 1929.

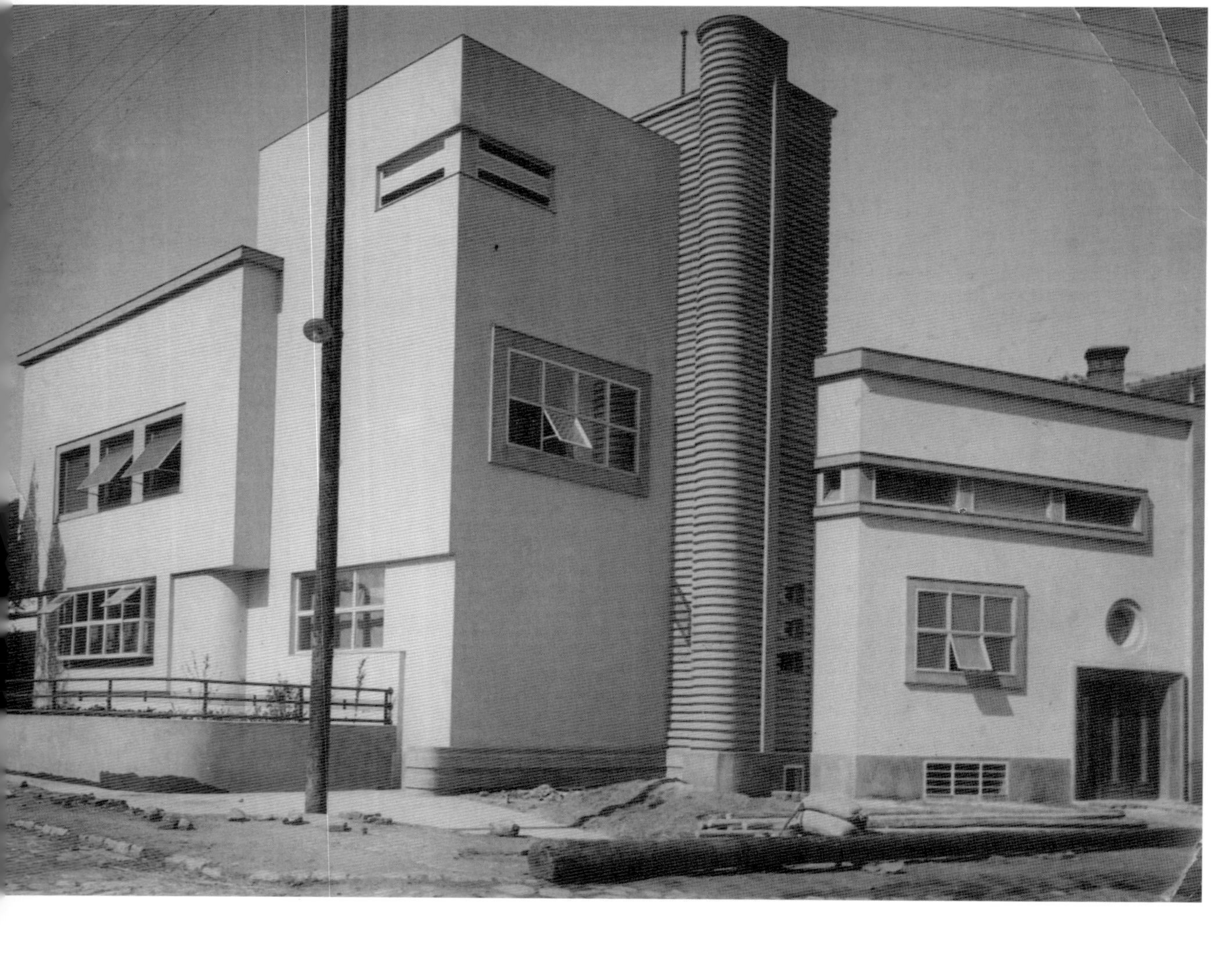

"Brašovan was inspired by the Renaissance and neoclassical, Palladian architectural paradigms," with the entrance zone "undoubtedly representing the most brilliant example of a citation of Alberti's and Palladio's models in the eclectic architecture of Belgrade."[90] But if the severe tectonics of the primary form, combined with the almost purist articulation of the geometric landscape of the flat roof terrace, are seen as dominating the eclectic paraphernalia, the shadow of doubt creeps in. Still, under no conditions can this be enough to make it a modern house; it is still a traditional massive decorated box, with no attempt on the architect's part to break from it. Yet, if Brašovan had followed his instinct and developed the very bone of this villa, its geometric potential and the latent power present in the planar articulation, and had constructively combined it with modern building techniques, would he not have come to a quite different substance of modernism from the one he presented in Barcelona, *nota bene*, the same year villa Genčić was finalized?

Even if we can detect traces of modernism in this house, Brašovan seems not to have, as he departed in the completely opposite direction. This becomes clear when villa Genčić is viewed against the house Brašovan built for himself and his wife Marija in Belgrade in 1931. This was his first modern project realized in Belgrade and showed the true face of his pseudo-modern identity. First, the house was expensive, among the most expensive villas of the period by far, its overall cost being comparable with that of a four-story apartment building. Second, it was a crossbreed, combining traces of expressionist aesthetic, modern style, and traditionalist planning. Quite contrary to his own feeling for tectonics and geometrical clarity in both the two previous villas, in his own house Brašovan demonstrated the instability of his position. This is most notable in the complicated, but not at all complex, articulation of the facades, which blurs the clarity of the primary forms: interplay of cubic geometry and rounded wall edges, styling and framing of elements in two-color variation, and dramatization of the effect by dense horizontal profiling on the most prominent vertical volume. Especially indicative of the architect's want of adornment is the design of windows, of which there are ten different types on the two street facades alone. And each type, notwithstanding its functional appropriateness, is distinctly utilized as a kind of cosmetic, or rather as costume jewelry designed to lift the drabness of the plain dress. The figure of a little nymphet by the entrance speaks for itself.

As success was built upon success, Brašovan was soon commissioned to design a modern villa for the rich merchant Dušan Lazić (1932) on a large site in the most prestigious area, only a block away from the main entry to the Royal Mansion. With this house he rounded off his style-seeking exercise and produced a synthetic expression of the typical period modernism. The fairly functional planning of distinctly separate public, private, and service areas is

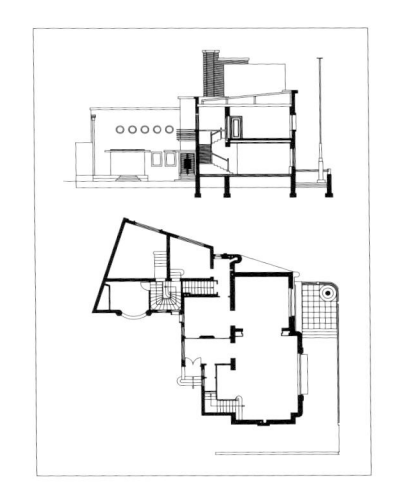

4.53 Dragiša Brašovan, Brašovan house, Belgrade, 1931. View from the street (courtesy City Museum, Vršac); ground-floor plan and section; detail of the main entrance (courtesy City Museum, Vršac).

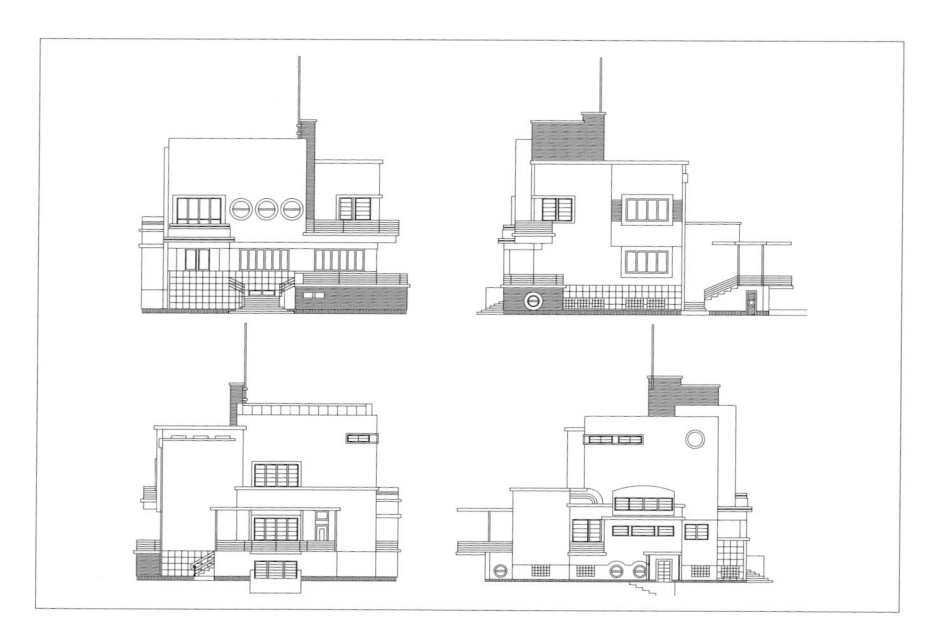

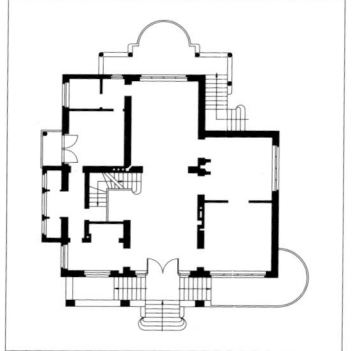

reflected in the external design. But, despite the pure stereometric geometry of the primary form and the attempt at functionality and free flow of space, there is no corresponding change of the structural system, and so the plan is lacking in backbone, to use Mies van der Rohe's words, not free "but chaotic and therefore constipated."[91] In the articulation of the facades, holding onto the pattern book already elaborated in his own house, Brašovan went to excess in the combination of various stucco textures, window types, handrails and metalwork details, and modernist symbols.

As Nikola Dobrović suggested in his critical study, there is something incomplete about Brašovan's modernism.[92] In the shift from historicism to modernism Brašovan did not investigate the ideas of the modern movement, nor did he experiment or struggle with the ideological issues or questions of authenticity. Quite simply, he interpreted what he presumed and perceived as the canon of modern architecture. Well versed in the manipulation of historical styles, he took modernism as another style, and put buildings together according to the new canon. In this he was little concerned with the economy of space or structural aspects of modern architecture. As has been noted in the accounts of his life and work, it was through foreign architectural magazines, and especially through publications of the Bauhaus, that Brašovan had become thoroughly aware of the advance of modernism when he said in 1929: "all that has been known until now has to be forgotten, and we have to start from the very beginning." It was, therefore, through the images diffused through the magazines that he judged, or more precisely gauged, what new architecture should look like. It

CHAPTER 4 **BYT MODE**

seems that Brašovan, in fact, took architectural magazines and publications as catalogues of patterns of multiple different modern styles, analogous to the multiplicity of historical styles. In the appropriation of the modern paradigm Brašovan acted from his own eclectic self, processing expressionist or Bauhaus models as easily as he had previously processed the "Budapest modernized baroque" (Dobrović), "Oriental baroque" (Kojić), "Renaissance" (Kadijević), etc. He first used the expressionist pattern for the contemporary architecture of the Workers' Chamber Hall in Novi Sad (1929–1931),[93] and also for the modern Yugoslav pavilion in Barcelona (1929). In the design of his own house in Belgrade (1931), the expressionist pattern is transmuted and styled to the more clean-cut fashion, while the dominant paradigm for the Yugoslav pavilion in Milan is the Bauhaus model and its characteristic transparency combined with the plain and smooth geometry of the walls. In all these buildings, Brašovan made no rupture with the concept of style, rather he acted self-consciously to process images of modernity and consequently to produce stylistic forms.

To return to Dobrović's critique and paraphrase its main points: being detached from the ideologically charged ideas of the modern movement, Brašovan's modernism was incomplete, predominantly formalistic, stylistic, and even superficial. In this, it was not too different from the way the ideas of the European modern movement were translated in America following the exhibition "Modern Architecture: International Exhibition," held in the Museum of Modern Art in New York in 1932. The exhibition launched what has since been known

4.54 (opposite page) Dragiša Brašovan, villa of Dušan Lazić, Belgrade, 1932. Ground-floor plan and elevations.

4.55 Dragiša Brašovan, Workers' Chamber Hall, Novi Sad, 1929–1931.

as the International Style, the principles of which were set down in Henry-Russell Hitchcock and Philip Johnson's publication of the same name.[94] As Beatriz Colomina has observed, in the American translation the European movement was understood only in aesthetic terms, reduced to a style devoid of its social, ethical, and political content.[95] Similarly, in Brašovan's translation, an economy of object and space, so central to modern architecture, is displaced into the economy of style.

In the period between 1933 and 1940 Brašovan finished his great modernist trilogy, since regarded as the canonic works of Serbian modernism: the Palace of the State Print Works in Belgrade (1933; 1937–1940), the Air Forces Headquarters in Zemun (1935), and the Palace of the Danube Regional Government in Novi Sad (1936–1939). All three buildings are large block structures of eminently autonomous character whose monumental presence dominates their respective cityscapes, giving them a characteristic identity.

In the Palace of the State Print Works in Belgrade, Brašovan produced a design that far transcended the limitations set by his usual stylistic approach, realizing a building that distinctly stands out as the most accomplished modern work of his opus. In the relatively poor and industrially underdeveloped Serbia of the period, it was this building of eminently industrial character that became the topos of Serbian modernism in architecture. It seems odd that the most celebrated achievement of the architect favored by an affluent clientele and the establishment would be a printing factory, the building type of the low aesthetic. But it is precisely the absence of high art in this project that is its most valuable asset. I would argue that, being forced to primarily investigate the technical and technological aspects of the complex program, Brašovan had to reverse his design strategy and renounce the pursuit of style. After his fairly conservative design in the modern style was awarded the first prize in the Yugoslav national competition in 1933, triumphing over more uncompromisingly contemporary concepts, most notably the scheme by architect Drago Ibler or the second-prize winners Kiverov, Korka, and Krekić (both offices from Zagreb), he was commissioned to carry out the project. The client arranged for him to be sent on a study tour of Germany, during which he learned about different technology systems and saw modern printing factories in that highly developed country. Through this direct contact with the source of modern thinking, he must have realized that for the factory the external appearance is unimportant to the space of production, and that production space has therefore to be constructed from within. In this sense, Brašovan's final design follows the innermost essence of production space, providing a neutral framework of structural skeleton and consequent free plan and free facade that are most appropriate for the organization of the production process.[96]

The building was not constructed until 1937–1940, and then it was on a different, much larger site in a suburban industrial zone. In its organization, as Nikola Dobrović observed, it represented a powerful struggle of Brašovan as architect/artist with a complex technical process of integrating various differentiated programs and technological requirements within a single building.[97] Critical of the resulting composition for reflecting this struggle, most notably in the uneasy complexity of the volumetric, which for him demonstrated the architect's flight from functionalistic unification and standardization, Dobrović suggested that the fragmentation of the body of the building verges on a disjunction of disparate forms, motifs, and substructures.[98] Notwithstanding the main point of the critique, I would argue that Brašovan deliberately used the potential of disjunction as his compositional strategy. The disparity of parts, pronounced as separate elements in the composition, is further elaborated in the various wall surface perforations developed for each of the facades enveloping various volumes, a series of different patterns that emphasize the textural quality of tautly stretched continuous wall surface. Belonging to the same register of expressive means, the patterns serve both to achieve the discreteness of each part and to provide for their unity. By treating the wall as a continuous perforated surface, in which all elements are of the same order of importance, Brašovan succeeded in creating a powerful composition of large plastic volumes of seamless quality. More importantly, the strict functionality, industrial design,

4.56   Dragiša Brašovan, Palace of the State Print Works, Belgrade, 1933; 1937–1940. View from the street; (following page) side facade (contemporary photograph by Marija Milinković) and facade articulation (contemporary photograph by Milica Lopičić).

183

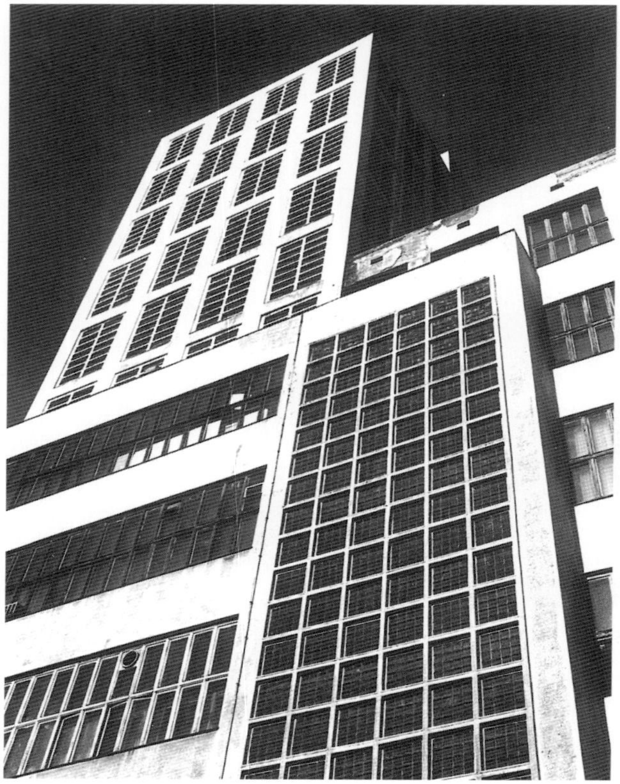

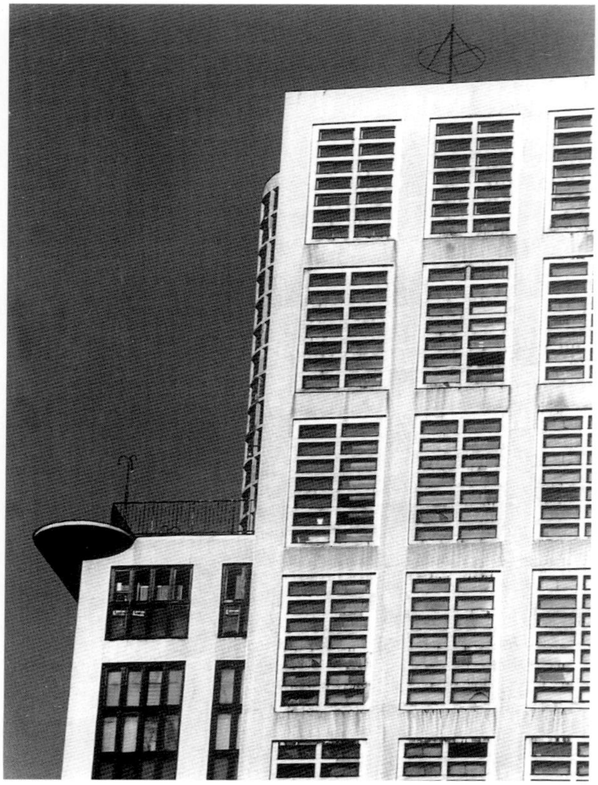

and lack of any overt symbolism have rendered this architecture contemporary throughout the years of constantly changing paradigms.

While the Belgrade building with its bold industrial character can be seen as an antinomy in Brašovan's opus, the other two works of the major trilogy represent the culmination of his particular version of the modern style. The compositional strategy of the Air Forces Headquarters in Zemun can be regarded as the architect's attempt to perfect, and perhaps canonize, the concept first employed in the Yugoslav pavilion at the Milan fair (1931). In both, the dramatic effect is achieved by the vertical feature juxtaposed against the dominant horizontal mass of the building. But, while the pavilion's central vertical volume is juxtaposed against the asymmetry of its horizontal volumes, in the Air Forces Headquarters the glazed prismatic vertical motif accentuates the strict symmetrical arrangement of the plan and the facade facing the main square. The lightness and transparency of the earlier scheme give way to the dogmatic rhythm of ribbon windows in the latter. Above all, the highly symbolic form of the Zemun building seems like a mannerist aberration of the simple period aesthetic of the pavilion in Milan. This aspect of the design was harshly criticized by Branislav Kojić in his text "Symbolism in Architecture," in which the building is cited as an example of structural symbolism: "the air forces command carrying airplane wings on its roof."[99]

The Palace of the Danube Regional Government in Novi Sad was by far the largest, the most important, and the costliest of Brašovan's three modernist monuments.[100] The building was to be the seat of the regional administration, set up in 1929 and presided over by the *ban,* a state functionary appointed by and responsible to King Aleksandar.[101] The architectural competition for the design of the new building was held in 1930, but the jury failed to award the first prize. The royal administration of the Danube Region decided to directly appoint Dragiša Brašovan, despite the fact that his entry had not been awarded any prize at the competition. As the construction of the building had been postponed due to the economic crisis and political instability of various *bans,* a completely new project was drawn up by Brašovan in 1936, when the construction finally commenced. As it happened, in the five years between the competition and the start of the final redesign, modern architecture gained a status of legitimacy that made it appropriate for state institutions. Himself one of the central figures in the legitimation of modernism, Brašovan now sealed the new state canon with the Palace of the Danube Regional Government.

The grand architectural composition of the Palace rests on the monumental horizontality of the primary volumetric juxtaposed against the asymmetrically positioned slender vertical tower. The strength of the building is achieved by the powerful massing of its 180-meter-long horizontal body, ending with the cylindrical form on one end and the tower with the anchoring parallelepiped

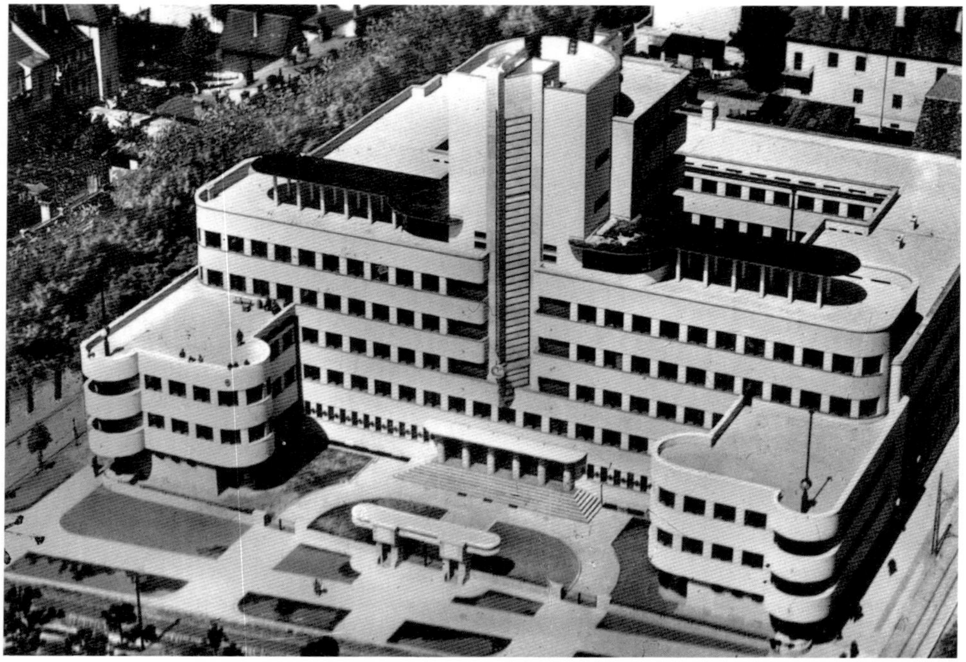

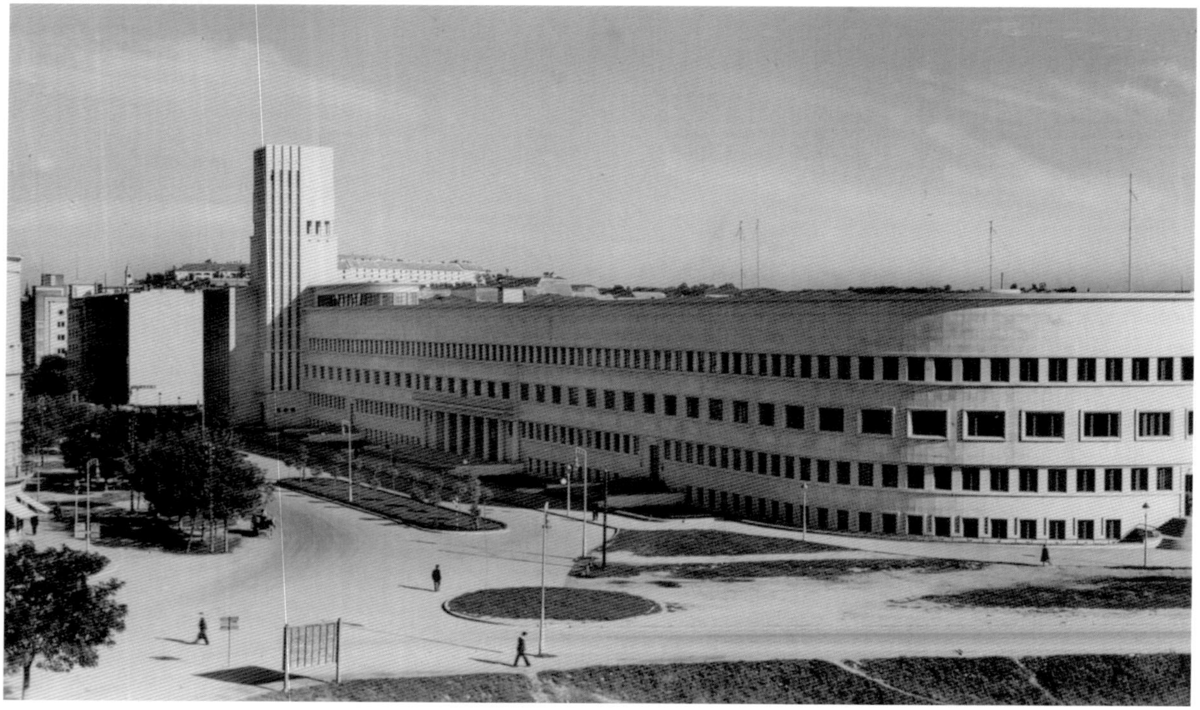

4.57 (opposite page) Dragiša Brašovan, Air Forces Headquarters, Zemun, 1935. Aerial view.

4.58 (opposite page) Dragiša Brašovan, Palace of the Danube Regional Government, Novi Sad, 1936–1939 (photograph from 1950s).

4.59 Bogdan Nestorović, PRIZAD Palace, Belgrade, 1937–1938. Views of the front and rear facades.

4.60 Bogdan Nestorović, Craftsmen's Hall, Belgrade, 1931–1933.

form on the other. It is quite important to note that Brašovan intended to clad the facades in red brick, which would have resulted in a very particular aesthetic, perhaps one evocative of the great Dutch tradition of Berlage or Dudok. The client, however, demanded that the cladding be done in white stone from the Adriatic island of Brač, on the basis of ever-arguable "aesthetic reasons," and, the architect went along and gave his vote for it at the Building Committee meeting.[102] I would contend that it was precisely at this point of radical alteration of cladding material, and the consequent drastic change of the character of the Palace, that its architecture lost the initial balance struck between monumental massing and fine brickwork detailing. Notwithstanding its dignified presence in the Novi Sad cityscape, the resulting white corpus, clad seamlessly in some 12,000 square meters of Brač stone, achieved a different, more monumentalist aesthetic than the one originally envisaged. This kind of aesthetic somehow earned Dobrović's unforgiving resentment: "not having felt the expressive power of the 'painterly' character of that huge wall surface, the master began to introduce artificial horizontal lines and sculptural individualization of windows and doors" and thus "weakened one architectural principle and, in doing that, lessened the quantum spatial energy."[103]

In the context of the development of the modern style and its application in large public and office buildings, Brašovan's monumental modernism became accepted as the canon. What Dobrović diagnosed as an "incomplete" modernism, and criticized as an exercise in modernist formalism, was in fact the substance of the architectural mainstream. Buildings by architect Bogdan Nestorović, such as Craftsmen's Hall (1931–1933) or the PRIZAD Palace (1937–1938), are representative of this trend. Even the two high-rises finalized in the late thirties, the Vreme building (1937–1938) by Branislav Kojić and the Mortgage Bank skyscraper Albania (1938–1940) by architect Miladin Prljević (after the winning competition project by Branko Bon and Milan Grakalić), carried the heavy artifice of monumentalism rather than daring to show their naked nature. By the end of the 1930s, it seemed as if *byt* had never really changed its mode.

4.61 (opposite page) Branislav Kojić, Vreme building, Belgrade, 1937–1938. (Courtesy Architecture Department in the Museum of Science and Technology, Belgrade.)

4.62 Branko Bon and Milan Grakalić, and Miladin Prljević, Albania Palace, Belgrade, 1938–1940. (Period photograph by Zvonimir Janović, courtesy Miloš Jurišić.)

5 DEPARTURE

The development of shipping in Boka Kotorska in the past, and the consequent relative prosperity of this region of our country, unique for its natural beauty, was particularly reflected in the rational architecture of the captains' houses built during the eighteenth and at the beginning of nineteenth century. "Ship" and "house" were correlative terms then, and money earned by cruising and trading in the Adriatic and the Mediterranean provided the basis for changing the fickle yet profitable deck of a ship for the solid ground of their own houses. The size and the equipment of the house expressed, in the manner typical of pioneers, the achieved earnings, the thought-out savings, and personal vanity. It is no wonder that these men, deeply immersed in the hard and monotonous life at sea, cramped in the narrowest spaces—the sailing ships from Boka were neither large nor comfortable— dreamed of a house on the coast of their homeland, with windows facing the sea.

Milan Zloković, **"Captains' Houses in Boka"**

MILAN ZLOKOVIĆ (1898–1965): THE ARCHITECT AND HIS SHIP — 5.1

The seminal role played by the architect Milan Zloković in Serbian modernism is the principal reason for extracting his work from the context of general contemporary practice and examining it more closely and in more detail. His work is the very substance of Serbian modernism, and his buildings form the most coherent testimony to the ethos of the epoch. The second but no less important reason is that the significance of his achievement becomes apparent only if the body of his work is investigated from its own center as it were, and against the influences he was subject to that were outside the architectural discourse of the zeitgeist. For this, we should focus on the Boka Kotorska background to his otherwise European sensibility, which may well have been the origin of his very particular habit of mind and his creative disposition.

Milan Zloković was born in 1898 in the northern Adriatic port city of Trieste, into a naval family of Serbs from Boka Kotorska, his father Đuro being a captain

Lloyd Triestino Pfo "Abbazia"

Coperta di Passeggio

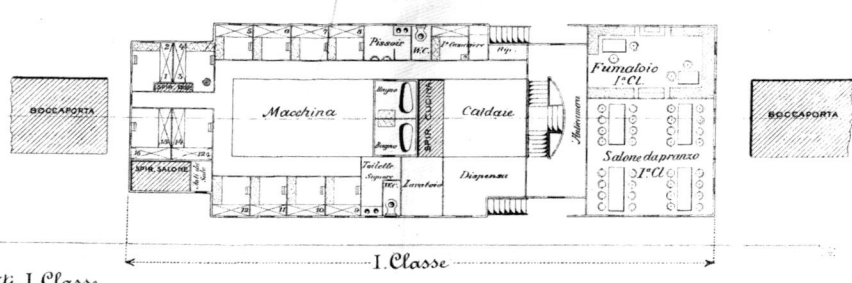

I. Classe

30 Letti I. Classe
26 Letti II. Classe

Coperta di Manovra

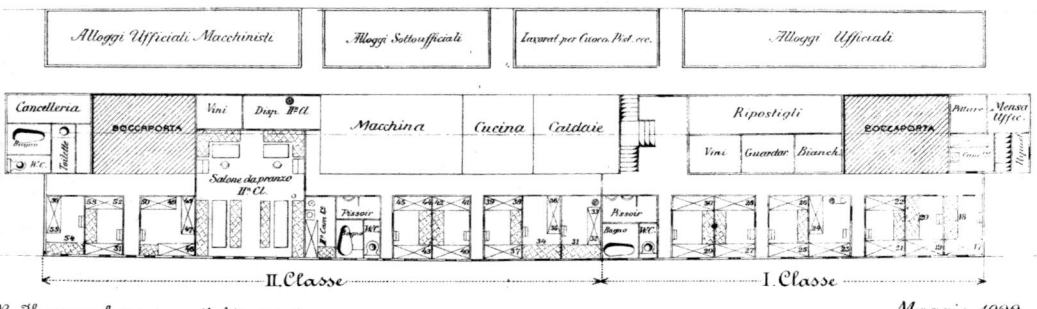

II. Classe — I. Classe

N.B. Il numero basso segna il letto di sotto, il numero alto quello di sopra.

Maggio 1922

and commander in the Trieste Lloyd merchant fleet.¹ The Zloković family came from Bijela, a small town in the bay of Boka Kotorska in the southeastern part of the Adriatic Sea. The bay of Boka, down to which the rugged mountains of Montenegro dramatically descend and sink into the sea, is a region of exceptional natural beauty and the site of three beautiful old towns: Kotor, Perast, and Risan. It is a region of historical multiculturalism, which gave Europe great seamen, merchants, captains, and famous admirals in the period of Venetian rule, from the beginning of the fifteenth to the end of the eighteenth century. Its towns of Roman-Dalmatian-Venetian type are renowned for the brilliant architecture of their stone churches, palaces, and captains' houses. Coming from this land and being from a naval family, one of the prime images of Zloković's childhood and adolescence must have been the great trinity of Mediterranean life: the sea, the ship, and the stone house. These three are most certainly the origin of the eternal loyalty and sense of belonging he felt for the rationality and aesthetic of both the ships and the traditional architecture of his region. The three are likewise fundamental to the ethos of his own architecture. The desire to become

5.1 (opposite page) Plans of the ship *Abbazia* (Lloyd Trieste).

5.2 Milan Zloković.

a ship captain like his father before him, which dominated his boyhood, was transformed into a deep understanding of the logic and rationale of the ship's economy of space and engineering. And the traditional captains' houses of Boka were the topos through which he intuitively internalized the great rules of harmony and proportion set in stone by the anonymous old master craftsmen.[2]

When, in the 1950s, Zloković wrote on the stone houses of Boka Kotorska, he in fact alluded to his own architectural credo.[3] He identified in these houses the rational economy of space and object, a concept that was so central to his own architectural concerns. His intention was not to evoke nostalgia for patriarchal handicraft culture, but to point to historical praxis and *technē* as the combination of practicality, economy, and social relations.[4] For Zloković, the building of stone houses was neither art nor handicraft, but *technē* immanent in the tectonics of architecture. He underlined the fact that the house owners, the ship captains, were at the same time the architects, for whom "ship" and "house" were correlative terms. The economy of the ship was thus the key to the economy of the house. More to the point, this architecture was not invented, but constructed according to traditional, practical, and economical premises. In this, Zloković opposed the notion of the architect as the dominating creator, the demiurge, who can be detached from the realities of the money economy. Like Adolf Loos before him, he also rejected the domination of artistic creation over learning, custom, and tradition. I would suggest that this parallel becomes clearer in the reading of Loos by Massimo Cacciari: "In the impatience for the new that is expressed in the architect's 'artistic creation,' Loos sees a pretense to erecting a work as text, or to erecting a work to serve as a central language, around which the other languages degenerate into means or instruments, and those of the past become an 'eternal image.'"[5] Similarly, in Zloković's writing, the past is not seen as the "eternal image" but as the language of old masters and the tradition of craftsmen, the innovative reading of which will yield new combinations and possibilities in contemporary practice.

In his texts, Zloković suggests that the owner/captain would set down exact dimensions of usable space around which the massive stone walls would be constructed. All dimensions, such as the width, length, and height of rooms, the intervals (center to center) between windows and doors, and wall thickness, were invariably stated numerically, as whole numbers in Venetian feet (sometimes with the addition of half-foot fractions).[6] Prior to construction, the owner would also have all the special stone elements ordered from the famous stonemasons of Vrnik islet by the island of Korčula in the Adriatic: stone slab frames for doors and windows, balconies, balustrades, eaves, steps, consoles, etc. The stone elements, which largely predetermined the architecture of the house, were cut to standard sizes and profiles, also measured in Venetian feet, from Korčulan stone, and shipped over to Boka as prefabricates to be assembled on the building site. The house would be built around the void of the internal space, which remained to be fitted out with timber structure floors and partitions, only after the outer stone shell and roof were finished. All construction was based on standard measurements in simple numerical interrelations, and it was, as Zloković demonstrated, a harmonically coordinated modular structure. The houses were built by unselfconscious craftsmen in a conventional and orderly manner: "The method of construction was traditional, and in no case had there been any deviation from it."[7] The old masters were unaware that the houses they constructed were "modern," as modern as Loos's master saddler's saddles.[8]

Milan Zloković, however, was fully aware of being modern, even though his work can be seen as a commentary on tradition and classical heritage, as much so as Loos's or Le Corbusier's. His work was new and dissociated from its connection to the past, yet it was related by radical and free transformation to the conception of the past as being usable for the present. The logic of transformation can be seen in Cacciari's terms as "the new space of the multiplicity of languages" as well as "the plurality of techniques and the conventional character of their names." In his study "Loos and His Angel: Being Loyal," Cacciari insists on the idea of the game:

One cannot play except by belonging, by habituating oneself to the rules that have shaped the game. In this "habit" new combinations, new possibilities emerge. The deeper one's participation in a game, the more these openings issue from practice itself, from habit. The truly present has deep roots—it needs the games of the old masters, the languages of posthumousness. The tradition therefore does not unfold from book to book, drawing to drawing, line to line, but follows the long detours, the waits, the labyrinths of the games among the languages, among linguistic *practices*.[9]

I would argue that Zloković had entered such a game in his architectural work, patiently, endlessly, continually reciprocating inputs of history, theory, and practice. In this, his modernism comes close to that of Adolf Loos, for he, like the

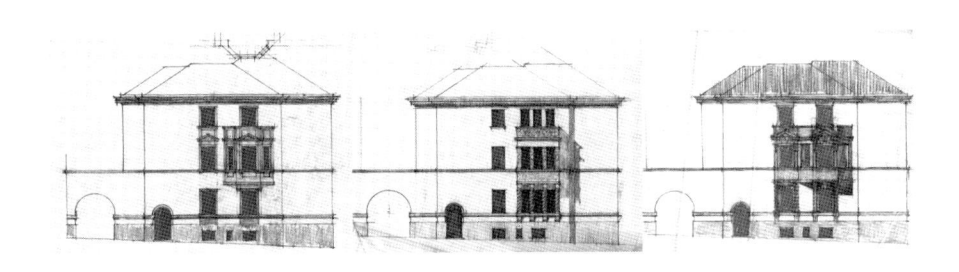

5.3   Milan Zloković, alternative sketches of the elevation for the house in Rankeova Street, Belgrade, 1926.

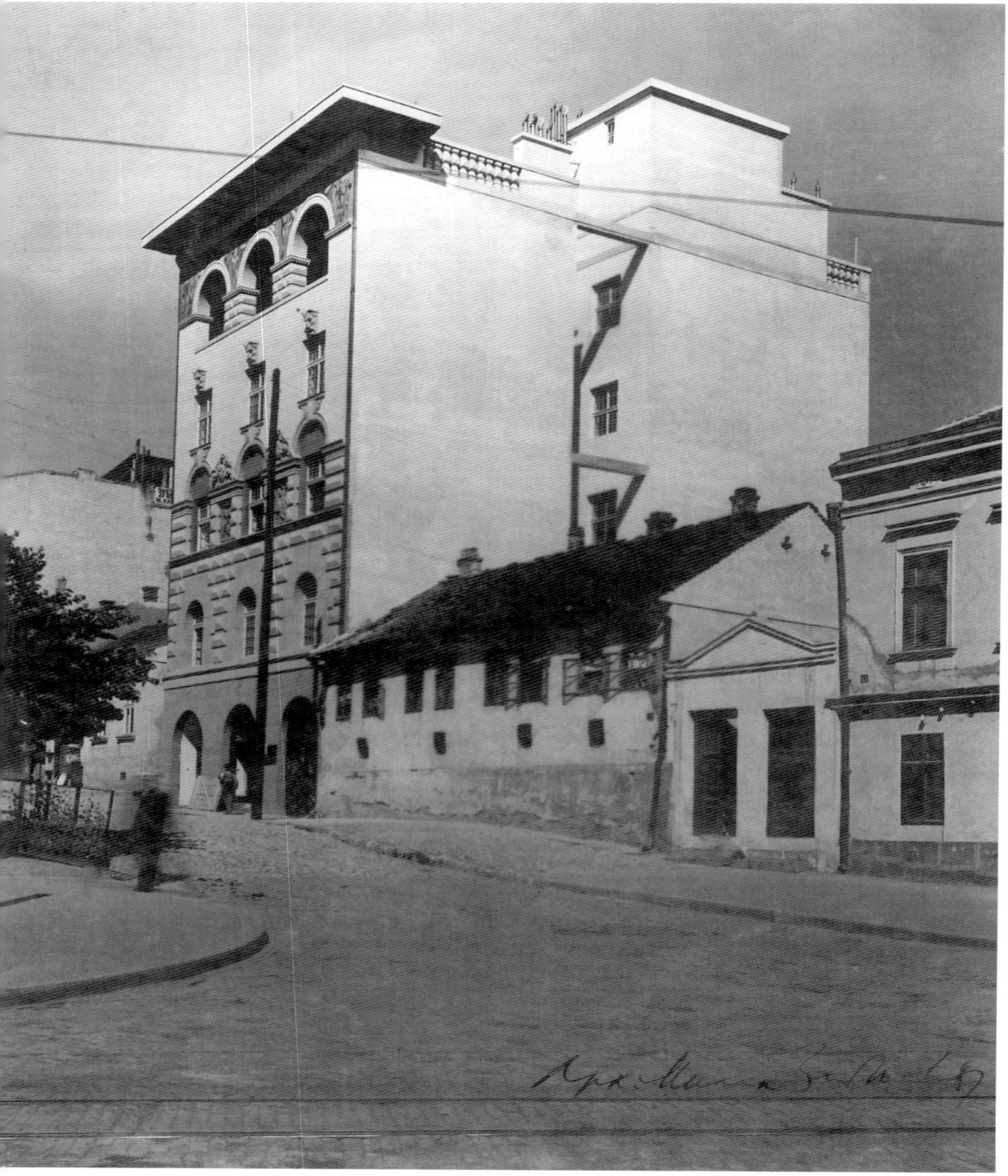

famous Viennese, played by belonging and played with loyalty to the beauty and logic of the natural forms of tradition. It is loyalty that binds him to the great master builders from Boka Kotorska, and that binds them back to what lasts—harmony and proportion in architecture. In recognizing the rules of the game, and without the slightest aim of inventing a new game, Zloković opened himself to the possibility of decision, of change and of artistic transformation within the set rules. In this he made up the game of different discourses relative to each other, questioned them, and established both harmony and contrast between them. They were the rules of geometry and proportion, the language of tradition and craftsmanship, the economy of space and object, and the rational logic of the ships and their engineering.

In his study of the anthropomorphic system of measurements in the old architecture of Boka Kotorska, Korčula, and Dubrovnik, Zloković noted that in his prewar design practice he had not worked on problems in the science of proportion and metrology, but that he had intuitively come to solutions that had harmonious proportions.[10] As it happened, during the German occupation of Belgrade when his practice had to cease, and in the post-Second World War period when he was marginalized by the actors of the new political order in the changed sociopolitical circumstances, he focused on theoretical work on problems of regulating systems, proportion, and modular coordination in architecture.[11] As Zloković himself seldom referred to his own projects in his theoretical works, current historiography has divided the two into separate compartments, with his praxis deemed representative and favored against the loss of direction in his theory.[12] It is my contention that the constituent facts of Zloković's architecture and its elaboration in building can be detected only through a reconciliation of his practice and his theory. The key to Zloković's game is in his work, in which the practices of modernity and of tradition, and of design and theory, are interrelated, without either claiming precedence over the other.

THE HOUSE RULES   **5.2**

In one of his rare comments relating to his own work, Milan Zloković pointed to his intuitive familiarity with the window dimension of 120 × 160 cm, i.e., a ratio of width to height of 3:4, which, he had ascertained, albeit much later in the 1950s, was the current window type of the traditional Mediterranean architecture in the Yugoslav coastal regions.[13] This note brings us back to Zloković's own house of 1927 in which he adopted that very size for the main window type, and directs

5.4   Milan Zloković, apartment block in Kralja Milutina Street, Belgrade, 1926–1927.

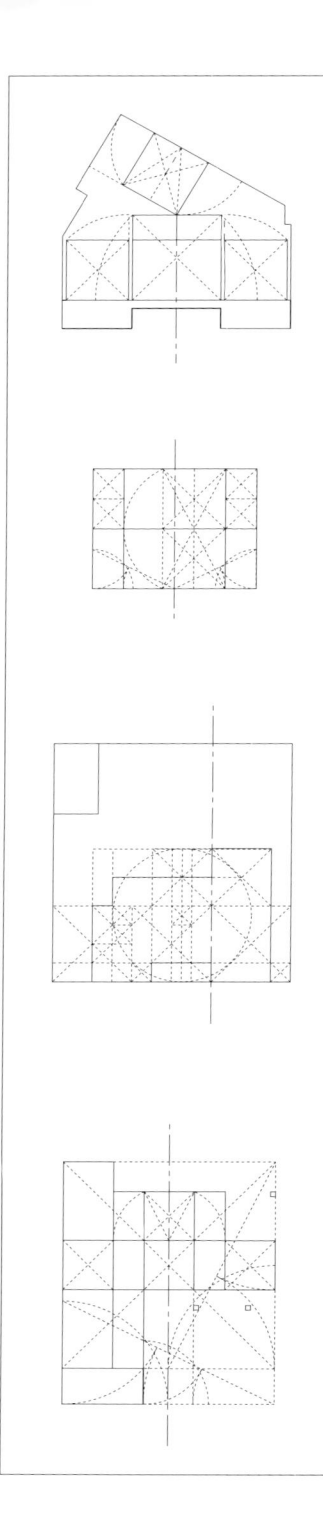

our investigation toward analysis of his intuitive use of regulating lines as a means of architectural design. There is a certain inevitability to Zloković's modernism—an elusive trace of the "Golden Section of Deception,"[14] a common denominator of authentically modern yet classical purity. The origin of its essentially modern character—the invisible signifiers of its guiding principles—have still to be traced. Zloković often made reference to *Vers une architecture,* in which Le Corbusier declared: "The choice of the regulating line is one of the decisive moments of inspiration, it is one of the vital operations of architecture."[15] In keeping with these words, Zloković based his designs on the values inherited from the great classical tradition, which he translated for the modern condition, much in the way Loos had taught: "Our culture is based on the recognition of the all-surpassing greatness of classical antiquity."[16] As demonstrated by proportional analysis diagrams, it can be argued with certainty that Zloković adopted geometrical systems for generating the structure, organization, and form of all his modern houses and villas, designed in the period 1927–1932.

In arranging the plan of his own house, Zloković opted for the combination of three geometrically related squares that define the function of the principal rooms on the first level.[17] The chosen basic module is a square, which corresponds to the sizes of side rooms, while the main room with its antechambers is inscribed into a central square, the dimensions of which are derived from the module's diagonal, following the principles of simple *ad quadratum* geometry. The module is entirely site-related, as the basic dimension chosen is the maximum width between structural walls that could fit on the corner cutoff of the irregular site. Furthermore, the complete three-dimensional plan of the house is resolved in relation to the position and dimensions of the central square, with the geometry of the square translated to section, determining the floor heights of the first two levels, and to elevation, in which it regulates the positions of openings.[18] The square thus turns into a regulating cube, just as Zloković's design method turns into Adolf Loos's lesson: "In this way I brought my students to think three-dimensionally, in the cube."[19]

Loos's basic premise, that design should proceed from interior to exterior, is reversed in Zloković's house, for the starting point here is the inherent geometry of the site into which the regulating cube is inserted. The form of the house becomes a three-dimensional resolution of two different volumetric systems dictated by the site geometry. Despite the acute angle of the intersecting perimeter streets, the composition rests on a combination of simple perpendicular volumes in two different axial systems. The perception of the house is a result of the montage of spatial experiences of interlocking cubes which can only be comprehended by walking around the site through a series of sequential urban frames. But, rather as Cacciari suggested of Loos's houses, the "exterior says nothing about the interior because they are two different languages,

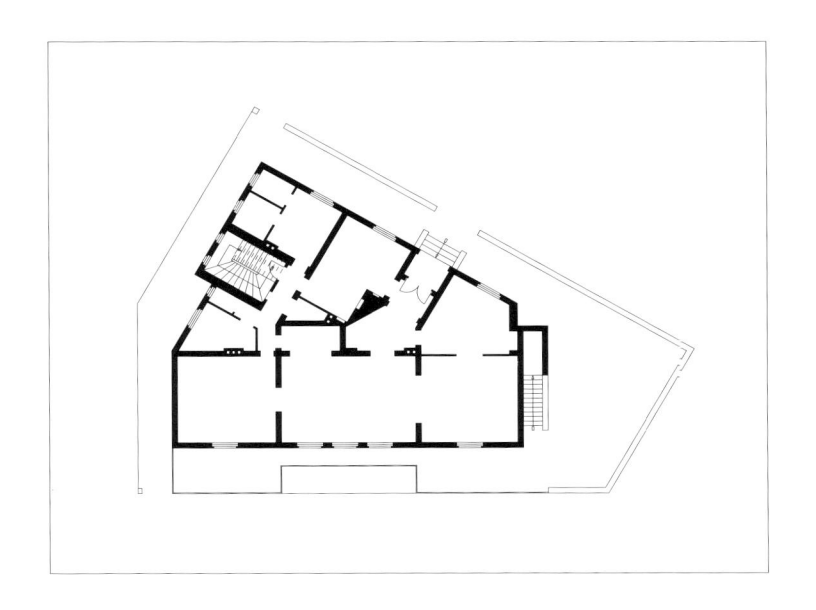

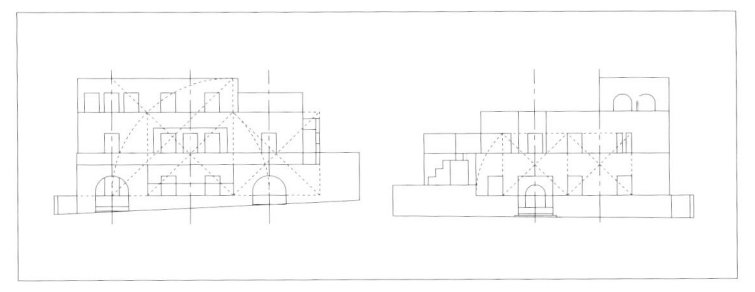

5.5 (opposite page) Schematic diagrams of proportional systems of four houses by Milan Zloković. Zloković house, 1927–1928; Žaborski house, 1928; villa Šterić, 1932; Prendić house, 1932–1933.

5.6 Milan Zloković, Zloković house, Belgrade, 1927–1928. Plan of first floor; elevations with the regulating lines; interior of the central room from the 1930s.

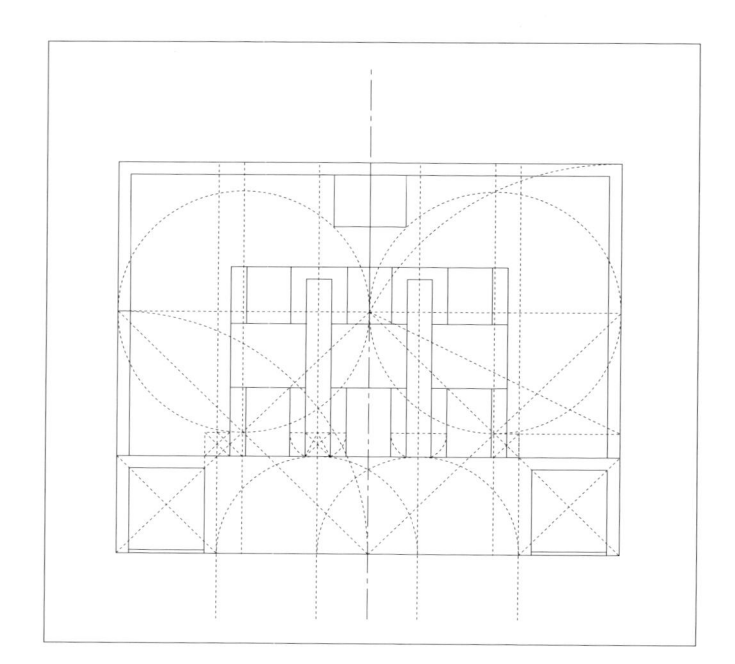

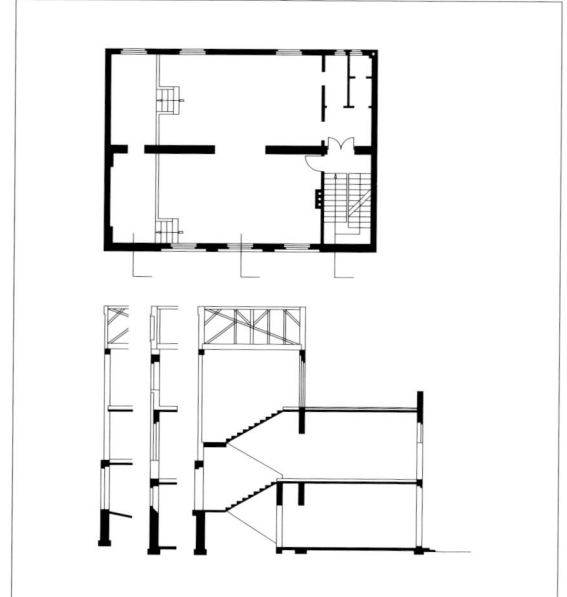

and each speaks of itself,"[20] and it is the wall that divides them into different linguistic practices. The difference posited between the interior and exterior recalls the traditional construction of captains' houses in Boka Kotorska, in which the stone walls were erected first and the interior was inserted as a separate internal substructure. In fact, the actual interior of Zloković's house was changed many times over the years, with no bearing on the ethos of the architecture, for behind the plain cubic form of the dumb exterior the essence of the house is kept; it is primarily a "letting dwell."[21]

Many aspects of Zloković's design method, therefore, invite comparison with that of Adolf Loos: the loyalty and belonging to traditional values, the formal likeness of their houses, the functional organization of served and serving spaces, the use of flat roofs as terraces, the three-dimensional planning of space, and the use of regulating systems, particularly of the system based on a square. For Loos, as Panayotis Tournikiotis suggested, the classical rules of composition were the timeless common language of Western civilization, which sought to be respected when translated into new architectural forms, so that order, beauty, and harmony might be achieved.[22] Similarly, for Zloković the use of regulating lines, passed down to him from the common architectural design practice of the nineteenth century, was an automatic design procedure, yet he used it in an undogmatic way, for he never allowed himself to be overtaken by the geometric system. His facades generally obey axial symmetry, but when the internal layout

CHAPTER 5 **DEPARTURE**

demands an exception to the rule, he resorts to asymmetry in the otherwise rigorous arrangement of openings. This functional understanding of rules of symmetry, simplicity and clarity of the primary volumetric, purity of plain rendered walls, and restraint in expression became characteristic of all his modern houses. Zloković developed his own design method as a synthesis of seemingly opposite operations. He uses regulating systems as an invisible law of the structure of the object, as opposed to the modernist experimentation with architectural form. He thus probes the modern formula with the classical means to architectural design, so that, as Manfredo Tafuri suggests, "the criticism of the work thus becomes an operation of the work itself."[23]

One of the most interesting examples of Zloković's tendency to radically modernize the plan while keeping the form restrained in a Loosian manner is the house of Nevena Zaborski (1928), where he realized what might be regarded as an authentic *Raumplan*. The house is located on a conventional narrow site of an urban perimeter block, and it is literally built into a street frontage. The facade is of a tripartite composition obeying axial symmetry, its division being regulated by the rules of the golden section. The point of departure for the internal planning is, however, not the external layout of the facade but the analysis of heights necessary for each particular space/room/*Raum,* and their position in the functional diagram of the house. The most compact planning is achieved by tight volumetric packing, whereby manipulation of room heights is used for spatial economy. The complexity of this project affords the most rational site exploitation while achieving luxury in the simplicity of the principal public space of the house's *piano nobile*. By composing the house "in the cube," as it were, Zloković adopted a method of *Raumplan* that is characteristic of houses by Loos. Even the names of rooms are associative: "musical niche" in the Zaborski house paraphrases "musical room" of the Moller house by Loos (Vienna, 1928). The Zaborski house was designed in October 1928, the same year the Moller house was built, and it therefore represents an authentic design based on thorough understanding of the most economic and intricate three-dimensional planning, which is in line with, and not a copy of, Loos's *Raumplan*.[24]

Further elaboration of a three-dimensional plan is evident in the house of Jovan and Dragojla Prendić (1932–1933), where Zloković employed the *Raumplan* logic to resolve a dual function of a house in the most economic manner. The program required inclusion of Mrs. Prendić's doctor's surgery, as a function separated from the residential space but integrated into the house. The plan is regulated by *ad quadratum* geometry resting on a modular grid derived from duodecimal division of the site width. The two principal functions—living and working—are geometrically and formally divided by the in-between zones, dedicated to services and circulation. The two programs are of different room heights and are set on different levels, so that the internal staircase, placed in the

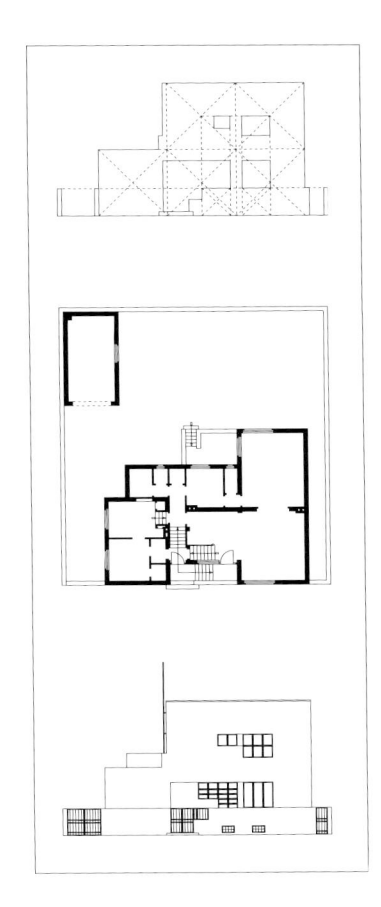

5.7 (opposite page) Milan Zloković, house of Nevena Zaborski, Belgrade, 1928. Elevation with the regulating lines; plan and sections indicating the *Raumplan*.

5.8 Milan Zloković, house of Jovan and Dr. Dragojla Prendić, Belgrade, 1932–1933. Diagram of facade with regulating lines, ground-floor plan, and front elevation.

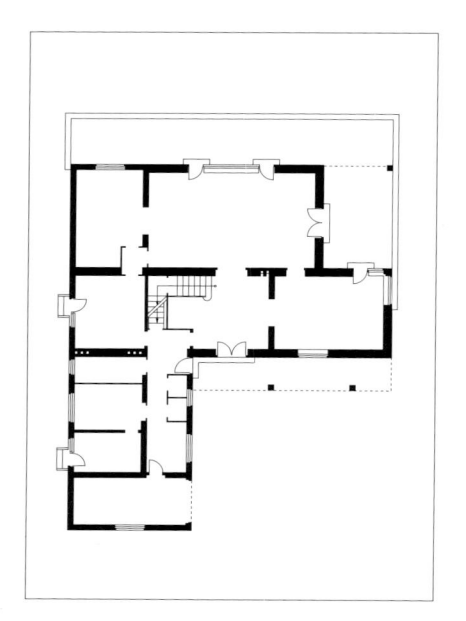

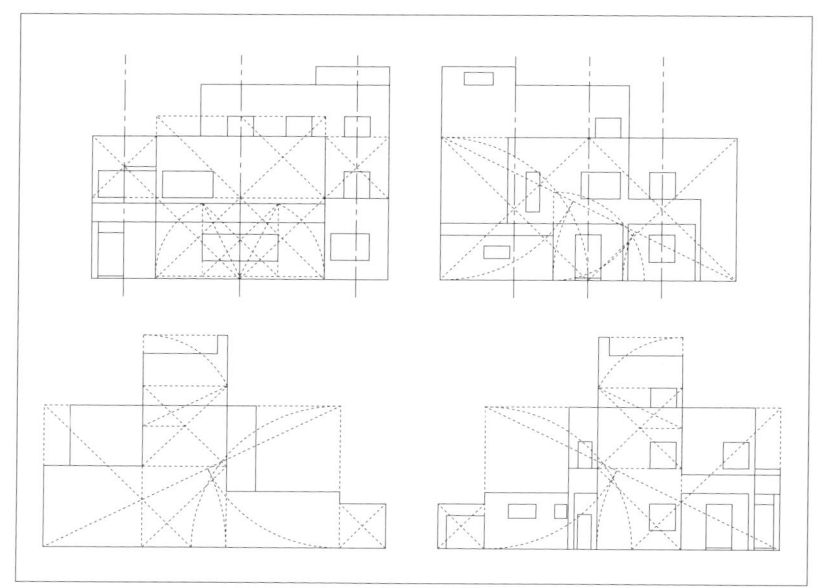

sliver between the surgery and the main hallway, serves both as a divider of the two parts and a point of connection. The circulation zone is reduced to minimum area by utilizing the potential of the stairs to restrict all circulation to vertical interconnection of different rooms. The design seems to follow the rules of the *Raumplan* or spatial plan as explained by Loos's collaborator, the Zagreb architect Zlatko Neumann: "The spatial plan, which is a consequence of different room heights consistently placed on different levels, allows for a vertical tendency of circulation routes, as the shortest and most direct connection between particular rooms . . . , thus creating the most intimate internal connection within the structure of the house."[25] In the same manner, the entrance zone is literally carved out of the body of the house, and the separation of public and private entrances is effectively provided by the change of level within this zone. Despite the restrictions of a tight urban site, the design of the Prendić house, based on the economy of the *Raumplan,* resulted in a spacious and generous living space on the raised ground level, combined with a strictly functional lateral distribution of service and work rooms. The form of the house is uncompromisingly pure, the main body implying a volume of simple cubic dimensions of 10 meters on a side, with the positions of openings corresponding to the central square inscribed on the facade surface.[26]

In the design of the villa of Dragoljub Šterić (1932), built on a large site in the most exclusive residential zone of Belgrade, Zloković attempted to address simultaneously what are usually mutually exclusive spatial concepts, the free

5.9 Milan Zloković, villa of Dragoljub and Vukosava Šterić, Belgrade, 1932. Plan of ground floor; schematic diagrams of elevations with the regulating lines; view from the garden.

flow of internal space toward the garden and the cubic composition of form. This duality is inherent in both the organization of internal spaces and the resulting form of the villa. The functional scheme rests on the traditional layout of interconnecting public rooms on the ground floor and private quarters on the first floor, with serving spaces plugged in as a separate servants' wing. The form follows function inasmuch as there is a clear distinction between the public front of the house, with a forecourt, and the private back of the house, with rooms opening out toward the garden. While on the south-facing side the stepping down of volume and long terraces imply a concept of fluidity, there is no effective Wrightian "destruction of the box," and the form of the villa is self-contained and static. The overall composition of villa Šterić is asymmetric and complex, but it is far from being arbitrary, as Zloković again resorted to laws of geometry to regulate his work. The three-dimensional plan of the house is resolved according to the rules of the golden section, for example the dimensions of the forecourt and consequent regulation of the primary volumetric, the planimetrics of the principal internal spaces, and so on. The general height of the villa corresponds to a half-cube, save the protruding volume of the top floor, the height of which is also regulated by the golden section. The cubic shape of the villa is reinforced by the use of color, which was studied in a large-scale wooden model painted in black, white, and gray in a neoplasticist manner. The use of color is subtle, in that it not only accentuates the relation of the wall to the openings but also hides the regulating lines, which are, nevertheless, essential to the design.

In each of these houses, as well as in other examples of small-scale residential projects such as the villa of Bruno Mozer in Zemun (1929–1931) and the small blocks of flats in Neimar (1932), Zloković employed what may well be called a one-off design strategy. Each design with its geometric system is autonomous, custom-made as it were, with no modularity developed across the type. Consequently, there is no seriality or standardization of elements, except in the modularity of windows and doors, and the construction is invariably massive brickwork load-bearing walls with some structural elements in reinforced concrete. More standard and economic, although far from standardized, were his designs for apartment buildings. Typically planned on narrow sites in perimeter urban blocks, these would have two rental apartments per floor, each with two principal rooms at the front, the central dining room in the middle, and the service rooms in the courtyard wing. The facade reflected the internal organization, but also the social status of the middle-class tenants. There is no inventiveness in this architecture; it simply followed the standard programmatic requirement with no exploration of the plan or the external appearance, except when the client required some refinement such as the application of cast reliefs. Representative of this line of Zloković's work are the Opel building (1930–1931) and the apartment block in Miloša Pocerca Street (1932), both in Belgrade.[27]

CHAPTER 5 **DEPARTURE**

In his subsequent projects for public buildings with complex technological programs, however, Zloković shifted toward the structured rationalization of architectural concept and design method as the dominant strategy. It can be argued that in resolving the composite structure of buildings such as a hotel, a hospital, or a school, he erased the boundaries, or rather minimized the distinction, between the aesthetic, the practical, and the cognitive functions of architecture. In this, the role of the image of the ship cannot be overlooked. It does not oversimplify Zloković's endeavor to insist on the process of internalization of the aesthetic and logic of the ship in his architectural work; rather it serves to point up the relevance of this appropriation in the context of modernist discourse.

READINESS TO DEPART 5.3

Recurring at the crossover between the point of departure and the endpoint of this research are the points raised in Le Corbusier's book *Vers une architecture* (1923), especially those referring to "eyes which do not see." The cover photograph of the book's first edition shows the long side deck of the ocean liner *Aquitania* (Cunard Line), which directly relates to the central chapter entitled "Eyes which do not see: I. Liners."[28] The same photograph is included as an illustration to the text, of which the caption, entitled "architect's note," serves to point to "the value of a 'long gallery' or promenade—satisfying and interesting volume; unity in materials; a fine grouping of the constructional elements, sanely exhibited and rationally assembled."[29] Le Corbusier considered the steamship to be "the first stage in the realization of a world organized according to the new spirit" and offered it as a point of departure to the "seriously-minded architect."[30]

In the context of the present analysis, Le Corbusier's rhetoric can be understood to be indicative of the emblematic value that might be assigned to the analogous series of photographs of ships taken by Milan Zloković. In 1924 he took a set of photographs of the *Carniola* (Lloyd Trieste), whose captain was his father Đuro Zloković. Even if these pictures primarily do "homage to the work of thought,"[31] they also testify to the young architect's intuitive tendency toward the basic notions of modernity. The choice of ambience and, in particular, the central perspective of the frame in Zloković's picture of father/captain on the deck of the *Carniola* can be seen as directly comparable to Le Corbusier's photograph of the *Aquitania* side deck. "The pictures stand as facts of seeing, as the

5.10   Milan Zloković, Opel apartment block, Belgrade, 1930–1931.

5.11   Milan Zloković, apartment block in Miloša Pocerca Street, Belgrade, 1932.

actual forms of knowledge of things," argues K. Michael Hays: "And their richness may therefore be recognized in terms of their ability to assimilate material and productive values to visual and psychological effects, to convert the qualities of one into the forms of the other, and thereby to reunite the two levels of subjective mental labor and the objective realities of production."[32] In this sense, the photographs of the *Carniola* which Zloković took at the beginning of his career can be seen as being assimilated into the visual and psychological effect of his later architectural enterprise. Yet the process of such an assimilation and appropriation was to be a long and a convoluted one, and it was not until Zloković found the clue to full employment of his intuitive understanding and technical knowledge of engineering and mathematics that his architecture became authentic. Judging by the photographic evidence, it was as late as 1940 that he managed to make a series of images of his own architecture that fully correlate with the ones of the *Aquitania* and the *Carniola* and confirm what is meant by the "house" being correlative to the "ship." These are the photographs of his most notable modernist work, the University Clinic for Children in Belgrade (1933; 1936–1940)—the hospital correlative to the ocean liner.

5.12 (opposite page) Photographs of the ship *Carniola* (Trieste Lloyd) taken by Milan Zloković, ca. 1924. Captain Đuro Zloković on the *Carniola;* ship's deck.

5.13 Milan Zloković, University Clinic for Children, Belgrade, 1933; 1936–1940. Internal space under construction.

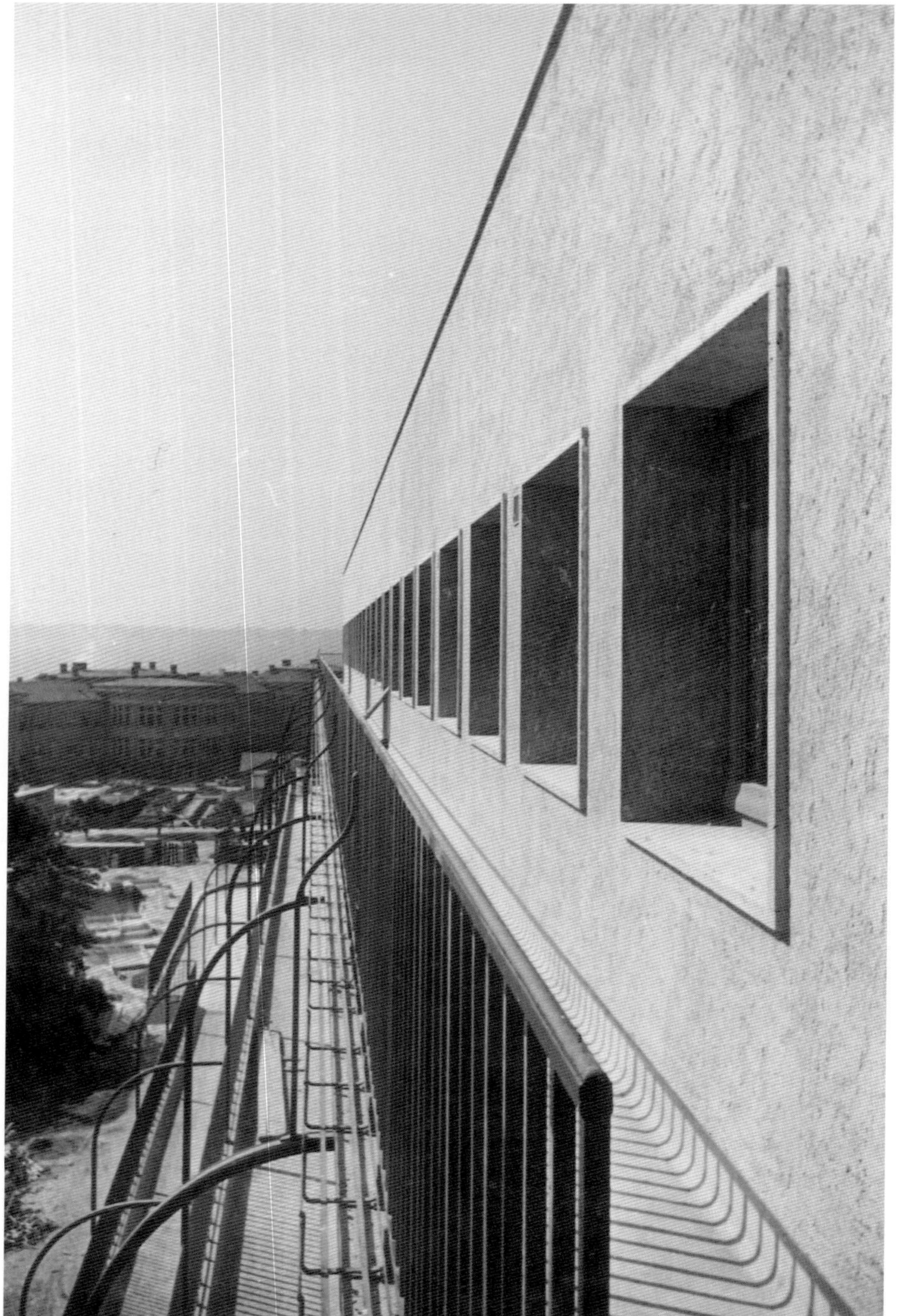

In a section of *The Principle of Hope* called "Building on Hollow Space," Ernst Bloch characterizes modern architecture, and particularly that of the *Neue Sachlichkeit,* as "houses like ships":

These days houses in many places look as if they are ready to leave [*reisefertig*]. Although they are unadorned or for this very reason, they express departure. On the inside they are bright and bare like sick-rooms, on the outside they seem like boxes on movable rods, but also like ships. They have a flat deck, portholes, a gangway, a deck rail, they have a white and southern glow, as ships they have a mind to disappear.[33]

On its surface, this describes the literal appearance of modern architecture, the aesthetic register of buildings or houses "like ships" and the elements of their formal vocabulary that are easily traced back to many an example of the International Style. But, seen within the context of Bloch's philosophy of hope, the text is instrumental in waging a polemic against functionalism as a totally misguided image of utopia and a manifestation of a bourgeois culture of late capitalism. It attacks high modern architecture as historyless and boring, seemingly brave but in fact trivial, hating ornament yet sunk into schematization much more than any of the nineteenth-century historical styles. As suggested in Hilde Heynen's reading of the principal propositions of this text, Bloch dismisses functional architecture, with its "purity" and "honesty," as an illusion, since it remains a social creation that "cannot blossom at all in the hollow space of late capitalism."[34] Furthermore, Bloch sees the openness, transparency, and lightness of modern buildings as being premature in the world of terror "The broad window, full of nothing but outside world, needs an outdoors full of attractive strangers, not full of Nazis; the glass door right down to the floor really requires sunshine to peer and break in, not the Gestapo."[35] The destiny of Zloković's University Clinic for Children sadly supports this thesis. Designed as a modern building in 1933 and constructed in the years leading up to the Second World War, only to be seriously damaged in the bombardment of Belgrade, the Clinic was repaired and finalized in the postwar period, to be poorly maintained and almost neglected in the course of the years to come, and finally disfigured by violent and ignorant interventions in the last decade of the twentieth century. The final blow came with the recent construction of a solid brickwork wall in place of the large-span, transparent glass free facade to the outpatient clinic on the raised ground floor. Could this walling-in signify anything else but the form of barbarian violence as an extreme opposition to the idealistic position of the emancipatory project that Zloković offered in his modernism?

Notwithstanding the significance of Bloch's text as a critique of the empty shell of modern architecture, and particularly that of the *Neue Sachlichkeit,* its

5.14   University Clinic for Children. Top-level terrace.

wording still evokes an elusive image of architecture's intriguing potential. This potential is inherent in the qualifications expressed by Bloch: modern architecture is *reisefertig,* it has "a mind to disappear," it uses abstract technology. It is precisely these qualifications that could apply to the University Clinic for Children in Belgrade. At first glance the building looks as if it were ready to travel, rather like a ship, with decks, railings, etc. Positioned asymmetrically on one side of the site, the tall freestanding slab, stretched between two perimeter streets, is singular and noncentralized. Its pure and simple form looks perfectly fitted into the length of the site, even though it might have a "mind to disappear" from the existing urban order. In the confused conditions of urbanization of interwar Belgrade, the Clinic acts rather as "a prosthetic apparatus for a crippled and crippling city," in the sense in which K. Michael Hays has written of the Petersschule project by Hannes Meyer.[36]

Another Zloković building, the Health Center in Risan (1938–1941), produces a similar effect in an entirely different environment. As the first large modern building erected in this small town on Boka Kotorska, it stands out tall and odd, contrasting the existing townscape yet strangely relating to the harsh rocky landscape behind. Constructed in the most contemporary building technique of the period, the concrete structure of the Health Center bears traces of the compositional strategies of traditional Mediterranean architecture. The simple pitched roof is designed with regard to the climatic conditions, quite like that of a local house, and the stepped geometry of the retaining walls with the pergola takes its lead from the traditional method of terracing the rocky landscape. But

CHAPTER 5 **DEPARTURE**

the building's functional and formal resolution does not give way to sentimental emulation of the traditional techniques. It is, rather, a case of rationalizing the design concept in conjunction with a thorough understanding of the construction logic immanent in Mediterranean architecture. The uncompromising functionality, strict modularity, and standardization of this architecture clearly manifests the departure from conservatism and sweet traditionalism.

In both the Belgrade clinic and the Health Center in Risan, the interior is composed by the hospital rooms themselves, functionally arranged along the longitudinal axis like ship's cabins, efficiency of planning being imperative for the tight social program budget. The resulting internal planning is pragmatic to the point of being utterly utilitarian, with a highly efficient ratio of circulation to usable area.[37] The consequent structuring of the composition, rather like that of an ocean liner, coupled with Bloch's notion of abstract technology that comes to the fore in the design for a modern hospital, resulted in the characteristic ship-like form. Yet there is more to this architecture than its functional organization, or the mere likeness of its form to a ship. A hidden mechanism can be traced by which it is constructed as both an expression of the epoch and a timeless structure of harmonic proportions. Against the machine aesthetic of "engineering as architecture," Bloch advocated a return to the principles set down by Vitruvius— *utilitas, firmitas, venustas*—which should all come together in a building. Similarly, in the two hospitals Zloković's design contains a critical resistance to the concept of the pure functionalism that is embodied in a humanistic notion of proportional harmony.

5.15   (opposite page) Panorama of Risan with the Health Center by Milan Zloković in the background, period photograph.

5.16   Milan Zloković, Health Center, Risan, 1938–1941. Two views of the building and its site.

The displacement of the center of gravity in Zloković's architectural discourse becomes comprehensible within the framework of his 1930s masterpieces, in which he succeeded in finding a form that was appropriate to their inmost essence, without anything superfluous or excessive. The Hotel Žiča in Mataruška Banja, realized in 1931–1932, is the first in this line of uncompromising designs. Set in the center of the small spa town, the anticontextual and antihistoricist white architecture of the hotel sits uncomfortably within the sleepy settlement of provincial *pensions*. Its functional organization is clear and simple: the double-height restaurant on the ground floor, accommodation units on the first floor, and the open-air cinema on the roof terrace level. The design rests on the logical distribution of functions, plain cubic treatment of the primary form of the building, and consistent modularity of the structural system and window and door apertures. As a period critic, Đurđe Bošković, noted, the hotel's "simplicity, calm surfaces, harmonic proportions, and rhythm of apertures represent the right model to which a contemporary architecture aims today."[38] And, quite like a ship, this building, with its flat roof terrace deck, cinema screen rigging, projection cabin navigating bridge, and smooth hull with rigorously arranged cabin windows, bids farewell to the town it leaves behind. In times to come, however, the natives took firm hold of the departing hotel, drastically reconstructing it in the 1960s and thus mooring it permanently to the backwater of their commonplace.

With another building of exceptional purity and clarity of geometric system, Zloković shifted the margins of the Serbian provincial townscape. In the Primary School in Jagodina (1937–1940), the point of departure and the route to an

5.17 (opposite page) Aerial view of Mataruška Banja, period photograph.

5.18 Milan Zloković, Hotel Žiča, Mataruška Banja, 1931–1932. View of the rear facade, view of the facade toward the park circus, and detail of the colonnade.

abstract aesthetic are somewhat different from those of the Hotel Žiča. In this building his explorations focused on the radical minimization of a number of constituent elements, and subsequent restraint in the use of expressive means. The whole design of the school rests on the consistent application of the modular grid, in both planning and the structural system and in formal resolution of the primary form and each individual element of the facades. From the street, the building appears as a half-cube block of smooth white walls, with no secondary surface articulation whatsoever. In the articulation of the facades, Zloković renounced all but the standardized window module and its expressiveness as a sharp cutout from the solid wall surface. By limiting himself to the surface, he took on the task of constructing a series of interrelated two-dimensional images of a totally abstract aesthetic. To do this, he made use of a discontinuous modular grid made up of a basic window type, the rectangular figure with width-to-height ratio of 9:4, and the reinforced concrete structural elements framing the opening. Such a closely knit grid enabled him to alternate brick wall infill, for example for parapets, with window openings all across the facade surface, and a subsequent free composition of the building image. By relating the basic rectangular figure to the geometric construction of the classic $1{:}\sqrt{5}$ rectangle, Zloković harmonized not only the various types of window and door openings but also the correlation of elements and the overall form of the building. Furthermore, inherent in the logic of the continuous trabeated-frame grid is a flexibility in manipulating the fenestration, which allows the volumetric character of the space behind the facade surface to be expressed. The fenestration of the main entrance facade clearly shows the variation of single- and double-height spaces of the internal volumetric.

    The architectural conception of the school in Jagodina may be seen as a distant reflection of the contemporary development of the Italian rationalist movement.³⁹ With no ambition to overrate the possible line of influence, I would still argue that Zloković's school bears some relation to the "canonical work of the Italian Rationalist movement" (Kenneth Frampton), the Casa del Fascio in Como by Giuseppe Terragni (1932–1936), especially in the use of regulating lines. However, even if this were a source of inspiration, it has to be seen in the context of Zloković's rigorous selection of design references. In this sense, his list of illustrations for a lecture he gave at the Faculty of Architecture is indicative, for he proceeds from the images of a steam engine, hangars, and the ship *Normandie* to the architecture of skyscrapers, including Le Corbusier's scheme for Buenos Aires, to pictures of an apartment building in Milan by Pietro Lingeri and Giuseppe Terragni, and finally to the Casa del Fascio in Como.⁴⁰

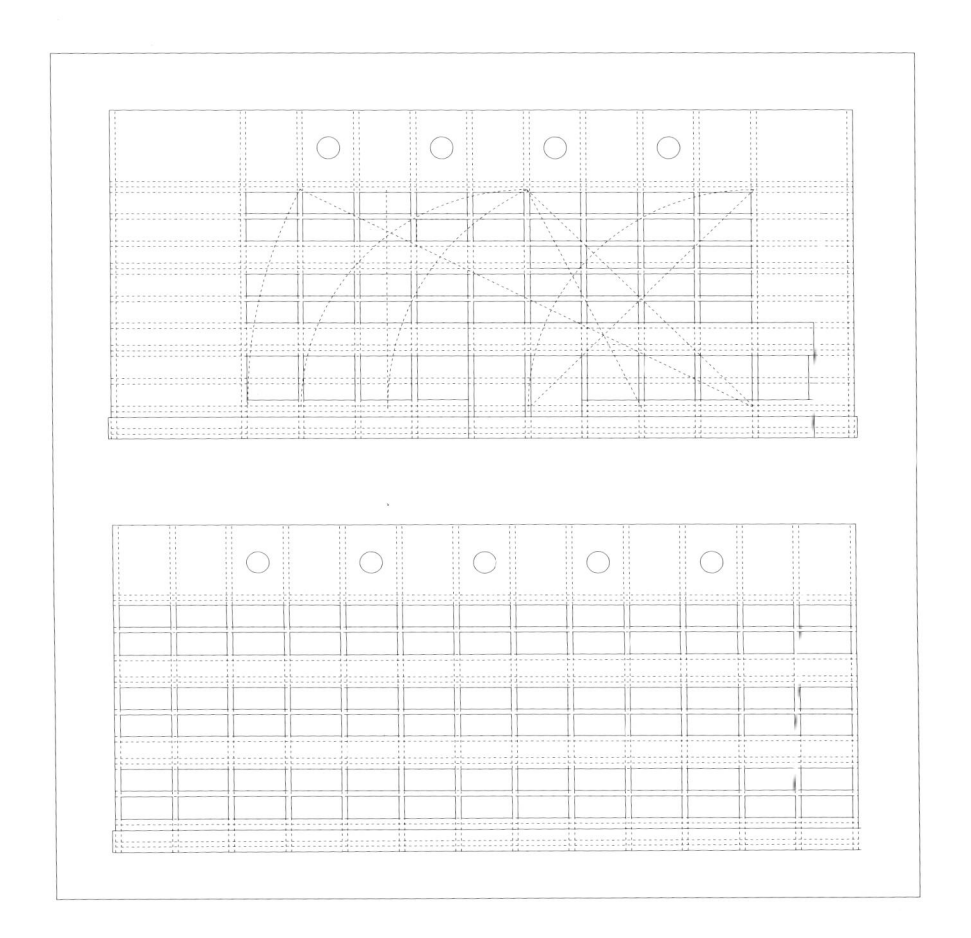

Another vague reference to Terragni, this time the Novocomum block in Como (1927), springs to mind when reviewing Zloković's design for Commerce Hall in Skopje (1933–1935). It has to do with the broad field of reference con-

5.19 (opposite page) Milan Zloković, Primary School, Jagodina, 1937–1940.

5.20 (opposite page) Primary School in Jagodina under construction.

5.21 Schematic diagrams of the elevations of the Primary School in Jagodina with regulating lines.

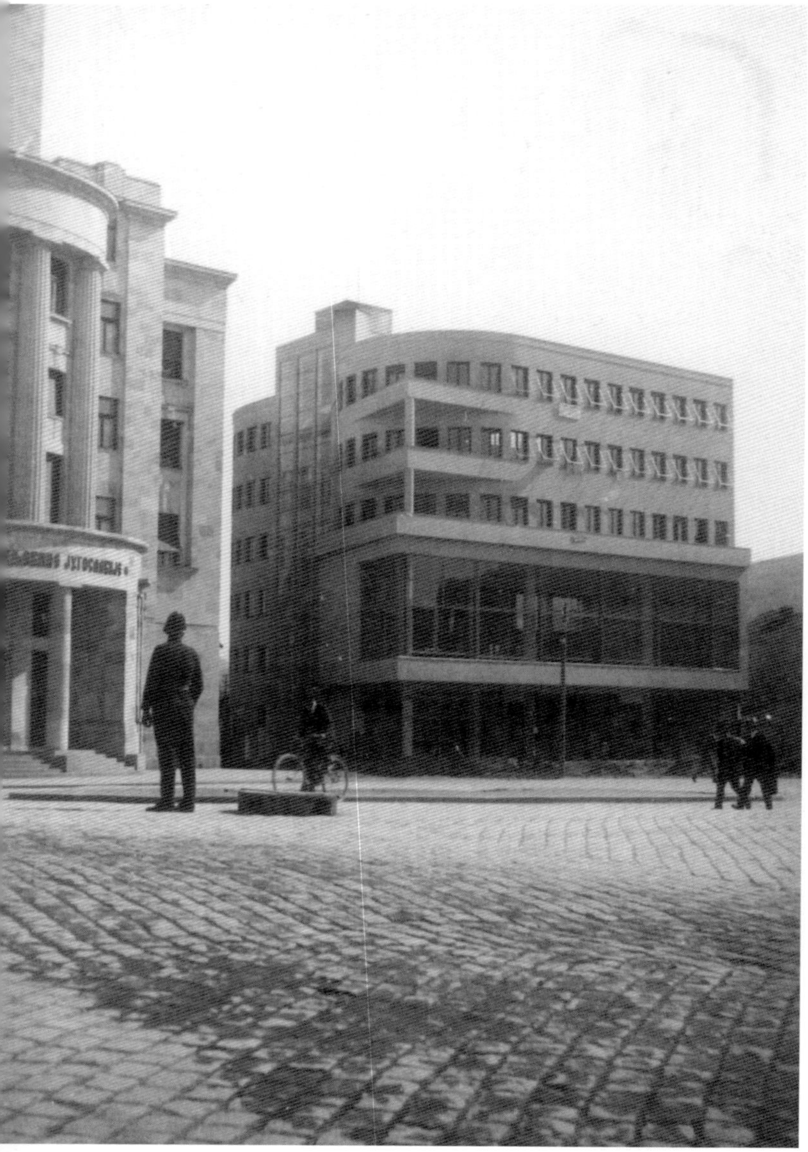

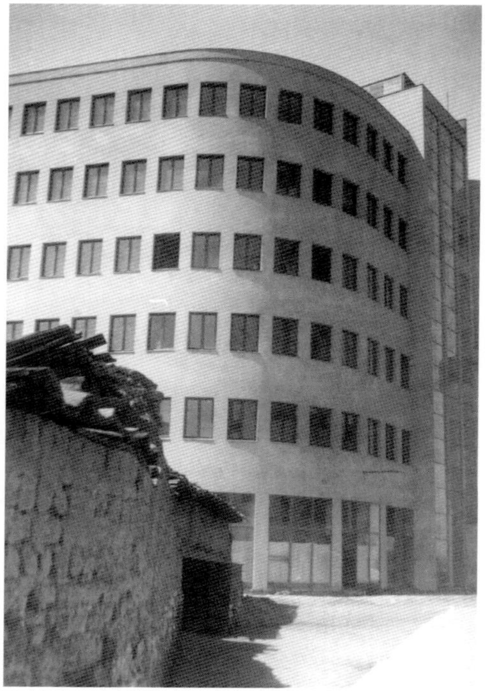

necting the architectures of Ilya Golossov's Club Žnjev in Moscow (1929), Terragni's Novocomum in Como, and Commerce Hall in Skopje. The interplay of cylindrical and cubic volumetric characteristics of all three buildings reduces to what Reyner Banham wrote of Novocomum: "Nothing could be more period and dated than the edgy alternation of bull-nosed and sharp-arrised corners that contribute most of the visible 'architecture' of the exterior."[41] Nevertheless, Zloković's building is one of the most innovative works of Serbian modernism in architecture, primarily in its bold manipulation of the concrete structural framework on which the composition of the building depends. By superimposing the heavy mass of the upper floors on the "suspended," double-height mezzanine volume clad in its wide-span transparent glass facade, Zloković inverts the traditional understanding of structural hierarchy.[42] And this is done in full consciousness of functionality, for the public areas in the lower floors are open and transparent, while the offices are organized in keeping with the strict, almost regimental order of window openings on the upper floors. In the less prominent part of the building at the back, the structure is integrated into the curved facade wall, thereby acting as a framework for the totally serialized fenestration. The resulting appearance is one of a pure abstract aesthetic, with no concessions to period stylization.

In these buildings, Zloković gradually developed a body of work that manifestly upheld the processes of abstraction and rationalization as the results of modernization and the consequent shift from the concept of subjectivity, as K. Michael Hays argues in his study of the shift from the humanist position of the modern subject: "seriality, the renunciation of narrative time, the disprivileging of the purely visual, and the thematization of incompleteness and uncertainty are aesthetic corollaries of the disenfranchisement of autonomous individualism."[43] The buildings and construction processes of Zloković's 1930s masterworks can be seen in this sense as having renounced narrative and disprivileged the purely formal or visual aspect of architecture, yet as having retained the concept of harmony and proportion as the form of protracted humanism.

In his last paper, on modular coordination, published in the year of his death, Zloković left a testamentary note concerning his design of the University Clinic for Children in Belgrade.[44] In a short and cryptic paragraph he points specifically to the Clinic as an example of consistent modular collimation, and writes: "From 1927 onward, the study of the convenience of modular measures in architectural design, especially adapted for public buildings, has continually been useful in ascertaining the determining procedure of composition." While the only comment concerning the Clinic's composition is that the stepped volumetric of the building is a consequence of the requirements for the therapeutic wards, the character of the building is explained numerically as a function of a modular grid. He specifically notes the combination of the continuous modular

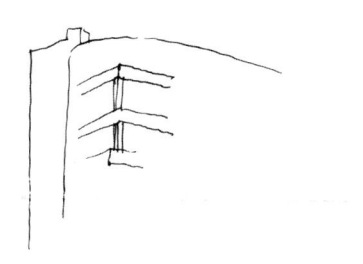

5.22 (opposite page) Milan Zloković, Commerce Hall, Skopje, 1933–1935. View from the main square and view of the rear facade.

5.23 Commerce Hall, Skopje. Zloković's sketches of the corner volume.

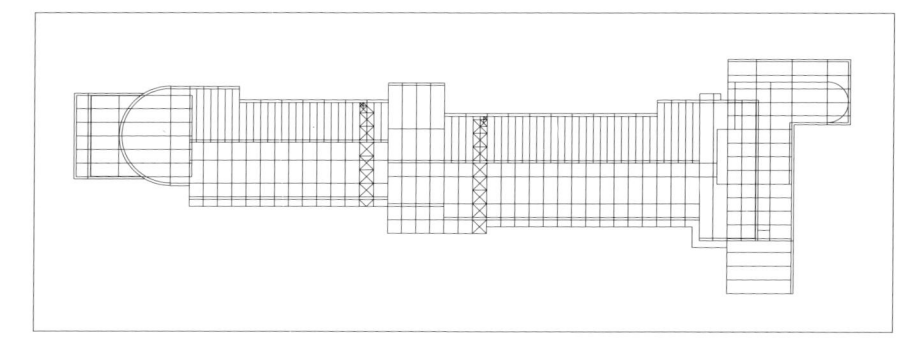

system in the longitudinal direction and the discontinuous spanning system between the structural brickwork walls in the transverse direction. The continuous axes are ordered in the rhythm of 3 × 2 meters and 2 × 3 meters, i.e., in 6-meter intervals, while the dimensions in the transverse direction are variable (8, 6, and 5 meters in the stepped segment, and 6.5 meters beyond). The text is supported by a diagram of the relevant portions of the plan in which the resulting harmonic modular correlations of 60M (6 meters) to 60M/2, 60M/3, 60M/6, and 60M/12 are shown graphically. What I would attempt to demonstrate here is that when the composite plan of the Clinic is reconstructed following these fragmentary diagrams, as I have done for this research, the whole design clearly appears to follow from the application of consistent modular collimation.

On the facades, the effect of the all-dominating module appears to result from the interplay of the plain wall surface and the standardized and serialized window and door openings. The basic window type consists of two elements cut out from the wall surface and lined with slightly protruding stone slab frames: the window and the *Oberlicht*.[45] Such a window unit is repeated in the hospital rooms, with the *Oberlicht* window opening around the horizontal axis providing the necessary minimum of ventilation and light, while the lower part is a standard double window type with Eslinger wooden blinds.[46] The balcony doors are directly derived from this basic type, using the standard window

CHAPTER 5 **DEPARTURE**

5.24 (opposite page) Milan Zloković, University Clinic for Children, Belgrade, 1933; 1936–1940. Model.

5.25 (opposite page) University Clinic for Children. Schematic drawing of the modular coordination of the composite plan.

5.26 University Clinic for Children. View from Pasterova Street.

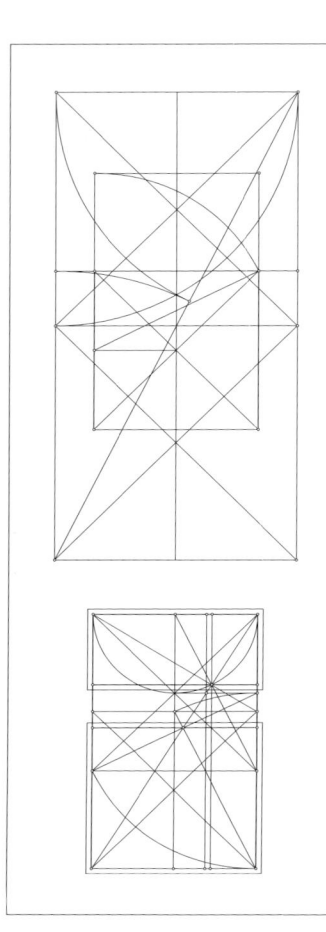

extended downward to the floor level, or the window without the transom where deemed functionally appropriate. Thus, the construction of the window unit is a consequence of pragmatic requirements, but its formal articulation calls for a geometric analysis. The paramount questions are those of the position and the intriguing dimensions of the two openings and the transom between them, as their proportion and modular coordination are clearly determined systematically and consistently throughout.

Starting from the basic modular unit of the facade wall, delineated by the modular gridlines in width and by the top levels of the two floor slabs in height, a rectangle of 1:2 ratio is arrived at. As the width of the window is fixed by the critical structural dimension of the brickwork section of the wall between the openings, the height and position of the two elemental figures had to be found geometrically. Again, it is a theoretical paper by Zloković that offers a clue to the design procedure.[47] As I have attempted to ascertain in constructing a proportional analysis diagram for the building based on Zloković's paper, in the first step the height of the rectangular figure of the facade unit is divided, using the rules of the golden section, in order to determine the main generating line for the construction of the window unit.[48] Thus, the outline figure of the window plus transom is determined by constructing the dynamic rectangle, that is, a rectangle with sides in relation of 1:φ, so that the generatrix divides it into a square and another rectangle of the same proportion. In the next step, the rectangle is further divided following the corresponding theoretical diagram from Zloković's paper, in order to demonstrate that all elements of the window unit can be (or in fact were) arrived at geometrically. Finally, when the dimensions calculated from the diagram are checked against the actual window elements on site, the proportional analysis proves accurate to the point that even the thickness of the framing stone slabs is exactly as it comes from the drawing.

As it unfolds, the proportional diagram departs from the actual object, the Clinic building, and starts to exist as an autonomous theoretical concept. Yet, when it is worked out as the basis for determining the form and exact proportion of the real architectural elements, it starts to relate to the whole structure and its inherent geometric system from which it receives meaning. This is analogous to what Theodor W. Adorno suggested the musical tone does: "The tone receives meaning only within the functional structure of the system, without which it would be a merely physical entity."[49] In designing the Clinic as an efficient "machine for medical treatment" with its structure and elements in spatial harmony of proportion, Zloković chose the middle path between active orientation toward machine technology and humanist principles of autonomy of artistic construction. Bearing the contradictions of being both autonomous and purpose-oriented, the architecture of the Clinic aims at beauty in the sense of Adorno's definition: "Beauty today can have no other measure except the depth to which a work resolves contradictions. A work must cut through the contradictions and overcome them, not by covering them up, but by pursuing them."[50] With regard to the contradictions pursued in Zloković's work—of which complexity and ambiguity of conception are corollaries—the architectural theoretician Aleksej Brkić attempted to explain the underlying reasons:

Firstly, it was because of his sense of the dynamic in spatial events that, by geometric operations, he tried to relate to the supposition of an absolute aesthetic order—which was not so strange, since polyhedral ornament-free modernism simply required a certain aesthetic justification, certain proofs of aesthetic credibility, thus leading to this sort of Euclidean reflection. And secondly, by still following functionalist doctrine, notwithstanding that he would be the first to oppose doctrinaire functionalism with his oeuvre, he attempted to give a practical rationalization for the abstract and purely theoretical regulations in a numerical directive system.[51]

Although it was Brkić who first pointed to the importance of synthetic analysis, his reading here seems somewhat simplified. The reasons noted in the passage above imply Zloković's resistance to the fundamental notions of modern architecture, and the need to justify its "plainness," but his architecture defies such a reading since spatial harmony is inherent in it, not something added on. I would suggest that in maintaining a distinction between the pragmatic-technical role of the engineer and the artistic-poetic role of the architect, Zloković, like Le Corbusier, who was certainly one of the figures most influential in his development, held to the duality inherent in the modern aesthetic. For him geometry and proportion were inextricably linked to architecture, in the sense of a passage of *Une maison—un palais* that Zloković underlined in his own copy: "Géométrie, production normale de notre cerveau et *fatale,* parce que participant à un rythme universel, nous avons reconnu que ce rythme était géométrique: figures qui sont *caractères.*"[52]

The architecture of Milan Zloković resists simple interpretation, for it is abstract and rational yet deeply humanist, functional and pragmatic yet artistic, self-referential in its modernity yet relating to the classical rules of proportion. Similarly, no single point of reference can be taken as a paradigm for his work, yet his architecture corresponds to the principal notions of the zeitgeist and to the contemporary practice of modernity. This is most notable in his last realized project in the period between the world wars, the Fiat Automobile Service building in Belgrade (1939–1940). At a time when modern architecture was retreating in the face of the rising monumentalism and totalitarianism, Zloković produced this model of a nonnarrative functionality and formal restraint. The building is made up of three separate sections with diverse programmatic requirements: an

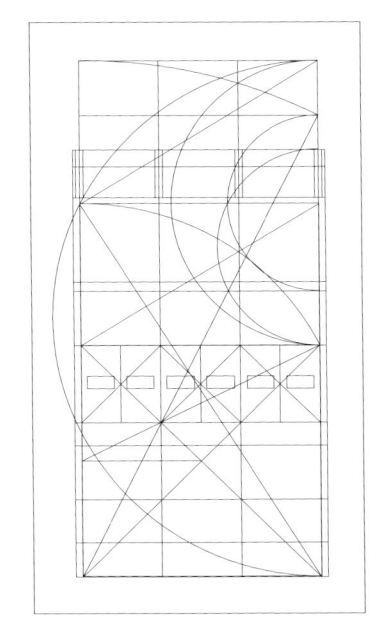

5.27 (opposite page) University Clinic for Children. Proportional diagrams of the facade section, and of window and *Oberlicht*.

5.28 University Clinic for Children. Schematic drawing of the elevation on Pasterova Street with the regulating lines.

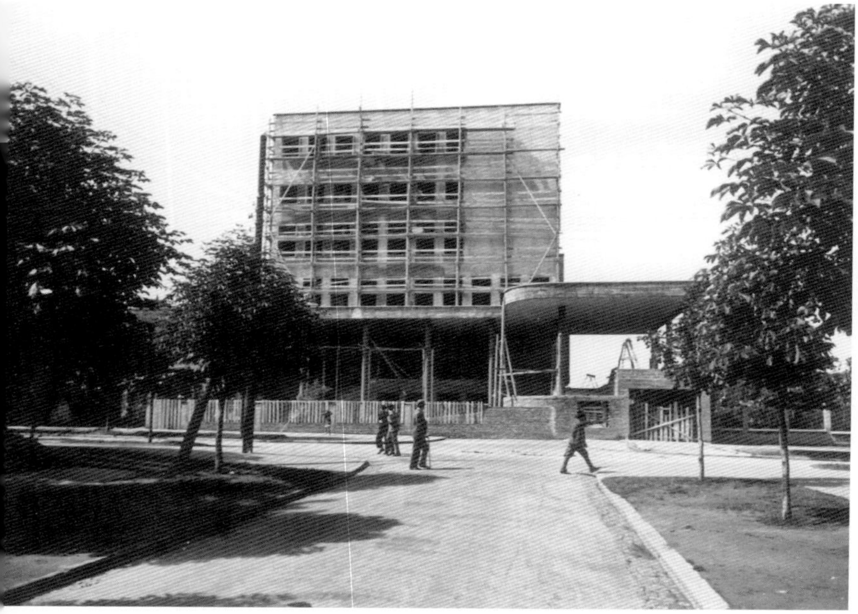
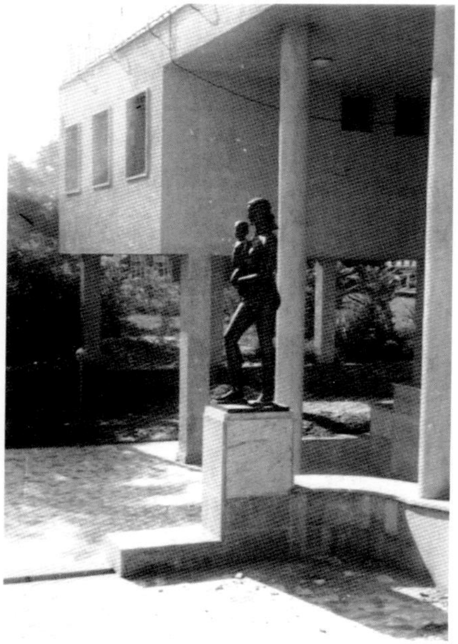

apartment block with the automobile showroom, a garage, and workshops. The composition of the whole was developed according to the need to address separately the different functional, structural, and formal aspects. It was in the resolution of this complexity that Zloković's creative potential burst forth. With no concessions to subjective compositional strategies, he resolved the complex as the result of a sequence of production processes, although in full correspondence with site-specific issues. The garage and the workshops are organized as a production line along the side street. The most prominent part of the building with the showroom takes up the exposed corner position, while the southwest-facing residential section forms the orderly frontage on the main street. The three parts are accordingly formally articulated as expressions of their respective functional and structural properties, but also as distinct architectural units. The effect of the balanced interplay of functional units expressed as solid and void, i.e., wall and trabeated frame structure, is enhanced by the use of facade materials: red brick cladding for the main body of the building, precast reconstituted stone cladding for the expressed structural frame and foundation of the building, serialized windows and a unified grid of mullions for the large openings. Although he was operating within the usual modernist register, Zloković departed from the pure white aesthetic of his previous works. As much as he was paving a safe white modernist path with the Clinic (which was being finalized at the same time), in the Fiat building he intuitively announced a new direction. It is as if in his last built work of the interwar period Zloković demonstrated his ever-present capacity to question the canon, and readiness to set sail for a new territory to explore.

5.29   (opposite page) University Clinic for Children. View of the building site from Tiršova Street; sculpture by Lojze Dolinar at the main entrance.

5.30   Milan Zloković, Fiat Automobile Service building, Belgrade, 1939–1940. Model.

5.31   Milan Zloković, Hall of the Christian Union of Young People, Belgrade, 1940 (project).

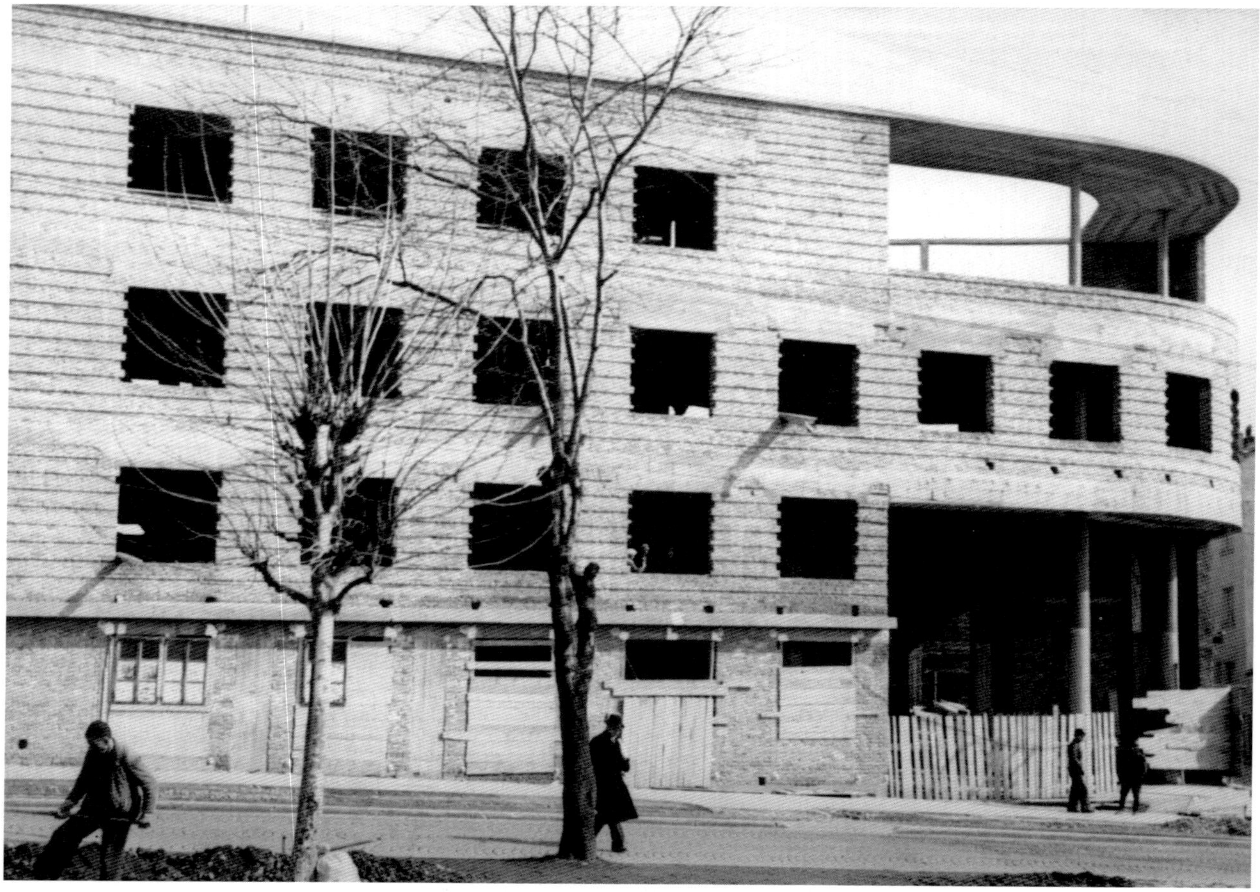

5.32 Fiat Automobile Service building. Building site; detail (contemporary photograph by Milica Lopičić).

VISION

The subjects of modern cultures have telescopes, microscopes, cameras for eyes; microphones, radios, telephones for mouths; ships, trains, cars and planes for legs; and all of these instruments-that-extend-our-grasp for arms.[1]

When the state-of-the-art instruments for astrography were finally installed in the new Astronomical Observatory in Belgrade in May 1932, the whole complex was photographed extensively. All relevant aspects of the complex were systematically covered in film frames zooming in from distant aerial views of the site with the landscape/cityscape in the background, to shots of particular groups of pavilions, to architectural portraits of individual buildings, to close-ups of the astronomical instruments from the interior of the pavilions' domes. It was only recently, when scanning some of these photos to make illustrations for this book, that I found that they were taken and developed by the Photographic Department of the Histology Institute of the Medical Faculty in Belgrade.[2] The Observatory and the Histology Institute both being part of the University of Belgrade at the time, it may have been only practical that the reputable Photographic Department of the Medical Faculty, notwithstanding that it specialized in microphotography, would carry out the task of documenting the architecture and equipment of the new complex.[3] But could there be more than just practical reasons that brought together the photographic laboratory especially renowned for its work in microscope photography with the Observatory being tuned up to embark on the new course in astrography, that of telescope photography?

Founded in 1922 by professor of histology Dr. Aleksandar Kostić, the Photographic Department of the Histology Institute had become the place of excellence for the use of photography in medical research, and particularly that of microphotography. In the preface to his histology textbook for medical students, Professor Kostić wrote that his main aim was to relate closely the morphological histology and the functional characteristics of the shapes being researched. Included in the textbook were over 400 original microphotograms—microscope photographs of histological samples—as the author considered this the most faithful medium for reproduction of the matter observed. In this, he continued, "we follow the modern movement, which wants to create physiological histology from the old descriptive histology."[4] The power of apparatus thus proved decisive, as it gave the power of vision that enabled the practice of modernity. Apparatus, whether scientific, technical, social, or ideological, providing visibility and consequently knowledge, as Michel Foucault has shown with the example of Bentham's Panopticon, is inseparable from power: "to induce . . . a state of conscious and permanent visibility . . . assures the automatic functioning of power."[5]

6.1   (opposite page) Window. (Milan Zloković, Mortgage Bank, Sarajevo.)

6.2   Telescope and astronomer. (Jan Dubovy, Astronomical Observatory, Belgrade.)

When expert professionals of microscope, telescope, and camera photography met at the 1932 Observatory photo session, they sought to document and render visible the new and "objective" reality. In their "being there," or rather in an awareness of their "having-been-there," as Roland Barthes put it, there is, however, something else added to the simple act of recording, which invests the action with more than just a documentary purpose. Notwithstanding that the photographs of the Observatory aimed to represent the flat facts of the new complex, and thus, as Barthes suggested, "must be related to a pure spectatorial consciousness and not the more projective, more 'magical' fictional consciousness," they manifest the intelligibility of a culture of the machine age.[6] The newly built Observatory provided ground for a kind of vision, one based on scientific observation, a vision that was not a revelation but the fact of seeing. And it is the fact, as a truth verifiable from experience and/or observation, that binds the new notion of vision to the new concept of architecture. The modern epoch opened the way to factual vision, as science, technology, and engineering took precedence over style and inspiration. At the Belgrade Astronomical Observatory, the design of the pavilions was by and large determined by the actual physical characteristics of astronomical instruments and requirements for their operation within the physical space of the building. The architecture Jan Dubovy produced there was, thus, architecture after the fact. And in opening up to the scientific content, as Walter Benjamin wrote, the architecture there developed its new forms, the forms delineating the new content.[7]

What the photographs of the Observatory did not show, however, was the absence of the gaze through the telescopes. Although three Zeiss instruments and two Askania refractors all equipped with cameras for astronomical photography were, just then, being put in place, no astrographic work was carried out until some three years later.[8] After being in storage since 1923–1924, when they first arrived in Serbia, the telescopes were not put into full function until 1935, when the first image of asteroids made with the Zeiss astrograph was produced by the astronomer Miodrag Protić.[9] Because of the need to study in detail all the optical characteristics of the apparatus, regular observation was further delayed until the following year. So, concealed in the photographs of the Observatory is the absence of functional vision that the whole major exercise was about. The photographic documentation, therefore, provided false evidence. I would argue that it is precisely the missing facts, primarily the hidden time lag and the absence of functionality, that are crucial for understanding the condition of modernism in Serbia. This takes us to the Lacanian position, as put forward by Joan Copjec:

Contrary to the idealist position that makes *form* the cause of being, Lacan locates the cause of being in the *informe:* the *unformed* (that which has no

signified, no significant shape in the visual field) and the *inquiry* (the question posed to representation's presumed reticence). The subject is the effect of the impossibility of seeing what is lacking in the representation, what the subject, therefore, wants to see. The gaze, the object-cause of desire, is the object-cause of the subject of desire in the field of the visible. In other words, it is what the subject does not see and not simply what it sees that founds it.[10]

If we were also to look at the linguistic message "Omnia in numero et mensura" inscribed on the front facade of the central administration building of the Observatory, and see it as what Roland Barthes called an "anchorage," then "we can see that it is at this level that the morality and ideology of a society are above all invested."[11] This brings me back to Dr. Aleksandar Kostić and his preface for another book, this time not on histology but on human sexuality. As a pioneer in sexology, Dr. Kostić was fully aware of the controversy his book would cause in 1932 when it was first published, as he wrote in his defense: "Everything said in this book is true, and for that reason it is moral."[12] Beauty, also, was widely seen as a corollary to truth, and consequently to morality. "The beautiful is that which is true," lectured architect Branislav Kojić, and he postulated truth and honesty as the main principles of the new architecture. Like Heidegger, we now ask what truth means in terms of architecture, as "it is necessary to make visible once more the happening of truth in the work."[13] None understood this better than Milan Zloković, who made number and measure, modularity and proportional harmony, structural rationality and abstract aesthetic the central regulating systems of his architectural objects. With Zloković truth has a twofold content: one of programmatic and economic facts and of those that come with the mathematical accuracy of the proportional diagram, and the other that is out of reach, the creation, the artistic component of architectural work. Yet some part of truth is always inaccessible, as Copjec points out in quoting Lacan: "I always speak the truth. Not the whole truth, because there is no way to say it all. Saying the whole truth is materially impossible: words fail. Yet it is through this very impossibility that the truth holds onto the real."[14]

In another project contemporary to the Observatory, and on a parallel plane of architectural representation, in the 1929–1930 competition for Terazije Terrace architect Nikola Dobrović had expanded the field of vision. He related it to the cinematographic character of cognition in the modern individual. For him it was, again, vision that had been central in setting out the new urban space of the Terrace which opens to views: "from the aesthetic-technical point the eye of the spectator cannot be allowed to come across any architectural obstacles."[15] Beatriz Colomina has shown how Le Corbusier's vision transformed the traditional architectural thinking about place and inhabitation, and argued: "The

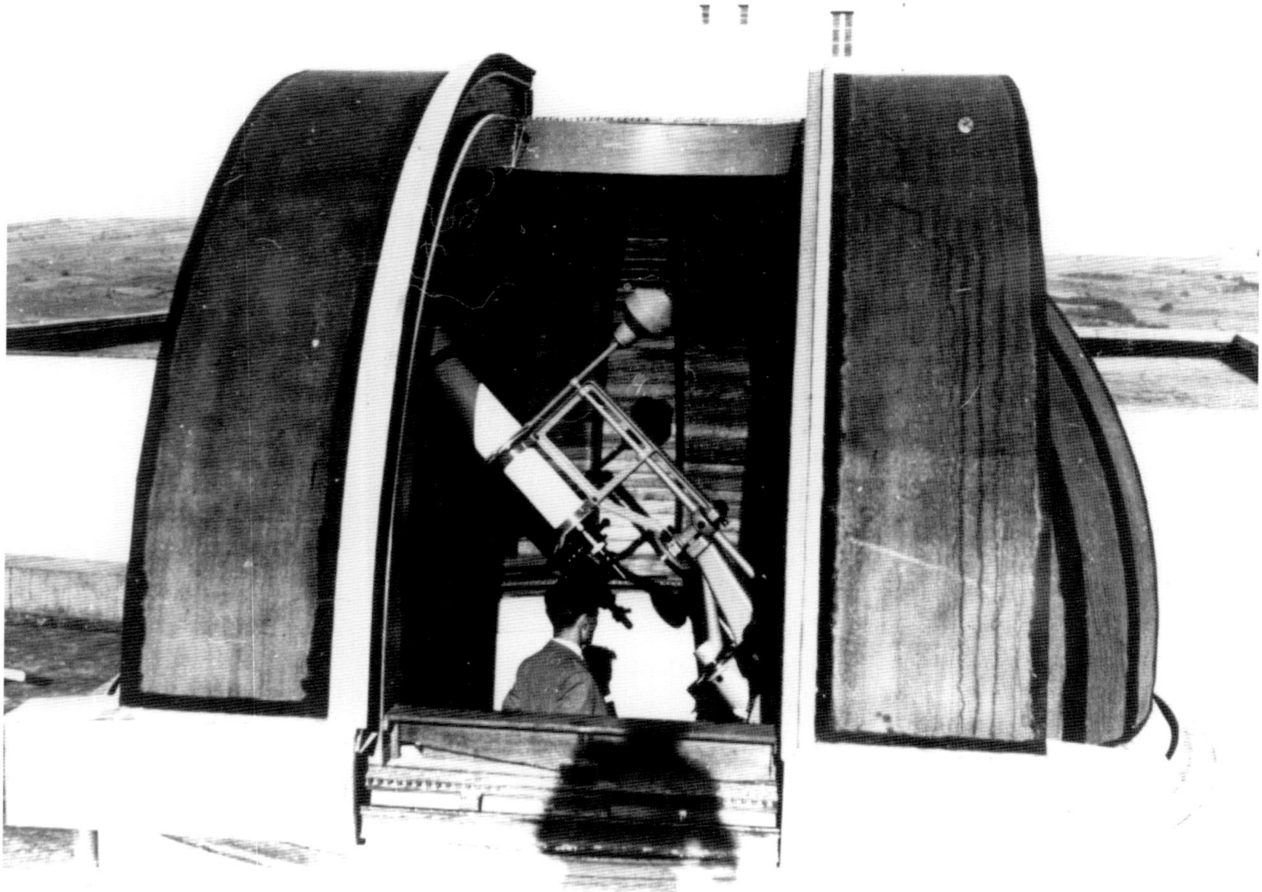

organizing geometry of architecture slips from the perspectival cone of vision, from the humanist eye, to the camera angle."[16] Dobrović well understood what Le Corbusier meant when he wrote: "Architecture is judged by eyes that see, by the head that turns, and the legs that walk. Architecture is not a synchronic phenomenon but a successive one, made up of pictures adding themselves one to the other, following each other in time and space, like music."[17] The space he himself aimed at was effected by Le Corbusier through the architectural promenade. And, as Colomina has shown, that space is the architectural correlative of the space of the movie camera.[18]

Yet, if we look at Serbian modernism, what did vision mean there? To return to Dobrović's spectator, the "mentally and physically worn-out" city dweller of whom he wrote in the 1930s, where did his or her vision end/extend? Did he or she not have to wait another thirty years to become the "homo spatiosus," the new urban individual of the 1960s who perceived and experienced the city as the "color film (macro film) on the Cinemascope of urban prospects"?[19] And even then, in the final act of construction of the Ministry of Defense Headquarters, was it not the architect's vision that remained incapable of being fully effected, and the building thus more of a belated realization of a once-visionary concept? Could we not then propose that it was time lag and incompleteness that were at the very foundation of modern architecture in Serbia? Architecture, as it were, floating in an elusive element of time.

6.3   Observation. (Jan Dubovy, Astronomical Observatory, Belgrade.)

NOTES

Where not otherwise attributed, all translations of quotations from Serbian sources are by the author.

INTRODUCTION

1. P. Morton Shand, "A Note on the New Belgrade," *Architects' Journal* (London), no. 1734 (11 April 1928), p. 504.

2. Reminiscence of Yugoslav architect Mate Baylon, who studied and practiced architecture in Vienna in the 1920s: "I remember also one answer Loos gave to a question posed to him either at one of his lectures or on one of his visits to Holzmeister's studio. Asked what he thought of Le Corbusier, he said: 'Er ist ein Prophet der nach Rückwärts schaut!'" Mate Baylon, "Studije arhitekture u Beču dvadesetih godina" [Studies of Architecture in 1920s Vienna], *Arh* (Sarajevo, 22 May 1991), pp. 56–59.

CHAPTER 1 SHIFT

Epigraph: Le Corbusier, *Journey to the East,* ed. and annotated Ivan Žaknić, trans. Ivan Žaknić in collaboration with Nicole Pertuiset (Cambridge: MIT Press, 1989), p. 35.

1. This voyage proved to be of the utmost importance for Charles-Édouard Jeanneret (later known as Le Corbusier) as an artist and architect. During the journey he kept a travel diary, took many photographs, and filled six *carnets* with drawings and sketches. Extracts from his travel notebooks were first published as articles in the La Chaux-de-Fonds newspaper *Feuille d'avis* during 1911. Of this journey he wrote fondly in many a later publication, e.g.: "I embarked on a great journey, which was to be decisive, through the countryside and cities of countries still considered unspoilt.... I saw the grand and eternal monuments, glories of the human spirit." Le Corbusier, *The Decorative Art of Today,* trans. James I. Dunnett (1925; Cambridge: MIT Press, 1987), p. 206. In 1965, he chose some of the articles, letters, and drawings from this journey for publication in his last book: Le Corbusier, *Le Voyage d'Orient* (Paris: Forces vives, 1966), of which *Journey to the East* is the English translation.

2. Le Corbusier, *Journey to the East,* p. 43.

3. See the inscription on the sketch "Pottery from the Balkans," ibid., p. 17.

4. "But to work, to draw, to understand the full richness that one must give one's work, and the degree of concentration, of transposition, of invention, of re-creation that is required, I settled where no one at that time put his easel—far from the *Grande Galerie.* I was always alone... with the attendants.... The popular arts, pots and carpets at the ethnographic Museum of Belgrade.... What lessons, what lessons! What drawings, conscientiously putting and then answering questions with the precise outline of an eloquent form!" Le Corbusier, *The Decorative Art of Today,* pp. 198, 200.

   Le Corbusier gave two drawings sketched at the Ethnographic Museum in Belgrade to Katarina Ambrozić (curator of the National Museum of Belgrade) when she visited him in Paris in 1963. The drawings are now in the National Museum in Belgrade. The inscription on the drawing of the jugs reads: "dessiné au musée à Belgrade (par Jeanneret) en 1911 (voyage d'Orient), Le Corbusier 21/2/1963." The inscription on the drawing of *gusle* reads: "Gocle, Guclé, Musée Ethnographic Belgrade, dessiné à Belgrade en 1911, Le Corbusier 21/2/1963."

5   Le Corbusier, *Journey to the East*, p. 16.

6   Seldom published, and regarded by Le Corbusier as lost, this drawing is in the National Museum in Belgrade (from Šlomović collection). The inscription on the drawing reads: "Knajewatz de Serbie, Charles Édouard Jeanneret." Milorad Pantović, a Belgrade architect who worked in Le Corbusier's Rue de Sèvres office in 1936–1937, recounted that Le Corbusier was surprised on hearing about this drawing, about which he had totally forgotten, and wondered how it had got to the National Museum in Belgrade. Milorad Pantović, "Atelje L. C.—Rue de Sèvres 35," *Arhitektura urbanizam* (Belgrade), no. 35–36 (1965), pp. 80–81.

7   Le Corbusier, *Journey to the East*, p. 15.

8   According to Milorad Pantović, Le Corbusier said that he gave the jug and "all those things" to his mother. Pantović, "Atelje L. C.—Rue de Sèvres 35," p. 80.

9   Le Corbusier, *The Decorative Art of Today,* p. 34. In the conclusion of the caption Le Corbusier writes: "This story from the land of fine culture and imperishable art contains one of the most powerful lessons to be learnt today: evolution due to economics is inexorable and irresistible; regret is useless; poetry which seemed immortal is dead; everything begins again; that is what is fine and promises the joys of tomorrow." Ibid., p. 35.

10 Ibid., p. 207.

11 *Putevi* (Belgrade), Summer 1924, p. 123.

12 "In intention the modern city was to be a fitting home for the noble savage. A being so aboriginally pure necessitated a domicile of equivalent purity; and, if way back the noble savage had emerged from the trees, then, if his will-transcending innocence was to be preserved, his virtues maintained intact, it was back into the trees that he must be returned." Colin Rowe and Fred Koetter, *Collage City* (Cambridge: MIT Press, 1978), p. 50.

13 After his visit in 1911, Le Corbusier never returned to Belgrade. Although his work was well appreciated by Belgrade architects, it was not until 1952 that they had the opportunity to see a comprehensive exhibition of his projects. See *Le Corbusier: Izložba,* exh. cat. (Belgrade: Savez društava arhitekata Jugoslavije, 1952). For Yugoslav architects, even the excitement of hosting the CIAM 10 conference in Dubrovnik in 1956 was shadowed by the absence of the great master they had always longed to meet. See Oliver Minić, "Neostvareni susret sa Le Corbusiercm" [Unrealized Meeting with Le Corbusier], *Arhitektura urbanizam* (Belgrade), no. 35–36 (1965), p. 84.

14 Branko Maksimović, *Problemi urbanizma* [Issues of Urbanism] (Belgrade: Geca Kon, 1932). "Around 1932/33 I sent a copy of my book *Problemi urbanizma* to my friend E. Weissmann in Paris. He showed and gave that book to Corbusier." Branko Maksimović, handwritten inscription on the

inside cover of his own copy of Le Corbusier, *Način razmišljanja o urbanizmu* [*Manière de penser l'urbanisme*], trans. Tijana Maksimović (Belgrade: Građevinska knjiga, 1974).

15   Cf. Branko Maksimović, "Združivanje i ponovna deoba gradilišta," in *Problemi urbanizma,* pp. 46–53; and Le Corbusier, *Način razmišljanja o urbanizmu,* pp. 71–72.

16   Another *collaborateur* from the famous Rue de Sèvres studio, Jovan Krunić, wrote about Le Corbusier's disgust at Belgrade: "When, during my stay in Paris in 1958, I presented him with my booklet *Arhitektura Beograda* [*Architecture of Belgrade*], printed in 1954 and illustrated with photographs of the most important buildings of the old and the new city, leafing through it he just commented: 'Bon dieu comme c'est laid,' as if for fifty years he had borne a grudge from his severe disappointment of 1911." Jovan Krunić, "Sećanje na Korbizjea (11)" [Remembrance of Le Corbusier], *Politika* (Belgrade), 13 June 1995.

17   Branko Ve Poliansky, *Toumbé* (Belgrade: Édition Zenit, 1926). Branko (Valerij) Ve Poliansky was the alias of Branko Micić (1898–1947).

18   Comment from an autobiographical note written by Micić in March 1926 and published in the Slovenian avant-garde magazine *Tank* (Ljubljana, no. 11/2, 1927). Ljubomir Micić (born 1895, Sošice/Jastrebarsko; died 1971, Belgrade) was a poet, critic, and author, founder of the avant-garde movement Zenitism. He graduated in philosophy from the University of Zagreb and was employed as a lyceum teacher until 1922, when he was fired for his Zenitist activities (biographical data based on the literature listed in note 21). He published books of poetry and one "dramatic mystery" before starting the magazine *Zenit,* but later scorned his early output. He was sole owner and editor of *Zenit,* "The International Review for Zenitism and New Art" (1921–1926), and author of a number of Zenitist publications, including *Manifest zenitizma* [Zenitist Manifesto], with Ivan Goll and Boško Tokin; *Arhipenko—Nova plastika* [Archipenko: New Plasticity]; *Antievropa* [Anti-Europe]; *Aero-plan bez motora* [Airplane without engine], etc. After the closing down of *Zenit,* he had to flee Belgrade, and he lived in Paris from 1927 to 1936, where he continued to publish Zenitist works, e.g.: *Hardi! À la barbarie:—Paroles zénitistes d'un barbare européen; Zéniton:—L'Amant de Fata Morgana; Les Chevaliers de Montparnasse; Être ou ne pas être; Barbarogénie le décivilisateur,* etc. He finally returned and settled in Belgrade in 1937, where his activities slowly ceased. In the years after the Second World War he lived in isolation, on the verge of poverty, and produced hand-made "bibliophile notebooks," which he sent to some institutions and to a few of his remaining friends. For an insightful account of Micić's last years, see Irina Subotić, "Sećanja na susrete sa Ljubomirom Micićem" [Remembrance of Meetings with Ljubomir Micić] (1981), in *Od avangarde do Arkadije* (Belgrade: Clio, 2000), pp. 37–44. After his death, a valuable collection of "Zenit's International Gallery of New Art" (including originals by Alexander Archipenko, Wassily Kandinsky, El Lissitzky, Marc Chagall, Robert and Sonia Delaunay, Albert Gleizes, László Moholy-Nagy, Hannes Meyer, and others, many of them signed with dedication to Micić) was found in his flat. The art collection is now kept in the National Museum, while books, letters, manuscripts, etc. are at the National Library in Belgrade.

19   Ljubomir Micić, "Čovek i Umetnost" [Man and Art], *Zenit* (Zagreb), no. 1 (February 1921), p. 1.

20   "'Optimal projection' does not signify ideally structured space of the future, it does not even try to define it, but instead it signifies *movement in choosing* an 'optimal variance' in the overcoming of reality." Aleksandar Flaker, "Optimalna projekcija" [Optimal Projection], in *Poetika osporavanja* (Zagreb: Školska knjiga, 1982), p. 68.

21   For more detailed studies of art aspects of *Zenit*, its publication activities, and Zenitism in general, see Vida Golubović and Irina Subotić, *Zenit i avangarda dvadesetih godina* [*Zenit* and the Avant-Garde of the 1920s], exh. cat. (Belgrade: Narodni muzej, 1983); Irina Subotić, "Avant-Garde Tendencies in Yugoslavia," *Art Journal* 49, no. 1 (Spring 1990), pp. 21–27; Irina Subotić, *Likovni krog revije "Zenit" (1921–1926)* [*Zenit* Magazine Art Circle, 1921–1926] (Ljubljana: Znanstveni inštitut Filozofske fakultete, 1995); Irina Subotić, "Likovno stvaralaštvo u časopisu 'Zenit'" [Art in *Zenit* Magazine] (1983), "Zašto Zenitizam ne može da bude (samo) srpski" [Why Zenitism Cannot Be (Solely) Serbian] (1996), and "Odblesci ruske avangarde u jugoslovenskom Zenitizmu" [Reflections of the Russian Avant-Garde in Yugoslav Zenitism] (1997), all reprinted in *Od avangarde do Arkadije*, pp. 26–36, 45–50, 51–57; Vida Golubović and Staniša Tutnjević, eds., *Srpska avangarda u periodici* [Serbian Avant-Garde in Periodicals] (Novi Sad: Matica Srpska; Belgrade: Institut za književnost i umetnost, 1996); Irina Subotić, "Les Avant-Gardes historiques: Dadaïsme, zénithisme et surréalisme," in *Un siècle d'histoire*, exh. cat. (Paris: Musée d'Histoire Contemporaine—BDIC, 1998), pp. 256–265.

22   "It [*Zenit*] often used the term *revolutionary*, yet by its essence it was anticlerical, antibourgeois, antibureaucratic, antitraditional, antiacademic—all in the name of the new: the new art, the new creative expression and language, the new models that would make up the new man in the struggle for humanity, primarily through art." Irina Subotić, "Avangardne tendencije u Jugoslaviji" [Avant-garde Tendencies in Yugoslavia], in *Od avangarde do Arkadije*, p. 13.

23   Ljubomir Micić, "Nova umetnost" [The New Art], *Zenit* (Belgrade), no. 34 (1924), not paginated.

24   Ljubomir Micić, "Savremeno novo i slućeno slikarstvo" [Contemporary New and Premonitory Painting], *Zenit* (Zagreb), no. 10 (1921), pp. 11–12. (Italics in the quotation denote expanded character spacing in the original text).

25   Boško Tokin, in Ljubomir Micić, Ivan Goll, and Boško Tokin, *Manifest zenitizma*, Biblioteka Zenit 1 (Zagreb, 1921), p. 14.

26   *Zenit* (Zagreb), no. 15 (1922), inside of cover.

27   Cf. Boško Tokin, "L'Esthétique du cinéma," *L'Esprit nouveau* (Paris), no. 1 (1920), p. 84; and Boško Tokin, "U atmosferi čudesa" [In the Atmosphere of Miracles], *Zenit* (Zagreb), no. 3 (1921), pp. 2–3.

28   As suggested by Irina Subotić with reference to Julia Szàbo, "La Tour de Tatline et son influence sur l'avant-garde de l'Europe Centrale et Orientale," *Ligeia* (Paris), no. 5–6 (1989), pp. 65–69. Cf. *Zenit* (Zagreb), no. 11 (February 1922), pp. 1–2.

29   Erenburg and Lisicki [Ilya Ehrenburg and El Lissitzky], "Ruska nova umetnost" [The Russian New Art], *Zenit* (Zagreb), no. 17–18 (1922), pp. 50–52.

30   The Yugoslav artists were Mihailo S. Petrov, Vjera Biller, Vinko Foretić Vis, Vilko Gecan, and Jo Klek. A catalogue of exhibited works was published in *Zenit* (Belgrade), no. 25 (1924).

31   Josip Seissel (born 1904, Krapina; died 1987, Zagreb) joined *Zenit*'s circle in 1922, and became one of the most important Zenitist artists under the pseudonym Josif or Jo Klek. In the period 1923–1924 he lived and worked with *Zenit* in Belgrade. He started to study at the Technical Faculty in Belgrade in 1923, but after breaking up with Micić he returned to Zagreb, became Josip Seissel again, and graduated in architecture from the Technical Faculty in Zagreb, in 1929, under Professor Hugo Ehrlich. He was the architect of the Yugoslav Pavilion at the International Exhibition in Paris of 1937, for which he was awarded the Grand Prix and *Légion d'honneur,* and continued his career as architect and urbanist in the postwar period. Member of the Yugoslav Academy of Arts and Sciences (JAZU). See Vera Horvat-Pintarić, *Jo Klek Seissel,* exh. cat. (Zagreb: Galerija Nova, 1978); Irina Subotić, "Jo Klek (Josip Seissel)," in Golubović and Subotić, *Zenit i avangarda dvadesetih godina,* pp. 121–126; Vlado Bužančić, *Josip Seissel* (Bol: Galerija umjetnina, 1989); Irina Subotić, *Seissel/Klek,* exh. cat. (Belgrade: Galerija Sebastian, 1990).

32   Micić, "Nova umetnost," not paginated.

33   For example, although there have been numerous publications on *Zenit*'s avant-garde activities in literature and the visual arts, there is not one systematic work on its architectural discourse.

34   Lajos Kassák, "Arhitektura slike" [Architecture of a Painting], trans. Ljubomir Micić, *Zenit* (Zagreb), no. 19–20 (1922), p. 67.

35   "For me, the three elements with the strongest potentials, for our and for future times, are opening up in the following perspective:
Zenitism: Poetry—Philosophy
Expressionism: Painting—Music
Cubism: Sculpture—Architecture."
Micić, "Savremeno novo i slućeno slikarstvo," p. 12.

36   Cf. Arhitekt P. T., "Novi sistem građenja" [New System of Construction], *Zenit* (Belgrade), no. 34 (1924); Walter Gropius, "Internacionalna arhitektura" [International Architecture], *Zenit* (Belgrade), no. 40 (1926); "Makroskop: Knjige Bauhausa" [Macroscope: Bauhaus Books], *Zenit* (Belgrade), no. 40 (1926), pp. 29–30.

37   [Ljubomir Micić], "Makroskop: Arhitektura" [Macroscope: Architecture], *Zenit* (Zagreb), no. 13 (1922), p. 24.

38   [Ljubomir Micić], "† Viktor Kovačić," *Zenit* (Belgrade), no. 34 (1924).

39   Micić, "Nova umetnost," not paginated.

40   Micić, "Savremeno novo i slućeno slikarstvo," p. 12.

41 *Zenit* (Belgrade), no. 40 (1926), front cover. An illustration (section showing a street profile) of Cornelis van Eesteren's winning competition entry for Unter den Linden in Berlin was also published in this issue.

42 Cf. the painting *Pafama*, 1922. Micić translated the name into Serbo-Croat as *arbos:* "Arbos is an acronym signifying Zenitist painting materials *ARtija-BOja-Slika,*" or in English, paper-paint-painting. Micić, "Nova umetnost," not paginated.

43 Jo Klek's letter to Ljubomir Micić dated 24 November 1923, in Vidosava Golubović, "Iz prepiske oko *Zenita* i Zenitizma" [From the Correspondence around *Zenit* and Zenitism], in *Ljetopis* (Zagreb: Srpsko kulturno društvo Prosvjeta, 1998), pp. 203–204.

44 Jo Klek's letter to Ljubomir Micić dated 24 August 1923, in ibid., p. 202.

45 Jo Klek, *Reklame,* illustration accompanying the text from ABC, "Moderna reklama," *Zenit* (Belgrade), no. 34 (1924). Also see Irina Subotić, "Tipografska i likovna rešenja *Zenita* i zenitističkih izdanja" [Typographic and Artistic Layout of *Zenit* and Its Publications], in Golubović and Tutnjević, eds., *Srpska avangarda u periodici,* pp. 443–454.

46 Photographs of Hannes Meyer's Theatre Co-op published in *Zenit* are *La Rêve Co-op* and *La Commerce Co-op, Zenit* (Belgrade), no. 37 (1925); and *Le Théatre Co-op, Zenit* (Belgrade), no. 39 (1926).

47 Jo Klek, *Nacrt za Zeniteum,* published in *Zenit* (Belgrade), no. 35 (1924).

48 Ješa Denegri, "Likovni umetnici u časopisu *Zenit*" [Artists in *Zenit*], in Golubovic and Tutnjević, eds., *Srpska avangarda u periodici,* pp. 431–442.

49 Subotić, "Jo Klek (Josip Seissel)," p. 122.

50 Title of a lecture Lissitzky gave at the Moscow Inkhuk (Institute of Artistic Culture) in 1921. See Camilla Gray, *The Great Experiment: Russian Art 1863–1922* (London: Thames and Hudson, 1962), p. 248.

51 Jo Klek, *Krčma,* published in *Zenit* (Belgrade), no. 34 (1924). Curiously, the reproduction of this painting is "assemblaged" next to Maxim Gorky's text entitled "Regarding the Revolution."

52 Piet Mondrian, quoted in Reyner Banham, *Theory and Design in the First Machine Age* (New York: Praeger, 1960), p. 152.

53 Jo Klek, *Vila Zenit,* published in *Zenit* (Belgrade), no. 36 (1925).

54 Cf. Beatriz Colomina, "Publicity," in *Privacy and Publicity: Modern Architecture as Mass Media* (Cambridge: MIT Press, 1996), pp. 140–199.

CHAPTER 2 **CONSTRUCT**

1   The first project for the house was submitted to the Belgrade City Council in April 1927, the amended project to which the house was built was resubmitted in October 1927, and the house was constructed in the period between July 1927 and December 1928.

2   "'The characteristic accessories of a photographic studio in 1865 are the pillar, the curtain, and the pedestal table. Posed there, leaning, seated, or standing up, is the subject to be photographed: full-length, half-length, or bust. The background is filled, according to the social rank of the model, with other paraphernalia, symbolic and picturesque.' ... Gisela Freund, 'La Photographie au point de vue sociologique' (manuscript, p. 106).—The pillars: emblem of a 'well-rounded education.' Haussmannization." Walter Benjamin, *The Arcades Project,* trans. Howard Eiland and Kevin McLaughlin (Cambridge: Belknap Press of Harvard University Press, 1999), p. 677 [Y4,4].

        Analogous photographic situations stem from the commercial use of modern architecture in fashion photography of the nineties. A series of stylish black and white fashion advertisements, photographed by Steven Meisel, use famous modern houses as a backdrop to sell frocks of style. In these photographs, the Maison de Verre in Paris by Pierre Chareau and Bernard Bijvoet (1933) or Villa dall'Ava by Rem Koolhaas (1992) is set behind the supermodel Linda Evangelista posing in Gianfranco Ferre evening gown. The full-length model is leaning against the emblematic modernist architectural element, steel staircase or concrete column, used as a symbolic background to support the implied social rank of the hypothetical dress wearer. Similarly, one of the best examples of British modern architecture, the Penguin Pool in the London Zoo by Berthold Lubetkin and Tecton (1933), serves the new Brit fashion design, giving the right styling to the advertisement for a little black suit by Paul Smith (photograph by Hugh Hales-Tooke).

3   Having already been responsible for more than ten built houses and apartment buildings, and becoming a chartered architect in 1926, Milan Zloković set himself to building his own house, and more importantly to stabilizing his architectural position. Three sets of drawings for the house were consecutively submitted to the Belgrade City Council, the first one being for another site which was soon to be given up. The building permit was originally given for the second set dated April 1927, which shows an awkward house with a hipped tiled roof of deep eaves over a plain body of the building set on a rusticated stone base, and a symmetrical arrangement of double windows with wooden shutters opening outward and classicizing stone balustrade. The project aimed at a Mediterranean style, not at the Mediterranean type. It was soon to be drastically reformulated in the changed project, the third set of drawings, which was endorsed in October 1927 and according to which the house was finally built. (Original projects in the Historical Archive of Belgrade.)

4   Cf. Massimo Cacciari, *Architecture and Nihilism: On the Philosophy of Modern Architecture* (New Haven: Yale University Press, 1993).

5   "Further on comes a very characteristic extract ... from *L'Art de la photographie* (Paris, 1862), by Disderi, who says, among other things: 'In making a portrait, it is not a question only ... of reproducing, with a mathematical accuracy, the forms and proportions of the individual; it is necessary also, and above all, to grasp and represent, while justifying and embellishing, ... the intentions of

nature toward this individual' ... Gisela Freund, 'La Photographie au point de vue sociologique' (manuscript, p. 108)." Benjamin, *The Arcades Project*, p. 677 [Y4,4].

6   The invention of the new technique of the daguerreotype, which was officially announced on 19 August 1839 at the Académie des Sciences in Paris, reached Belgrade less than a year later: "Of special interest is the information reported in *Srbske narodne novine* [The Serbian Popular Newspaper], dated 12 May 1840, which states that Dimitrije Novaković made a daguerreotype of Belgrade." The first photographs (i.e., calotypes) of Belgrade were made in 1850 by the great pioneer of Serbian photography, Anastas Jovanović. By the end of the nineteenth century photography was gaining widely in popularity, and in 1901 a "First Exhibition of Amateur Photography" was held in Belgrade (thirty-five photographers exhibited their works). Milanka Todić, *Istorija srpske fotografije, 1939–1940* [The History of Serbian Photography, 1839–1940] (Belgrade: Prosveta, 1996); quotation from p. 195.

7   M.B., "Izložba beogradskog Foto-kluba" [The Exhibition of the Belgrade Photo Club], *Srpski književni glasnik* (Belgrade) 28, no. 2 (1929), p. 157.

8   On the relationship of photography and avant-garde art in Serbia, see Milanka Todić, "Nikola Vučo: Fotografija i nadrealizam u Srbiji" [Nikola Vučo: Photography and Surrealism in Serbia], in *Nikola Vučo* (Vienna: Muzej primenjene umetnosti u Beogradu and Österreichisches Fotoarchiv am Museum moderner Kunst Wien, 1990), pp. 71–83; Milanka Todić, "Fotografija i avangardni pokreti u umetnosti: Zadržano bekstvo nadstvarnosti" [Photography and the Avant-garde Movements in Art: The Captured Escape of Superreality], in Vida Golubović and Staniša Tutnjević, eds., *Srpska avangarda u periodici* (Novi Sad: Matica Srpska; Belgrade: Institut za književnost i umetnost, 1996), pp. 455–463; and Milanka Todić, "Fotografija i avangardni pokreti u umetnosti" [Photography and the Avant-Garde Movements in Art], in her *Istorija srpske fotografije, 1939–1940*, pp. 87–96.

9   For example, the photograph documenting *Zenit*'s stand at the "Exhibition of the Revolutionary Art of the West and America" in Moscow, published in *Zenit* (Belgrade), no. 43 (December 1926), p. 9.

10 Cf. "The photographic reproduction of artworks as a phase in the struggle between photography and painting." Benjamin, *The Arcades Project*, p. 673 [Y1a,3].

11 Marko Ristić, "Čeljusti dijalektike" [Jaws of Dialectics], in *Nemoguće/L'Impossible* (Belgrade, 1930), p. 45, referring to André Breton, *Nadja* (Paris, 1928).

12 The Belgrade surrealist movement evolved, in the late 1920s, out of the activity of thirteen main protagonists, the artists, poets, and publicists Marko Ristić, Aleksandar Vučo, Oskar Davičo, Milan Dedinac, Mladen Dimitrijević, Đorđe Jovanović, Đorđe Kostić, Dušan Matić, Branko Milovanović, Koča Popović, Petar Popović, and Stevan (Vane) Živadinović Bor, and the painter Radojica Živanović Noje. Nikola Vučo was also closely associated with the group, and his photographs from the period constituted an important contribution to the development of the movement. The key members had all belonged to a group of Serbian students who received their secondary education in exile in Switzerland and France during the First World War, and were to continue their

studies in the postwar period at the Sorbonne in Paris (e.g., Vane Živadinović, Aleksandar Vučo, and Nikola Vučo all graduated in law from the Sorbonne in Paris during their active surrealist period, Oskar Davičo studied there at the department of Romance languages, and Koča Popović studied law and philosophy). The movement's key figure was Marko Ristić (1902–1984), himself also a publicist and author, who kept in close contact with André Breton and the French surrealists. Although they started with surrealist experimentation in 1924 (in parallel with the Paris circle around Breton), the Belgrade group did not declare their adherence to surrealism until 1930, when they published the almanac *Nemoguće/L'Impossible*. This group was to evolve into one of the most influential and forceful intellectual circles of the postwar communist era; through their largely directive interpretation of cultural history in those years, surrealism was promoted to the status of the principal avant-garde movement in interwar Serbian art, often by playing down the role of other avant-garde movements such as Dada and Zenitism. Although of great significance to the development of Serbian culture in general, surrealism had no direct bearing on architecture. Notwithstanding this fact, I would argue that surrealism acted as an important catalyst of the zeitgeist, and thus had an influence on the perception of the new architectural and urban conditions.

13 Jovanka Iličić, "*L'Esprit nouveau*," *Putevi* (Belgrade), no. 2 (February 1922), pp. 31–32.

14 *La Révolution surréaliste* (Paris), no. 1 (December 1924). See Miodrag B. Protić, *Treća decenija: Konstruktivno slikarstvo* [The Third Decade: Constructivist Painting] (Belgrade: Muzej savremene umetnosti, 1967), p. 11.

15 Ibid.

16 "Naselja prognanih iz raja," *Svedočanstva* (Belgrade), no. 7 (1925), not paginated. In her studies on the relationship of photography and surrealism in Serbia (see note 8 above), Milanka Todić points out the importance of these photographs to the discourse of surrealism.

17 Todić, "Nikola Vučo: Fotografija i nadrealizam u Srbiji," p. 73.

18 As ascertained by Tournikiotis, Loos's essay "Ornament and Crime" first became widely known through its publication in *L'Esprit nouveau,* on 15 November 1920. Panayotis Tournikiotis, *Adolf Loos* (New York: Princeton Architectural Press, 1994), p. 23.

19 Adolf Loos, "Ornament and Crime" (1908), in *The Architecture of Adolf Loos* (London: Arts Council of Great Britain, 1985), p. 100.

20 Kurt Schwitters, "Die Merzbühne" (1919), quoted in Manfredo Tafuri, *The Sphere and the Labyrinth,* trans. Pellegrino d'Acierno and Robert Connolly (Cambridge: MIT Press, 1990), p. 101.

21 This type of blind is formed of thin horizontal wooden slats linked into a continuous flexible surface, which slides from a roller down a metal frame on the outside of the window. Its main characteristic is that the frame has a central joint, which means that the bottom half can be pushed outward, providing effective shading and allowing good ventilation, at the same time enabling a view through the window. These blinds proved excellent in Belgrade's harsh climate, where sum-

mers are extremely hot and sunny and winters windy, snowy, and cold, and were used extensively in this period.

22 It seems certain that no historian of architecture would ever consider putting the blinds into play. In this research, however, they provide us with an insight into another facet of the architect's creative personality. They make him into a living dramatic character in the play staged here. The actual action of going up and down the stairs to push and pull the blind frames so they do something for the photograph puts color in the cheeks of the main character—it makes him real and alive, enabling a transition from the story of a historical figure whose portrait gathers dust in a provincial museum. Even if the blinds' frames were only extended out for the paint to dry, it is worth noting that it was precisely at that point that the majority of the photographs were taken.

23 Adolf Loos, "Architektur" (1910), in *The Architecture of Adolf Loos,* p. 106.

24 Dušan Matić and Marko Ristić, "Uzgred budi rečeno" [Just in Passing], in *Nemoguće/L'Impossible,* pp. 117–136.

25 Ibid., p. 132.

26 Ibid., p. 122.

27 Todić, "Fotografija i avangardni pokreti u umetnosti," p. 93.

28 Dejan Sretenović, "Murder Happens Not Like the Arrow Strikes Not," in *2nd Annual Exhibition Catalogue,* English trans. Srđan Vujica, Aleksandar Bošković, and Branislav Dimitrijević (Belgrade: Fund for an Open Society and Center for Contemporary Arts, 1997), p. 131.

29 Benjamin, *The Arcades Project,* p. 216 [I2,6].

30 Dr. Đorđe Đorđević, Professor in the Medical Faculty, and his wife Krista (cousin of the famous Serbian painter Sava Šumanović), the vice president of the Society of Friends of the Arts "Cvijeta Zuzorić," had been given the existing house by Krista's guardians, her aunt and uncle Mr. and Mrs. Vladimir Matijević, as a dowry. (Information kindly provided from his family's sources by Miloš Jurišić.) The initial project for a radical reconstruction of the old house was made in 1921 by architect Danilo Vladisavljević but was scrapped, as was the second one, made in 1923 by architect Milan Sekulić. The final project to which the house was reconstructed was signed by engineer Vinko Đurović. Being great lovers and patrons of the arts, Krista and Đorđe Đorđević specially commissioned wooden reliefs for the hall in their new Belgrade home from sculptor Sreten Stojanović, whose work and education they had supported from his student days in Vienna and Paris. The house with all its contents was completely destroyed by fire in the German bombardment of Belgrade in 1941. (Original plans for the reconstruction are kept in the Historical Archive of the City of Belgrade.)

31 Reliefs, in wood, stone, and reconstituted stone, were a very important segment in this sculptor's opus. The influence of Antoine Bourdelle, whose student Stojanović was at the Grande Chaumière in Paris between 1919 and 1922, cannot be overlooked. In his study on the sculptor, Lazar Trifunović

notes that the first thing the young artist went to see on arriving in Paris, almost rushing off straight from the railway station, were the old master's reliefs on the Théâtre des Champs-Élysées. Lazar Trifunović, *Sreten Stojanović* (Belgrade: Srpska akademija nauka i umetnosti, 1973), p. 13.

32 Cf. Sreten Stojanović, "Reljefna plastika" [Relief Modeling], in Trifunović, *Sreten Stojanović*, pp. 228–233.

33 Trifunović, *Sreten Stojanović*, p. 26.

34 Sreten Stojanović, "Šta je skulptura" [What Is Sculpture], in Trifunović, *Sreten Stojanović*, p. 214.

35 According to the owner's son, who now lives in the house, the cost of the reliefs almost equaled the total cost of the house.

36 Stojanović, "Reljefna plastika," p. 230.

37 Benjamin, *The Arcades Project*, p. 216 [I2,6].

38 Cf. "The twentieth century, with its porosity and transparency, its tendency towards the well-lit and airy, has put an end to dwelling in the old sense." Ibid., p. 221 [I4,4].

39 Ibid., p. 218 [I3,1].

40 Paintings by Mladen Josić, Ivan Radović, Jovan Bijelić, sculptures by Sreten Stojanović, etc.

41 The reliefs on the facade and in the interior are by Belgrade sculptor Dušan Jovanović.

42 This passage quoted from Hilde Heynen, *Architecture and Modernity: A Critique* (Cambridge: MIT Press, 1999), p. 121. Cf. Ernst Bloch, *The Utopian Function of Art and Literature: Selected Essays*, trans. Jack Zipes and Frank Mecklenburg (Cambridge: MIT Press, 1988), p. 79.

43 Ivan Zdravković, "Savremeni enterijer u Beogradu" [Contemporary Interior in Belgrade], *Umetnički pregled* (Belgrade), no. 4 (1938), p. 122.

44 Le Corbusier on the experience of movement in the Villa Savoye at Poissy, as quoted in Beatriz Colomina, *Privacy and Publicity: Modern Architecture as Mass Media* (Cambridge: MIT Press, 1994), p. 6.

45 For a detailed and documented account of GAMM, see Branislav Kojić, *Društveni uslovi razvitka arhitektonske struke u Beogradu 1920–1940. godine* [Societal Conditions of Development of the Architectural Profession in Belgrade, 1920–1940] (Belgrade: Srpska akademija nauka i umetnosti, 1979), pp. 169–198.

46 The café where this historic union took place was one in which Belgrade intellectual circles of the period often met and fervently discussed issues of art and politics. The avant-garde Weltanschauung, atmosphere, and spirit of Paris café society was brought over to the Russian Tsar by

Marko Ristić and other surrealists, who held their meetings there as well. It is an intriguing coincidence that in the building directly opposite the café Ljubomir Micić once sited the offices of *Zenit* (1924–1926), and that in 1928 the Belgrade Photo Club installed themselves at the same address.

47   As confirmed by the document Matrikel-Nr. 182-1913/14 (courtesy of Universitätsarchiv der Technischen Universität Wien), Dušan Babić finalized his studies with the "2. Staatsprüfung" on 5 May 1923, acquiring the title Ingenieur. I am grateful to Dejana Kabiljo for obtaining this document for me.

48   Kojić, *Društveni uslovi razvitka arhitektonske struke u Beogradu 1920–1940*, p. 171.

49   The Architects Club was formed at the first regular assembly of the Union of Yugoslav Engineers and Architects (UYEA) in Zagreb on 24 May 1920. Membership in the Club required a Diploma in Architecture, membership in UYEA, and two recommendations by Club members. Around 1930, the Club numbered 76 members, of whom 20 were women (altogether, women comprised about 25 percent of the practicing architects in Belgrade at that time). Architects Club regulations were issued in 1930. Ibid., pp. 45–97.

50   Oblik [Form] was formed in 1926 by the artists Branko Popović, Jovan Bijelić, Sava Šumanović, Petar Dobrović, Petar Palavičini, Veljko Stanojević, Marino Tartalja, Toma Rosandić, and Sreten Stojanović. The group was soon joined by Ivan Radović, Ignjat Job, Milan Konjović, Stojan Aralica, Kosta Hakman, Mihailo S. Petrov, and others. Some of the members exhibited their works at the "First Salon of Architecture" in June 1929, and GAMM exhibited their projects with Oblik at the latter's "First Exhibition" at the Arts Pavilion in December 1929–January 1930. Works by the architect Nikola Dobrović, who was not a member of GAMM (but, presumably, came through his brother Petar, painter and member of Oblik), were also presented at this exhibition. Jan Dubovy took part at the "11th Exhibition" of Oblik in Sofia (Bulgaria), in 1934.

51   Zograf was formed in 1927 by Živorad Nastasijević, Vasa Pomorišac, Ilija Kolarović, and Josip Car. Pomorišac exhibited his paintings at the "First Salon of Architecture" (1929), and Kojić took part in the exhibition of Zograf in Osijek in 1931.

52   Branislav Kojić, "Arhitektura Beograda" [Architecture of Belgrade], *Vreme*, 6 January 1929.

53   Branislav Kojić, handwritten notes for a lecture given at the Architects Club in 1929. Architecture Department in the Museum of Science and Technology, Belgrade.

54   The building, designed by Branislav Kojić, was criticized as a nonfunctional gallery space of an arbitrary and tasteless form. Branko Popović, "Umetnički paviljon u Beogradu" [The Arts Pavilion in Belgrade], *Srpski književni glasnik* (Belgrade), no. 3 (February 1929), pp. 209–213.

55   Branko Popović, "Jesenja izložba beogradskih umetnika" [The Belgrade Artists Autumn Show], *Srpski književni glasnik* (Belgrade), no. 4 (February 1929), pp. 298–305.

56   Milan Zloković, "Moderní architektura v Bělehradě," *Stavba* (Prague), no. 12 (1929), p. 182.

57 The exhibition, organized by the Architects Club in Prague, was a sort of return visit following the show of contemporary Czechoslovakian architecture held in Belgrade in 1928, which gave a strong impetus to the development of Belgrade modern architecture.

58 *Výstava sdružení moderních architektů z Bělehradu*, exh. cat. (Prague, 1930), not paginated.

59 Zoran Manević, "Beogradski arhitektonski modernizam (1929–1931)" [Belgrade Architectural Modernism (1929–1931)], *Godišnjak grada Beograda* (Belgrade), no. 26 (1979), pp. 209–224.

60 I am grateful to Rade Bogdanović for providing me with the catalogue of the exhibition and a reference to a newspaper note: J.C., "Výstava sdružení moderních architektů z Bělehradu," *Lidove Noviny*, 11 June 1930, p. 7.

61 Of lesser importance was the "Second Salon of Yugoslav Contemporary Architecture," held in 1933, in which Slovenian architects declined to participate. This was also to be the last exhibition organized by GAMM.

62 Branko Maksimović, "Prva izložba savremene jugoslovenske arhitekture" [The First Exhibition of Contemporary Yugoslav Architecture] (1931), in *Srpska arhitektura 1900–1970* (Belgrade: Muzej savremene umetnosti, 1972), p. 72.

63 On this competition, see *Concours pour l'érection d'un phare à la mémoire de Christophe Colomb*, Union Panaméricaine, 1928 (competition announcement), and ibid. 1931 (competition results).

64 Đurđe Bošković, "Jugoslovenska arhitektura" [Yugoslav Architecture] (1931), in *Srpska arhitektura 1900–1970*, p. 75.

65 Kojić, *Društveni uslovi razvitka arhitektonske struke u Beogradu 1920–1940*, p. 180.

66 Jan Dubovy (born 1892, Lazce, Austro-Hungarian monarchy; died 1969, Liberec, Czechoslovakia) graduated from the Technical University in Prague (ČVUT-Fakulta Architektury v Praze) in 1921, under Professor Jozef Fanta, architect of Franz Joseph Station in Prague (1901–1909) and the fin de siècle Hlahol house (1904–1905). Dubovy settled permanently in Belgrade in 1922. Initially employed there by the Prague firm Architekt Matej Blecha (1922–1923), from 1923 he worked as an architect in his own private practice, and from 1926 to 1934 he was employed in the Planning Department of the Technical Administration of the Belgrade City Council. In 1934 he moved to Bitola and Skopje in Macedonia. After the Second World War he moved back to Czechoslovakia, and from then on he had no further contact with Serbian architecture. For a detailed account of Dubovy's life and work see Zoran Manević, *Dubovi* (Belgrade: Društvo istoričara umetnosti, 1985); and Dijana Milašinović Marić, *Arhitekta Jan Dubovi* (Belgrade: Zadužbina Andrejević, 2001).

67 Kojić, *Društveni uslovi razvitka arhitektonske struke u Beogradu 1920–1940*, p. 169.

68 Stjepan Planić, ed., *Problemi savremene arhitekture* (Zagreb: Jugoslovenska štampa d.d., 1932), p. 95.

69 In 1931 Dubovy started to use the title, but there are no documents to prove where he acquired his doctorate. Zoran Manević cites an account by a friend of Dubovy that it was at "a German university," while Dijana Milašinović Marić confirms the doctorate being noted in the protocol of the Astronomical Observatory in Belgrade on 17 April 1931.

70 The Astronomical and Meteorological Observatory in Belgrade was founded in 1887 by Professor Milan Nedeljković, who was also appointed the first director. As it was equipped with a small number of instruments of modest capabilities, the early activities of the Observatory were of very limited scope. Thanks to the initiative and persistent action of Professor Nedeljković, the government finally agreed in 1922 to use part of the monies received as war reparations (paid to the Kingdom of Serbs, Croats and Slovenes after the First World War) to buy astronomical and meteorological instruments of a total value of over 4 million gold German marks. By 1923, the cost of the astronomical instruments bought from the German firms (Zeiss and Askania) amounted to some 3 million gold German marks, or US $600,000. The instruments started to arrive in Belgrade in 1923, and although some were used in temporary buildings at the old site, others were stored until the new Observatory was finished in 1932. See B. M. Ševarlić and J. Arsenijević, "Sto godina rada Astronomske opservatorije u Beogradu" [One Hundred Years of Work in the Astronomical Observatory in Belgrade], in *Sto godina Astronomske opservatorije u Beogradu* (Belgrade: Astronomska opservatorija, 1989), pp. 25–40.

71 Cf. Jan Dubovy, "Vrtarski grad" [Garden City], *Tehnički list* (Zagreb), nos. 1, 2, and 3 (1925), pp. 7–11, 19–24, and 42–46; "Nešto o gradovima u vrtu" [On Garden Cities], *Savremena opština* (Belgrade), no. 4 (1926), pp. 66–68; "Budući veliki Beograd" [The Future Greater Belgrade], *Savremena opština* (Belgrade), no. 6–7 (1927), pp. 1166–1171.

72 The following buildings were finished and moved into in 1932: the Central Administration Building (with the library, specially constructed 10-meter-deep cellar for the chronological instruments, astronomers' offices, management and administration offices, director's apartment, and observation dome with Zeiss comet-searching telescope); Large Refractor Dome Pavilion (with the powerful Zeiss refractor 65/1055 cm); Small Refractor Dome Pavilion (with the small Zeiss refractor 20/302 cm); Astrograph Pavilion (with Zeiss astrograph 16/80 cm); pavilion with two Askania instruments; Workshops Pavilion; Gate Pavilion; ten apartments for astronomers; and water reservoir tower. Ševarlić and Arsenijević, "Sto godina rada Astronomske opservatorije u Beogradu," pp. 26–27.

73 Dragan Aleksić, "Izložba moderne arhitekture u Umetničkom paviljonu" [Exhibition of Modern Architecture in the Arts Pavilion], *Vreme* (Belgrade), 10 June 1929, p. 3.

CHAPTER 3 **EXPOSURE**

1 Invitation sent to Milan Zloković in 1929. (Bothe & Ehrmann may be an absurd reference to the name of a well-known, Zagreb-based furniture company.)

2 "'The world exhibitions have lost much of their original character. The enthusiasm that, in 1851, was felt in the most disparate circles has subsided, and in its place has come a kind of cool calculation.

In 1851, we were living in the era of free trade.... For some decades now, we have witnessed the spread of protectionism.... Participation in the exhibition becomes... a sort of representation...; and whereas in 1850 the ruling tenet was that the government need not concern itself in this affair, the situation today is so far advanced that the government of each country can be considered a veritable entrepreneur.' Julius Lessing, *Das halbe Jahrhundert der Weltausstellungen* (Berlin, 1900), pp. 29–30." Walter Benjamin, *The Arcades Project,* trans. Howard Eiland and Kevin McLaughlin (Cambridge: Belknap Press of Harvard University Press, 1999), p. 183 [G5a,5].

3   Susan Buck-Morss, *The Dialectics of Seeing: Walter Benjamin and the Arcades Project* (Cambridge: MIT Press, 1989), p. 323.

4   "'Europe is off to view the merchandise,' said Renan—contemptuously—of the 1855 exhibition." Paul Morand, *1900* (Paris, 1931), p. 71, in Benjamin, *The Arcades Project,* p. 180 [G4,5].

5   "Srbija na Pariskoj izložbi" [Serbia at the Paris Exposition], *Brankovo kolo* (Sremski Karlovci), no. 16 (1900), p. 505.

6   "All collective architecture of the nineteenth century constitutes the house of the dreaming collective." Benjamin, *The Arcades Project,* p. 844 [H°,1].

7   This is explained well in Susan Buck-Morss's reading of Benjamin: "Paradoxically, collective imagination mobilizes its powers for a revolutionary break with the recent past by evoking a cultural memory reservoir of myths and utopian symbols from a more distant ur-past. The 'collective wish images' are nothing else but this." Buck-Morss, *The Dialectics of Seeing,* p. 116.

8   These monumental artworks depicted themes from the national history and were largely commissioned by the state for the exhibition. Among the paintings were Paja Jovanović, *The Crowning of Tsar Dušan,* 500 × 390 cm; Marko Murat, *Arrival of Tsar Dušan in Dubrovnik,* 500 × 320 cm; Đorđe Krstić, *The Fall of Stalać,* 255 × 180 cm; and Rista Vukanović, *The First Victims of Turkish Dahija,* 200 × 270 cm. See Lazar Trifunović, "Učešće Srba na svetskoj izložbi u Parizu 1900: rekonstrukcija" [Participation of Serbs at the World Exposition in Paris 1900: Reconstruction], in *Umetnici članovi SANU* [Artist Members of SANU] (Belgrade: Srpska akademija nauka i umetnosti and Beogradski sajam, 1980), pp. 500–501; and Boža Nikolajević, "Srpska umetnost na pariskoj izložbi" [Serbian Art at the Paris Exposition], *Brankovo kolo* (Sremski Karlovci), no. 1 (1900), rpt. in ibid., pp. 502–506.

9   Minor modifications of the project were made by the French architect Baudrie, whose intervention amounted to closing off the arcades of the perimeter porch with decorative glass panels. The interior of the pavilion was designed by Kapetanović in collaboration with another French architect, Viterbeau, "in such a way that everything was adapted to the taste of the Parisian public." Aleksandar Kadijević, *Jedan vek traženja nacionalnog stila u srpskoj arhitekturi* [One Century of the Quest for the National Style in Serbian Architecture] (Belgrade: Građevinska knjiga, 1997), pp. 68–71.

10 "As part of the new imperialism, 'national' pavilions promoted national grandeur, transforming patriotism itself into a commodity-on-display." Buck-Morss, *The Dialectics of Seeing,* p. 89.

11 Of the total of 220 awards that Serbian exhibitors won, 7 were Grand Prix (one of which was for tobacco) and 35 were Gold Medals, mostly awarded for agricultural and food industry products.

12 *Kilims* proved to be merchandise of a very good currency. A great number of the exhibited *kilims* were purchased directly by the office of the French president. "Srbija na pariskoj izložbi," *Brankovo kolo* (Sremski Karlovci), no. 25–26 (22 June 1900), p. 830.

13 Eight freight carriages of exhibits were sent to Paris from Belgrade, seven of products to be displayed in the pavilion and one containing paintings. "Srbija na pariskoj izložbi," *Brankovo kolo* (Sremski Karlovci), no. 16 (1900), p. 505. The text in the official Exposition guide said of the pavilion that "une riche décoration intérieure rappelle les fresques brillantes qui décorent certains sanctuaires de l'Orient." *L'Exposition pour tous, visites pratiques à travers les Palais* (Paris: Montgredien & Cie, 1900), p. 44.

14 Sigfried Giedion, *Bauen in Frankreich* (Leipzig and Berlin, 1928), p. 33, in Benjamin, *The Arcades Project*, p. 154 [F2a,3].

15 Cf. Dušica Živanović, "Život i delo arhitekte Milorada Ruvidića, 1863–1914" [Life and Work of the Architect Milorad Ruvidić], unpublished master's thesis, Faculty of Architecture, University of Belgrade, 1997.

16 Document of the Prussian Ministry of Construction published in *Zentralblatt der Bauverwaltung*, no. 40 (1904), translated by Milorad Ruvidić as "Odredbe za izvođenje konstrukcija iz betona sa gvožđem," *Srpski tehnički list* (Belgrade, 1904), pp. 58–61; (1905), pp. 20–25.

17 Walter Benjamin, "The Ring of Saturn," in *The Arcades Project*, p. 887.

18 "Attempt to develop Giedion's thesis. 'In the nineteenth century,' he writes, 'construction plays the role of the subconscious.' [Giedion, *Bauen in Frankreich*, p. 3.] Wouldn't it be better to say 'the role of bodily processes'—around which 'artistic' architectures gather, like dreams around the framework of physiological processes?" Benjamin, *The Arcades Project*, p. 391 [K1a,7].

19 The German pavilion designed by Albrecht Speer, and the Soviet pavilion designed by Boris Iofan.

20 This Trocadéro, or Palais de Chaillot (by the architects Azéma, Carlu, and Boileau), was built for the 1937 exposition. It replaced the old Trocadéro to which the following refers: "It is characteristic of these enormous fairs to be ephemeral, yet each of them has left its trace in Paris. The exhibition of 1878 was responsible for the Trocadéro, that eccentric palace clapped down on the top of Chaillot by Davioud and Bourdais, and also for the footbridge at Passy, built to replace the Pont d'Iéna, which was no longer usable." Lucien Dubech and Pierre d'Espezel, *Histoire de Paris* (Paris: Payot, 1926), p. 461, in Benjamin, *The Arcades Project*, p. 180 [G4,4].

21 The mosaic *Three Girls* (2.7 × 4.5 m) is today in the Presidency of the Republic of Serbia in Belgrade; cf. Ivana Simeonović Ćelić, *Milo Milunović: Boundless Striving towards the Essence of the Painter's Matter and Colour* (Belgrade: SANU and CANU, 1997), pp. 107–108, 137–138, and 411.

22 Josip Seissel, *Jugoslavenski paviljon na Međunarodnoj izložbi u Parizu 1937* [Yugoslav Pavilion at the International Exposition in Paris 1937] (Zagreb: Tisak Zaklade tiskare Narodnih novina, 1937).

23 The pavilion of the Kingdom of Serbia at the previous, 1905 World Exposition in Liège (Belgium) had been designed by a Belgian architect, F. Dainef, in a version of the Serbian-Byzantine style. Catalogue: *Exposition Universelle de Liège (1905), Parc de la Boverie, Pavillon Royal de Serbie*.

24 For a more detailed account see Katarina Ambrozić, "Paviljon Srbije na međunarodnoj izložbi u Rimu 1911. godine" [Pavilion of Serbia at the International Exposition in Rome 1911], in *Zbornik radova Narodnog muzeja*, III, 1960/61 (Belgrade: Narodni muzej, 1962), pp. 237–269; and Lazar Trifunović, "Srpski paviljon u Rimu 1911: rekonstrukcija" [Serbian Pavilion in Rome 1911: Reconstruction], in *Umetnici članovi SANU*, pp. 520–521.

25 Ivan Meštrović started to work on the sculptures of the Vidovdan cycle in 1908, when he lived in Paris. Sculptural fragments were first exhibited at the Paris Autumn Salons of 1908 and 1909, and in the Manes artists' association in Prague (1908). In 1910 he exhibited 80 sculptures (most of which were part of the Vidovdan cycle) in the Viennese Secession, after which the exhibition traveled to Zagreb. After the great success at the Rome exposition in 1911, the most notable presentations were held at the Venice Biennial (1914), the Victoria and Albert Museum in London (1915), and the Brooklyn Museum in New York (1929). For a more detailed account see Ana Adamec, *Ivan Meštrović 1883–1962*, exh. cat. (Belgrade: Srpska akademija nauka i umetnosti, 1984). For Meštrović's architectural work, see Neven Šegvić, "Ivan Meštrović i arhitektura," *Arhitektura* (Zagreb), no. 186–188 (1983–1984), pp. 2–9.

26 Dimitrije Mitrinović, "Srbi i Hrvati na Međunarodnoj umetničkoj izložbi u Rimu" [Serbs and Croats at the International Art Exposition in Rome], *Srpski književni glasnik* (Belgrade), no. 26 (1911), rpt. in *Umetnici članovi SANU*, pp. 522–528.

27 Curiously enough, at roughly the same time as he designed the pavilion in Rome, Petar Bajalović designed a house for the mathematician Mihajlo Petrović, inventor of the 1900 "hydro-integrator." Divna Đurić-Zamolo, *Beograd 1898–1914, iz arhive Građevinskog odbora* (Belgrade: Muzej grada Beograda, 1980), plate 65.

28 Only one of the two projects has survived, presumably the winning one; it has been presented in Marina Đurđević, *Arhitekti Petar i Branko Krstić* (Belgrade: Republički zavod za zaštitu spomenika kulture i Muzej nauke i tehnike, 1996), pp. 18–19; and in Kadijević, *Jedan vek traženja nacionalnog stila u srpskoj arhitekturi*, pp. 130–131.

29 Kadijević, *Jedan vek traženja nacionalnog stila u srpskoj arhitekturi*, p. 131.

30 Headline in *Politika*, 26 December 1925.

31 On the whole, this epilogue may have been of benefit to the state budget, given that the Philadelphia exposition proved a disappointment, at least in terms of the number of visitors, of whom only 10 million were recorded instead of the 50 million expected.

32 Interior decoration was to be carried out by a Serbian decorative artist, Dušan Janković, who was then living and working in Paris, but as the project fell through his design was never finalized. Only two drawings, now in the Museum of Applied Art in Belgrade, indicate his intention to decorate the architectural elements of the interior (such as an arched colonnade) with highly stylized and modernized folklore motifs.

33 For a detailed account of the national presentation in Paris, see Bojana V. Popović, 'Učešće Kraljevine SHS na međunarodnoj izložbi modernih primenjenih i industrijskih umetnosti u Parizu 1925. godine" [Participation of the Kingdom of Serbs, Croats and Slovenes at the International Exposition . . . in Paris 1925], *Zbornik Narodnog muzeja* (Belgrade), no. 16/2 (1997), pp. 233–243; and Željka Čorak, "The Yugoslav Pavilion in Paris," trans. Rajka and David Davison, *Journal of Decorative and Propaganda Arts* (Miami), Yugoslavian Theme Issue, no. 17 (Fall 1990), pp. 36–41.

34 Đura Đurović, "Naš paviljon na pariskoj izložbi" [Our Pavilion at the Paris Exposition], *Politika* (Belgrade), 5 July 1925, p. 4. The "Bosnian room" was put up in the part of the exhibit on within the Grand Palais.

35 Benjamin, *The Arcades Project,* p. 396 [K3a,2].

36 The phrase is inspired by Musil's "Principle of Insufficient Cause" and Bank Director Leo Fischel: "Thanks to the above-mentioned Principle the Parallel Campaign becomes a tangible reality before anyone knows what it is." Robert Musil, *The Man without Qualities,* trans. Sophie Wilkins (London and Basingstoke: Picador, 1995).

37 I am in debt to Quetglas's account of the German Pavilion at the 1929 exposition in Barcelona, which starts by commenting on the responses of contemporary observers ('natives," in his metaphor): "In order to obtain this reencounter with the primitive object, not any native will do: only the ingenious ones. Never the pedantic ones, who add surprises on their own, who create false tracks that lead nowhere, who describe emotions produced only with the desire to interest the foreigner." José Quetglas, "Loss of Synthesis: Mies's Pavilion" (1980), trans. Luis E. Carranza, in K. Michael Hays, ed., *Architecture Theory since 1968* (Cambridge: MIT Press, 1998), pp. 384–391.

38 According to the Belgrade newspaper *Politika,* the Spanish daily *El Dia Grafico,* 29 June 1929, published ten illustrations of the pavilion. "Španska štampa o našem paviljonu u Barseloni" [Spanish Press on Our Pavilion in Barcelona], *Politika* (Belgrade), 30 June 1929, p. 7.

39 "More examples, because those perverse natives form part of a tough and prolific race: the person who writes, in no. 57 of the *CAU* magazine, that perhaps it is time to oppose 'new interpretations' to the 'old interpretations' that have always granted the monopoly of quality and interest to the German Pavilion. It is very possible that there is more than one person who would be interested in the pavilions of Yugoslavia, of the Casa Jorba Warehouses, of the Ebro Hydrographic Confederation, or in any other of the rancid exercises that vulgarly combine futurist jokes, poorly evoked expressionist effects, and quickly suspended neoplastic decompositions. And perhaps someone will enjoy this." Quetglas, "Loss of Synthesis," pp. 384–385.

40 Buck-Morss, *The Dialectics of Seeing,* p. 323.

41   On the work of Dragiša Brašovan see chapter 4.3 of this book.

42   For example, all construction and carpentry work was carried out by Dušan Branković and Mihailo Krašević.

43   Cf. Sigfried Giedion's understanding of modernism: "The typical features of modern architecture, then, are simultaneity, dynamism, transparency, and many-sidedness; it is a play of interpenetration and a suggestive flexibility." Hilde Heynen, *Architecture and Modernity: A Critique* (Cambridge: MIT Press, 1999), p. 40.

44   Ignasi de Solà-Morales, *La Exposición Internacional de Barcelona 1914–1929: Arquitectura y ciudad* (Barcelona: Feria de Barcelona, 1985), pp. 114–115.

45   Possible, but arguable, references for the design of the pavilion may have been Fritz Höger's Chilehaus in Hamburg (1923), or the project for Josephine Baker's house in Paris by Adolf Loos (1927). Cf. Zoran Manević, "Naši neimari: Dragiša Brašovan" [Our Architects: Dragiša Brašovan], *Izgradnja* (Belgrade), no. 8 (1980), p. 52; Aleksandar Kadijević, "Život i delo arhitekte Dragiše Brašovana, 1887–1965" [Life and Work of Dragiša Brašovana], *Godišnjak grada Beograda* (Belgrade), no. 37 (1990), p. 156; and Solà-Morales, *La Exposición Internacional de Barcelona*, p. 114.

46   J., "Naš uspeh na međunarodnoj izložbi u Barceloni" [Our Success at the International Exposition in Barcelona], *Politika* (Belgrade), 5 November 1929, p. 7.

47   A.A., "Kraljevska poseta našem paviljonu u Barseloni" [The Royal Visitation to Our Pavilion in Barcelona], *Politika* (Belgrade), 5 October 1929, p. 4.

48   "Uspeh naše izložbe u Barceloni" [Success of Our Exhibition in Barcelona], *Politika* (Belgrade), 24 October 1929, p. 9.

49   Stanislav Vinaver, "Veliki uspeh našeg paviljona" [The Great Success of Our Pavilion], *Politika* (Belgrade), 5 July 1929, p. 6.

50   See Stanislav Vinaver, *Gromobran svemira* [Cosmic Lightning Rod] (Belgrade, 1921), which represented a seminal attempt at deconstruction of narrative and genre. Cf. Gojko Tešić, *Antologija srpske avangardne pripovetke, 1920–1930* [Anthology of Serbian Avant-garde Stories] (Novi Sad: Bratstvo-jedinstvo, 1989).

51   Cf. Buck-Morss, *The Dialectics of Seeing*, p. 146: "The paradox is that precisely by giving up nostalgic mimicking of the past and paying strict attention to the new nature, the ur-images are reanimated. . . . The moment of sublation reveals itself visually, in an instantaneous flash wherein the old is illuminated precisely at the moment of its disappearance."

52   Vinaver, "Veliki uspeh našeg paviljona."

53   Benjamin, *The Arcades Project*, p. 857 [O°,5].

54 Vinaver, "Veliki uspeh našeg paviljona."

55 "The nineteenth century, like no other century, was addicted to dwelling. It conceived the residence as the receptacle for the person, and it encased him, with all his appurtenances, so deeply in the dwelling's interior that one might be reminded of the inside of a compass case, where the instrument with all its accessories lies embedded in deep, usually violet folds of velvet." Benjamin, *The Arcades Project,* p. 865 [P°,3], and p. 220 [I4,4].

56 "Today this world is highly precarious. Dwelling is diminished: for the living, through hotel rooms; for the dead, through the crematorium." Ibid.

57 Werner Blaser, *Mies van der Rohe: The Art of Structure* (Basel, Boston, and Berlin: Birkhäuser Verlag, 1993), p. 28.

58 "Naš paviljon na Milanskom sajmu" [Our Pavilion at the Milan Fair], *Politika* (Belgrade), 7 April 1931, p. 4.

59 The original study was written in 1965, but Brašovan's family objected to it and stopped its publication. It was finally published ten years later, when both architects were dead. Nikola Dobrović, "Brašovan," *IT novine* (Belgrade), no. 697–732 (1976–1977), not paginated.

60 In comparison with the overall budget for the pavilion, estimated at some 2 million dinars, i.e., 240,000 Spanish pesetas, the prize money seems to have been very generous.

61 In e-mail correspondence sent to me on 21 February 2001, Ignasi de Solà-Morales wrote: "Honestly, it is the first time I heard about the competition and prizes for architectural proposals. I do not affirm it is not true but, certainly, I have not noticed it before and I never found information about it in my research. In relation to the general opinion about the reception of Mies Pavilion, what has been always said is it did not receive important recognition in Barcelona during the time. Also being quite exaggerated, I never found mention of any prize." Apart from being the author of the aforementioned book on the Barcelona exposition, Ignasi de Solà-Morales was one of the authors of the reconstruction of the German pavilion in 1983–1986, together with Cristian Cirici and Fernando Ramos.

62 Dobrović, "Brašovan," not paginated.

63 Ibid.

64 Miloš R. Perović has compiled two important publications of texts by Nikola Dobrović and reproductions of his works as well as critiques from the period, accompanied by the editor's own research studies: Miloš R. Perović, ed., *Dobrović,* special issue of *Urbanizam Beograda,* no. 58 (Belgrade: Zavod za planiranje razvoja grada Beograda, 1980); and, Miloš R. Perović and Spasoje Krunić, eds., *Nikola Dobrović: Essays, Projects, Critiques,* trans. into English by Ann Vasić (Belgrade: Arhitektonski fakultet Univerziteta u Beogradu and Muzej arhitekture, 1998). In the more recent study "of the unknown Dobrović" and of the possible sources of his architectural inspiration, Perović writes: "Dobrović is certainly the greatest name of Serbian Modernism in architec-

ture, a man who, unlike his contemporaries, never questioned the propriety of his progressive viewpoints." And: "Today, when the entire Yugoslav architectural, scientific and professional world marks a hundred years since the birth of the greatest architect of Serbian Modernism, it is entirely clear that our knowledge of some crucial aspects of his work, for example the cultural background and influences which formed his strong and impressive artistic expression, is no greater than 60, 40, or 10 years ago." Miloš R. Perović, "Nikola Dobrović: The Sources of His Artistic Language," in Perović and Krunić, eds., *Nikola Dobrović: Essays, Projects, Critiques,* pp. 21 and 34–35.

65   The Headquarters is an ensemble of two buildings: the Yugoslav Army General Staff Building and the Federal Ministry of Defense Building. For a comprehensive analysis of the Ministry of Defense Headquarters in Belgrade, see Bojan Kovačević, *Arhitektura zgrade Generalštaba: Monografska studija dela Nikole Dobrovića* [Monograph on the Architecture of the Yugoslav Army General Staff Building and the Federal Ministry of Defense Building] (Belgrade: Novinsko-informativni centar "Vojska," 2001).

66   Theo van Doesburg, "Yugoslavia: Rivaling Influences—Nikola Dobrović and the Serbian Tradition," in *On European Architecture: Complete Essays from Het Bouwbedrijf (1924–1931)* (Boston: Birkhäuser Verlag, 1990), pp. 289–295; translated into Serbian by M. Roter-Blagojević and N. Truhar-Pejnović in Perović and Krunić, eds., *Nikola Dobrović: Essays, Projects, Critiques,* pp. 214–216.

67   Nikola Dobrović was born in 1897 in Pécs in the Austro-Hungarian monarchy. He received his education as an architect at the Department of Architecture, King Franz Josef University in Budapest (1915–1916), and at the Department of Architecture, Technical University in Prague (1919–1923). Perović and Krunić, eds., *Nikola Dobrović: Essays, Projects, Critiques,* p. 23.

68   Ljiljana Babić, "Arhitekt Nikola Dobrović (12. 2. 1897.–11. 1. 1967.)," *Arhitektura Urbanizam* (Belgrade), no. 43 (1967), pp. 22–31. Dobrović confirmed his direct involvement with the above article in his notes from 5 October 1965 "that I have dictated to Ljiljana [Babić] the most important moments of my life and work." See "Unpublished Notes," in Perović, ed., *Dobrović,* p. 145.

69   For a study of Dobrović's Prague opus, see Tanja Damljanović, "Prilog proučavanju praškog perioda Nikole Dobrovića" [Contribution to the Study of Nikola Dobrović's Prague Period], *Saopštenja* (Belgrade), 27–28 (1995–1996), pp. 237–251.

70   Ibid., pp. 242–245. Cf. *Stavba* (Prague), no. 7 (1929), p. 136.

71   Kosta Strajnić, "Savremena arhitektura Jugoslovena: Nikola Dobrović i njegovo značenje" [Contemporary Architecture of Yugoslavs: Nikola Dobrović and His Significance], *Arhitektura* (Ljubljana), no. 4 (1932), pp. 108–114; originally published in *Architekt* (Prague), no. 10 (1930).

72   Cf. V. Jos de Hrajter, "Schilderkunst v. Petar Dobrovitsj en Architectuur van Nicola Dobrovitsj in Pulchri Studio," *Het Vaderland* (The Hague), 24 February 1931; V. V. Šteh, "Výstava Petra a Nikoly Dobroviče," *České slovo* (Prague), 23 February 1932; etc. There are translations into Serbian in Perović and Krunić, eds., *Nikola Dobrović: Essays, Projects, Critiques,* pp. 217–227.

73 Nikola Dobrović, "Jugoslavenski dom u Pragu" [Yugoslav Hall in Prague], *Československo-Jihoslovanská Revue* (Prague), 1931–1932, p. 194.

74 The large construction firm Kapsa & Müller, with offices in Prague, Pilsen, and Bratislava, employed nearly ten thousand people. One of the partners, František Müller, was the owner of the famous villa Müller in Prague which was designed by Adolf Loos (1928–1930). For an insightful account of Müller and the house construction, see Leslie van Duzer and Kent Kleinman, *Villa Müller: A Work of Adolf Loos* (New York: Princeton Architectural Press, 1994).

75 Dobrović, "Jugoslavenski dom u Pragu," p. 195.

76 For an insightful review of Dobrović's villas in the Dubrovnik region, see Marina Oreb Mojaš, "Graditeljska ostvarenja Nikole Dobrovića na Dubrovačkom području" [Architectural Works of Nikola Dobrović in the Dubrovnik Region], *Arhitektura urbanizam* (Belgrade), no. 93 (1984), pp. 4–10; and Marina Oreb Mojaš, "Simetrija, materijal i brod" [Symmetry, Material, and Ship], *Arhitektura* (Zagreb), no. 186–188 (1983–1984), pp. 60–63. For a review of the Grand Hotel see Krunoslav Ivanišin, "Hotel Grand na Lopudu" [Grand Hotel at Lopud], *Oris* (Zagreb) 3, no. 3 (1999), pp. 126–139.

77 Ranko Radović, "Nikola Dobrović ili o povećanju s vremenom" [Nikola Dobrović, or on Enhancement with Time], *Urbanizam Beograda* (Belgrade), no. 52 (1979), p. 27.

78 As noted in Babić, "Arhitekt Nikola Dobrović," Dobrović gave much of the credit for the success of the Grand Hotel to his client, maritime captain Antun Sesan, whom he much appreciated for the "brave and prophetic" decision to build a veritably modern hotel. According to this article, Sesan resisted the pressure of the conventional and conservative environment and rejected reactionary and clerical forces that campaigned against Dobrović on the grounds that he promoted Bolshevism in his architecture. It is not incidental that Dobrović's first client in the homeland had been a ship's captain, a man who by grace of his profession had seen the world and understood the spirit of the epoch, and as such could have a good rapport with his architect. In this connection, I would recall what the architect Milan Zloković wrote of the maritime captains of his family's home town of Boka Kotorska (Montenegro): "There are numerous signs that speak toward the alluring hypothesis that former captains from Boka, being shipowners and merchants, were at the same time responsible for the design of their houses. Of sober and practical mind, they demonstrated a developed talent for logical organization of rooms in the house and its correct urban position." Zloković also points out that at the time of building of the great captains' houses in Boka (eighteenth and nineteenth centuries), "house" and "ship" were correlative terms. Milan Zloković, "Građanska arhitektura u Boki Kotorskoj u doba mletačke vlasti," *Spomenik* (Belgrade), no. 103 (1953), pp. 131–146.

79 See chap. 4 of Kovačević, *Arhitektura zgrade Generalštaba,* pp. 75–96.

80 Nikola Dobrović, "Šest sličica iz sveta arhitekture" [Six Pictures from the World of Architecture], text of a lecture given at the Serbian Academy of Science and Arts in 1965, in Nikola Dobrović, *Savremena arhitektura 5* (Belgrade: Zavod za izdavanje udžbenika SR Srbije, 1971), p. 92.

81 The grid of joints was, however, made to match the stone color, as the client deemed white joints too "strong and conspicuous." Ibid.

82 Todor Manojlović, "Kolektivna izložba Petra Dobrovića, Riste Stijovića i Nikole Dobrovića" [Group Exhibition of . . .], originally published in *Vreme* (Belgrade), 19-20 November 1930; cf. Đurđe Bošković, "Platno, drvo, beton" [Canvas, Wood, Concrete], originally published in *Vreme* (Belgrade), 21 November 1930, and Stefan Hakman, "Zajednička izložba g.g. Petra Dobrovića, slikara, Riste Stijovića, vajara, i Nikole Dobrovića, arhitekte" [Joint Exhibition of . . .], originally published in *Misao* (Belgrade) 12, no. 263-264 (December 1930); all rpt. in Perović and Krunić, eds., *Nikola Dobrović: Essays, Projects, Critiques,* pp. 203-205, 206-208, 210-211.

83 Bošković, "Platno, drvo, beton," p. 208.

84 "Unfortunately, according to Dobrović's words, Dragiša Brašovan, who, as an influential member of the jury, had himself some unclear ambitions toward this project, simply 'pushed' the project out." Zoran Manević, "Naši neimari: Nikola Dobrović," *Izgradnja* (Belgrade), no. 1 (1981), p. 46.

85 Manojlović, "Kolektivna izložba Petra Dobrovića, Riste Stijovića i Nikole Dobrovića," p. 205.

86 Nikola Dobrović, "Konkurzni radovi za pozorišnu zgradu u Novom Sadu" [Competition Projects for a Theater Building in Novi Sad], *Arhitektura* (Ljubljana), no. 3 (1931), pp. 76-78.

87 Strajnić, "Savremena arhitektura Jugoslovena: Nikola Dobrović i njegovo značenje," p. 113. For a detailed account of the Split competitions, see Darovan Tušek, *Arhitektonski natječaji u Splitu* (Split: Društvo arhitekata Splita, 1994), pp. 55-59, 63-70.

88 Nikola Dobrović, "U odbranu savremenog graditeljstva" [In Defense of Contemporary Construction], *Arhitektura* (Ljubljana), no. 2 (1931), pp. 33-36.

89 Nikola Dobrović, "Pokrenutost prostora—Bergsonove dinamičke sheme—nova slika sredine" [Space Set in Motion—Bergson's Dynamic Schemes—New Image of Environment], originally published in *ČIP* (Zagreb), no. 100 (1960), pp. 10-11; rpt. in Nikola Dobrović, *Savremena arhitektura 3: Sledbenici* (Belgrade: Građevinska knjiga, 1962), pp. 234-247.

90 Ibid., p. 234.

91 Ibid., p. 237.

92 Nikola Dobrović, "Terazijska terasa: Jedan savremeni problem prestonice" [Terazije Terrace: One Contemporary Problem of the Capital City], originally published in *Vreme* (Belgrade), 26 and 27 February 1932, rpt. in Perović, ed., *Dobrović,* p. 63.

93 Nikola Dobrović, *Obnova i izgradnja Beograda* [Reconstruction and Construction of Belgrade] (Belgrade: Urbanistički institut NR Srbije, 1946).

CHAPTER 4 **BYT** MODE

1   Cf. Aleksandar Flaker, "Byt," in *Pojmovnik ruske avangarde 2* [The Glossary of the Russian Avant-Garde, 2] (Zagreb: Grafički zavod Hrvatske, 1984), pp. 9–21.

2   Milan Zloković, "Stara i nova shvatanja" [Old and New Notions], *Arhitektura* (Ljubljana), no. 5 (1932), pp. 143–144.

3   Milan Zloković, "Glavna obeležja savremene arhitekture" [The Main Characteristics of Contemporary Architecture], *Smena* (Belgrade), 1938, p. 86.

4   Ibid., p. 87.

5   Summary figures are given in table 4.1. For the 1921 population, see Slobodan Vidaković, "Arhitektura Beograda i komunalna politika" [Architecture of Belgrade and Communal Policy], *BON*, no. 12 (1932), pp. 797–802; for the 1929 population, Slobodan Vidaković, "Rezultat pop sa stanovništa Beograda 15. april 1929" [Results of the Census 15 April 1929], *BON*, no. 7 (1929), pp. 3–10. For the 1938 population and the growth in built-up area throughout this period, see Oliver Minić, "Razvoj Beograda i njegove arhitekture između dva rata" [Development of Belgrade and Its Architecture between the Wars], *Godišnjak grada Beograda* 1 (1954), pp. 177–187.

6   See Slobodan Ž. Vidaković, "Stambeno pitanje i asanacija" [Housing Issues and Its Improvement], in *Naši socijalni problemi* (Belgrade: Geca Kon, 1932), from which my table 4.2 is reproduced (p. 112). The author points out that at least 29,800 new small flats were needed for the number and social status of new inhabitants, instead of just some 8,000 realized in the period.

7   Ibid., p. 109.

8   Ibid., p. 118.

9   According to the official statistics, out of the total number of dead, every second inhabitant of the poor quarter of Savamala died of tuberculosis, and every fifth in the central area of Terazije. Mortality of newborn children in Belgrade reached as high as 220 of every 1,000 babies (compared to, e.g., 128–134 per 1,000 in the industrial cities of England). Ibid., pp. 118–119.

10 Cf. Siegfried Kracauer, "On Employment Agencies: The Construction of a Space," in Neil Leach, ed., *Rethinking Architecture: A Reader in Cultural Theory* (London: Routledge, 2000), pp. 59–64.

11 Stanislav Vinaver, "Stremljenja savremenih gradova" [Aspirations of Contemporary Cities], *BON* (Belgrade), no. 18 (1931), p. 1209.

12 Cf. Georg Simmel, "The Metropolis and Mental Life," in Leach, ed., *Rethinking Architecture*, pp. 69–79.

13 The lecture was published in the official magazine of the UYEA: Jan Dubovy, "Vrtarski grad" [Garden City], *Tehnički list* (Zagreb), nos. 1, 2, and 3 (1925), pp. 7–11, 19–24, and 42–46. The text was

illustrated with Ebenezer Howard's garden city diagrams and photographs of Letchworth Garden City and Hampstead Garden Suburb.

14   Simmel, "The Metropolis and Mental Life", p. 76.

15   Ibid.

16   Dubovy, "Vrtarski grad," p. 10.

17   Ibid., p. 11.

18   In practice, garden city ideas were only partially implemented in the middle-class residential areas, such as those named Kotež (Cottage) Neimar, Professors Colony, and Clerks Colony. Funded through private loans granted to the members of cooperatives, and thus largely cleared of the social aspect and also of the ideological layers professed by Dubovy, these did little to resolve the widespread housing problem.

19   Jan Dubovy, "Radenička kuća i radenički dom" [Workers' House and Workers' Hall], *Savremena opština* (Belgrade), no. 2 (1926), pp. 75–79; and Jan Dubovy, "O regulacionom planu sela" [On Regulation Plans for Villages], *Savremena opština* (Belgrade), no. 4 (1926), pp. 66–68.

20   Dubovy, "Radenička kuća i radenički dom," p. 76.

21   Ibid., p. 79.

22   Cf. Hannes Meyer, quoted in K. Michael Hays, "Contra the Bourgeois Interior: Co-op Zimmer," in his *Modernism and the Posthumanist Subject: The Architecture of Hannes Meyer and Ludwig Hilberseimer* (Cambridge: MIT Press, 1992), pp. 68–69.

23   For example, the house of Jozef Paroci (certified bricklayer) of 89 square meters total area, which cost 48,000 dinars; or that of Petar Paroci, of 67 square meters total area, which cost 38,000 dinars. The quotation is from Zoran Manević, *Dubovi* (Belgrade: Društvo istoričara umetnosti Srbije, 1985), not paginated.

24   Kracauer, "On Employment Agencies," p. 59.

25   The social program was financed from the Fund for the Construction and Maintenance of Workers' Institutions, established with a loan granted to the Belgrade City Council by the Ministry of Social Policy following an agreement with the Workers' Chamber. The loan of 10 million dinars (over 25 years, with 4 percent interest per annum) was granted to the Council in 1927 for the construction of workers' shelters, kitchens, bath houses, libraries, job centers, workers' flats, and institutions for the care of workers' children. See "Radnička skloništa opštine beogradske," *BON* (Belgrade), no. 4–5 (1930), pp. 207–216.

26   Ibid., pp. 210–211.

27 In the period of the worst economic crisis, between 1932 and 1935, the shelters were used by 100,000 men, 20,000 women, and 26,000 children yearly. Milica Milenković, "Radničke socijalne ustanove u Srbiji, Međunarodna organizacija rada i proces modernizacije radničkog zakonodavstva u Jugoslaviji i Srbiji 1918–41" [Workers' Social Institutions, International Labor Organization, and Modernization of Labor Legislation in Yugoslavia and Serbia 1918–41], in *Srbija u modernizacijskim procesima XX veka*, conference proceedings (Belgrade: Institut za noviju istoriju Srbije, 1994), pp. 289–296.

28 Simmel, "The Metropolis and Mental Life," p. 70.

29 Among other European countries, 72 per 100,000 inhabitants per annum died of tuberculosis in Denmark in this period, 106 in England, 133 in Germany, and 156 in Norway. Slobodan Ž. Vidaković, *Tuberkuloza i sifilis sa gledišta socijalne politike* [Tuberculosis and Syphilis from the Aspect of Social Policy] (Belgrade: Izdanje S. B. Cvijanovića, 1931), p. 21.

30 Ljuba Stojanović, "Tuberkuloza i njene posledice" [Tuberculosis and Its Consequences], *BON* (Belgrade), no. 10 (1938), p. 689.

31 Ibid., p. 690.

32 Ibid., p. 688. Compare Loos's call for hygiene forty years earlier: "An increase in the use of water is one of our most critical cultural tasks. May our Viennese plumbers fulfill their task and bring us closer to that most important goal, the attainment of a cultural level equal to the rest of the civilized Western world." Adolf Loos, "Plumbers" (1898), in *Spoken into the Void: Collected Essays 1897–1900,* trans. Jane O. Newman and John H. Smith (Cambridge: MIT Press, 1982), p. 49.

33 Cf. Dragomir Popović, "Opštinski stanovi u Beogradu" [Council Flats in Belgrade], *BON* (Belgrade), no. 21–22 (1931), pp. 1384–1392.

34 Branko Maksimović, "Problem vangradskih naselja" [Problem of Suburban Settlements], *BON* (Belgrade), no. 1 (1930), pp. 17–19. Of all Belgrade modern architects, only Maksimović wrote about the contentious themes of the *Existenzminimum,* the minimum requirements of a decent existence, which were discussed at the 1929 CIAM congress in Frankfurt. Cf. Branko Maksimović, "Racionalizam modernih stanova za minimum egzistencije" [Rationalism of Modern Apartments for the *Existenzminimum*], *BON* (Belgrade), no. 5 (1930), pp. 486–490; and Branko Maksimović, *Problemi urbanizma* [Problems of Urbanism] (Belgrade: Geca Kon, 1932).

35 According to statistics, some 170,000 citizens of Belgrade lived on a monthly income ranging from 720 to 1,800 dinars; the average monthly salary of skilled workers was around 1,400 dinars; and the average worker's daily wage was 24.50 dinars. Vidaković, *Tuberkuloza i sifilis sa gledišta socijalne politike,* pp. 38, 44.

36 For this concept to be realized, Maksimović had to wait another twenty years for the change of sociopolitical circumstances after the Second World War, when he was appointed to design the workers' housing estate in Novi Železnik (1947). Being a product of the new spirit of collectivization, it was, however, of arguable architectural merit.

37 T. K. Fodor, "Beograd, naličje jednog grada," *Nova literatura* (Belgrade), no. 3 (February 1929), pp. 86–88. (The article was illustrated with perspective drawings of Le Corbusier's Ville Contemporaine and the Chicago Tribune competition entry by Walter Gropius.) The author of the article, Toša Fodor, also known as Teodor Balk or by his pseudonym (T.) Fjodin, was a medical doctor and writer and a regular contributor to *Nova literatura* (a magazine of leftist orientation published in 1928–1929).

38 Ibid., p. 87.

39 P. Morton Shand, "A Note on the New Belgrade," *Architects' Journal* (London), no. 1734 (11 April 1928), p. 506.

40 It is curious that both in the text and in the caption under the photograph, the names of the brave new architects are missing. As Shand was simply recapitulating the information sent to him from Belgrade by Branislav Kojić, he may have regarded these as being inadvertently overlooked. But, in light of the local circumstances of the period, could this be seen as a deliberate omission on Kojić's part? The building featured in the article has since been totally ignored by all accounts of the modern movement in Serbia, never to be mentioned, republished, or exhibited again. The main reason for the neglect may be that its author was not an architect but an engineer, Professor Vojislav Zađina of the Technical Faculty. At the time he provided the information and photographs for the article, neither Kojić nor his colleagues had had any of their modernist projects realized; thus a proxy to save face had to be provided instead. This building of simple form, symmetrically composed around a rounded corner volume, with facade largely purified of decoration, nevertheless correctly represented the character of the emerging sensibility. Ljiljana Blagojević, *Moderna kuća u Beogradu, 1920–1941* [The Modern House in Belgrade, 1920–1941] (Belgrade: Zadužbina Andrejević, 2000), p. 22.

41 It may be worth quoting the whole passage, for it gives an exact picture of the extent of change the modern times and technology brought to the Balkans: "If a man came to Vienna from the Balkan states, where they still wear foot wrappings, and went in search of a lingerie shop where he could buy his customary foot covering, he would be met with the news—incomprehensible to him—that foot wrappings cannot be bought in Vienna. He could, of course, order them. 'Well, what do people wear here then?' 'Socks.' 'Socks? Why, they are very uncomfortable. And too hot in the summer. Doesn't anyone wear foot wrappings anymore?' 'Oh, yes, the very old people. But the young people find foot wrappings uncomfortable.' And so the good man from the Balkans decides with a heavy heart to make the attempt to wear socks. In doing so, he arrives at a new rung of human culture." Adolf Loos, "Underclothes" (1898), in *Spoken into the Void,* pp. 72, 74.

42 Walter Benjamin, *The Arcades Project,* trans. Howard Eiland and Kevin McLaughlin (Cambridge: Belknap Press of Harvard University Press, 1999), pp. 71–72 [B4a,1].

43 Original manuscript for the speech given by Branislav Kojić at the Conference of the Group of Architects of the Modern Movement in Belgrade in 1932, kept in the Architecture Department in the Museum of Science and Technology, Belgrade.

44 Comment jotted down by Branislav Kojić in the margin of the text for a lecture on the origins of modern architecture given in 1934. Original manuscript in the Architecture Department in the Museum of Science and Technology, Belgrade.

45 Mary McLeod, "Undressing Architecture: Fashion, Gender, and Modernity," in Deborah Fausch et al., eds., *Architecture in Fashion* (New York: Princeton Architectural Press, 1994), p. 139.

46 Although women's right to vote was recognized under §70 of the 1921 Constitution of the Kingdom of Serbs, Croats and Slovenes, in practice women had no right to vote until 1941. Also in effect were other legal provisions that sanctioned inequality of women in business and ownership matters, which were not changed either until 1941. Under §920 of the Civil Act, for example, married women were included among those who had no right to govern their own property: "the feeble-minded, squanderers noted by court, libertines, debtors whose property is in bankruptcy, and married women during their husbands' life." Women were particularly discriminated against in the inheritance law, as a widow could only inherit the right of use of her husband's property but not the full ownership, while daughters could inherit from their fathers only if there were no male heirs.

47 Cf. Bojana Popović, *Moda u Beogradu, 1918–1941* [Fashion in Belgrade, 1918–1941] (Belgrade: Muzej primenjene umetnosti, 2000).

48 Branislav Kojić, "Arhitektonski život prestonice" [Architectural Life of the Capital City], unpublished article written for the magazine *Arhitektura*. Original manuscript in the Architecture Department in the Museum of Science and Technology, Belgrade.

49 According to information kindly passed to me by Miloš Jurišić, the building was constructed in 1939, but the original owner never took possession of his estate. As the building was drawing close to completion, it caught the eye of the Soviet delegation which insisted it should be the seat of the first legation of the USSR in Yugoslavia. Pera Milanović was made to sell the building to the government for this purpose, and in late 1940 it was finalized as the USSR legation (it was listed as such in the 1941 telephone directory). As the internal organization had to be adapted for the new users, the White Russian émigré architect Matvej Eisenberg, who, despite his origins, inclined to the left, was appointed to carry out the supervision of the work. It is outside the scope of this study to investigate this example in more detail and explore the related ideological discourse, but I would still pose a dilemma: Could it have been the very dazzle of the highly eclectic facade that was deemed the most appropriate mode of representation for the first mission of one communist regime in Belgrade? Curiously, the Palazzo continued to fascinate even in the new sociopolitical conditions of the postwar period, when the building was used as the Embassy of the Peoples Republic of China.

Documentation: The request by Pera Milanović to make the facade a "true copy" of Palazzo Principe Dorio was confirmed in a letter submitted to the Municipal Building Council, signed by the architect Đorđe Đorđević, dated 26 April 1939. Included with the letter were two photographs of the Roman palazzo supplied by the client. It seems, however, that the project of the facade was carried out by Professor Dante Petroni from Rome, as stated in a subsequent document of the Belgrade Engineers Chamber, dated 8 June 1939, in which Belgrade architect Josif Najman was permitted to certify the project as the local architect in charge. On 10 June 1939, Najman submitted the project and the technical brief to the Council in order for the building permit to be obtained. This document specifies the use of the building, the organization of the program, and the building materials. It also confirms that the facade is a copy of the Roman palace and that the principal material of the facade is stucco, but with columns in the entrance zone made of natural stone. This correspondence is kept in the Historical Archive of the City of Belgrade (the original project is not available).

50   As observed by Katarina Mladenović, Belgrade fashion designer, in 1923. Popović, *Moda u Beogradu, 1918–1941,* p. 59.

51   Critique by Mirko Brun, a designer with Jean Patou in Paris, in 1929. Ibid., p. 59.

52   Fodor, "Beograd, naličje jednog grada," p. 87.

53   Val K. Warke, "'In' Architecture: Observing the Mechanisms of Fashion," in Fausch et al., eds., *Architecture in Fashion,* p. 133.

54   Dušan Janković (born 1894, Niš; died 1950, Belgrade) started to study architecture at the Technical Faculty in Belgrade (1913–1914) but was interrupted by the First World War. He continued his studies at the private architectural school in the Parisian suburb of Arcueil (1917–1918), which he left after being admitted to the painting department at the École Nationale Supérieure des Arts Décoratifs in Paris, where he graduated in 1921. He lived and worked in Paris until 1935, when he returned to Serbia and permanently settled in Belgrade. Painter, graphic artist, and designer, he is best known for his work in the field of applied arts (fashion, design of textiles, porcelain, ceramics, furniture design, books and graphic design, etc.). During the 1920s he worked as a fashion designer and operated a fashion house in Paris, which was registered under his wife's name: "La mode d'Art de l'atelier Colette Janković, 126 av. Philippe Auguste, Paris XIe." His architectural designs include a number of interiors (e.g., the "Tic-Tac" room at the Moulin Rouge in Paris, 1925) and the total design of a modernist villa in Saint-Cloud near Paris, 1932–1934. For a detailed account on his life and work, see Vladimir Rozić, *Dušan Janković 1894–1950: Život i delo* (Belgrade: Muzej primenjene umetnosti, 1987).

55   Julijan, "Hiljadu druga noć" [Thousand and Second Night], *Preporod* (Belgrade), 18 February 1923.

56   Branislav Kojić, "Vila na Topčiderskom brdu," *Arhitektura* (Ljubljana), no. 6 (1932), p. 161.

57   As all great modern houses tend to leak, so would Dubovy's villa have, had it been constructed. As architectural historian Zoran Manević ascertained, the client rejected the plans on grounds that the roof drainage was not and could not be resolved, and asked the architect to revise the scheme. In the revised project Dubovy uncompromisingly kept his original design intent, offering minor changes in the arrangement of rooms but leaving the flat roofs and doing nothing to overcome the drainage problem. As a consequence he lost the commission, and a new project was carried out by his fellow modernist Dušan Babić, who complied with the client's wishes and produced a conventional suburban house with hipped roof and pretty ornamentation and detailing (such as the little heart-shaped cutouts in the wooden shutters).

58   Henri Focillon, *Vie des formes* (Paris, 1934), quoted in Benjamin, *The Arcades Project,* p. 80 [B9a,2].

59   This reflected the dual interests and talents of the younger of the two brothers, Branko Krstić (born 1902, Belgrade; died 1978, Belgrade), who was educated both as an architect and as a sculptor. In parallel to studying architecture at the Technical Faculty in Belgrade, where he graduated in 1927, he was a student at the sculpture department of the Belgrade Art School. After graduation he spent a year as an assistant in the studio of the well-known sculptor Đorđe Jovanović. For most of his active years he taught at the Secondary Technical School in Belgrade, and in the period 1946–1950 he taught architectural drawing at the Faculty of Architecture. Petar Krstić (born 1899, Belgrade; died 1991, Belgrade) graduated from the Technical Faculty in Belgrade in 1924; from 1925, when he was elected an assistant, he remained employed at the Faculty until his retirement in 1970. While they practiced architecture as a team, the younger brother had an independent career as an artist, often exhibiting his sculptural works in the art shows at the Arts Pavilion. The brothers Krstić are best known for their monumental eclectic trilogy realized in Belgrade: St. Marko Church (1930, 1932–1939), the Agrarian Bank (1931–1934), and Igumanov Palace (1936–1937). Through less prestigious projects for private houses and apartment buildings, they developed a very particular modernist sensibility, and they joined GAMM in 1930. See Marina Đurđević, *Arhitekti Petar i Branko Krstić* (Belgrade: Republički zavod za zaštitu spomenika kulture and Muzej nauke i tehnike, 1996).

60   Dušan Tomić was a great lover of architecture who initiated and financed a yearly award for "the most beautiful facade in Belgrade." Cf. note 87 below.

61   To cut costs, the marble cladding was changed to the cheaper finish of Terranova stucco plastering.

62   Branko Krstić, "Stambena zgrada gđe Jelinić," *Arhitektura* (Ljubljana), no. 6 (1931), pp. 167–168.

63   Dušan Babić (born 1896, Banja Luka; died 1948, Belgrade) graduated from the Technische Hochschule in Vienna in 1923, after which he returned to Sarajevo where he was employed in the Municipal Building Department. He moved to Belgrade in 1928 and was employed in the Department of Architecture of the Ministry of Construction. In his own private practice he realized a number of private houses and apartment buildings in Belgrade and a church in Doboj. Zoran Manević, "Dušan Babić," *Izgradnja* (Belgrade), no. 2 (1981), pp. 43–47.

64   Branislav Kojić (born 1899, Smederevo; died 1987, Belgrade) graduated from the École Centrale des Arts et Manufactures in Paris in 1921. He was first employed by the Department of Architecture of the Ministry of Construction (1921–1928), and after that was a principal in the private office with his wife Danica (1928–1941). In 1925 he was elected an assistant at the Department of Architecture of the Technical Faculty in Belgrade, later Faculty of Architecture (elected associate professor in 1946, professor in 1950, dean in 1963–1964), where he stayed until retiring from his academic career in 1965. He held positions of chief executive, president of the board, and director of the Institute of Architecture and Urban Planning in Belgrade (1955–1970). His titles include Doctor *honoris causa* of the University of Belgrade (1977) and corresponding member (1955) and regular member (1963) of the Serbian Academy of Sciences and Arts. In his active architectural

career he carried out some 100 projects and competitions and realized some 40 buildings. For a detailed account of the architect's life and work, catalogue of works, and complete bibliography, see Snežana Toševa, *Branislav Kojić* (Belgrade: Građevinska knjiga, 1998).

65 Among other projects he exhibited at the autumn show of 1928, Kojić included his survey of an old house in Simina Street, and in the "First Salon of Architecture" in 1929 he displayed two drawings titled *Interior à la Le Corbusier* alongside a survey drawing of the *konak* of Princess Ljubica and *Sketch in the National Style*. Branislav Kojić, *Društveni uslovi razvitka arhitektonske struke u Beogradu 1920–1940. godine* (Belgrade: Srpska akademija nauka i umetnosti, 1979), p. 187. Less prominent, but indicative of Kojić's versatility, or perhaps his lack of principle, are the eclectic projects he produced on demand by clients. A good example, though not the only one, is the house of Dr. Đorđe Radin (1931–1932), which he initially designed as a house with modern facade; he had the drawing of the elevation published in the magazine *Arhitektura* (Ljubljana), no. 4 (1932), p. 103. The building was finalized, however, with no drastic change to the internal organization but with the facade in the prevailing style of the period academicism, presumably on demand by the owner.

66 See, for example, Branislav Kojić, *Stara gradska i seoska arhitektura u Srbiji* [Old Urban and Rural Architecture in Serbia] (Belgrade: Prosveta, 1949); *Seoska arhitektura i rurizam* [Rural Architecture and Ruralism] (Belgrade, 1958); *and Stari balkanski gradovi, varoši i varošice* [Old Balkan Cities, Towns, and Small Towns] (Belgrade, 1976). Kojić's diligent and rational attitude was well characterized by the academician Đorđe Zloković in a speech given at the opening of the exhibition marking the centenary of the architect's birth: "As the *ancien élève d'École centrale,* the academician Branislav Kojić applied the analytical method of the French school in all his architectural and research projects. In his course on rural and industrial architecture, which he taught at the Faculty of Architecture in Belgrade, he cherished systematic research and the method of deduction in the quest for the optimal solution." Đorđe Zloković, "Branislav Kojić—neumorni istraživač i analitičar" [Branislav Kojić: A Tireless Researcher and Analyst], in *Branislav Kojić: In Remembrance of the Architect on the One-Hundredth Anniversary of His Birth,* exh. cat. (Belgrade: Serbian Academy of Sciences and Arts, 2001).

67 The mansion house of *Kneginja* (Princess) Ljubica was built in 1829–1831 by Hadži-Nikola Živković, who was the first qualified master builder in the period when Serbia was striving for independence from Ottoman rule, under *Knez* (Prince) Miloš Obrenović. It represents a transitional type between Oriental and Western architecture.

68 Danica Kojić (born 1899, Belgrade; died 1975, Belgrade) graduated from the Department of Architecture at the Technical Faculty in Belgrade. She was first employed by the Department of Architecture in the Ministry of Construction (1924–1928), after which she worked in private practice with her husband, where she was particularly involved in interior and furniture design. Cf. Snežana Toševa, "Danica Kojić (1899–1975)," *Godišnjak grada Beograda* 43 (1996), pp. 109–121.

69 The year after it was finished, the building was awarded the prize for one of the three most beautiful facades in Belgrade constructed in the previous year.

70   Cf. the initial designs for the house of Dr. Đorđe Radin (1931) and the house of Svetislav Marodić (1932), the competition proposal for the Tanurdžić Palace in Novi Sad (1931), as well as one undated proposal for an apartment building.

71   Warke, "'In' Architecture: Observing the Mechanisms of Fashion," p. 133.

72   Mir-Jam, "Beogradska moda: Ovog leta su sve Beograđanke uniformisane" [Belgrade Fashion: All Women of Belgrade Are Uniformed This Summer], *Nedeljne ilustracije* (Belgrade), 4 August 1935, pp. 8–10.

73   A. V. Herenda, "Pitanje kirije i otkazni rokovi u Beogradu" [Question of Rental Prices and Notices in Belgrade], *BON* (Belgrade), no. 24 (1931), pp. 1560–1562.

74   There was probably no family that had not moved 5, 10, or 15 times in 20 years, and the number of those living in the same flat for more than 5 years was very small. Petar Đorđević, "O selidbama u Beogradu" [On Moving in Belgrade], *BON* (Belgrade), no. 14 (1930), pp. 697–703.

75   Cf. Ljiljana Blagojević, "Ulaz u stambenu zgradu: prikaz perioda od 1918–1941. godine u Beogradu" [Entrance Zone in Apartment Blocks, 1918–1941, Belgrade], unpublished specialist thesis, Faculty of Architecture, University of Belgrade, 1989.

76   Dragomir Popović, "Uređajni osnovi za Beograd" [Land Use Plan of Belgrade], *BON* (Belgrade), no. 10 (1932), pp. 635–639; and "Izvadak iz novog Građevinskog zakona" [Excerpt from the New Construction Act], in Stjepan Planić, ed., *Problemi savremene arhitekture* (Zagreb: Jugoslovenska štampa d.d., 1932), pp. 55–59.

77   Table 4.3 is based on *Statistički godišnjak 1938–39* [Statistical Yearbook 1938–39] (Belgrade: Državna štamparija, 1939), pp. 206–207.

78   Milivoje Tričković, "Naši arhitektonski gresi" [Our Architectural Sins], *BON* (Belgrade), no. 12 (1932), pp. 770–772.

79   Momčilo Belobrk (born 1905, Valjevo; died 1980, Belgrade) graduated from the Department of Architecture at the Technical Faculty in Belgrade in 1930 and became a member of GAMM in 1932. After three years of employment in the design and construction firm of Đura Borošić (also a member of GAMM), he started his own practice in 1933. Through the outbreak of the Second World War, he realized some 40 residential buildings (including houses and villas). In the postwar period he specialized in the architecture of performing arts buildings. In 1943 he started his academic career at the School for the Applied Arts (latter to become the Academy), where he stayed until his retirement in 1972. See Marta Vukotić, *Arhitekta Momčilo Belobrk* (Belgrade: Republički zavod za zaštitu spomenika kulture and Muzej nauke i tehnike, 1996).

80   Quoted in Reyner Banham, *Theory and Design in the First Machine Age* (New York: Frederick A. Praeger, 1960), p. 211.

81 Joan Copjec, "The Sartorial Superego," in her *Read My Desire: Lacan against the Historicists* (Cambridge: MIT Press, 1994), pp. 76–77.

82 Benjamin, *The Arcades Project*, p. 68 [B3,1] and p. 79 [B9,1].

83 Dragiša Brašovan (born 1887, Vršac; died 1965, Belgrade) graduated from the Technical University in Budapest, Department of Architecture, where he studied under Professors Alajos Hauszmann, Frigyes Schulek, Emil Tőri, and others (1907–1912). First employed in the office of Emil Tőri and Móric Pogáni in Budapest, in 1918 he moved back to the Kingdom of Serbs, Croats and Slovenes, first to Veliki Bečkerek and, in 1920, to Belgrade. He established a private practice in partnership with Milan Sekulić, then his own practice from 1925 to 1941. His titles include President of the Association of Artists, President of the Oblik Art Society, and President of the Architects Club. In 1953 he was elected Honorary Corresponding Member of the Royal Institute of British Architects, in 1961 Corresponding Member of the Serbian Academy of Sciences and Arts. On the life and work of Dragiša Brašovan, see Nikola Dobrović, "Brašovan," *IT novine* (Belgrade), no. 697-732 (1976-1977), not paginated; Zoran Manević, "Život jednog graditelja" [Life of an Architect], *IT novine* (Belgrade), no. 697-710 (1976), not paginated; Zoran Manević, "Naši neimari: Dragiša Brašovan," *Izgradnja* (Belgrade), no. 8 (1980), pp. 49-57; Aleksandar Kadijević, "Život i delo arhitekte Dragiše Brašovana, 1887–1965" [Life and Work of Architect Dragiša Brašovan], *Godišnjak grada Beograda* 37 (1990), pp. 141-172.

84 Manević, "Život jednog graditelja," not paginated.

85 For example, the Discount Bank in Belgrade (1921–1922), an apartment block with the Bank's premises for one of the wealthiest people in Serbia of the period, bank director and majority shareholder Dragiša Matejić; a rental apartment building (1927–1928) for the former governor of the National Bank Dobrivoje Lazarević; villa Genčić (1929) for the former government minister and wealthy entrepreneur Đorđe Genčić.

86 Manević, "Život jednog graditelja," not paginated.

87 In 1930, villa Škarka, of the "Oriental baroque" style, was awarded one of the four *ex aequo* prizes for the most beautiful facade in Belgrade (for the year 1927), by the foundation of Professor Dušan Tomić. The other three prize winners were villa Marinković, in the national vernacular style, by Branislav Kojić; an apartment building in Njegoševa Street, "with elements of domestic medieval architecture," by Aleksandar Deroko; and villa Milosavljević, "in the spirit of the Renaissance architecture from our coastal regions," by Dragomir Tadić. Having chosen only houses of the "styles," it is not strange that the jury had bypassed the house of Milan Zloković, also submitted to the competition for the prizes. Kojić, *Društveni uslovi razvitka arhitektonske struke u Beogradu*, pp. 89-90.

88 Kadijević, "Život i delo arhitekte Dragiše Brašovana," p. 153.

89 Nikola Dobrović, "In memoriam: Stvaranje arh. Dragiše Brašovana," *Arhitektura urbanizam* (Belgrade), no. 33-34 (1965), pp. 42-44.

90   Kadijević, "Život i delo arhitekte Dragiše Brašovana," p. 153.

91   "The free plan and a clear construction cannot be kept apart. The structure is the backbone of the whole and makes the free plan possible. Without that backbone the plan would not be free, but chaotic and therefore constipated." Mies van der Rohe, quoted in Christian Norberg-Schulz, *Meaning in Western Architecture* (London: Studio Vista, 1975), p. 364.

92   Dobrović, "Brašovan" (1976), not paginated.

93   As ascertained in the chronological analysis of Brašovan's life and work by Aleksandar Kadijević, the first building in which Brašovan announced his departure from academicism was the Workers' Chamber in Novi Sad.

94   Henry-Russell Hitchcock and Philip Johnson, *The International Style: Architecture since 1922* (New York: Norton, 1932).

95   "For Johnson and Hitchcock the International Style was thus specifically established by a few masters and masterpieces, and 'the canon of executed works'." Beatriz Colomina, *Privacy and Publicity: Modern Architecture as Mass Media* (Cambridge: MIT Press, 1996), pp. 201–202.

96   The building was the first one in Serbia to have a totally consistent structural framework in reinforced concrete. Due to the low stability parameters of the ground, the building had to be constructed on a one-meter-thick reinforced concrete foundation slab, which also represented an engineering innovation in Belgrade. Although the horizontal windows appear to have metalwork frames, they are made of wood.

97   Dobrović, "Brašovan" (1976), not paginated.

98   "The disjunction of the composition implies a departure from functionalist uniformity. The technical program had given Brašovan the opportunity to handle things more bravely and to play with expressive means of contemporary architectural narrative. The division of the overall massing among a number of sets of motifs and substructures, and the separation of the composition taken to the limit, already creates a disunion, and only one step further the impression would be that the whole building mass comprises a number of independent objects. . . . Speaking generally of the architecture of this building today, a question could be posed: are all the elements of this powerful composition perfectly fitted together in the best interrelation?" Ibid., not paginated.

99   Branislav Kojić, "Simbolizam u arhitekturi" [Symbolism in Architecture], *Tehnički list* (Zagreb), no. 15–16 (1939), pp. 185–187.

100   The total area was some 5,700 square meters (ca. 570 rooms), the final cost 56,350,501 dinars. For a documented account of the construction of the Palace of the Danube Regional Government, see Donka Stančić and Miško Lazović, *Banovina* (Novi Sad: Prometej, 1999).

101   Following the dismissal of parliament and the dictatorship of 6 January 1929, King Aleksandar reorganized the country into nine large regions (Banovinas) to which some economic and

political governance was passed from the central state. The Danube Region, of which the administrative center was Novi Sad, was the second largest in the country. The area spread over some 28,000 square kilometers, with a population of more than 2 million. Although the city of Belgrade with Zemun and Pančevo were geographically a part of the Danube Region, they had a separate administration.

102 Stančić and Lazović, *Banovina*, pp. 57–60.

103 Dobrović, "Brašovan" (1976), not paginated.

CHAPTER 5 **DEPARTURE**

Epigraph: Milan Zloković, "Kapetanske kuće u Boki" [Captains' Houses in Boka], *Politika* (Belgrade), 13 April 1958, p. 19.

1 Milan Zloković (born 1898, Trieste; died 1965, Belgrade) finished German primary and *Realschule* (secondary school, in which sciences and modern languages are stressed in the curriculum) in Trieste (Italy), then started his studies in engineering at the Superior Technical School in Graz (Austria) in 1915. In May of the next year his studies were interrupted by the First World War, when he was mobilized into the Austro-Hungarian army. After demobilization, when Trieste was assigned to Italy by the Paris peace conference, he refused to take Italian citizenship, and in 1919 he moved to the Kingdom of Serbs, Croats and Slovenes and continued his studies in Belgrade. He graduated from the Department of Architecture of the Technical Faculty, University of Belgrade, in 1921. After graduation, in 1922–1923 he went to Paris on a grant from the French government, and later as a bursar of the Ministry of Education of the Kingdom of Serbs, Croats and Slovenes. There he studied in the design studio of Professors Godefroy and Freynet at the École Nationale Supérieure des Beaux-Arts, attended lectures in Byzantine and Serbian medieval art at the Sorbonne (Professor Charles Diehl) and at the École des Hautes Études (Professor Gabriel Millet), and regularly attended courses in drawing at the Académie de la Grande Chaumière. For a short period he was employed as an architectural assistant in the Paris office of Auburtin and Parenty. In April 1923, Zloković returned to Belgrade, where he was elected to the university position of assistant in the Department of Architecture of the Technical Faculty (later the Faculty of Architecture). His academic career continued uninterrupted until his death; he was elected assistant professor (*Docent*) in 1932, associate professor in 1939, and professor in 1950. In the period 1952–1954 he was dean of the Faculty of Architecture. He also taught at the Technical Faculty in Skopje (1956–1960). In parallel he taught at the Belgrade *Realschule* in 1924–1925 (descriptive geometry), the Technical School in 1924–1928 (descriptive geometry, building construction, and design of public buildings), the Graphic School in 1927–1928 (science of styles), and the Pedagogical College in 1925–1936 (on ornaments). In addition to his academic career, he actively practiced in his own architectural office until 1941, and took part in architectural competitions in which he was awarded some 20 prizes and 16 commendations (honorariums). In his private practice Zloković realized some 40 buildings, from private houses and villas to large public buildings. In the interwar period he published articles that promoted modern architecture and a few papers on the architecture of the past, most notably on the old churches in the region of Prespa and Ohrid, the Gradac Monastery church, and the traditional architecture in the coastal regions of the Adriatic. His study

"Jugoslaviens balkanische Holzarchitekturen—Baukünstlerische Analogien zwischen Japan und der Balkanhalbinsel als Grenzgebiste orientalisch-asiatischer Kulturzonen" (illustrated with more than 300 original images of the Balkan vernacular timber architecture) was submitted to the international competition organized in Japan to celebrate 2,600 years of the Japanese empire in 1941; due to the outbreak of the Second World War, the outcome remained unknown. In the postwar period his private practice had to cease due to the new sociopolitical circumstances, but he continued to participate in architectural competitions. Between 1960 and 1965, together with his son Đorđe and daughter Milica, also architects, he realized the Teachers College in Prizren (the first prefabricated building in Yugoslavia with consistently applied modular coordination) and the Tourist Complex in Ulcinj. In this period he focused on theoretical work on problems of regulating systems, proportion, and modular coordination in architecture, and published numerous articles and theoretical papers in this field.

2   In an autobiographical sketch note for a letter, Zloković wrote that he decided to study architecture only when he realized that due to his imperfect sight he could not enroll in the naval academy and follow in the footsteps of his father. I would suggest that the text of this letter is indicative of the origins of his architectural concept. The sketched text was written in English, Zloković's fifth language (after Serbian, Italian, French, and German), and I am here reprinting it verbatim: "I didn't think nothing special about architecture in my childhood. My greatest ambition at that time was to be captain in the merchant fleet as my father was. He didn't support my proposa to go to see, but never said that to me; his ambition on the other hand was to see his only son as an engineer. My destiny was sealed when I was fourteen years old and ready to pass from the middle school in the Nautical Academy. You certainly know that one had to have a good sight to be accepted in the Academy. A doctor visited me and he was sorry to declare that I was unable for the sea career; one eye was weaker. I was depressed for a time, but not for long, and I accepted definitively father's proposition to become an engineer. I didn't like architecture at that time because I found that it was an easy job to build houses: I wanted to build harbors, bridges and tunneling." (Courtesy Đorđe Zloković.)

3   Zloković, "Kapetanske kuće u Boki," p. 19; and Milan Zloković, "Gradanska arhitektura u Boki Kotorskoj u doba mletačke vlasti" [The Civil Architecture in Boka Kotorska in the Period of Venetian Rule], *Spomenik* (Belgrade), no. 103 (1953), pp. 131–146. See also an earlier article: Milan Zloković, "O gradenju na primorju" [On Building in the Coastal Regions], *Pomorski Lloyd* (Belgrade), no. 8 (1936), pp. 4–5.

4   The term *technē* is used here in the meaning explained by Martin Heidegger: "To the Greeks *technē* means neither art nor handicraft but, rather, to make something appear, within what is present, as this or that, in this way or that way. The Greeks conceive of *technē*, producing, in terms of letting appear. *Technē* thus conceived has been concealed in the tectonics of architecture since ancient times. Of late it still remains concealed, and more resolutely, in the technology of power machinery." Martin Heidegger, "Building Dwelling Thinking," in *Martin Heidegger: Basic Writings*, ed. David Farrell Krell (London: Routledge, 1993), p. 361.

5   Massimo Cacciari, "Loos and His Angel" (1981), in his *Architecture and Nihilism: On the Philosophy of Modern Architecture* (New Haven: Yale University Press, 1993), pp. 150–151.

6   Very occasionally the stated dimensions would use fractions in ¼, ⅓, ⅔, or ¾ foot. Zloković, "Gradanska arhitektura u Boki Kotorskoj u doba mletačke vlasti," p. 136.

7   Ibid., p. 133.

8   Cf. Adolf Loos, "The Master Saddler," translated into Serbo-Croat by architect Ernest Weissmann, *Arhitektura* (Ljubljana), no. 11 (1993), pp. 166–169.

9   Massimo Cacciari, *Architecture and Nihilism: On the Philosophy of Modern Architecture*, p. 152.

10 Cf. Milan Zloković, "Antropomorfni sistemi mera u arhitekturi" [Anthropomorphic Systems of Measurements in Architecture], *Zbornik zaštite spomenika kulture* (Belgrade) 4–5 (1955), pp. 181–216.

11 For the complete bibliography of texts by Milan Zloković, see Zoran Manević, *Zloković* (Belgrade: Institut za istoriju umetnosti and Muzej savremene umetnosti, 1989).

12 In the most detailed monographic study on Zloković produced to date (ibid.), architectural historian Zoran Manević focused on his interwar practice, leaving out the postwar period of his work. Failing to find any relevant connection between the two sides of Zloković's creative personality, in fact regarding him as a split personality and setting aside the latter side as an "obsession" with proportion and numbers, he only mentioned the theoretical work in a few general comments in the final paragraph of his study. Notwithstanding Manević's colossal contribution to the systematic and thorough research of Zloković's opus and bibliography, this disregard calls for a revision. Similarly, in her study of Zloković's life and work, art historian Marina Đurđević does little to integrate pre- and postwar phases. By and large she reinterprets Manević's findings, with added reviews of his postwar buildings as well as some general consideration of his theoretical work. Cf. Marina Đurđević, "Život i delo arhitekte Milana Zlokovića (1898–1965)" [Life and Work of Architect Milan Zloković], *Godišnjak grada Beograda* 38 (1991), pp. 145–168.

13 Because such comments are so rare from him, but more importantly because it is indicative of Zloković's design method, the comment deserves to be quoted in full: "It is interesting that in 1935, when I still had not worked on problems in the field of the science of proportions and metrology, I intuitively applied the above-mentioned type of window [the traditional window analyzed in the study] in the new Community Hall in Bijela (Boka Kotorska), with the single difference that, for the dimension of the stone frame, I adopted 20 cm instead of 17.385 cm (½ Venetian foot), and this was for a width of opening of 120 cm, the consequence being that the ratio between the two is 1:6, a fact to which I did not give much importance. For the dimensions finally adopted for the window opening, 160/120 cm (4:3), with which I felt a general familiarity, I did not find it necessary to relate them to the dimensions of the frame, (20 + 160 + 20)/(20 + 120 + 20) cm = 200/160 cm (5:4). For me it was important that I liked the shape of that window and that I found its dimensions convenient. I was far from realizing that I had achieved the absolute planimetric similarity of my window to the current window type in our coastal region, all the more in that the above-mentioned project was worked on in Belgrade and that at the time I had not known the exact dimensions of the window types of traditional architecture." Zloković, "Antropomorfni sistemi mera u arhitekturi," p. 193.

14 Alluding to the title of a surrealist text: Aleksandar Vučo, "Zlatan presek obmane" [The Golden Section of Deception], *Nemoguće/L'Impossible* (Belgrade, 1930), pp. 109–112.

15 Le Corbusier, *Towards a New Architecture* (1923), trans. Frederick Etchells (London: Architectural Press, 1948), p. 71.

16 Adolf Loos, "Meine bauschule" (1913), in his *Sämtliche Schriften: Trotzdem* (Vienna and Munich: Verlag Herold, 1962), p. 323.

17 The house contains three completely independent apartments: a rental apartment in the lower ground floor, the owner's apartment at the principal level, and another rental apartment on the floor above.

18 For example, at the lower ground level the central square determines the positions of two protruding volumes with arched openings and the consequent position of the lightwell; the plan of the first floor is one square module less than that of the ground floor, thus regulating the geometry of the setback (e.g., the length of the stepped section multiplied by the square root of 2 equals the whole length of the principal level); the position of openings is derived from the rotation of its diagonal; etc.

19 Loos, "Meine bauschule," p. 325.

20 Massimo Cacciari, "Loos and His Contemporaries" (1975), in *Architecture and Nihilism,* p. 107.

21 "The essence of building is letting dwell." Heidegger, "Building Dwelling Thinking," p. 361.

22 Cf. Panayotis Tournikiotis, *Adolf Loos* (New York: Princeton Architectural Press, 1994), pp. 59–69.

23 Manfredo Tafuri, "The Historicity of the Avant-Garde: Piranesi and Eisenstein," in his *The Sphere and the Labyrinth* (Cambridge: MIT Press, 1990), p. 59.

24 Loos's work was not widely known in the 1920s as there were very few books about his work at the time. The first definitive monograph was published in 1931: Heinrich Kulka, *Adolf Loos, das Werk des Architekten* (Vienna: Verlag von Anton Schroll & Co, 1931). Milan Zloković owned the book's first edition, signed in handwriting: "Belgrade, April 1931, Zloković." There is no evidence that Zloković knew Loos's work before 1931, although there may have been indirect points of connection, such as through architect Dušan Babić who, being a Vienna graduate, came to Belgrade from the source, and who lived in Zloković's house at the time of GAMM. Also, Zloković may have been acquainted with monographs in the Czech language written by Karl Marilaun (Brno, 1929) or Bohuslav Markalous (Prague, 1929) through the Czech architectural circles with which Belgrade architects kept in close contact.

25 Zlatko Neumann, "O problemu prostora u arhitekturi" [On the Problem of Space in Architecture], *Tehnički list* (Zagreb), no. 11–12 (1939).

26 The balance of solid and void is accentuated by the materials and coloring: the base is in reconstituted stone plaster, the facade is plain render, and the entrance niche is colored in deep earth red.

27 The reliefs on the Opel building, of an appropriate thematic content ("Man Racing the Automobile," "Sacrifice to the God Mercury," and "Industrial Workers"), are by architect Branko Krstić.

28 Le Corbusier, *Vers une architecture* (Paris: Éditions G. Crès et Cie, 1923).

29 Le Corbusier, *Towards a New Architecture*, p. 92.

30 Ibid., p. 97.

31 "And are we really to imagine that the daguerreotype has murdered art? No, it kills the work of patience, but it does homage to the work of thought." A. J. Wiertz, quoted in Walter Benjamin, *The Arcades Project*, trans. Howard Eiland and Kevin McLaughlin (Cambridge: Belknap Press of Harvard University Press, 1999), p. 671 [Y1,1].

32 K. Michael Hays, *Modernism and the Posthumanist Subject: The Architecture of Hannes Meyer and Ludwig Hilberseimer* (Cambridge: MIT Press, 1992), p. 72.

33 Ernst Bloch, *The Principle of Hope*, trans. Neville Plaice, Stephen Plaice, and Paul Knight (Cambridge: MIT Press, 1986), p. 733.

34 Cf. Hilde Heynen, "Building on Hollow Space: Ernst Bloch's Criticism of Modern Architecture," in her *Architecture and Modernity: A Critique* (Cambridge: MIT Press, 1999), pp. 118–128.

35 Bloch, *The Principle of Hope*, p. 734.

36 "Like a prosthetic apparatus for a crippled and crippling city unable to function adequately on its own, the Petersschule [like the Clinic] organizes its elements in such a way as to reveal the present order as unsatisfactory, physically and socially, and to propose an antisocial response as a possible way out: the Petersschule [like the Clinic] would like to disappear, to leave the old city behind." Hays, *Modernism and the Posthumanist Subject*, p. 107.

37 In the period of intense work on the Clinic, Zloković was also concerned with the problem of the efficiency of planning, and in 1938 he presented a paper to the Architects Club on this issue, which unfortunately has since been lost. The topic of this paper was "The analytical research of plan arrangement in relation to use ratio and to various structural systems in architectural design."

38 Đurđe Bošković, "Jugoslovenska arhitektura" [Yugoslav Architecture] (1931), in *Srpska arhitektura 1900–1970* (Belgrade: Muzej savremene umetnosti, 1972), p. 75.

39 As Kenneth Frampton noted in *Modern Architecture: A Critical History* (London: Thames and Hudson, 1980), p. 207, the rationalist approach was concerned with "the total integration of conceptual, structural and symbolic form," which, as a principle, could also be applied to Zloković's

concerns in his 1930s buildings. Himself a native of what became Italian territory, and spending his holidays in Italy every year after the war (his family being situated permanently in Trieste), Zloković could easily have been familiar with the rationalist movement.

40   Milan Zloković, manuscript notes for a lecture at the Faculty of Architecture, Belgrade (not dated); courtesy Đorđe Zloković.

41   Reyner Banham, *Age of the Masters: A Personal View of Modern Architecture* (1962; London: Architectural Press, 1982), p. 91.

42   The puzzling insertion of the corner column on the upper floors a posteriori is well worth noting. Contrary to the customary practice of constructing the structural framework first, it is clear from period photographs that the columns between the sharp parapet projections on the upper floors were added after the installation of windows and finalization of the facade finish. Presumably, it was not Zloković's intention to have columns in this position, and their odd, belated appearance surely seems contrived.

43   Hays, *Modernism and the Posthumanist Subject*, p. 5.

44   Milan Zloković, "La coordinazione modulare," in *Industrializzazione dell'edilizia* (Bari: Istituto di Architettura della Facoltà di Ingegneria, Università degli Studi di Bari, 1965), pp. 140–196. See section 18: "Un esempio di collimazione modulare del 1931: La Clinica Pediatrica della Facoltà di Medicina di Belgrado realizzata nel periodo d'anteguerra," pp. 177-179.

45   *Oberlicht*, German for the glazed opening above the window or door, with the transom between the two.

46   The roller mechanism for the blinds is hidden on the internal side and incorporated within the thickness of the transom between the two apertures.

47   Milan Zloković, "Uloga neprekidne podele ili 'Zlatnog preseka' u arhitektonskoj kompoziciji" [The Role of Continued Proportion or "Golden Section" in Architectural Composition], parts I, II, and III, *Pregled arhitekture* (Belgrade), no. 1 and no. 2 (1954) and no. 3 (1955), pp. 11–17, 44–48, and 80-85.

48   The golden section is "the proportion of the two divisions of a straight line or the two dimensions of a plane figure such that a smaller is to the larger as the larger is to the sum of the two. If the sides of a rectangle are in this proportion and a square is constructed internally on the shorter side, the rectangle that remains will also have sides in the same proportion." (*The Collins English Dictionary*.) The numerical value of this proportion, designated by the symbol φ, is:
$$\varphi = \frac{\sqrt{5}+1}{2} = 1.618\ldots$$

49   Theodor W. Adorno, "Functionalism Today," in Neil Leach, ed., *Rethinking Architecture: A Reader in Cultural Theory* (London: Routledge, 2000), p. 14.

50   Ibid., p. 19.

51 Aleksej Brkić, *Znakovi u kamenu: Srpska moderna arhitektura 1930–1980* [Signs in Stone: Serbian Modern Architecture 1930–1980] (Belgrade: Savez Arhitekata Sabije, 1992), p. 109.

52 Le Corbusier, *Une maison—un palais: À la recherche d'une unité architecturale* (Paris: Crès et Cie, 1928), p. 3.

VISION

1 Joan Copjec, "Cutting Up," in her *Read My Desire: Lacan against the Historicists* (Cambridge: MIT Press, 1994), p. 40.

2 As stamped and annotated on the back of the prints provided for this research courtesy of the Astronomical Observatory in Belgrade.

3 From 1927, when the laboratory was moved into the new building of the Histology and Physiology Institute, the Photographic Department often provided services not only to the other departments of the Medical Faculty but to other university departments and institutions, as well as to some state institutions. Mileta Magarašević, "Medicinska fotografija" [Medical Photography], in Miodrag Đorđević, ed., *Serbian Photography 1839–1989* (Belgrade: Srpska akademija nauka i umetnosti, 1991), pp. 146–147.

4 Aleksandar Đ. Kostić, *Osnovi histologije* [The Basics of Histology] (Belgrade: Napredak, 1927), p. 7.

5 "Hence the major effect of the Panopticon: to induce in the inmate a state of conscious and permanent visibility that assures the automatic functioning of power." Michel Foucault, "Panopticism," in Neil Leach, ed., *Rethinking Architecture: A Reader in Cultural Theory* (London: Routledge, 2000), p. 361.

6 Roland Barthes, "Rhetoric of the Image," in his *Image Music Text,* selected and trans. Stephen Heath (London: Fontana Press, 1977), p. 45.

7 "Scientific method is distinguished by the fact that, in leading to new objects, it develops new methods. Just as form in art is distinguished by the fact that, opening up new contents, it develops new forms." Walter Benjamin, *The Arcades Project,* trans. Howard Eiland and Kevin McLaughlin (Cambridge: Belknap Press of Harvard University Press, 1999), p. 473 [N9,2]. Also: "The dialectical method is thus distinguished by the fact that in leading to new objects, it develops new methods, just as form in art is distinguished by the fact that it develops new forms in delineating new contents. It is only from without that a work of art has one and *only* one form, that a dialectical treatise has one and *only* one method." Ibid., p. 474 [N10,1].

8 "Included in the extensive set of astronomical instruments, expertly chosen after the First World War by Professor Nedeljković, there were three Zeiss instruments for astrographic work: visual refractor 65/1055 cm with photo-camera, visual refractor 20/302 cm with two astro-cameras 16/80 cm, and astrograph 11/128 cm with camera 16/18 cm, as well as two types of Askania photo-

visual refractors 13.5/100 cm and 16/240 cm." Vojislava Protić-Benišek, "Astronomska fotografija" [Astronomical Photography], in Đorđević, ed., *Serbian Photography 1839–1989*, pp. 153–157.

9   The main reason for the delay was that there were not enough expertly trained staff to carry out work previously undertaken and to start in with the observation at the same time. Also, additional adjustment and improvement of access to the instruments were needed before the observation could start. Vojislava Protić-Benišek, "Pet decenija aktivnosti grupe za male planete, komete i satelite Astronomske opservatorije u Beogradu" [Fifty Years of Activity: Minor Planets, Comets, and Satellites Department of Belgrade Astronomical Observatory], in *Sto godina Astronomske opservatorije u Beogradu* [One Hundred Years of the Astronomical Observatory in Belgrade] (Belgrade: Astronomska opservatorija, 1989), pp. 89–96.

10   Joan Copjec, "The Orthopsychic Subject," in *Read My Desire,* pp. 35–36.

11   Barthes, "Rhetoric of the Image," p. 40.

12   Aleksandar Đ. Kostić, *Polni život čoveka* [Sexual Life of Man] (Belgrade: Panteon, 1932), p. iv.

13   Martin Heidegger, "The Origin of the Work of Art," in *Martin Heidegger: Basic Writings,* ed. David Farrell Krell (London: Routledge, 1993), p. 167.

14   Jacques Lacan, quoted in Copjec, "The Orthopsychic Subject," p. 15.

15   Nikola Dobrović, "Uređenje 'Terase' na Terazijama u Beogradu" [Planning of the Terrace at Terazije in Belgrade], *Arhitektura* (Ljubljana), no. 4 (1932), p. 117.

16   Beatriz Colomina, *Privacy and Publicity: Modern Architecture as Mass Media* (Cambridge: MIT Press, 1994), p. 335.

17   Le Corbusier, *The Modulor,* trans. Peter de Francia and Anna Bostock (Basel, Boston, Berlin: Birkhäuser, 2000), pp. 72–73.

18   Colomina, *Privacy and Publicity,* p. 134.

19   Nikola Dobrović, "Pokrenutost prostora—Bergsonove dinamičke sheme—nova slika sredine," in his *Savremena arhitektura 3: Sledbenici* (Belgrade: Građevinska Knjiga, 1962), p. 237.

ILLUSTRATION CREDITS

Reproductions from Periodicals

Architects' Journal, London: figure 4.15

Arhitektura, Ljubljana: figures 2.20, 2.21, 2.22, 2.24, 2.25, 2.26, 2.27, 2.28, 2.36, 2.37, 2.38, 2.39, 2.40, 2.43, 2.47, 3.18, 3.19, 3.22, 3.24, 3.25, 3.26, 3.27, 3.28, 3.30, 3.31, 4.20, 4.21, 4.23, 4.26, and 4.30

Beogradske opštinske novine, Belgrade: figures 4.9, 4.10, 4.11, 4.12, and 4.14

Československo-Jihoslovanská revue, Prague: figure 3.20

Godišnjak našeg neba za godinu 1935, Belgrade: figure 2.55

Nadrealizam danas i ovde, Belgrade: figure 4.1

Nemoguće/L'Impossible, Belgrade: figure 2.11

Nova iskra, Belgrade: figures 3.3 and 3.7

Politika, Belgrade: figure 3.13

Savremena opština, Belgrade: figures 4.4 and 4.5

Svedočanstva, Belgrade: figure 2.6

Tehnički list, Zagreb: figure 4.3

Umetnički pregled, Belgrade: figures 3.21, 3.23, 4.27, 4.38, 4.39, 4.40, and 4.49

Zenit, Zagreb and Belgrade: figures 1.8, 1.9, 1.10, 1.11, 1.15, and 1.18

Reproductions from Other Publications

L'Art décoratif et industriel dans le Royaume S.H.S. (Belgrade: Narodna misao, 1925) (courtesy University Library, Belgrade): figure 3.9

Dobrović, Nikola, *Obnova i izgradnja Beograda* (Belgrade: Urbanistički institut NR Srbije, 1946): figure 3.32

Dobrović, Nikola, *Savremena arhitektura 5* (Belgrade: Zavod za izdavanje udžbenika SR Srbije, 1971): figure 3.29

Exposition Internationale des Arts Décoratifs et Industriels Modernes, Paris 1925, Section du Royaume des Serbes, Croates et Slovènes, Photo Album (courtesy Museum of Applied Art, Belgrade): figures 3.10, 3.11, and 3.12

Le Corbusier, *L'Art décoratif d'aujourd'hui* (Paris: G. Crès et Cie, 1926), p. 34 (courtesy Fondation Le Corbusier, ©FLC 46): figure 1.5

Meštrović (Zagreb: Nova Evropa, 1933): figure 3.8

Micić, Ljubomir, Ivan Goll, and Boško Tokin, *Manifest Zenitizma* (Zagreb, 1921): figure 1.7

Planić, Stjepan, ed., *Problemi savremene arhitekture* (Zagreb: Jugoslovenska štampa d.d., 1932): figure 2.44

Seissel, Josip, *Jugoslavenski paviljon na Međunarodnoj izložbi u Parizu 1937* (Zagreb: Tisak Zaklade tiskare Narodnih novina, 1937): figure 3.6

Umetnici članovi SANU, exhibition catalogue (Belgrade: SANU, Beogradski sajam and Narodni muzej, 1980): figure 3.5

Reproductions from Archival Sources

Architecture Department in the Museum of Science and Technology, Belgrade: figures 2.30, 2.32, 3.17, 4.17, 4.33, 4.34, 4.35, 4.37 (center), and 4.61

Archive of the Serbian Academy of Sciences and Arts, Belgrade: figure 3.4 (Historical collection 14410/I-B-957)

Astronomical Observatory, Belgrade: figures 2.49 and 2.50

City Museum, Vršac: figures 3.14, 3.16, 4.50, and 4.53 (left and bottom right)

Fondation Le Corbusier: figure 1.6

Historical Archive of the City of Belgrade: figure 4.31

Institute of Architecture and Urban Planning of Serbia, Belgrade: figure 4.32

Library of the Faculty of Architecture, Belgrade: figures 4.37 (left and right) and 4.44

Museum of Applied Art, Belgrade: figures 2.5, 2.9, 2.10, 4.18, and 4.19

Museum of Contemporary Art, Belgrade: figure 2.12

Museum of the City of Belgrade: figures 2.48, 2.51, 2.53, 2.54, 4.16, 4.42, 6.2, and 6.3

National Museum, Belgrade: figures 1.2, 1.3, 1.4, 1.12, 1.13, 1.14, 1.16, 1.17, and 1.19

Photo-documentation Center Politika: figures 2.35, 2.45, 3.1, 3.15, 4.7, 4.8, 4.51, 4.52, and 4.59

Reproductions from Private Sources

Courtesy Nikola Belobrk: figures 4.45, 4.46, 4.47, 4.48, and 4.49

Courtesy Viktorija Brašovan: figure 2.17

Courtesy Miloš Jurišić: figures 1.1, 2.46, 3.2, 4.2, 4.13, 4.28, 4.41 (left), 4.43, 4.55, 4.56 (left), 4.57, 4.58, 4.60, and 4.62

Courtesy Vojislava Protić-Benišek: figure 2.52

Courtesy Đorđe Zloković: figures 2.1, 2.2, 2.3, 2.4, 2.7, 2.8, 2.13, 2.14, 2.15, 2.16, 2.17, 2.18, 2.19, 2.23, 2.29, 2.31, 2.33, 2.34, 2.41, 2.42, 5.1, 5.2, 5.3, 5.4, 5.6 (bottom), 5.9 (right), 5.10, 5.11, 5.12, 5.13, 5.14, 5.15, 5.16, 5.17, 5.18, 5.19, 5.20, 5.22, 5.23, 5.24, 5.26, 5.29, 5.30, 5.31, 5.32 (left), and 6.1

Ljiljana Blagojević: figures 4.6, 4.22, 4.24, 4.25, 4.29, 4.36, 4.41 (right two), 4.53 (top right), 4.54, 4.56 (right two), 5.5, 5.6 (top and center), 5.7, 5.8, 5.9 (left), 5.21, 5.25, 5.27, 5.28, and 5.32 (right)

ILLUSTRATION CREDITS

INDEX

ABC, 11, 15
Academicism, 50, 52, 57, 134, 177
Adorno, Theodor W., 220
Aleksandar (Karađorđević), king, 60, 96, 185
   Dictatorship of 6 January 1929, 60, 81
Aleksić, Dragan, 74
Alfonso XIII (king of Spain), 96
Après le cubisme (Jeanneret and Ozenfant), 6
Arbos, 15, 237 (n. 42)
Archipenko, Alexander, 12, 14
Architecture d'aujourd'hui (exhibition, Paris, 1933), 68; fig. 2.43
Architecture d'aujourd'hui (film by Chenal and Le Corbusier), 148
Architecture vivante, 14
Architekt, 106
Arhitektura, 52, 151
Art décoratif d'aujourd'hui (Le Corbusier), 5; fig. 1.5
Arvatov, Boris, 125

Babić, Dušan, 58, 68, 152, 154, 261 (n. 63)
   Lektres building, Belgrade, 68
   UYEA building, Belgrade, fig. 2.40
   villa of Jelena Plevan, Belgrade, 154; fig. 4.31
   villa Protić, Belgrade, 152; fig. 4.30
   villa of Karl and Maria Reich, Belgrade, 152; fig. 4.29
   villa of Dragutin Smejkal, Belgrade, 154; fig. 4.32
Babić, Ljiljana, 106
Bajalović, Petar, 89
   pavilion of the Kingdom of Sebia, Rome, 89; fig. 3.7
Baldesar, Helen, 92
   "Bosnian room" (with Mijić and Smiljanić), 92; fig. 3.11
Banham, Reyner, 217
Barbarogenius, 8, 10
   cultural barbarism, 9, 10
Barcelona, 176, 179
   International Exposition (1929), 83, 95, 96
Barthes, Roland, 228, 229
Bauhaus, 180, 181

Bayer, Herbert, 17
Behrens, Peter, 3
Belgrade
   Architects Club, 59, 62
   Arts Pavilion, 29, 62, 68, 110, 146
   Central Department of Hygiene, 136
   Chief Urbanist, 119
   City Council, and housing, 136, 137, 139; fig. 4.11
   construction of flats, 128 (table 4.2)
   fashion show, 165; fig. 4.42
   Helena Rubinstein Beauty Institute, fig. 4.16
   Hotel Casina, 144
   increase in population and built-up area, 128 (table 4.1)
   Master Plan (1923), 58, 130
   New Belgrade, 119–120
   panorama, fig. 1.1
   Regulation Plan (1938), 119
   Skadarska Street, fig. 4.2
   Technical Faculty, 15, 58
   Town Planning Department, 119
   Urban Planning Institute of Serbia, 119
Belobrk, Momčilo, 65, 169, 174; fig. 4.45
   apartment block in Bosanska Street, Belgrade, fig. 4.46
   apartment block in Dobračina Street, Belgrade, fig. 4.46
   apartment block in Dositejeva Street, Belgrade, fig. 4.46
   apartment block in Francuska Street, Belgrade, fig. 4.47
   apartment block in Njegoševa Street, Belgrade, fig. 4.47
   apartment block in Svetogorska Street, Belgrade, fig. 4.47
   entrance doors to apartment blocks, fig. 4.48
   interior of underground carpark, fig. 4.48
   student project, fig. 4.44
   villa in Kaćanskog Street, Belgrade, fig. 4.49
Benjamin, Walter, 29, 44, 48, 49, 50, 83, 84, 86, 92, 100, 142, 176, 228
Bergson, Henri, 11, 117
Berlage, H. P., 143, 188

Bloch, Ernst, 52, 96, 209, 210, 211
   reisefertig, 209–210
Bohemian Ball, 144; fig. 4.19
Boka Kotorska, 58, 191, 193, 194, 197, 200, 210
Bon, Branko, 188; fig. 4.62
Borošić, Đura, 63
   Hotel Prague, Belgrade, 63; fig. 2.35
Bošković, Đurđe, 63, 68, 212
Braniš, Vojta, 92
Brašovan, Dragiša, 65, 83, 95, 100, 103–104, 165, 176–188, 264 (n. 83); figs. 3.15, 4.50
   Air Forces Headquarters, Zemun, 182, 185; fig. 4.57
   apartment block in Braće Jugovića Street, Belgrade, fig. 4.38
   house of Dragiša Brašovan, Belgrade, 50, 179; figs. 2.17, 4.53
   Palace of the Danube Regional Government, Novi Sad, 68, 103, 182, 185, 188; fig. 4.58
   Palace of the State Print Works, Belgrade, 103, 182–183; fig. 4.56
   villa of Đorđe Genčić, Belgrade, 177, 179; fig. 4.52
   villa of Dušan Lazić, Belgrade, 179–180; fig. 4.54
   villa of Richard Škarka, Belgrade, 177; fig. 4.51
   Workers Chamber Hall, Novi Sad, 181; fig. 4.55
   Yugoslav pavilion, Barcelona, 65, 83, 95–103, 181; figs. 3.13, 3.14
   Yugoslav pavilion, Milan, 100, 181, 185; fig. 3.16
   Yugoslav pavilion, Thessalonica, 100
Breton, André, 33
   Nadja, 32
Breuer, Marcel, 52
Brkić, Aleksej, 221
Buckingham, James Silk, 130
Buck-Morss, Susan, 95, 100
Burmazović, S., fig. 4.14
Byt, 125, 127, 144, 165, 188

Cacciari, Massimo, 27, 194, 195, 198
Chenal, Pierre, 148

Colomina, Beatriz, 182, 229, 231
Contimporanul, 11
Copjec, Joan, 174, 228, 229

Dalmatia, 108, 109
Damljanović, Tanja, 106
Dedinac, Milan, 33
Delaunay, Robert, 12
Denegri, Ješa, 17
De Solà-Morales, Ignasi, 96, 102
De Stijl, 11, 14
De Stijl Manifesto (Mondrian and van Doesburg), 19
Devětsil (magazine and group), 11, 106
Dimitrijević, Mladen, 33
Dobrović, Nikola, 57, 83, 102–112, 117, 119, 123, 177, 180, 181, 183, 188, 229, 231, 252 (n. 67); fig. 3.17
   Agrarian Bank, Belgrade, 112
   bathing complex at Bačvice Bay, Split, 111; fig. 3.25
   Danube Station, Belgrade, 57, 112; figs. 2.26, 3.27
   Grand Hotel on Lopud, 108; fig. 3.21
   hotel at Lapad, fig. 3.22
   Hotel-Kursaal, Dubrovnik, 112; fig. 3.28
   house of Dr. Burliž, Prague, 106; fig. 3.18
   house with a pharmacy, Krč, 106; fig. 3.19
   King Aleksandar I College, Prague, 106; fig. 3.20
   Ministry of Defense Headquarters, Belgrade, 104, 108, 109, 110, 117, 123, 231
   Municipal (or City) Café, Dubrovnik, 57, 112; fig. 2.27
   Palace of the Coastal Regional Government, Split, 112
   Palace of the Vardar Regional Government, Skopje, 112; fig. 3.26
   PRIZAD building, Belgrade, 109
   railway station, Skopje, 112
   Regional Hospital, Split, 111, 112
   Student Vacation Association Hall, Dubrovnik, 108, 109
   Terazije Terrace, Belgrade, 57, 83, 106, 111, 112, 117–123, 229; figs. 2.28, 3.29, 3.30, 3.31, 3.32

Dobrović, Nikola (cont.)
   theater, Novi Sad, 111; fig. 3.24
   villa Vesna on Lopud; fig. 3.23
Dobrović, Petar, 106, 110, 111
Doesburg, Theo van, 11, 104, 105
   Rosenberg house, 14
Dolinar, Lojze, fig. 5.29. *See also* Hus, Herman
Đorđević, Đorđe and Krista, 44, 241 (n. 30)
Dubovy, Jan, 58, 62, 63, 68, 71, 74, 76, 130–134, 144, 146, 148, 228, 244 (n. 66)
   Astronomical Observatory, Belgrade, 71–79, 226, 228, 229, 245 (n. 70); figs. 2.44, 2.45, 2.47, 2.48, 2.49, 2.50, 2.51, 2.52, 2.53, 2.54, 2.55, 6.2, 6.3
   Cvetni trg Market Hall, Belgrade, fig. 2.34
   Evangelical church, Ostojićevo, 68; fig. 2.37
   house of Jozef Paroci, Belgrade, 132; fig. 4.6
   pan-Slavic idea, 130–131
   Serbian Orthodox Church boarding school, Novi Sad, 65; fig. 2.36
   Triangulation Point of Belgrade, 62, 74; fig. 2.47
   typical peasant's house, 131; fig. 4.5
   typical worker's house, 131–132; fig. 4.4
   villa of Arkadije Miletić, Belgrade, 146; fig. 4.22
   Workers' Shelters, Belgrade, 132, 134; figs. 4.7, 4.8, 4.9
Dubrovnik, 108, 109, 112, 197
Dudok, Willem Marinus, 140, 188

Eesteren, Cornelis van
   Rosenberg house, 14
Ehrenburg, Ilya, 11, 12
Ehrlich, Hugo, 52
   Yugoslav Associated Bank, Belgrade, 52; figs. 2.20, 2.21, 2.22
Eslinger (wooden blinds), 25, 35, 218
Esprit nouveau (magazine), 11, 33, 34
Existenzminimum, 128

"First Exhibition of the Photo Club," 29
"First Salon of Architecture," 29, 62, 74

"First Yugoslav Salon of Contemporary Architecture," 68, 74
Flaker, Aleksandar
   on *byt,* 255 (n. 1)
   optimal projection, 127, 235 (n. 20)
Fodor, Toša, 140
Foucault, Michel, 226
   on Bentham's Panopticon, 226
Fourier, Charles, 130

GAMM. *See* Group of Architects of the Modern Movement in Belgrade
Garden city, 74, 130, 131, 137
Garnier, Tony, 130
Geometrical or regulating system, 197, 198, 200, 201, 204; fig. 5.5
   ad quadratum, 198, 201
   consistent modular collimation, 217, 218
   golden section, 201, 204
   harmony and proportion, 194, 197, 211, 212, 217, 221, 229
   modular, 195, 211, 214, 220
   regulating line, 198, 200, 204
Giedion, Sigfried, 85, 86
Gleizes, Albert, 12
Golossov, Ilya
   Club Žnjev, 217
Grakalić, Milan. *See* Bon, Branko
Graz
   Technische Hochschule, 58
Gropius, Walter, 140
Grossstadt, 27
Group of Architects of the Modern Movement in Belgrade (GAMM), xii, 29, 57–63, 65, 68, 71, 74, 76, 83, 104, 142, 169, 176
   at Damascus Sword café, 71
   Rules of, 59–60, 71
Gusle, 5; fig. 1.3

Hague, The
   Pulchri Studio, 106
Hays, K. Michael, 206, 210, 217
Heidegger, Martin, 229
Heynen, Hilde, 209

Hitchcock, Henry-Russell, 182
Howard, Ebenezer, 130
Hribar, Stjepan, 92
   pavilion of the Kingdom of Serbs, Croats and Slovenes, Paris, 91–92; fig. 3.10
Hus, Herman
   house of Lojze Dolinar, fig. 4.41

Ibler, Drago, 182
International Style, 182

Janković, Dušan, 144
   interior decoration of buffet at Bohemian Ball, 144; fig. 4.19
   villa, Belgrade, 144, 146; fig. 4.18
Jeanneret, Albert, 6; fig. 1.6
Jeanneret, Charles-Édouard. *See* Le Corbusier
Johnson, Philip, 182
Josić, Mladen, 81
Journey to the East (Le Corbusier), 3, 232 (n. 1)

Kadijević, Aleksandar, 177, 181
Kandinsky, Wassily, 12
Kapetanović, Milan, 84
   pavilion of the Kingdom of Serbia, Paris, 84–85, 91; figs. 3.2, 3.3, 3.4
Kapsa & Müller, 108
Kassák, Lajos, 13
Kiesler, Frederick
   Cité dans l'Espace, 92
Kilim, 5, 50, 85, 92, 100
   from Pirot, 84, 88, 96
Klek, Josif (Jo), 12, 13, 15–21, 27, 86, 236 (n. 31). *See also* Seissel, Josip
   Advertisements, 15, 17; fig. 1.12
   Bayadere, 19; fig. 1.17
   "Exhibition of the Revolutionary Art of the West and America," Moscow, 12
   "Internationale Ausstellung junger Kunst," Bielefeld, 12
   Pafama, 15
   Playing Cards, 19; fig. 1.16
   "La Prima Expozitie Internationala a 'Contimpuranul,'" Bucharest, 12
   Tavern, 19; fig. 1.15
   Villa Zenit, 21, 27; fig. 1.19
   Zenitheum I, fig. 1.13
   Zenitheum II, fig. 1.14
Klipstein, Auguste, 3
Kljaković, Jozo, 92
Knjaževac, 5, 6; fig. 1.4
Kojić, Branislav, 52, 58, 60, 62, 71, 130, 142, 154, 157, 159, 165, 176, 181, 185, 229, 261–262 (n. 64); fig. 2.30
   apartment block of Dr. Đurić, Belgrade, 159; fig. 4.37
   Arts Pavilion, Belgrade, 62, 243 (n. 54)
   Đura Jakšić School, Skopje, fig. 2.24
   erker, 157
   folkloric style, 154, 157
   Hall of the Sokol organization, Belgrade, fig. 2.39
   house of Branislav and Danica Kojić, Belgrade, 157; fig. 4.34
   house of Svetislav Marodić, Belgrade, 157, 159; fig. 4.36
   Interior à la Corbusier, 62; fig. 2.32
   Municipal Administration Center, Novi Sad, 68; fig. 2.38
   national shop, Paris, 92; fig. 3.12
   Tsar Dušan School, Skopje, fig. 2.24
   Urology Hospital, Belgrade 62
   villa Đorđević, Belgrade, 157
   villa for a small family, Belgrade, 146; fig. 4.20
   villa Marinković, Belgrade, 157; fig. 4.35
   villas for artists, 146; fig. 4.21
   Vreme building, Belgrade, 188; fig. 4.61
Kojić, Danica, 143; fig. 4.33
   interior of the house of Mihajlo Kojić, Belgrade, 143; fig. 4.17
   interior of Kojić house, 157 fig. 4.34
Korčula, 194, 197
Kostić, Aleksandar, 226, 229
Kovačević, Bojan, 109
Kovačić, Viktor, 13–14, 105
   Slaveks building, 13

Kovaljevski, Đorđe, fig. 4.13
Kracauer, Siegfried, 129, 132
Krejček, Miroslav, 92
Krizman, Tomislav, 92, 96; fig. 3.9
Krstić, Branko and Petar, 65, 91, 111, 148–152
   apartment building in Brankova Street, Belgrade, 152; fig. 4.27
   apartment building in Kumanovska Street, Belgrade, 151; fig. 4.26
   Igumanov Palace, Belgrade, 152; fig. 4.28
   pavilion of the Kingdom of Serbs, Croats and Slovenes, Philadelphia, 90
   Veterinary Foundation apartment block, Belgrade, 151
   villa of Olga Lazić, Belgrade, 150; fig. 4.25
   villa of barrister Milićević, Belgrade, 148; fig. 4.23
   Villa Vukosava, Belgrade, 149–150; fig. 4.24

Labrouste, Henri, 143
Lacan, Jacques, 228, 229
La Chaux-de-Fonds, 6
Lazarević, Đorđe, 165
   Ta-ta Department Store, Belgrade, 165; fig. 4.41
Lazić, Svetomir, 131
   family houses in the Serbian style, 131; fig. 4.3
Le Corbusier (Charles-Édouard Jeanneret), 3–8, 10, 27, 52, 108, 139, 140, 143, 146, 148, 195, 198, 205, 221, 229, 231; figs. 1.2, 1.3, 1.4, 1.5, 1.6
   apartment of Charles de Beistegui, 146
   Aquitania (steamship), 205–206
   Buenos Aires scheme, 215
   "eyes which do not see," 27, 119, 205
   five points, 106
   Maison Dom-ino, 91
   Normandie (ship), 215
   Pavillon de l'Esprit Nouveau, 92
   Pavillon des Temps Nouveaux, 88
   Ville Contemporaine, 130
   Ville Radieuse, 7
LEF, 125
Lingeri, Pietro, 215. *See also* Terragni, Giuseppe

Lissitzky, El (Lazar), 11–13, 15, 17; fig. 1.11
   Construction, 11
   Prouns, 13, 17
Ljubica (Obrenović), princess, 157
   konak, 157
Ljubljana, Architects Club, 68
Loos, Adolf, 14, 21, 25, 34, 39, 50, 142, 143, 194, 195, 198, 200, 201, 202
   Moller house, 201
   "Ornament and Crime," 34
   Raumplan, 201, 202
   Villa Moïssi, 14
Lozowick, Louis, 12
Lukić, Đorđe, 74. *See also* Tatić, Rajko

Ma, 11
Maksimović, Branko, 7, 65, 137
   colony for the poor, Belgrade, 137; fig. 4.12
Malevich, Kazimir, 12, 125
   bespredmetny, 125, 134
   suprematism, 12
Manević, Zoran, xii, 63, 176
Manière de penser l'urbanisme (Le Corbusier), 8
Mann, Thomas, 136
Manojlović, Todor, 111
Man Ray, 41
Marinković, Branislav, 165
   apartment block in Kićevska Street, Belgrade, fig. 4.41
Matić, Dušan, 33
McLeod, Mary, 143
Melnikov, Konstantin
   pavilion of the USSR, Paris, 92
Mendelsohn, Erich, 15, 17
   Einstein Tower, 15
Meštrović, Ivan, 88–89
   Vidovdan cycle, 89
   Vidovdan Temple, 89; fig. 3.8
   Yugoslav idea, 89
Metropolis, 27, 130, 131
Meyer, Hannes, 11, 17
   Co-op works, 17
   Petersschule, 210
Micić, Anuška, 11

Micić, Branko. *See* Ve Poliansky, Branko
Micić, Ljubomir, 8–9, 10–15, 17, 32, 234 (n. 18); fig. 1.7
Mies van der Rohe, Ludwig, 102, 103, 180
   German pavilion, Barcelona, 95, 96, 100, 102
   Tugendhat house, 146
Mijić, Karlo. *See* Baldesar, Helen
Milunović, Milo, 44, 49, 87
   Three Girls, 87
Mišković, Vojislav, 74
Modern style, 142, 144, 148, 149, 152, 168, 177, 179, 181, 182, 185, 188
Moholy-Nagy, László, 12
Mondrian, Piet, 19
Museum of Modern Art, New York, 181

Nadrealizam danas i ovde, 41
Najman, Josif, 52
   Mint, Belgrade, fig. 2.25
   photocollage of buildings designed by, fig. 4.43
National style, 57, 61. *See also* Serbian-Byzantine style
Nedeljne ilustracije, 49
Nemoguće/L'Impossible, 34, 39, 41
Nestorović, Bogdan, 188
   Craftsmen's Hall, 188; fig. 4.60
   PRIZAD Palace, 188; fig. 4.59
Neue Sachlichkeit, 106, 130, 209
Neumann, Zlatko, 202
Nina-Naj. *See* Micić, Anuška
Noble savage, 3, 5, 6, 10, 84
Noi, 11
Nova literatura, 140

Oblik [Form] (group of artists), 60, 146, 243 (n. 50)
Oreb Mojaš, Marina, 108
Ozenfant, Amédée, 6; fig. 1.6

Paris
   École Centrale des Arts et Manufactures, 58
   École des Hautes Études, 58
   École Supérieure des Arts et Métiers, 58

Eiffel Tower, 84
Exposition Internationale des Arts Décoratifs et Industriels Modernes (1925), 92
Exposition Internationale des Arts et Techniques dans la Vie Moderne (1937), 86
Exposition Universelle Internationale (1900), 83
fashion, 143
Galerie des Machines, 84
Grand Palais, 84
Petit Palais, 84
Pont Alexandre III, 84
Pont de l'Alma, 84
Sorbonne, 58
Trocadéro, 86
Universal Exposition (1889), 83
Passagen-Werk [Arcades Project] (Benjamin), 83, 142
Peinture moderne (Le Corbusier and Ozenfant), 169
Perret, Auguste, 130
Petrik, Dragan, 136
   village for tuberculosis sufferers, 136; fig. 4.10
Petrović, Mihajlo (journalist), 31
Petrović, Mihajlo (mathematician), 85
   hydro-integrator, 85; fig. 3.5
Petrović, Rastko, 33
Philadelphia, 91
   Sesquicentennial International Exposition (1926), 90
Photography
   Askania instruments, 74, 228
   astrography, 226
   Belgrade Photo Club, 29
   Benjamin's notes on, 238 (n. 2), 270 (n. 31)
   history of, in Serbia, 239 (n. 6)
   microphotography, 226
   photogram, 41; fig. 2.11
   Photographic Department of the Histology Institute of the Medical Faculty, Belgrade, 226
   on photographic studio, 238 (n. 2)

Photography (cont.)
   rayograph (*see* Photography: photogram)
   in surrealism, 29, 32, 34, 41
   by Vučo, 39
   Zeiss, 74, 228
   by Zloković, 35, 41
Plečnik, Jože, 105, 111, 112
Politika, 81, 96–97
Popović, Branko, 60
Prague, 3, 65, 106, 108, 111, 131
   Architects Club, 106
   architectural firm of Bohumil Hübschmann and Antonin Engel, 106
   architectural firm Dušek-Kozák-Maca, 106
   Czech functionalism, 63, 106
   Denisův Institut, 106
   Technical University, 58, 106
   Umělecká Beseda, 63
Principle of Hope (Bloch), 209
Prljević, Miladin, 165, 188
   Albania Palace (after Bon and Grakalić), 188; fig. 4.62
   apartment block in Kneza Miloša Street, Belgrade, fig. 4.39
   apartment block in Kosančićev Venac Street, Belgrade, fig. 4.40
Problemi urbanizma [Issues of Urbanism] (Maksimović), 7
Problems of Contemporary Architecture [Problemi savremene arhitekture] (Planić), 74
Protić, Miodrag, 228
Protić, Miodrag B., 34
Putevi, 33

Quetglas, José, 95

Radović, Ranko, 108
Reconstruction and Construction of Belgrade [Obnova i izgradnja Beograda] (Dobrović), 119
Révolution surréaliste, 33
Ristić, Marko, 32, 33, 39, 144; fig. 2.5
Rodchenko, Aleksandr, 11
   Constructive Form in Space, 11

Rome
   International Exposition of Art (1911), 88
   Palace of Fine Arts, 88
   Palazzo Principe Dorio, 144
Rosandić, Toma, 87
Russian Tsar café, 32, 58, 242–243 (n. 46)
Ruvidić, Milorad, 84, 86; fig. 3.2. *See also* Kapetanović, Milan

Sant'Elia, Antonio, 17, 130
Sarajevo, 92
Savremena opština, 131
Schwitters, Kurt, 35
"Second Yugoslav Salon of Contemporary Architecture," 74
Seissel, Josip, 21, 86, 87, 236 (n. 31). *See also* Klek, Josif
   pavilion of the Kingdom of Yugoslavia, Paris, 86; fig. 3.6
Serbian Academy of Sciences and Arts, 102
Serbian-Byzantine style, 68, 84, 88, 90, 91, 100, 111, 112, 157
Servant's Broom, The (ballet by Ristić, Milojević, and Isačenko), 144
7 Arts, 11
Shand, Philip Morton, x, 140
Siedlung, 137, 146
Simić, Vojin, 65
Simmel, Georg, 130, 131, 142
   "The Metropolis and Mental Life," 130
Smiljanić, Dušan. *See* Baldesar, Helen
Societal Conditions of Development of the Architectural Profession in Belgrade, 1920–1940 [Društveni uslovi razvitka struke u Beogradu, 1920–1940] (Kojić), 71
Spencer, Thomas, 130
Sretenović, Dejan, 41
Srpski tehnički list, 86
Stavba, 11, 62, 65, 106
Stijović, Rista, 110, 111
Stojanović, Ljuba, 136
Stojanović, Sreten, 44, 48, 49, 60, 146; figs. 2.14, 2.15
Strajnić, Kosta, 106
Sturm, Der, 11

Subotić, Irina, 15, 17
Surrealism, 29, 32–34, 41, 239–240 (n. 12)
Survage, Léopold, 19
    La Ville, 19; fig. 1.18
Svedočanstva, 33, 34; fig. 2.6

Tafuri, Manfredo, 201
Tanazević, Branko, 90
Tatić, Rajko, 74
    Belgrade Fair (with Lukić and Tričković), 74; fig. 2.46
Tatlin, Vladimir, 11, 12, 14
    Monument to the Third International, 11, 14; fig. 1.10
Teige, Karel, 106
Terragni, Giuseppe, 215, 217
    apartment building, Milan (with Lingeri), 215
    Casa del Fascio, 215
    Novocomum, 215, 217
Tesla, Nikola, 10
Thonet (firm), 39
365, 11
Todić, Milanka, 34, 41
Tokin, Boško, 11
Tomorrow: A Peaceful Path to Real Reform (Howard), 130
Toumbé (Ve Poliansky), 8
Tournikiotis, Panayotis, 200
Tričković, Milivoje, 74, 168. *See also* Tatić, Rajko
Trieste, 58, 191
Trieste Lloyd, 193
    Abbazia, fig. 5.1
    Carniola, 205–206; fig. 5.12
Trifunović, Lazar, 44
Tuberculosis, 134, 136
    Anti-Tuberculosis Conference, 130
    Anti-Tuberculosis League, 136
Turin
    International Exposition of Industry and Labor (1911), 90

Une maison—un palais (Le Corbusier), 221
Union of Yugoslav Engineers and Architects, 59, 130

Ve Poliansky, Branko (Branko Micić), 8, 234 (n. 17)
Vers une architecture (Le Corbusier), 198, 205
Veshch/Gegenstand/Objet, 11, 15
Vienna
    Secession, 89
    Technische Hochschule, 58
Vinaver, Stanislav, 96–97, 100, 130
Viollet-le-Duc, Eugène-Emmanuel, 143
Vitruvius (Marcus Vitruvius Pollio), 211
Vreme, 60
Vrnik (islet), 194
Vučo, Aleksandar, 33, 269 (n. 14)
Vučo, Nikola, 39
    Wall of Agnosticism, 39; fig. 2.10
    We Have to Convince No One, 39; fig. 2.9

Warke, Val, 144, 148, 165
Werk, Das, 11
Wright, Frank Lloyd, 143
    destruction of the box, 204

Zađina, Vojislav, fig. 4.15
Zadkine, Ossip, 12
Zagreb, 9, 10, 13, 15, 19, 21, 44, 92, 110, 202
    Architects Circle, 68
    architectural firm Kiverov, Korka, and Krekić, 182
    Technical Faculty, 15
Zenit, 9–15, 17, 19, 21, 29, 32, 34, 97; figs. 1.8, 1.9, 1.10, 1.11, 1.18
    Balkanization of Europe, 9, 10
    constructivism, 11, 14, 17
    cubism, 13, 14, 21
    "First International Exhibition of New Art," 12, 14
    primitivism in art, 10
    supranationalism, 9
    Zenitheum, 14, 17; figs. 1.13, 1.14
    Zenitism, 8, 9, 10, 13, 14, 86, 87, 91
    Zenitosophy, 10
Zenitist Manifesto [Manifest Zenitizma] (Goll, Micić, and Tokin), 10
Zeppelin, Count, airship, 81, 123; fig. 3.1

Živadinović Bor, Stevan (Vane), 41; fig. 2.11
 Milica S. Lazović Like a Shadow, 41; fig. 2.12
 One Minute before a Crime, 41; fig. 2.12
Živanović Noje, Radojica, 239–240 (n. 12); fig. 4.1
Zloković, Đuro, 191, 205; fig. 5.12
Zloković, Milan, 21, 25–29, 35, 41, 44, 48, 49, 50, 52, 57, 58, 62, 68, 81, 125, 127, 130, 191, 193–225, 229, 266–267 (n. 1); figs. 2.29, 5.2
 apartment block in Kralja Milutina Street, Belgrade, fig. 5.4
 apartment block in Miloša Pocerca Street, Belgrade, 204; fig. 5.11
 blocks of flats in Neimar, Belgrade, 204
 "Bosnian Hall" in the house of Đorđe and Krista Đorđević, 44, 48–49; fig. 2.14
 Columbus Tower, Santo Domingo, 68; fig. 2.42
 Commerce Hall, Skopje, 35, 215, 217; figs. 2.7, 5.22, 5.23
 Fiat Automobile Service building, 221, 223; fig. 5.31
 Hall of the Christian Union of Young People, fig. 5.30
 Health Center, Risan, 210–211; figs. 5.15, 5.16
 Hotel Žiča, Mataruška Banja, 39, 52, 68, 212, 214; figs. 2.8, 2.23, 2.41, 5.17, 5.18
 house in Rankeova Street, Belgrade, fig. 5.3
 house of Đorđe Dragutinović, Zemun, 48; fig. 2.15
 house of Jovan and Dragojla Prendić, Belgrade, 201–202; fig. 5.8
 house of Nevena Zaborski, Belgrade, 201; fig. 5.7
 Museum of the Adriatic Guards, Split, 62; fig. 2.31
 Opel building, Belgrade, 204; fig. 5.10
 Primary School, Jagodina, 212, 214; figs. 5.19, 5.20, 5.21
 railway station, Obrenovac, 62; fig. 2.33
 State Mortgage Bank, Sarajevo, 50; figs. 2.18, 2.19, 6.1
 University Clinic for Children, Belgrade, 206, 209, 210, 217, 218, 223; figs. 5.13, 5.14, 5.24, 5.25, 5.26, 5.29
 villa of Bruno Mozer, Zemun, 204
 villa of Dragoljub Šterić, Belgrade, 202, 204; fig. 5.9
 Zloković house, Belgrade, 27, 29, 35, 41, 50, 197–198; figs. 2.1, 2.2, 2.3, 2.4, 2.13, 2.16, 5.6
Zograf, 60, 243 (n. 51)